Secular Mysteries: Stanley Cavell and English Romanticism

Secular Mysteries: Stanley Cavell and English Romanticism

Edward T. Duffy

BLOOMSBURY
NEW YORK • LONDON • NEW DELHI • SYDNEY

Bloomsbury Academic
An imprint of Bloomsbury Publishing Plc

175 Fifth Avenue	50 Bedford Square
New York	London
NY 10010	WC1B 3DP
USA	UK

www.bloomsbury.com

First published 2013

© Edward T. Duffy, 2013

All rights reserved. No part of this publication may be reproduced or transmitted in any form or by any means, electronic or mechanical, including photocopying, recording, or any information storage or retrieval system, without prior permission in writing from the publishers.

No responsibility for loss caused to any individual or organization acting on or refraining from action as a result of the material in this publication can be accepted by Bloomsbury Academic or the author.

Library of Congress Cataloging-in-Publication Data
Duffy, Edward T.
Secular mysteries: Stanley Cavell and English romanticism/Edward T. Duffy.
p. cm.
Includes bibliographic references and index.
ISBN 978-1-4411-2678-8 (pbk.: alk. paper) – ISBN 978-1-4411-1718-2 (hardcover: alk. paper) 1. Cavell, Stanley, 1926- 2. Literature–Philosophy. 3. Romanticism. I. Title.
B945.C274D84 2013
191–dc23
2012036725

ISBN: HB: 978-1-4411-1718-2
PB: 978-1-4411-2678-8
ePub: 978-1-4411-9536-4
ePDF: 978-1-4411-8647-8

Typeset by Deanta Global Publishing Services, Chennai, India

What should we be without
The dolphin's arc, the dove's return,

These things in which we have seen ourselves and spoken?
Ask us, prophet, how we shall call
Our natures forth when that live tongue is all
Dispelled, that glass obscured or broken

In which we have said the rose of our love and the clean
Horse of our courage, in which beheld
The singing locust of the soul unshelled,
And all we mean or wish to mean.

Richard Wilbur, "Advice to a Prophet"

for Barb
così m'hai dilatata mia fidanza
come 'l sol fa la rosa quando aperta
tanto divien quant' ell' ha di possanza

Contents

Preface and Acknowledgments   x

1   Stanley Cavell's Redemptive Reading: A Philosophical Labor in Progress   1
2   Reading Romanticism   35
3   A Wordsworthian Calling of Thinking   85
4   Bursting from a Congregated Might of Vapors: Desire, Expression and Motive in Shelley   117
5   "The Breath Whose Might I Have Invoked in Song": *Epipsychidion* and *Adonais*   133
6   Reviewing the Vision of *The Triumph of Life*   201

Notes   225
Bibliography   241
Index   247

Preface and Acknowledgments

This book on Stanley Cavell, William Wordsworth, and Percy Bysshe Shelley does not pretend to be a documented inventory of the influences exerted on Cavell by the English romantic poets. If it did, it would be a much shorter book. Instead, struck by the fervor with which Cavell midway on the career of his professional life in "ordinary language philosophy" announced that his philosophy was "calling for"[1] romanticism, I propose to place him side by side with the two romantic poets to whom I have found myself most attracted. The aim is to show how Cavell and my romantic relay of Wordsworth and Shelley call out and answer to each other in ways that sound out the depths of the questions and purposes informing their poetry and Cavell's philosophy.

In an interview on his only extended reading of English romantic texts—the pages of *In Quest of the Ordinary* devoted to Coleridge's "Ancient Mariner" and Wordsworth's "Immortality Ode"—Cavell acknowledges that he turned to these perhaps too representative "Romantic war horses"[2] in order to test his intuition that the romantic movement was as a whole and in principle committed to the two-part labor of composing works that would be both "records of losses"[3] and "texts of recovery" (*IQ*, 50), and the one by way of the other. This double-edged task that Cavell acknowledges his philosophical own is, from the outset, buried in the punning title of *In Quest of the Ordinary*. (The pun, more apparent to the ear than the eye, is on a chivalric *quest* and a coroner's *inquest*. Spelled out early in the book, it can be retrospectively found lurking in the title-page's layout of its first two words.) Cavell's finding of a romanticism that, like him, is in quest of an ordinary that is still vitally alive for us even in the aftermath of all our casual slaughters of it represents its romantic champions as not only committed to the recovery of a lost ordinary of human language but also called to an endless series of inquests into the myriad deaths of an ordinary that, as Cavell tells it, constantly provokes both him and his belatedly discovered romantic precursors on to a path whose point is the recovery of "the (my) (ordinary) (human) voice" (*IQ*, 26), but where in accord with Emerson's very Wordsworthian allegiance to the near and the common the questing protagonist is constrained "to find the journey's end in every step of the road"[4] or as Cavell puts it "in every word, with every breath."[5]

Cavell's acknowledgment of English romantic poetry as a collective "major mind" (*CH*, 1) in which he could sound the depth and bearings of his own was my cue for going on (in "The Romantic Calling of Thinking: Stanley

Cavell on the Line with Wordsworth" (*Studies in Romanticism* 37: Winter 1998)) to a passage in Wordsworth's *Prelude* that Cavell does not touch upon, but which is charged not only with several of his master-tones but also with a very Cavellian practice of "the writer's faith"(*SW*, 104) that despite all the "terrors, miseries, vexations and lassitudes" suffered in a dark time there yet remains (in further words of Wordsworth) "the calm existence that is mine when I/Am worthy of myself" (1805, I. 356–61).[6] This going on to some Wordsworth unnoted by Cavell led me further to the hardly calm Shelley, the other romantic poet I was most attracted to and the one about whom I had most written. In Cavell's work, Shelley appears only twice and each time briefly, but to my mind and with the possible exception of William Blake, he most thoroughly exemplifies Cavell's passionate philosophical interest in the expression and recovery of desire that is for him the distinguishing feature of the perfectionist authorship he finds everywhere in literature but most signally in the American romanticism of Emerson and Thoreau.

My working assumption that Wordsworth and Shelley are sufficiently representative of one half of my subject could be justified by claiming that, leaving aside the belatedly recognized Blake, English romantic poetry divides neatly into two generations, that Wordsworth is its seminal figure and acknowledged as such with varying degrees of Oedipal resistance by Keats, Shelley, and Byron, that the desire driving this poetry into existence is generally agreed to be more thoroughly unloosed upon the world in the character and writing of a younger generation that is, like Blake, more fiercely concerned with the unbinding (and consequently the repression) of desire, and that for better or for worse the younger romantic most unguardedly committing his desire to what Byron calls the "burning page" was Percy Bysshe Shelley. In short, I could have argued that just these two vastly different poets are representative of the movement as a whole because in Wordsworth we find its founding impulse and in Shelley its most uncompromised expression. I could have so argued, but given that I wanted before all else to place these two interests of mine side by side in a conversation where the depth of the one would call out to the depth of the other, I remain wary of leaning too heavily on a train of thought that could only have occurred to me *ex post facto*, only after the *fact* of my interests and where these interests did and did not lead me. In explanation of my choice of Wordsworth and Shelley, then, I feel that it would be more pertinent to provide some personal history as to how I came to my professional bearings in the charged magnetic field continually at play in my head between Cavell's voice in contemporary philosophy and the quite differently inflected voices of just these two English romantic poets, one of whom is hardly mentioned by Cavell.

The beneficiary at Manhattan College of a full four years of historically sequenced and rigorously text-based courses in philosophy, I nonetheless went on to graduate study in my first love, literature. Enrolled in the English and Comparative Literature Program at Columbia, I went on to write a dissertation on Rousseau and Shelley that increased my admiration for the perennially underappreciated mind and poetry of Shelley, even as semester by semester I found myself more and more drawn to Wordsworth. But for no discernible practical reason and with a formidable amount of catching up to do in French as well as English literature, I nonetheless kept returning to two philosophers whose writing I had excitedly pored over in my senior year: John Austin and the later Wittgenstein of *Philosophical Investigations*. Repeatedly drawn back to these most unlikely of guilty pleasures, I could neither help nor explain myself, and it was only a decade later with my chance introduction to Cavell's work on Austin and Wittgenstein that I began more clearly to understand and more confidently to treasure this ostensibly distracting interest. And then when almost another decade further on Cavell announced, with particular emphasis on Wordsworth, that his "philosophy was calling for romanticism" and that this movement was (in his account of it) calling on its readers to slough off the world-historical "torpor" Wordsworth deplored and begin again to take an "interest in their own lives,"[7] I realized that these two interests of mine could no longer be insulated from each other, and happily resolved to take on the protracted labor of conducting an exploratory conversation between them, where it was precisely my own interest that brought the philosophy and the poetry together in a spirited interplay and mutual questioning, from whose perspective I might better see the "depth of the ideas on both tracks,"[8] might, as it turned out, even pursue that conceptual depth further on to its always receding origin and incentive in what I long knew Shelley to have figured as a "burning fountain," Wordsworth as a "fixed, abysmal, gloomy, breathing-place/[from which] Mounted the roar of waters" (1850, XIV. 58–9).

As Cavell might say, this was something to go on with and work out. But, as the two pictures of conceptual genesis just now invoked from *Adonais* and *The Prelude* may suggest, this necessarily imagined and conventionally "mysterious" depth of conceptual formation is not itself reducible to just another of the concepts for which it is the putative *fons et origo*. (Compare Wittgenstein's *Tractatus*, 4.121[9]: "What expresses *itself* in language, *we* cannot express by means of language" (Wittgenstein's emphases)). As different as they are in their imagining of our beginnings as members of the talking, thinking form of life, Shelley's burning fountain and Wordsworth's fixed abysmal breathing-place are alike in that each is represented as what comes before and leads on to the concepts with which, in Cavell's language, we relate what our world and our others in it are (called). But while any thus conjectured first quickening toward the distinctively human and necessarily communal work of conceptual production cannot, without distortion, be turned into a concept, it is nonetheless a seriously real constituent of our life. Not unlike the Lucretian *Alma Venus Genetrix* that Shelley was so taken with, it engulfs us and incessantly streams into us as a force of (our) nature that is capable of being demythologised into, and understood as, the attractively creative power of the *interest* which Wordsworth called for with such urgency that what he calls this "immense word" in both Thoreau and Wordsworth went, he testifies, "absolutely through him."[10] Went right through him and, I assume, drew out of him his eventual claim that it was this torpor-overcoming interest that provoked the poetry of Wordsworth (and of Coleridge) no less than his own philosophy of ordinary language into a labor of "conceptual investigation,"[11] aimed not so much at achieving an encyclopedic mastery of all things knowable as at staying the course of "the most forbearing act of thinking (this may mean the most thoughtful), to let true need, say desire, be manifest and be obeyed."[12]

For Cavell, the most telling exponent of such conceptual investigations as would make the achievement of desire their final end or "exit" (*IQ*, 28) is Emerson, endlessly calling for the subversion of a dominant mode of "Western conceptualizing," where the clutching hand stands for a "kind of sublimized violence" (*CH*, 39) that enacts the "most unhandsome part of our condition" (*CH*, 38) and condemns us to the "evanescence and lubricity of all objects, which lets them slip through our fingers then when we clutch hardest" (*EL*, 473). In aversion to this understanding of what counts as thinking, Cavell proposes an Emersonian turning away from it and toward what he (Cavell) calls the "most handsome part of our condition," where the gracelessly clutching hand devoted to emptiness is itself turned around into, and succeeded by, the same hand opening and readying itself for that "most forbearing act of thinking" by which, in case after case, the "*partiality*" (*CH*, 42) of our thinking is made manifest and constraining.

Cavell's *partiality* is another way he has found to talk about what he elsewhere calls *desire* or *interest*. For while Emerson's apodictic "Thinking is a partial act" (*EL*, 62) may start out from the word's primary sense, telling us that a thinking that necessarily does not include its own genesis or genius must be incomplete, it quickly turns out that in Cavell's reading of it the curt predication of this utterly specific sentence (in just this paragraph in just this essay) is already on its way toward amplifying itself into its further and commonly available sense of the inclination of thinking, what it is attracted or drawn to. Cavell's most comprehensive formulation of this "most handsome part of our condition" comes to him when in a phrasing uncannily reminiscent of the *Venus Genetrix* of Lucretius and Shelley he names it the "specifically human form of attractiveness, naming the rightful call we have on one another, and that I and the world make upon one another." (*TN*, 86–7). This is (Cavell claims) "a reasonable sense of intelligence-not the sense of applying it but that of receiving it." It is "a stopping to think (say not for action but for passion), as if to let our needs recognize what they need" *(CH*, 20).

In a preliminary survey of the spiritual landscape Cavell finds himself sharing with romantic poetry, he declares, in reference to the *omnium gatherum* of Coleridge's *Biographia Literaria*, that "the general idea [he has] of what constitutes serious romanticism's self-appointed mission" (*IQ*, 43) is its "contesting" of philosophy, poetry, religion and politics "with one another" where, consequent upon a conviction (shared by Cavell) that "there is a life and death of the world [and of us in it] dependent on what we make of it" (*IQ*, 68), the "stakes appear sometimes as the loss or gain of our common human nature, sometimes as the loss or gain of nature itself" and where these stakes are put further at risk by what Cavell himself calls the "disreputable sense that the fate of this contest is bound up with one's own writing"(*IQ*, 43) so that, on a final accounting several pages later, "[romantic] poetry takes itself, its own possibility, as its subject" (*IQ*, 66), this a final and not especially heterodox word on romantic poetry's self-reflexiveness that recalls Cavell's frequently expressed doubts about the feasibility of writing his philosophy up to the standard of an Emerson for whom the "path of his faith and redemption" (*T*, 19) is not backed by any theses or propositions but, punningly, "fronted" by the "character" (*CH*, xxx) of Emerson's essays and so "proven on the way, *by the way*" (*SW*, 137, Cavell's emphasis).

For Cavell, romanticism is, uncontroversially, a trans-Atlantic as well as a European phenomenon and Emerson is one of its major exponents, but not so much because of what is generally thought to be his vaguely sublime thoughts as because of his conviction that the fate of its truly extravagant ambitions depends on the thin reed of a written expression bent, like Emerson's, on "submitting" itself "to the condition of acquiring whatever authority and conviction is due to it by looking at its countenance and surface" (*IQ*, 23). That Cavell chose so forcefully to insist on the mountainous divide between romanticism's Promethean ambitions and the slenderness of its individualist and writerly means was interesting in itself. But even more so was how the specific terms of this insistence recalled the haunting phrase from Cavell's work that I have chosen for my title: *secular mysteries*. Cavell uses this (I believe) coinage only once and not in any direct reference to romanticism. It comes to him in the course of his effort (in *The World Viewed: Reflections on the Ontology of Film*) to draw his life-long fascination with the movies into explicitly philosophical conversation with what the philosopher of ethics in him knows to be the inevitable "mismatch" in any human life between the "intention" of the human subject and the "consequences" in the world of any actions deriving from that intention.[13] Speaking generally of this mismatch, Cavell remarks that its "natural province" in theater was tragedy, in film comedy. But he then adds that film also became the venue for something that is "neither tragedy nor comedy," and something that, apparently, could not be safely filed away under the stale rubric of the "tragic-comic." For this evidently new thing on the screen draws out of Cavell this new name and genre of "secular mysteries," defined by him as "forms" where "the mismatch between intention and consequence appears as the distance between the *depth* to which an ordinary human life requires expression and the *surface* of ordinary means through which that life must, if it will, express itself" (*WV*, 180, emphases added). (It seems appropriate to mention here that *The World Viewed* is widely regarded as Cavell's most difficult and inchoate production and that when he acknowledged its tentative and unfinished quality, he cautioned that the book's "difficulty lies as much in the obscurity of its promptings as in its particular surfacings of expression" (*WV*, 162).

As examples of cinematic secular mysteries, Cavell suggests a triple bill of films by De Sica, Fellini, and Bresson, all of them directors who were, he reminds us, "famous for their interest in unknown physiognomies" (*WV*, 180). From there, he turns to Carl Dreyer's silent classic, *The Passion of St. Joan*, and its lingering close-ups of inquisition, martyrdom, and immolation for a particularly telling demonstration of film's natural attraction toward the wordlessly expressive "mystery of the individual human face" (*WV*, 181), and then, finally, to the talkies of Hollywood's Golden Age and the recurring "mystery of the familiar [as] caught memorably" (*WV*, 182) in the screened faces of even the most celebrated stars. As a consequence of an obscure prompting of my own, I hear all this from Cavell on the "ontology of film" as anticipating not only his subsequent insistence on the surface expression and "countenance" of Emerson's writing but also his still later claim (and qualm) that Wordsworth's prized gift for "communicating with objects," while dismissed by Coleridge as virtually meaningless, nonetheless found an intelligible though suspiciously "animistic" description in what Coleridge himself itemized as the fourth of the "characteristic excellences" of his friend's poetry: its "perfect truth of nature, as taken immediately from nature, and proving long and genial intimacy with the very spirit which gives the *physionomic expression* to all the works of nature" (*IQ*, 72, emphasis added).

In *The Senses of Walden*, Cavell touches on how Thoreau's affinity with the "uncanny homeliness" of ordinary-language philosophy "stubbornly resting within its relentless superficiality" (*IQ*, 176) no more conflicts with his obvious and acknowledged gravitation toward, as we say, the bottom of things than it does with Wittgenstein's revolutionary way of discovering "essence" and "reaching bedrock" through "grammatical" investigations into "the *kind of statement* that we make about phenomena."[14] For Cavell, there is no question but that *Walden*, originally subtitled *Life in the Woods*, demands a deep reading, but "this deep reading is not one," he adds, "in which you sink away from the surface of words. Words already engulph us. It is one in which you depart from a given word as from a point of origin; *you go deep as into woods*. Understanding is a matter of orientation, of bearings, of the ability to keep to a course and to move in natural paths from any point to any other. The depths of the book are nothing apart from its surfaces. Figurations of language can be thought of as ways of reflecting the surfaces and depths of a word onto one another." (*SW*, 65, emphasis added).

Justly called by Charles Altieri "*the* poet of philosophical grammar,"[15] Wordsworth would likewise go deep into the darkened wood of our words and find orientation in what, in widest commonality spread, the things of his world are (called). His most deeply sworn vow is to keep his eye steadily and watchfully on "Nature's daily face" (III.133) so as to preserve the prompting of those "holy powers" (III. 83) that made him from before the dawn of memory "conversant" (III.103) with "the common countenance of earth and heaven" (III. 111) and would in time make him over into both the hero and author of *The Prelude*, a poetic endeavor for which you need but hear the formulation, "a book of losses, a text of recovery," to see its rightness for this autobiographical work in which Wordsworth both writes himself down (and almost off) as the perverse pursuer of a downward and darkening way toward chaos, and also, in recoil, writes himself up as the self-recovering "composer" of both himself and his world. In this connection, I cannot forbear mentioning that it was only after several years of teaching it and some time before Cavell's turn to romanticism that it dawned on me that *The Prelude* was a text whose subject/author finds himself compelled to "(re)compose" himself (and his world) in more than one sense of the word, and that hence it was one massively sustained instance of Robert Lowell's dictum that poetry is not the report of an event but the event itself, in this case the event of this individual poet having to "(re)compose" himself and his world. Or, to apply Cavell's packed phrasing of the same thought to this long poem on the "growth of a poet's mind," *The Prelude* is an instance of "the making of it happen, the poetry of it" (*SW*, 134) as, verse by verse, this poet's mind comes into its own at the provocation of "the depth to which [this]ordinary human life requires expression" but with the patiently developing understanding that this quest for expression has nothing else to go on aside from the "surface of ordinary means through which that life must, if it will, express itself."

Besides its coinage of *secular mysteries*, *The World Viewed* contains one of Cavell's earliest and more enigmatic references to Wordsworth. In the book's opening pages, he constructs a sweeping panorama of modern cultural history, organized around a "wish" that he claims has haunted "the West since the Reformation" and has worked itself out historically in ways that call for the inclusion of Wordsworth in the philosophical company of Kant, Hegel, Heidegger and Wittgenstein (*WV*, 22). As a tracker of the ways, detours and dead ends of modern philosophical skepticism since even before Descartes, Cavell identifies this wish as the culture's desire for "the power to reach this world, having for so long tried, at last hopelessly, to manifest fidelity to another." In the world-historical drama of this wish to "escape subjectivity and metaphysical isolation" and reach the "reality" of Thoreau's craving, Wordsworth is assigned the role of the romantic poet compelled to "[compete] with the history of poetry by writing out himself, writing himself back into the world," a densely worded declaration of where Wordsworth wrote and what he wrote for that strikes me as an uncanny anticipation of Cavell's later more general and explicit description of the English romantic venture as one whose "stakes" appear "sometimes as the loss or gain of our common human nature, sometimes as the loss or gain of nature itself," and always, to a scandalous or disreputable effect, "bound up with one's own writing."

In Cavell's staging of this world-historical drama, Wordsworth owes his starring role to the Copernican Revolution of Kant, in whose aftermath "our subjectivity [became] the route back to our conviction in reality." To speak in this way, continues Cavell in the tones of one saying what goes without saying, is "to speak of romanticism." Nearer to Cavell's disciplinary home, it is also to speak of the need not only for "the acknowledgement of that endless presence" of our subjectivity in (literally) all that is before and between us, but for the further acknowledgment that since the a priori endowment of this subjectivity has, in Cavell's Wittgensteinian inheriting of it, ramified out from Kant's 12 categories of the understanding into "our terms as our conditions"(*IQ* 38), we are dependent on these *con-ditions* (what we say together) not only for knowing anything at all but for even so much as our "having" a self or a world to be interested in. This is a formulation of where we presently find ourselves which, I will be claiming, comes to Cavell largely as a result of his initially wary acknowledgment of something he finds more self-consciously and unavoidably present in English romanticism than in either Emerson or Thoreau: namely, the "romantic animism" that he first takes notice of in Wordsworth and in the generally representative and specifically neo-Kantian dread of Coleridge that we "[carry] the death of the world in us" (*IQ*, 44) and so, in aversion to this morbidity, call upon the "calling of poetry" to salvage our humanity by "giving the world back, as to life" (*IQ*, 45). And doing this with the unstinting acknowledgment that the nature and dynamics of such a quest necessitates the shared romantic and Emersonian insistence on cultivating the near and the common into such forms as "one may call ... secular mysteries," because their point of departure and provocation is "the distance between the depth to which an ordinary human life requires expression and the surface of ordinary means through which that life must, if it will, express itself."

From the moment I settled on "secular mysteries" as an apt title, I knew that on the general grounds of making myself intelligible to my reader, I had imposed on myself the obligation of providing a timely explanation of the connection between Cavell's *ad hoc* use and definition of the term and his indefatigable championing of a thoughtful writing "to be proven only on the way" and "by the way" of its surface *expression*. But if this obligation initially seemed a mildly onerous chore, it soon assumed a more inviting face as its details began to yield at least a preliminary, say a *prima facie*, warrant for a marked feature of this book that may, to many, seem hopelessly outmoded: namely, the fact that it is more than half composed of insistently slow and close readings of Wordsworth and Shelley. Similarly close and painstaking readings (of Emerson, of Thoreau, of movies, of Heidegger and Wittgenstein) comprise a great part of Cavell's written work, and in the first chapter of *In Quest of the Ordinary*, he merges these correlative acts of reading and writing into each other with the remark that just as "reading is a variation of writing, where they meet in meditation and achieve accounts of their opportunities," so writing is "a variation of reading, since to write is to cast words together that you did not make so as to give or take readings"(*IQ*, 18), readings, Cavell quickly adds, of what we find before us in the world first and only derivatively or reflectively in books. This ontological expansion and mutual interpenetration of the concepts of writing and reading is a salient feature of each of the selections from Wordsworth and Shelley that I have chosen as characteristic of their work and purposes. In each, the writer is overheard taking a reading of his world, whose latter end is the reader himself becoming the one read. This, I dare say, is a common feature of romantic poetry as well as a persistent complaint lodged against its supposed narcissism or solipsism. But for Cavell, as will be detailed shortly in the first chapter, this turn toward the reading of the poet's subjectivity marks the "success" of any reading of the world, since it is a reading of one's own human hand and interest in all that we find before us. It is, in other words, the fruit and flower of that "most forbearing act of thinking," that "mode of conceptual accuracy" which Cavell explicitly calls "reading" (*IQ*, 14) through which one sees one's way clear toward "[letting] true need, say desire, be manifest and be obeyed" (*TN*, 45) in what elsewhere Cavell calls the "achievement" and "exit" of desire (*IQ*, 28) with (take my word for it) the implication that this is a devoutly to be wished exodus or redemption of desire.

This is where the religiously inflected title of my first chapter, "Stanley Cavell's Redemptive Reading: A Philosophical Labor in Progress," comes from. A synoptic history of Cavell's philosophical progress up through the late 1980s, this opening chapter provides an overview of his philosophy, organized around his comparatively early call for a "redemptive reading"[16] which, given the stakes and potential yield of reading in his philosophy, constitutes (again in Cavell's own phrase) a "theology of reading" (*T*, 53), a perhaps extravagant way of expressing the thought but one not at all unexpected from someone constantly problematizing the very idea of "the philosopher in American life" and forever claiming that in his reading of him not only did Emerson "found thinking for America," he also gave notice that for the running of this enterprise he would necessarily be "putting the *calling* and the *act* of his writing in the public place reserved in both of the founding testaments of our culture for the word of God" (*T*, 19). The chapter begins with Cavell's own philosophical beginnings in John Austin and Wittgenstein and then goes on to characterize his subsequent turning to Emerson (and Thoreau) as also a staying with Wittgenstein because it was Wittgenstein's call back to "the language of life" that Cavell eventually heard calling for Emerson's differently placed emphasis on the "life of language," understood as the incentive(s) constraining our human, talking form of life toward wording the world as we do "in every word, with every breath" (*CH*, 55).

The second chapter, "Reading Romanticism," extends the tracking of Cavell's philosophical progress up to the present day, but with a sharper focus on the place in, and consequences for, that progress of his turn to English romanticism and especially Wordsworth. On the one hand, this chapter tracks the nature and prehistory of this turn in Cavell's thought. On the other, it contends that Cavell's reading of the openly "animistic" Coleridge and Wordsworth led him on toward locating in the latter "a truer, newer animism" of animating interest, which in turn acted upon Cavell as a powerfully "obscure prompting" toward later work of his where the signifiers of *wind, air, breath* and *spirit* are of the essence for his (and Emerson's) master-theme of the condition of human freedom, as Cavell belatedly comes to see it figured in the remark of Emerson's "Fate" that "We should be crushed by the atmosphere but for the reaction of the air within the body.... If there be omnipotence in the stroke, there is omnipotence in the recoil," the aversively thoughtful recoil (Cavell glosses) of "our breath made words." Along with this continuation of the history of Cavell's philosophical progress, I move on to two openly "animist" passages in Wordsworth's *Prelude*, neither of which has received any of Cavell's direct attention. From there I return to "Fate," an essay written in the spirit of Emerson's own "all I know is reception" and Wordsworth's "wise passiveness," but one that Cavell dares to call a "tragic essay" because it is leavened with the acknowledgement that, as with Wordsworth's "ministry of fear," the reception in question must be of a fallen or lost world, filled to bursting with (in Emerson's words) "odious facts" and "savage accidents."

Most of the third chapter, "A Wordsworthian Calling of Thinking," is devoted to detailed readings of two passages from the *Prelude*, not anywhere noted by Cavell: its first "official" spot of time calling the poem's autobiographical hero back to what he discovers to be "the hiding places of his power," and the poem's conclusion on "the perfect image of a mighty mind" that Wordsworth was favored with on the top of Mount Snowdon. An unpacking of the *calling* in the chapter's title will suggest the drift of my purposes in moving beyond Cavell's direct engagements with Wordsworth. In one sense, the *calling* of the title names thinking as Wordsworth's vocation. In another, it points to a necessary reconceiving or recalling of thinking as if in response to the questioning Heideggerian title "Was heisst Denken?"—so often invoked by Cavell. Wordsworth's poetry contests what is conventionally called thinking, and in that endeavor, it displays a striking family resemblance with the way the philosophical investigations of Cavell, Emerson and Wittgenstein all question how a privileged mode of "Western conceptualizing" enacts a "kind of sublimized violence" that in regard to both us and our world effects a desolation and calls it a clearing.

The fourth chapter, "Bursting From a Congregated Might of Vapors: Desire, Expression and Motive in Shelley," moves on to a romantic poet who, in the absence of any direct or sustained notice from Cavell, uncannily illustrates the profound and mutually illuminating similarities of spiritual horizon obtaining between Cavell and English romanticism. The chapter focuses on the constantly recurring scene of poetic initiation in Shelley's work, characterized here (in terms drawn from Cavell) as the event of desire unleashed, obeyed and made manifest in "flowers of thought." My initially stated intuition—to be tested in the two subsequent chapters on Shelley's poetry—is that what Shelley calls "the mind in creation" is his no less than Cavell's master-theme, and that for both, this recurrent event of "lively origination" gets on its endlessly reiterated way only through that reception or impressionability, which Cavell sees accumulating into the "demand upon Emerson's writing, and his readers, to let the pain of his thought, theirs, collect itself" (*PP*, 31), so as, at the last, to turn itself into what is variously called a "flowering of mentality," a prophetically recoiling tongue of fire, or the "uncommunicated lightning of one's own mind."

The fifth chapter "The Breath Whose Might I Have Invoked in Song," is comprised of extended and intertwined readings of *Adonais* and *Epipsychidion*. It builds on the common understanding of each of these two very different poems as both a discourse of desire and an enactment of our form of life's desire and need for discourse. The extremely ambitious, self-reflexive and "highly wrought" *Adonais* epitomizes these qualities of its composition in its strategic naming of the pyramid of Gaius Cestius (dominating Keats' final resting place in Rome's Protestant Cemetery) as "flame transformed to marble." This way of calling Cestius's pharaonic bid for immortality takes note of the marmoreal monumentality often claimed for the highest reaches of "immortal" literary art, but less conventionally it also gives expression to the desire driving Shelley toward such constitutions of words as might attain the standing of work *aere perennius*, because they are powered by, in the words of *Epipsychidion*, a "burning, yet ever inconsumable" desire. Along with a sustained thinking through of fire as the figure in both these poems for the passionate incentive at the base or root of their construction, I go, as it were, behind or beyond fire into the circulating oxygen that is the breath of its being. I explore the way Shelley repeatedly (and (in *Adonais*) climactically) makes the breath of a world and of a culture (and especially that culture's "breath made words") into the attractive provoker of such bursting fires of the mind and flowerings of mentality as Shelley would receive and inherit as "incarnations of the stars" constituting an ever-renewed constellation of those (implicitly perfectionist) writers who waged contention with their time's decay and so have become star-like members of the "enduring dead" who "live . . ./And move like winds of light on dark and stormy air."

In the Shelley portion of this book, Cavell has been up to this point only an intermittent presence. In this sixth and final chapter—"Reviewing the Vision of 'The Triumph of Life'"-—he is self-consciously brought back into evidence as I endeavor to (re)hear Shelley's Dante-inspired masterpiece with, as it were, a Cavell-trained ear, and endeavor, likewise, to (re)hear what the last major but unfinished work of Shelley's hand can bring out of what, in a phrase stolen from Shelley, I am inclined to call the "secrets of an elder day" in the progress of Cavell's philosophy. Perhaps the innermost of these secrets and one (as Thoreau might say) "not involuntarily kept but inseparable from its very nature," is that lying even deeper than the poem's fairly obvious contendings with and between darkness and light is a more deeply pitched "breath battle"—a literal psychomachia—between the "enamored air" of the *Triumph*'s opening lines and what so disastrously becomes of this original or constitutive airing of things in "the clime/Of that cold light whose airs too soon deform." The chapter concludes with an extended (re)reading of the *Triumph*'s opening and conspicuously self-contained lines on the theme and hope of an "enamored air" that involves an elaborate figure not only for Shelley's reiterated trope of the flowers of poesy but also for what more than a century later Cavell will call "the great philosophical power" of passiveness or impressionability issuing into "flowerings of mentality."

Substantial portions of my first and third chapters originally appeared in, respectively, "Stanley Cavell's Redemptive Reading: A Philosophical Labour in Progress," *University of Toronto Quarterly* 65 (1996): 561–83 and "The Romantic Calling of Thinking: Stanley Cavell on the Line with Wordsworth," *Studies in Romanticism*, 37 (1998): 615–45. From the latter, several paragraphs have, with modifications, been moved to the first chapter, and its pages on Cavell's readings of Coleridge's "Ancient Mariner" and Wordsworth's "Immortality Ode" have, again with modifications, found their more appropriate place in the second chapter.

My epigraph is an excerpt from "Advice to a Prophet" from COLLECTED POEMS 1943–2004 by Richard Wilbur. Copyright © 2004 by Richard Wilbur. Reprinted by permission of Houghton Mifflin Harcourt Publishing Company. All rights reserved.

The work of this book benefited greatly from two Marquette Summer Faculty Fellowships and from several Marquette Faculty Development Grants. Other varieties of help have come from students, teachers, friends and colleagues who have modified or deepened some interest of mine or revealed a new one. Among the most memorable of these are: Alfred DiLascia, James Mullaney, Peter Gay, Karl Kroeber, Donald Reiman, Michael Riffaterre, Carl Woodring, Bob Gordon, Joel Grossman, Richard Helgerson, Linda Kauffman, Michael O'Connell, Milton Bates, Rebecca Ferguson, Tom Jeffers, Claudia Johnson, Christine Krueger, Michael McCanles, Cliff Spargo, James Swearingen, Mary-Beth Tallon, Amelia Zurcher, Kenneth Dauber, Richard Eldridge, Tim Gould, Walter Jost, and Garrett Stewart.

My most profound and heartfelt thanks is reserved for her to whom I dedicate this book. For her abiding love and nurturing of me and my works and for all that she does and is besides, she must there stand single.

1

Stanley Cavell's Redemptive Reading: A Philosophical Labor in Progress

> *Again he said to me, "Prophecy to these bones, and say to them, O dry bones, hear the word of the Lord. Thus says the Lord God to these bones: Behold, I will cause breath to enter you, and you shall live."*
>
> Ezekiel, 37.4–5

Although Stanley Cavell opens *The Senses of Walden* with the self-deprecating shrug, "What hope is there in a book about a book?," it soon becomes clear that, far from undervaluing the pages he has readied for the hands of his reader, he is claiming their worthiness to do spiritual battle with our all-too-average and depressed estimate of what reading counts for in the economy of what we do and in the substance of things we let ourselves hope for (*SW*, xiii). Finding himself in receipt of the burden of Thoreau's song that those he addresses are dead to the world, Cavell labors toward an account of the writing of *Walden*, which would resubmit the book's claim that the reading of the "bulk of these pages" is gathering toward the advent of a Scripture, now (if anytime) at hand, and big with either (as *Walden* puts it) "the dumps or a budding ecstasy."[1] Like William Blake, Cavell says to his reader, "Mark well my words! They are of your eternal salvation."

And as if this were not offense enough for one professor of philosophy, Cavell persistently claims that what he is doing is not literature or religion. It is philosophy, and *Walden* "the major philosophical text in my life—other than [Wittgenstein's] *Philosophical Investigations*" (*IQ*, 169).

If Cavell's career in professional philosophy finds itself drawn to what many would call extravagant therapeutic and redemptive claims, that career commences in (and never completely abandons) the very different offense Cavell notes as so often taken at "the ferocious knowledge the ordinary language philosophers will claim to divine by going over stupidly familiar words that we are every bit as much the master of as they" (*IQ*, 161). With the likelihood of offense its only apparent constant, the initial progress of this American philosopher is from John Austin's crisp precisions to these impassioned claims of his subsequent work: that Wittgenstein is a prophet for our dark time; that *every* [Cavell's repeated emphasis] word of Thoreau and Emerson is calling for redemption; that, in turn and as a continuing inheritance of these writers who (he repeatedly testifies) found thinking for America, every one of Cavell's own words must be about the same redeeming business.

Given the stark difference of (at least) style between Cavell's professional beginnings and his present voice in our culture, the first necessary business of this introductory chapter is to track how this self-styled "philosopher in American life" (*IQ*, 3) found himself taking steps along a little explored and idiosyncratically posted route, which is somehow "a path beyond, or through the ordinary language philosophy of the later Ludwig Wittgenstein and J. L. Austin."[2] My working intuition in tracking this "hobo of thought" (*TN*, 116) is that, first and last, he has set his heart on what our human form of life has found to say to and for itself. Cavell's unhedged investment in how we have worded the world will subsequently turn toward the "grammar" and criteria of Wittgenstein and toward the complex and encompassing forms of literary art, but by Cavell's own testimony, this commitment commenced when, as a listener and reader of Austin on "what we would say when," he found himself "being read" in a way that left him struck (and even stricken) with how little he knew of the terms of his own existence.

A claim and fervor of reason

John Austin is a writer very different from either Thoreau or the later Cavell, but for every word on which each trains his close philosophical attention, the task is, as Cavell says of Thoreau, to raise it "up to the light" (*SW*, 28) so as "to let it speak for itself; and in a way that holds out its experience to us, allows us to experience it, and allows it to tell us all it knows" (*SW*, 16). If Austin's practice of "linguistic phenomenology" serves to remind us of the way we use such familiar words as *believe* and *know*, and if a recurrent outcome of this activity of recollection is that we are surprised that we have just learned something about our world by learning something about our words, "perhaps" writes Cavell, "it is because we forget that we learn language and learn the world *together*, that they become elaborated and distorted together, and in the same places."[3] If a child just past the age of reason innocently says she *knows* something which her parents know she cannot possibly know, then that may be a cue for some parental instruction as to how she doesn't *know* this, she just *believes* it. And what "this scene of instruction" is addressing is not just the word *know* but whatever this thing called knowing *is*. Unearth the uses and consequences of our words, and with each one of them you "seem further to unearth the world?" (*T*, 40).

If Jacques Derrida is set on disclosing the deferred and differential "structurality of the structure" of *langue*, Austin concentrates on the occasionality of that form of life of us talkers which is speech or utterance, Saussure's *parole*. As either writers or talkers, our words occur (and endlessly recur) to us as our occasions call for them, and as listeners and readers we are well practiced in what is differently meant, on their differing occasions, by an identical sequence of words. Because "The coffee is hot" may be (among other possibilities) an observation, a hint, or a warning, what these four words in that order mean is not identical with what, on their differing occasions, is meant by these words (*IQ*, 131). But this distinction between the grammar and the rhetoric of a phrase is not a cue for a predictable set deconstructionist piece on undecidability. Rather, it unmelodramatically indicates something (logically) needed if someone is to be counted as a competent user of the language: "Words come to us from a distance; they were there before us; we were born into them. Meaning them is accepting that fact of their condition. To discover what is being said to us, as to discover what we are saying, is to discover the precise location from which it is said; to understand why it is said from just there, and at that time" (*SW*, 64).

With little apparent effort and as part of our initiation into the form of life of our shared language, we competent users of English have learned both to pick up on the pragmatic implications of others' speech and to take responsibility for our own. This does not mean that we are any less liable to error (and worse than error) here than in our statements of fact; it does not mean that we will never under- or overread implicatures or that we will never seek to disown what the words out of our own mouths clearly betray as our meaning, conviction or bias. It means only that this is one of the things we do when we talk and write. Whether we do it felicitously or not, it remains in place as one of the things we must do if we are to talk to each other at all. Because this mastery of the pragmatics of language is a condition of the form of life of us talkers, one of the driving forces of early Cavell is toward the increasingly solid conviction that in sufficiently imagined or described cases he (but he no more than anyone else) has the authority to say that if we say X then we *must* mean Y. To a science-bewitched view that the use of the first-person plural in the "must we mean what we say?" formula of Cavell's first book is presumptuous and empirically unwarranted mind-reading, he responds that the question is not asking for the empirical evidence of a head count or for the magic of a *pre*-diction. Rather it is appealing to, or bringing to mind, our presently shared diction. And for such things, Cavell insists, we speakers of the language do not need, and could not benefit from, evidence.

We *are* the evidence as we go on patiently asking ourselves what we should say when (*MW*, 4).

The inescapable and incalculable pertinence of asking "what we should say when" accounts for how Austin's work must be a philosophy of examples, must include the literariness of staging little dramas whose protagonists are *know* and *believe*, or *mistake* and *accident*. By their copious and pertinent specificity of detail, Austin's examples repeatedly drive it home that "the sounded utterance is only a salience of what is going on when we talk" (*MW*, 33), and that the rigorous matching of words like *mistake* or *accident* to the goings-on around them is a philosophical labor yielding its practitioners not just a more finely articulated inheritance of their native language, but also, and *through* this process of imaginative articulation, a disclosure of what these quite real things of mistakes and accidents *are* in our world, what for us (in a Cavellian master-tone) "count" as mistakes and accidents.

Austin's philosophical example to Cavell on his way to Wittgenstein was that, if we but avail ourselves of its distinguishing criteria, such an expression as the word *mistake* can tell us about ourselves and our world "through mapping the fields of consciousness lit by the occasions of [that] word" (*MW*, 100). Cavell will retain Austin's tenaciously nuanced attention to individual words; he will testify that it was Austin who "knocked him off [his] horse." But precisely as "thus grounded,"[4] precisely as an "ordinary language" philosopher given to this way of going on in philosophy, he will find his interest and his investigations gravitating toward the most common of our words, words more common and more indivisible than even *mistake*, words so common that they seem to have come to be as they are, not by the dictates of the kind of criteria unearthed in Austin's philosophical practice, but by the workings of those incalculably more basic (and hence routinely unnoticed) "Wittgensteinian" or "grammatical" criteria by which, as a matter of course and at an unfathomable depth of confidence, we call *this* that is throbbing in us our *pain*, or *this* routine bodily posture in reference to *this* most ordinary piece of furniture "to *sit* on a *chair*."

Cavell's turn from Austin's to Wittgenstein's concept of a criterion is most thoroughly rehearsed in the first part of *The Claim of Reason*, entitled "Wittgenstein and the Concept of Human Knowledge." There, Cavell characterizes his and Wittgenstein's "concept of knowledge" as "the human capacity for applying the concepts of a language to the things of a world" (*CR*, 17) where the application of concepts is both prompted and regulated by criteria that are constantly in play throughout the most common passages of our life with one another and with objects. The question Cavell wants this chapter to bring into focus about Wittgensteinian criteria is: As opposed to the manifest (but perhaps philosophically trivial) usefulness of Austinian criteria for purposes of identification, what is the good of Wittgensteinian criteria? "What," he writes, "is the *force* of *his* [that is, Wittgenstein's with Cavell's emphasis] habitual claims and questions about what a thing is called?" (*CR*, 66).

For Cavell, philosophy begins when "we 'don't know our way about,' when we are lost with respect to our words and the world they anticipate" (*CR*, 34). Wanting to understand something about which we suddenly feel at a loss (e.g. *opinion, faith, see, certain*), we remind ourselves of what kinds of statement we make about it; we perform what in Remark 90 of the *Investigations* Wittgenstein calls a "grammatical investigation." Wittgenstein acknowledges that in such straits we will "feel as if we had to *penetrate* phenomena," and then declines to go that route, turning instead to this act of overt self-presentation: "our investigation, however, is directed not toward phenomena, but, as one might say, toward the '*possibilities*' of phenomena. We remind ourselves, that is to say, of the *kind of statement* that we make about phenomena.... Our investigation is therefore a grammatical one" (*Investigations*, §90, all Wittgenstein's emphases).

Wittgenstein seeks not a parting of the phenomenal veils to reveal the "thing-in-itself" but a persistent explication of the tissue of possible statements that would "establish the position of an 'object' in our system of concepts" (*CR*, 76), that would leave "explained, unwrinkled before us" (*CR*, 78) the texture of assertion whereby we "[relate] various concepts to the concept of that object" (*CR*, 73). To effect these unwrinkling investigations, we are peremptorily told "don't think, but look!" (*Investigations*, §66)—and look not at anything calling itself hard and resistant reality, but look at what we *say* about the phenomena in question. Because "*Essence* is expressed by grammar" (*Investigations*, §371), it is just such superficially pedestrian but endlessly alert and painstakingly complex tracking of our grammar that will tell us "what kind of object anything is" (*Investigations*, §373).

As tracked by Wittgenstein, criteria bring up to the light our most common and unremarkable concepts and thus lay out in "perspicuous representation" the endlessly specific details of all we are in agreement on as our shared language. "It is," writes Wittgenstein, "what human beings *say* that is true and false; and they agree in the *language* they use. That is not agreement in opinions but in forms of life" (*Investigations*, §242, Wittgenstein's emphases). As the provider of the conditions for our knowing, saying or proving anything at all, forms of life are not themselves a matter of opinion. They are neither to be verified nor falsified. They are to be accepted or acknowledged, received or trusted. They are the given, the unconditioned. And their obscurely recurring good is that they give us the world, secure it to us in (and as) a net of conceptual articulation.

In Cavell's account of modern philosophy, Wittgenstein's *Investigations* "go on" from what he calls the Kantian "settlement," a settlement of philosophy ventured in response to the threat of skepticism and condensed into the axiom that "the conditions of the *possibility of experience* in general are at the same time the *possibility of the objects* of experience" (*TN*, 102).⁵ As continually remembered and reassessed in Cavell's work, this settlement, which famously represented itself as a Copernican revolution that would understand "the behavior of the world by understanding the behavior of our concepts of the world," is to be "radicalized so that not just twelve categories of the understanding are to be deduced, but every word in the language" (*IQ*, 38). And so, we are to deduce every word—we are, for example, to unknot "the conditions . . . in human thinking controlling the concept of condition" (*IQ*, 38)—in a way that will not bargain away the world for the mixed solipsistic pottage of sense data and the categories of the understanding, but will instead claim Thoreau and Emerson as "inheritors of Kant's transcendentalism [who write] out of a sense of the intimacy of words with the world, or of intimacy lost" (*IQ*, 170).

To a Cavell progressively more convinced that criteria do not "limit" but "constitute our access to the world" (*CH*, 22), Wittgenstein's grammatical investigations cleared the way toward a new "space of investigation" (*TN*, 81) in Thoreau and Emerson, where he could even more confidently go on with the effort of his earlier philosophical days "to identify Wittgenstein's *Investigations* (together with Austin's practice) as inheritors of the task of Kant's transcendental logic, namely to demonstrate, or articulate, the a priori fit of the categories of human understanding with the objects of human understanding, that is, with objects" (*TN*, 80). But because the going price for the Kantian settlement of human knowledge had turned out to be the positing of some necessarily unknowable (but still unappeasably sought) "thing-in-itself," Cavell found at least a piece of him responding to this offer with a sardonic "thanks for nothing" (*IQ*, 53). For Cavell, Kant's recuperation of human knowledge was itself in need of recuperation, and to its rescue he sees coming Thoreau and Emerson, "working out . . . the problematic of the day, the everyday, the near, the low, the common, in conjunction with what they call speaking of necessaries, and speaking with necessity" (*TN*, 81). But as Cavell retrospectively maps this eccentric philosophical itinerary, he does not envisage a complete break from the Kantian teaching of our conditionedness. Instead, he proposes and enacts his representative human need for repeatedly having to recover from (or get out of the grip of) this giant Kantian hand's "*picture*" of the thing-in-itself (*IQ*, 47) as irretrievably withheld behind an unbreachable epistemological line dividing appearances from whatever they are the appearances of. Moreover, he can find it in himself to sight the prospect of this recovery from within his own Wittgensteinian inheriting of Kant. He sights it in Wittgenstein's pressure to turn the skeptic's self-defeating rhetorical question "(how) can we know what there is in the world?" into what Cavell wants to get in place as the very real question, "what makes our knowledge *of* a world of objects at all?" (*CR*, 225, Cavell's emphasis).

If human knowledge has limiting conditions, either Kantian or Wittgensteinian, we are as a species fated to a dissatisfaction with those conditions and hence fated to overreach ourselves into what Kant calls the "transcendental illusion" that we can "know what transcends the conditions of possible knowledge" or into what Wittgenstein speaks of as "the illusions produced by our employing words in the absence of the (any) language game which provides their comprehensible employment" (*MW*, 65). As positioned within what Cavell calls the argument of the ordinary, the skeptic represents a never finally stilled voice within each of us that will seek a way of leaving or repudiating the game whenever our criteria are found to disappoint. And disappointing they will always and repeatedly be found because, as ours and only ours, they must at times strike us as arbitrary or merely conventional.

The originality of the *Investigations'* necessarily incessant response to skepticism is the way the book "takes [philosophy's] drift toward skepticism as the *discovery* of the everyday, a discovery of exactly *what* it is that skepticism would deny" (*IQ*, 170, Cavell's emphases): i.e. the everyday "home" (*TN*, 32) of our ordinary concepts as they deliver a world of "objects" to us within those human forms of life which "grow language" (*CR*, 170) and which "alone provide the coherence of our expression" (*MW*, 61). For Cavell, ordinary language philosophy rightly does not seek to *refute* skepticism. Instead it takes its stand in the necessity for an always renewed *response* to the skeptical "threat of world-consuming doubt by means of its own uncanny homeliness, stubbornly resting within its relentless superficiality" (*IQ*, 176). Cavell calls for "an acknowledgement of human limitation which does not leave us chafed by our own skin, by a sense of powerlessness to penetrate beyond the human conditions of knowledge" (*MW*, 61). The form this acknowledgement will have to take is not that "of philosophical construction but of *the reconstruction or resettlement of the everyday*" (*IQ*, 176, emphasis added).

The philosophical skepticism that pictures its clinically exact handling of human knowledge as a scrupulously impartial critique Cavell sees rather as a co-conspirator in a mode of "Western conceptualizing" for which (in both Heidegger and Emerson) the clutching hand, with which we "grasp" things, emblematizes a "kind of sublimized violence," that makes a desert and calls it a clearing. Cavell summarizes this region of Kant (the region of only sense percepts received and intellectual concepts only synthesized) as "no intellectual intuition," and adduces as its knowingly aversive counter Emerson's "all I know is reception" (*TN*, 80). From this recuperation of Western philosophical history, Cavell sees the post-Kantian survival of skepticism powering its way toward the disappearance of the world not on the nice epistemological rigor of its own accounting, but "on some other power, less genteel, call it repression" (*IQ*, 47). Call it, in one of Cavell's titles, a disowning of knowledge, a refusal to know what we cannot just not know.[6] Or, call it (as Cavell after Emerson does) that "most unhandsome part of our condition" (*CH*, 38) which causes us endlessly to come to grief with the "evanescence and lubricity of all objects, which lets them slip through our fingers then when we clutch hardest," and in aversion to which Cavell would draw himself and his readers to what Emerson calls the "most handsome part of our condition," that "specifically human form of attractiveness . . . naming the rightful call we have on one another, and that I and the world make upon one another" (*TN*, 86–7).

To disown the knowledge encoded in our agreements in forms of life is a form of repression because, on the Wittgensteinian principle that concepts follow interests, everything given to us in the counts and recountings of our shared language traces what has mattered to us. We count only what counts or matters to us, and so we count along the lines of an "aesthetics and economics of speech" (*CR*, 94–5) according to which we shear out a continually reforming "constitution" of words, which is not arbitrary but *natural*. For if we follow Cavell's example and take Wittgenstein's central concept of "form of life" as principally directed to the biological or "vertical" differentiation of the form of life of us talkers (both [horizontally] Greek and Jew, but neither plant nor animal), the yield is of an intuition as to what (in Cavell's polemically unfashionable emphases) *naturally* draws our "form of *life*" to construct for itself, in whatever language and with whatever refinements of distinction, such conceptual underpinnings and verbal spaces as are expressed in words like *hope* and *expectation*, *horror* and *home*, *intention* and *excuse*, *chair* and *pain* (*TN*, 41ff). Any social grouping will have to fix into place a multitude of conventions for its common business, but by the level of his address to the concepts of *criterion* and *agreement*, Wittgenstein would have his others and interlocutors consider "attunements" which, as evidence of our "natural history, go deeper than the more or less explicit adjustments any one cultural or historical grouping will call its conventions. He would have us consider what we settle on as a consequence of the "human fix itself" (*CR*, 110).

Our attunements expressed through criteria and gathered into a language (to imagine which is to imagine a form of life) witness what we have found *worth* saying. They are, before all else, agreements in valuing—agreements about "how we individuate things and name, settle on nameables, why we call things as we do—... how we determine what *counts* as instances of our concepts, this thing as a table, this as a chair, this other as a human, that other as a god. To speak is to say what counts" (*IQ*, 86, Cavell's emphasis). For any thing in our world to *be* a thing of our world, we must beforehand have settled on it as worth the candle of conceptualizing. We must care about it, take such interest in it as to drive it into what Heidegger calls unconcealment.

Because the "idea of valuing is the other face of asserting" (*CR*, 94), Cavell regularly finds himself pondering "what we have it at heart to say," an expression that strikes me as a remembering of the kerygma that there where we have laid up our treasure, there will we find what we have set our heart on. Where we have laid up our conceptual treasure (as in the keep and gathering of Heidegger) is, case by case, the evidence of something that has counted for us, mattered to us. And because a word or concept is both the expression of our interests and a schema of connectedness with other concepts, the issue is always how we are to settle (with) these words of ours as they endlessly call for a way to voice their proper individual interests and still "come to terms with" their others in a newly trued basis of constitution. This is what the bringing-our-words-back-home of ordinary language philosophy comes to or from. It is a response to what, by Cavell's account, stands at the heart of Thoreau's "book of losses" where "it is no set of desired things he has lost, but a connection with things, the track of desire itself" (*SW*, 51). And if these lost words of ours call out to be resettled, the venue for this mission is what, following Thoreau, Cavell calls writing or the second ("reborn") inheritance of language when the slap-dash mouthings of the mother tongue give way to the "father tongue" and its autonomously "reserved and select expression" (*Walden*, 69) in which every written element or word "preserves its integrity" under the pressure of differing occasions but still allows itself (and each of its fellows) to exit into and be adjusted by the company it keeps on each of these occasions (*SW*, 34).[7]

The father tongue of writing is "not a new lexicon or syntax at our disposal, but precisely a rededication to the inescapable and utterly specific syllables upon which we are already disposed" (*SW*, 16). Language so conceived and taken on is not a banner raised on high in order to *enforce* the unity of a human group. It is the standard of an attunement which is already there, only lost and tattered in the dark wood of our words as we are ordinarily given to blather them. If every word is a sign of (and a motion toward) bonds which we are always already violating, and if increasingly in Cavell our faithlessness to these commitments presents itself as the allegorical "first blight" for the legion of all our other forms of dereliction, then against this condition of chronic backsliding, the "writer's faith" stakes its hopes on the furthering and rational good that will come of recollecting the bearings of *every word* we find we have had it at heart to enter into an account of our condition. The aspiration of this faith is that, place by place and time after time, we may yet labor toward a fullness of term and so bring (back) to life-signaling circulation and currency whatever portions of our commitments and conditions have become dead and lost to us.

If Cavell's conviction in the hiding places of power to be found in our wordings of the world takes fire from the flinty Austinian mask of superficiality, what becomes of this abiding conviction in subsequent Cavell is a very un-Austinian ambition still to raise our words up to the light and still thereby, as Heidegger's *What Is Called Thinking?* puts it, "to let the truth happen" (*TN*, 3) of ourselves and our world, but now in the service of nothing less than the saving of the human as it now stands in need of what Cavell calls the second creation of a deliverance or a redemption. As provoked and deepened by the *Investigations*, Cavell's philosophical vision comes to see that what is all too commonly lost on us in our most ordinary words amounts to nothing less than a pit of perdition, from which the only promise of an exit is what *The Senses of Walden* is already calling not just a "rescue" but a "redemption" of language (*SW*, 63, 92). While remaining an American philosopher committed to the procedures and promises (and something of the stinting self-denials) of the ordinary language school, Cavell migrates from the Oxford don making virtuoso distinctions in the common room to the prophet crying in the wilderness. As the animus of his writings increasingly betrays its inspiration in the underlying current of moral fervor he makes such a point of in Wittgenstein, Heidegger and Emerson, one cannot help but be struck at the way later Cavell requires that the attending *to* his words be reconceived as attendance *at* his words (as in our attendance at some public and sacred enactment), the way he demands that—as in his "lectures after Emerson after Wittgenstein"—the reading of his readings be not just an intellectual engagement but a spiritual exercise. In this spiritual exercise, the interlocked reader and writer are to take steps together toward a wording of human condition, the success and profit of which will be less tallied up in the coin of instruction than proved experientially in such modes of responsiveness as his readers must learn to call *deliverance* (as from bondage) or *recovery* (as from an illness) or *redemption* (as from perdition).

A writer's testament and faith: Staying with Wittgenstein, going on with Emerson

"You only need sit still long enough in some attractive spot in the woods that all its inhabitants may exhibit themselves to you by turns" (*Walden*, 153). This is a sentence from *Walden*'s "Brute Neighbors" reiteratively honored by Cavell as all of the book's healing waters condensed into a few drops. Cavell's most extended draw on it occurs in his contribution to a 1981 symposium on "The Politics of Interpretation" (*T*, 50–1). There, in the course of again claiming Thoreau for philosophy, he brings the attractively stilled sitting (and setting) counseled by this sentence into close affinity with the therapeutic posture of psychoanalysis. As the persistent reader of *Walden* is to be drawn ever more deeply into its attractive pool of words so that, under the stillness of its gaze, she may in turn be read or found (out), so likewise with the dynamics of attraction and discovery at play in psychoanalytic practice. In the talking cure, the aptly named analysand suffers herself (the apposite pronoun in Freud's ground-breaking studies of Dora and hysteria) to be read under the all-gathering, all-inscribing gaze of a resolutely still analyst. By transference to this analyst as the archive of her own history, the patient subjects herself to what has come to settle just there as the text or constitution of herself, the therapeutic aim being to "get the hang of oneself" (*MW*, 85) and hence the freedom or run of one's self, a voice in one's history.

In Cavell's staging of the talking cure, the resolutely still therapist is "one human being [who] represents to another all that that other has conceived of humanity in his or her life, and moves with that other toward an *expression of the conditions which condition* that utterly specific life" (emphases added).[8] To Cavell, this one-on-one drama of reading and acknowledgment concretizes the philosophical call for our condition(s) to be brought up to the light, even as its directors or practitioners aggressively deny any philosophical origin for the theory and practice bearing Freud's name. In Cavell's intellectual progress, philosophy and psychoanalysis come to figure as mutually repressing others. Analysis denies its origins in philosophy, while philosophy, particularly in its Anglo-American guise, clearly wants to continue repressing any claims to healing that might have been advanced at its Socratic origins.

If *The Senses of Walden* directly affirms the need for the "redemption" both of our lost lives and of our lost words, the 1981 invocation of Freud presents psychoanalysis as the model for this "redemptive reading": "For most of us, I believe, the idea of redemption or redemptive reading and interpretation will not be credible apart from a plausible model or picture of how a text can be therapeutic, that is, apart from an idea of the redemptive as psychological.... I imagine that the credible psychological model of redemption will have to be psychoanalytic in character" (*T*, 51–2). When Cavell conflates psychoanalytic practice both with philosophy as revised in Thoreau and redemption as urged in the prophets, he might be taken as (merely) engaging in a patently "secularizing" example of his constant attempt "to fit together into some reasonable, or say convivial, circle, a collection of the main beasts in my jungle or wilderness of interests" (*IQ*, 153). But as Cavell strives to call psychoanalytic practice to its rightful and companionable place at the table of his interests, he seems drawn less to ruining some sacred truths of redemption down into the kind of recovery promised by analysis than to bringing up to the light the unacknowledged religious conditions of what we call psychotherapy. In *The Claim of Reason*, Cavell himself cautions that "nothing is obvious about 'secularization,' especially not whether in a given case it looks like, as one might call it, eternalization" (*CR*, 471–2). I think, then, of what Cavell's words here enact as a (not totally acknowledged) religious analog to what Cavell will more openly and more confidently write about the *philosophical* origins of psychoanalysis in his later "Freud and Philosophy: A Fragment." In again pursuing the claim that psychoanalysis is an inheritor of philosophy, this short piece climaxes on a decidedly religious note. Cavell cannot quite bring himself to end on the speculation that Freud's clinical methods make the task set by Wittgenstein's idea of grammar "concrete." Instead he goes one (guarded) step further toward the functional identity of Wittgensteinian grammar with the all-creating Logos of the Gospel of John: "The matter is to express the intuition that fantasy shadows anything we can understand reality to be. As Wittgenstein more or less puts an analogous matter: the issue is not to explain how grammar and criteria allow us to relate language to the world but to determine what language relates the world to be. This is not well expressed as the priority of mind over reality or of self over the world . . . It is better put as the priority of grammar—the thing Kant calls conditions of possibility (of experience and of objects), the thing Wittgenstein calls possibilities of phenomena—over both what we call mind and what we call the world. If we call grammar the Logos, we will more readily sense the shadow of fantasy in this picture."[9]

To return to Cavell's earlier offer of a psychoanalytic model for redemptive reading. There, he seems less sure of his ground; he betrays an anxiety about which discourse is to be master, the religious or the psychoanalytic. For his one thing needed of redemptive reading he clearly wants to appropriate psychoanalytic procedures as a model of great and shareable explanatory power. But he doesn't seem to say this with the sound of full conviction. The way he clears his throat—"For most of us, I believe"—is just halting enough that it carries with it a whiff of momentarily bad intellectual conscience, as if the speaker knows that what is driving him toward this conversational tic is the sense that, as he prepares to issue a call for redemptive reading, he had better quickly send his audience an ingratiating signal about the like-minded reasonableness known to subsist between them.

What I am taking as (in part) a gambit of accommodation edged with frayed uneasiness is, to my ear, amplified by Cavell's manifest impatience with what he sees as the typical inability of psychoanalytic interpreters to let their reading of texts turn into that experience of "being read" which is his touchstone for an authentic act of (and success in) what he wants reading to become. Addressing himself to psychoanalytic readers of all stripes who programmatically subject the text at hand to the truths of the master discipline, Cavell asserts that too often this routine has "seemed typically to tell us something we more or less already knew, to leave us pretty much where we were before we read." And he goes on to say "that from the point of view of psychoanalytic therapy the situation of reading has typically been turned around, that it is not first of all the text that is subject to interpretation but we in the gaze or hearing of the text" (*T*, 52).

The signs and wonders of recovery sought by Cavell haunt that region of the Kantian philosophical settlement where one is (as Cavell writes of Emerson and Thoreau) called to "the speaking of necessaries, and speaking with necessity" (*TN*, 81). Some of Cavell's (mostly) Wittgensteinian pictures of this region are: *forms of life*, *ground*, the *given*, the *unconditioned*, the *ordinary*. At the level at which we all have our various and specific ways of going astray from these necessities and thus of darkening ourselves to ourselves, the workings of what analysis would call repression or alienation are so fundamentally a portion of our human fate that the familiarly available grammatical possibilities of the phenomenon we conventionally call *therapy* are miscast as what to these griefs would count as recovery. Indeed, to try to make what we call *therapy* play this role strikes me as a variation on Cavell's abiding grief that nothing is more human than this way we have of mistaking our metaphysical finitude for some intellectual lack. It strikes me as letting some contingent developmental mischance stand in for the ground-level given that we're finite, that (as Beckett's Hamm says) "we're on earth, there's no *cure* for that" (*MW*, 129, Cavell's pointed emphasis).

"No *cure* for that," Cavell goes on, "but perhaps there is something else for it—if we could give up our emphasis upon cure. There is faith, for example." But *is* there faith when we do not as yet (or any longer?) have any way of saying how "that faith [could be] achieved, how expressed, how maintained, how deepened, how threatened, how lost" (*CR*, 243), when (as Cavell will some time later explain) we are not in command of even the "opening pieces" of this word's grammar as, for example, "that *this* is what we call "to lose one's faith," this to maintain it and so on (*IQ*, 136)? Because what Cavell is struggling to find words for does not fill the ready-to-hand bill of *therapy* or *cure*, he is provoked toward trying such "religious" caps as *faith* and *redemption*—even as in so doing he becomes more alive to the fact that "we do not understand a word of all this" (*SW*, 59).[10]

If there is no *cure*, then perhaps there is *faith*, and specifically there is what, speaking of Thoreau, Cavell calls the "writer's faith" that "human forms of feeling, objects of human attraction, our reactions constituted in art, are as universal and necessary, as objective, as revelatory of the world, as the forms of the laws of physics" (*SW*, 104). With all the fraudulent dreck and slipshod babble abroad in the world, the abandon with which Cavell expresses his trust in our "constitutions of words" or "our reactions constituted in art" must seem extravagant. But neither Thoreau nor Cavell harbors any illusions about how "before a true gaze" the bulk of our constructions would, in the former's memorable words, "all go to pieces in your account of them" (*Walden*, 65). What, on the contrary, Cavell proposes for the expenses of our spirit and the investments of our trust is at hand, for example, in the construction of *Walden* as it newly inhabits or settles our words. What Cavell commends to us is just this edification, the offering or boon of which is its own "primary evidence" (*EL*, 263) that the constituting has happened, that the art of writing is here doing its work of wording the world together. Call this how Cavell, keeping faith with the intuitions of ordinary language philosophy, receives Thoreau's counsel that we are to allow our "anxious wakefulness" (with our words maddening and haunting us) to give way to that "constant awakening" (*SW*, 98) in which "our words need not haunt us. [For] if we learn how to entrust our meaning to a word, the weight it carries through all its computations [i.e. "as it recurs page after page, changing its company and modifying its occasions"] will yet prove to be just the weight we will find we wish to give it" (*SW*, 34–5).

If all the little local discoveries on the common ground of our ordinary language make it clear that we are always failing to inherit the full measure to which our words express our character and our constitution and our world, then it is against the background of "this chagrin with the way the world is given to use words" (*CH*, 65) that the work and progress of philosophy must be seen as enjoining an endless vigilance and an exhaustive rigor about just how we have not let now this word and now that tell us all that it knows. On the threshing-floor of such aspirant "constitutions of words" as *Walden*, the deeply weighed and capaciously extended words of the "father tongue" would bring to light both that and how "our faithlessness to our language repeats our faithlessness to all our shared commitments" (*SW*, 66). The promise of Cavell's writing—and its fervent claim to and for reason—is that what has been repressed or cast out into darkness can be brought back to light and (our) life. In Wittgenstein's philosophical practice, the lost sheep of our words are, in Cavell's word, to be "shepherded" (*TN*, 35) back home from perdition. Taken up in faith, this pastoral work can be a sustained and sustaining joy, but it is surely labor, a philosophical and spiritual work in progress of a very exacting (and unending) kind. By the requirements of this labor, any and every word, either out of our mouth or at hand in print or script, can become something of our own in the use of which we are either justified or condemned.

Cavell acknowledges that his vision of writing assumes a posture toward "every word" that we have come to expect (if at all) only in poetry of the highest scriptural or prophetic ambition. But, like Thoreau, he would shoulder the burden in prose, his every word so pondered as to bear a part, and that a needful part, toward a gathering of itself and company toward a constitution or (justified) city of words. As Virgil famously has the Cumaean Sybil say about getting *back* from the dead, "Hoc opus, hic labor est." This is the real task and the real undertaking. It is what is called redemption. And redemption not just of our alienated grammar, but also a (continuing) redemption of that world which skepticism's denial of our grammar would deprive us of, but which Thoreau and Emerson as the American "inheritors of Kant's transcendentalism" would recover in their way of writing "out of a sense of the intimacy of words with the world, or of intimacy lost" (*IQ*, 170). What makes our knowledge *of* a world of objects is (in a phrase from Emerson) "the mysteries of human condition" (*EL*, 966; *IQ*, 37)—not some familiar and constant entity all too routinely called "*the* human condition," but the provisionality of a form of life had only on condition. We are, in other words, to accept and acknowledge that by the terms of human condition, "thought is not confined *by* language (and its categories) but *to* language" (Cavell's emphasis).[11] John Austin's trust in ordinary words represents one exemplary posture toward the form of life which is the life of our language; others are the later Wittgenstein and the Heidegger of *What Is Called Thinking* with his "confidence in a mode of argumentation which invests itself in what is apt to seem at best the child's play of language and at worst the wild variation and excesses of linguistic form that have always interfered with rationality" (*CH*, 38). And still another is to be found in Cavell's reading of Emerson as indeed a philosopher, but one whose characteristic call for, and practice of, a radical "abandonment of and to language and the world" (*IQ*, 175), while it earned the unstinting admiration of Nietzsche, has repeatedly provoked his American readers into denying him any serious philosophical standing.

Cavell first testifies to the "writer's faith" in Thoreau, but it is to Emerson that he eventually and then habitually turns for the recurring advent of this faith in what he characterizes as the essayist's own parable for the promptings, character, and bearing of the words he commits to paper and to the hands of his reader: "I shun father and mother and wife and brother, when my genius calls me. I would write on the lintels of the door-post, *Whim*. I hope it is somewhat better than whim at last, but we cannot spend the day in explanation" (*EL*, 262).¹² Cavell draws repeated attention to how the "genius" here calling on Emerson—genius as not some special endowment but the "capacity for self-reliance" (*CH*, 26)—occupies the commanding position of Jesus calling on his disciples to come and follow him unconditionally, and how the marking of the lintel reinscribes the discriminating sign which, in Pharaoh's Egypt, warded off the angel of death from the chosen people.

Cavell emphasizes the apparent blasphemy of Emerson's claims for a vocation commenced under the sign of shunning departure and opened toward an exodus undertaken in the hope that it alone is the way to life, freedom and deliverance. "Emerson," writes Cavell, "is putting the *calling* and the *act* of his writing in the public place reserved in both of the founding testaments of our culture for the word of God. Is he serious?" (*T*, 19). The temptation here is too quickly to affirm that Cavell definitely thinks so, no two ways about it. But perhaps the trailer about seriousness should be left there as a real and standing question, one which, far from impeding Cavell's writing, provokes him to a style, which, while often appearing to court dismissal, is deliberately penned in the hope that, at the last, it will indeed be taken to heart as deadly serious, but on the dauntingly estranging terms of a precursor who in "presenting the credentials of his vocation" (*IQ*, 22) is "submitting his writing to the condition of acquiring whatever authority and conviction is due to it by looking at its countenance and surface" (*IQ*, 23).

By whatever marks of writing Emerson blazes his trail "as from an Intuition of what counts to a Tuition of how to recount it" (*TN*, 102), these marks have, for Cavell, no foundation or authority other than themselves. Emerson's writing is not *backed* by anything; it is "fronted by the character of the judger" (*CH*, xxx). There is no guarantee that anyone will take Emerson at his word, no assurance that he will not be laughed out of countenance. That is up, by turns, to each reader of each essay. The writing itself is the "path of [Emerson's] faith and redemption" (*T*, 19), and if the self-reliant inscription of Whim is to prove better than whim at the last, then that will "be proven on the way, *by* the way" (*SW*, 137, Cavell's emphasis).

To Cavell, the "readings" of Thoreau and Emerson originate from thinkers repressed into amateur status by professional philosophy because, in marked contrast to what is commonly called argument or consecutive reasoning, "they propose, and embody, a mode of thinking, a mode of conceptual accuracy, as thorough as anything imagined within established philosophy, but invisible to that philosophy because based on an idea of rigor foreign to its establishment" (*IQ*, 14). This "foreign rigor" Cavell calls "reading." Coming to this account of reading with a faith that *our* terms constitute the conditions or possibilities of phenomena, Cavell "*sees*" reading "*as*"¹³ a process of "being read" (*IQ*, 16), and, like Thoreau, includes within it much more than the literal act of reading: "But while we are confined to books, though the most select and classic, and read only particular written languages, which are themselves but dialects and provincial, we are in danger of forgetting the language which *all things and events* speak without metaphor, which alone is copious and standard. Much is published, but little printed.... [The best course of study is] the *discipline of looking at what is to be seen*. Will you be a reader, a student merely, or a *seer*? Read your fate, *see what is before you*, and walk on into futurity" (*Walden*, 75, emphases added). Cavell comments that "what is before you is precisely not, if you catch Thoreau's tune, something in the future; what is before you, if you are, for example, reading, is a text. He asks his reader to see it, to become a seer *with* it. Only then can you walk beyond where you are" (*IQ*, 16, emphases added). As "writing is a variation of reading, since to write is to cast words together that you did not make so as to give or take readings," so reading is "a variation of writing, where they meet in meditation and achieve accounts of their opportunities" (*IQ*, 18). The lesson from either direction of this writing/reading exchange is: Words are not your private property. They were there before you as your grounding terms and conditions. If you want to walk, you need the friction of this "rough ground" (*TN*, 56; *Investigations*, 107). You need to see that it is the traction-affording grammar of this form of life which is before you as your tract of possibilities and instruction. Only then can you take your own steps beyond where you are. While Cavell insists that for him "philosophizing is a product of reading, the reading in question is not especially of books, especially not of what we think of as books of philosophy. The reading is of whatever is before you" (*IQ*, 18).

And the hoped-for success or "progress" of such reading is for the reader to become the one read, the one called out. For a preliminary example of this in Cavell's own practice of reading, consider how he turned to his own account this sentence from Emerson's "Divinity School Address": "Truly speaking, it is not instruction, but provocation, that I can receive from another soul" (*EL*, 79). Cavell manifestly found provocation in this sentence; he placed it at the epigraphic head to the entire enterprise of *The Claim of Reason*. And a decade later, he confessed that the sentence still "echoes" for him when he finds himself asking of an American English, uncannily like Heidegger's turns on one commonly used German word after another, "What translation will capture the idea of provocation here as calling forth, challenging?" (*CH*, 37).

If one applies to Cavell's reading of Emerson his interpretation of reading as "being read," then it seems inescapable that this reading of Emerson on the "act and calling" of his writing repeatedly turns up in Cavell's own writing because it constitutes a perpetually renewed occasion for his own writing to be read and understood in the character of a philosophical precursor who here and now claims for himself the callings of *both* Moses and Jesus. What does it say about Cavell's conception of his own work in progress that he continually returns to this spot in Emerson's writing where (by Cavell's own account) this writing imagines itself as recounting for itself the two dramas of "calling forth" in which the two "founding testaments of our culture" cast the word of God as summoning either the Israelites out of Egypt or all of us out of what Paul (*Romans* 7:24) calls this body of death?

My thought here about what might be called the religious conditions of Cavell's philosophical practice is that in his work of "revising mythology" (*IQ*, 53), Wittgenstein and Emerson are drawn on as the two needed characters or heroes of the two founding testaments of our culture, the one handing down, or drawing out, the law, the other aversively proclaiming a "new" instauration of the spirit to fulfill and so succeed the law. This is extremely treacherous terrain, and some cautionary signposts are in order. First of all, the institutional Christian step from so-called Old to New Testament may still enjoy an incalculable cultural privilege, but about the broad intertextual way the one testament has of going on from the other, there is precisely nothing new.[14] As Robert Alter authoritatively puts it, the Hebrew Bible is so much "a set of texts in restless dialogue with one another"[15] that it may rightly claim to have itself taught the writers of its successor testament that their tidings, to have any hope of a hearing, would have, like Second Isaiah, to say "behold I show you a new thing." When this "Old Testament" prophet calls for and celebrates a New Exodus from a new Egypt, he is as out "to make it new" as the author of *Revelations*. In addition, the religiously charged words saturating Emerson and Cavell's writing are invariably directed toward what is at hand in the near and the ordinary, and although most of the writers attracting Cavell's attention are (by his own testimony) "bone by bone" (*CR*, 471) reinterpreters of Christianity, "nothing," he notes, "is obvious about 'secularization', especially not whether in a given case it looks like, as one might call it, eternalization" (*CR*, 471–2). When, for example, Cavell first finds himself moved to write of Emerson answering the call of his genius and writing Whim on the lintel, he hits upon these words: "Something has happened; it is up to us to name it, or not to. Something is wrestling for our blessing" (*SW*, 137). The allusion to Jacob wrestling with the angel (and as a consequence receiving a blessing and a new name) could scarcely be more open, but Cavell has turned the onus of naming and blessing around to the self-reliant human agent. Here, the human striver is the one called out to the naming of where, at this juncture and thigh-stressing step of experience, he finds himself. To me, this looks less like a secularization of Jacob with the angel than an "eternalization" of Emerson's (and Cavell's) stake in and way with words.[16]

Cavell pictures Emerson and Wittgenstein as bound by a certain trust (and a certain distrust) of words. But if, for Wittgenstein, this trust issues into a call back to the "language of life," for Emerson it provokes a call onward to the "life of language" that can be received in "every word" as a potential vehicle for carrying out what Cavell calls thinking. This thinking attitude toward "every word" Cavell finds epitomized in Emerson's description of the poet as one who "in every word he speaks rides on them as the horses of thought" (*CH*, 22):

> Given that the idea of "every word" is not a generalization but bespeaks an attitude toward words as such, toward the fact of language, the horse suggests that we are in an attitude or posture of a certain grant of authority, such as humans may claim, over a realm of life not our own (ours to own), in view of some ground to cover or field to take. That words are under a *certain* control, one that requires that they obey as well as that they be obeyed, is captured in Wittgenstein's idea that in his philosophizing words are seen to be away and as having to be returned home (to their *Heimat*). What he says is not quite that 'what we do is to bring words back,' but more strictly that we *lead* them (*führen die Wörter*)—from metaphysical to everyday; suggesting that their getting back, whatever that is, is something they must do under their own power, if not quite, or always, under their own direction (Cavell's emphases).

Emerson's "horses of thought" picture our ordinary language as the "given" of the form of life of us talkers, which, while not ours to own, is nonetheless granted to us with a certain corresponding grant of authority. We don't own it but we have the run of it, and the successful pursuit of our claims on and with it is to be grounded on a life with our language such that our obedient readiness to inherit and "go on" with the words portioned out to us might (as in the ideal of poetry) find one of its exemplars in the posture of the capable equestrian perpetually on the *qui vive* for every slightest turn in the pulse and flection of a spirited mount.

But in the very act of praising Emerson's "life of language" as something like Elijah's "horses of fire," Cavell keeps himself in continuing conversation both with the kind of "every word" the European Wittgenstein "in our poverty" typically bears down on, and with the even more different kind of "every word" which three decades earlier the Harvard graduate student witnessed the Oxford don clinically palpating into the natural history of such microscopically intertwined verbal tissue as *inadvertently*, *automatically* and so on. Grant to Emerson that "[all language] is vehicular and transitive, and is good, as ferries and horses are, for conveyance, not as farms and houses are, for homestead"

(*EL*, 463), it would still seem to be a condition of any transit to the Emersonian life of language that we get back to the Wittgensteinian language of life. It is from there that, as from a hard bottom with words in place, each "crescive self" may begin to spring its arch toward a "constitution of words" which, in truing itself into its own "due sphericity," would stand ready for whatever, wheel without wheel, it finds to be its newly real needs and (at)tractions along the hard-bottom ground of "where we live and what we live for."

This dual (but not divided) allegiance of Cavell's is his way of making his own what he finds common to such heroes of his as Wittgenstein, Thoreau, Rousseau, and Luther: a clearly admired "sensibility" (*TN*, 44), the effect of whose provocative "attempts to conserve a project [respectively, philosophy, America, Community, Christianity] is to bring on deep revolutionary changes." Quoting Jesus, Cavell trenchantly asserts that "to demand that the law be fulfilled, every jot and tittle, will destroy the law as it stands, if it has moved too far from its origins (*CR*, 121). This is an old story about the letter that killeth and the spirit that giveth life, a story that gets translated into Cavell's Thoreauvian conception of his writing as a neighborly call upon his reader not to let the dead letter of these offered words evidence a slaying and themselves kill, but rather, with a correspondent and "congening" (*TN*, 12) spirit, to take them in and so recuperate them (back) up into the spirit in which they live and move and have their being. (As Thoreau says in the "Conclusion" to *Walden*, "The volatile truth of our words should continually betray the inadequacy of the residual statement. Their truth is instantly translated; its literal monument alone remains.")

The "sensibility" that fulfills the law by destroying it is that of the prophet who takes the "project" he was born into and, instead of consenting to it as it stands, aversively subjects what has come to seem the dead letter of its conventions to a corrosive inquest meant to reveal and make newly alive what these hidebound conventions were originally in service of, in what spirit framed. Any "reading" of where one finds oneself and one's form of life requires what John Keats called a "greeting of the spirit."[17] Without the latter's perpetually renewed advent, any writing "penned" into the residual statement of the dead letter will, for all its monumental bulk, lie stillborn. It will not be (in Cavell's play on words) *ex-pounded* (*IQ*, 126). It will not be raised up into the unseen force and flight of its volatile truth.

Cavell continues to inherit Wittgenstein (and Austin) because, as disclosed in criteria, the bedrock ground or origin (the "home") of our language games is something we are continually called to acknowledge as positioning us at one of the two Kantian "standpoints," the one that situates the human as subject to, and determined by, the concept of law. As the critic of culture "declining decline" (*TN*, 29) and calling our words back to the language games in which they are at home, Cavell's Wittgenstein is like a Moses insisting to his backsliding flock that to get back on what *Deuteronomy* calls the "way of life" they must return to the law given to them. But the tablets of this law are not for Cavell a stone of stumbling and offense to be put behind him once he has come into his own as a faithful receiver of the spirit wafting his way from Emerson. On the contrary, the law retains its claim on this representative ζῷον ἔχον λόγον. For if the law or home of our "pervasive and systematic agreements" (*CR*, 30) in language is bedrock—if this is where, as Wittgenstein repeatedly insists, justifications come to an end and we find ourselves without grounds or reasons and little more to say for ourselves than "this is what I do"—the story does not end just there. For this bedrock or grounding calls on us to attend to that reiterated Wittgensteinian moment in Cavell when, spade turned and criteria found disappointing, he feels called upon to "remind myself of the sorts of expressions in which Wittgenstein presents what I understand as the background against which our criteria do their work; even make sense" (*CR*, 83). At such junctures, Wittgenstein calls for (or reminds us of) the posture of acceptance or acknowledgment that alone provides the background against which criteria can be criteria, the law can be the law: "What has to be accepted, the given, is—so one could say—*forms of life*" (*CR*, 83, quoting *Investigations*, p. 226, Wittgenstein's emphasis). Such backgrounding expressions are not handed down as the law inscribed in stone. They are voiced, rather, as appeals toward a specifically human capacity for response and acknowledgment. They intimate that if we withhold the greeting spirit of acknowledgment—if we refuse to count— then our criteria go dead, all the breath gone out of them. "Words [then] have no carry. It is like trying to throw a feather; for some things, breath is better than strength; stronger" (*CR*, 84).

If it is within the breath of our acknowledgment alone that our criteria can live and have their all too human being, then, in addition to being the subjects of the law, we are, in necessarily successive acts of "lively origination" (*IQ*, 75), the bringers of the law. As a "stupendous antagonism" (*EL*, 953), we each of us constitute a scene for the playing out of the polarity of Emerson's Man Thinking as the latter finds himself positioned at both Kantian standpoints as a common subject of the law and "the inventor of the game" (*EL*, 469), the lordly claimant of autonomy. For Cavell, Wittgenstein is the self-described tenant of "the darkness of this time" (*Investigations*, x), remanding him back to the "rough ground" traction of our language games, but as just such an exponent of the possibilities of phenomena he also affords his American successor a way of "going on" from him. He provokes Cavell into a posture toward the given fact of language such that, in the face or reception of this fact, neither he nor his others need "imitatively declare our [unknowable] uniqueness (the theme of skepticism)" but may "originally declare our commonness (the theme of acknowledgement)" (*IQ*, 132). In this latter spirit of acknowledgement, Cavell turns to Emerson on the near, the low and the common; counts this too as a (re)turning to the "language of life"; but also claps, with a rebirth of infantine joy, when he finds that these essays in and of the New World draw him extravagantly on toward the "life of language" as it is constituting itself in the "new yet unapproachable America" of this writing (*TN*, 92).

In directing interest and giving thought to the ordinary terms of our existence, both Cavell's Wittgensteinian investigations and his Emersonian essays would bring up to "complete clarity" not only *what* the terms or conditions of our existence are, but (*Investigations*, §242) *that* these terms express the interests and indeed the necessities of the life-form of us talkers. In Wittgensteinian terms, our attunements in language register what, at the level not of opinions but of forms of life, counts for us, and one cardinal, say hinging, necessity of the form of life of us talkers is what Cavell will come to call the necessity of our freedom. For if there is to be any counting or criteria or grammar at all—if there is to be any language at all—then we have to be the ones originating it, all our countings a matter of what counts or matters for us. In the chapter of *In Quest of the Ordinary* entitled "Emerson, Coleridge, Kant (Terms as Conditions)," Cavell succinctly articulates the paradox of a necessary human freedom in a reading of Emerson's "Fate" as an effort to resituate the twin Kantian standpoints of freedom and necessity in language. Bearing down on a short and seemingly lightweight run of Emersonian sentences, Cavell makes them yield the provocative contention that although we are "victims of meaning," with the "character" of our language wording our world into intelligibility and so laying out before us what Cavell calls the law or "fatefulness of the ordinary," it is still the case that our "Lordship" (of a language that is no one else's but our own) "polarizes" this subjection to language. If we are fated to the ordinary and thus victims of meaning, we still "have a say in what we mean, [and] our antagonism to fate, to which we are fated, and in which our freedom resides, is as a struggle with the language we emit, of our character with itself" (*IQ*, 40). In addressing itself to the "old knots of fate, freedom, and foreknowledge," then, the *character* of Emerson's "Fate" "is meant to enact" an attractively penned (and pent) "struggle against itself, hence of language with itself, for its freedom" (*IQ*, 40).

If the emphasis of Wittgenstein's *Investigations* falls on bringing up to "total clarity" the "language of life" (*CH*, 21), by a contrast mostly of emphasis, the romantic nineteenth-century writing exemplified in the sentences of Emerson would raise itself up as a standard for the animating "life of language" (*CH*, 21). With the genius of Emerson's writing said by

Cavell to spring "from an Intuition of what counts to a Tuition of how to recount it" (*TN*, 102), such writing is, like Wittgenstein's, less interested in the assertion of any determinate theses or propositions than in giving voice and expression to the "*partiality*" of thinking as such, "what Kant calls (and Freud more or less calls) its incentive or interest (*Triebfeder* [a German word that, in this case of thinking, speaks of the trigger or spring for our drive toward intelligibility])" (*CH*, 42). What Cavell calls the "constitution of Emerson's writing," then, is conceived to be a series or course of words laid out before its thinking readers in the hope of "attracting [this thinking of theirs] to its partiality" (*CH*, 42). For our partiality—what counts or matters for us—is "the life of language," what animates it and brings it to life.

Perhaps nowhere does Cavell so dramatically represent this undergirding of the grammar of our life-forms by our shared partialities of desire and interest than in one highly charged and carefully staged moment of self-fashioning in the writing of *The Claim of Reason* (94–5). The scene is an argument about the natural and the conventional in Wittgenstein. But then, in a groundbreaking access to and of desire, there rises up before the eye and progress of the argument two pages of densely packed and breathlessly performed parenthesis, in which the language philosopher represents himself as drawn irresistibly to the question why we ever so much as begin to articulate the world into such conceptual constellations as we find in widest commonality around us spread. Cavell's answer (which he computes as fragments toward an "economics" and an "aesthetics" of speech) is that everything given to us in the counts and recountings of our shared language traces what has mattered or counted for us. Around this axis, the lathe of the strenuous tongue shears out a continually reforming "constitution" of words. Since we count only what counts or matters to us, the play of our re-countings should be keyed to this question of what matters to us. They should be pitched toward what Cavell calls "the achievement [or "exits"] of desire" (*IQ*, 28).

In reference to *Walden*—a book that "takes it upon itself to tell all and say nothing" (*CR*, 95)—Cavell puts the point more openly (still on pp. 95–6 of *The Claim of Reason*): "If we formulate the idea that valuing underwrites asserting as the idea that interest informs telling or talking generally, then we may say that the degree to which you talk of things in ways that hold no interest for you . . . is the degree to which you consign yourself to nonsensicality, stupefy yourself. . . . I think of this consignment as a form not so much of dementia as of what amentia ought to mean, a form of mindlessness. It does not appear unthinkable that the bulk of an entire culture, call it the public discourse of the culture, the culture thinking aloud about itself . . . should become ungovernably inane." In Cavell's account of it, Thoreau's ambition "to be a track-repairer somewhere in the orbit of the earth" (*SW*, 98; *Walden*, 78) is precisely not the pushing of a private agenda. To the contrary, Thoreau's draw toward *resolution* as "[comprising] both hardening and melting, the total concentration of resources and the total expenditure of them" (*SW*, 109) is directed toward "speaking of necessaries, and speaking with necessity" (*TN*, 81) as these necessities will be found to be encrypted in our ordinary and publicly shared language, the face value of whose every word is a fragment of our natural history and thus an open secret about what (in Cavell's brashly unfashionable emphasis) the human has *naturally* set its heart on.

For Cavell, the achievement of desire has become the one pressing philosophical task, a task signally taken on by Emerson and Thoreau but also to be found in Wittgenstein. Take the latter's remark, already invoked, that "it is what human beings *say* that is true and false; and they agree in the *language* they use" (*Investigations*, §241), this latter an agreement not in opinions but in forms of life. It is agreement in what matters. And discovering the depth of this systematic *Übereinstimmung* or "mutual attunement" was not, Cavell insists, "Wittgenstein's intellectual goal." It was his "instrument" (*CR*, 30), because "nothing is deeper than the fact, or extent, of [this] agreement itself" (*CR*, 32). It is the bedrock organon—what we have to go on—for exposing false necessities and discovering what really counts for us. So, in Wittgenstein's description of philosophy as "[leaving] everything as it is" (*Investigations*, §124), Cavell hears not reassurance for the temperamentally conservative but the most radical requirement for "the most forbearing act of thinking (this may mean the most thoughtful) to let true need, say desire, be manifest and be obeyed" (*TN*, 45).

As it now stands, our culture may profess to understand its would-be self-defining step from an Old Testament (of Law) to a New Testament (of Spirit) as having been successfully taken a long time ago, but in aversion to this conformist picture of our success, Cavell would, at Emerson's lead, turn toward the ways by which one might, word by word, "find the journey's end in every step of the road" (*EL*, 479; *TN*, 114). Reiteratively setting out on his own philosophical work in progress, Cavell comes to conceive of this work and progress in Emerson's terms of "stepping, lasting, grounding, achieving succession" (*TN*, 115). He comes to sense his calling as continually present in the systole and diastole of what he has it at heart to say about our human finitude as called to be both the obedient subject of the law's dictation and the autonomously mastering and spirited bringer of the law's character. In a word—a word he applies to just about every writer he cares about—Cavell *diurnalizes* the passage from Old to New Testament. He makes it an everyday thing, a daily posture of "diurnal devotedness" (*IQ*, 176), a stance toward words that would be fully responsive to their knotted call for *both* a pedestrian taking of legitimately authorized steps *and* an aversively volatile "leaping free of enforced speech, so succeeding it" (*TN*, 118). It is, so to speak, the law of a word that its meaning cannot legitimately be "up for decision" (*IQ*, 135). The meaning a word has is not totally (is not at all) at our disposal. But if a verbal concept is "stable," it must also be "tolerant." It must be graced with the "play" required for an "indefinite number of instances and directions of projection" (*CR*, 185). As it deals in the words given to it for its expression, any human form of life only stiffs itself with any stiff-necked try at "an attempted choice of meaning" (*SW*, 64) such as the one perpetrated by the American government when, on the way to a civil war within a house divided against itself, it persuaded itself to pass an abomination called the Fugitive Slave Law, as if "a man is a fugitive who is merely running from enslavement," (*SW*, 64). The alternative to such doomed "attempted choices of meaning," will appear subtle only because its demands are so utterly specific and incessant. That alternative is endlessly to take steps toward coming into one's own by acknowledging that it is but one's human due and responsibility to keep going on with "an autonomous choice of *words*" (*SW*, 64, emphasis added).

The edification of a book about a book

It is Cavell's fate as a reader to find himself caring about and letting himself be instructed by texts that are, as eventually he will say specifically of romantic works both "[account-] books of losses" and provocative "texts of recovery." *Walden*, "the major philosophical text in my life other than the *Philosophical Investigations*" (*IQ*, 169), is the first and still perhaps the most pertinent example in this regard. To Cavell's mind, we truly do want to turn toward Thoreau's "infinite expectation of the dawn" (*Walden*, 61), but to accomplish this turn—to bring off this "miracle" of change—we must be drawn out of the "sack of nostalgia" (*IQ*, 74). If "we crave change (say therapy) but are appalled by the prospect," then from this acknowledged position of impasse, we must be shown that "in our capacity for loss there is the chance for ecstasy" (*T*, 53). As in Freud's work of mourning, we must work toward a returning to (and of) the world by accepting, strand by strand, the verdict of reality that whatever we had before invested in is now, in fact, lost to us, gone. Far from leading us down a dead end, this "morning of mourning, [this] dawn of grieving" (*T*, 54) enables progress toward a newer day, whose Chanticleerian kerygma Cavell hears succinctly packed into Thoreau's twinned call to "see what is before you, and walk on into futurity" (*IQ*, 16). For to see what is before you is to achieve an account of it, to get it settled; and "only then can you walk beyond where you are" (*IQ*, 16). Only then can you shake off the unacknowledged vengefulness of your nostalgias, forego grievance and give yourselves to the present as your utterly specific "experiment," as your only opportunity for "lively origination" (*IQ*, 75). Only then, as in Thoreau's wisecrack, can you stop killing time and damaging eternity. And so Thoreau "completes the building of his house"—which means, being interpreted, both the resolution of himself and the edification of his book—"by showing how to leave it" (*T*, 54), by showing how neither he nor his reader is to take it (or embalm it) in the grievously deadening spirit of idolatry.

But to forego grievance and revenge is no easier a task than to put that Satan behind one who is the adversary sounder of souls, out to get even and clamoring for his due. Indeed, at its moment of truth or commitment, it is not a task at all. That "we do not know where the inspiration to give up revenge comes from" (*IQ*, 75) harks back to a remark made by Cavell almost two decades earlier: "it is [this] thing we do not know that can save us," this thing which, as opposed to works, "theology knew as grace" (*MW*, 326). But if grace (thought of as, I will venture, "the rightful call [or attractiveness] we have upon one another, and that I and the world, make upon one another" (*TN*, 86–7)), prompts a change of heart not to be accomplished by any determinate act of the will, nonetheless its way may be made straight or its channel opened up by the exhaustive "settling of one's accounts." As the settling of an estate may often be the necessary condition for turning to new ventures free of liens and encumbrances, so Thoreau must achieve the "settling" of himself if either he or his reader are to give themselves over to "the present moment, to toe that line" (*Walden*, 11). That this prevenient work of settling accounts is as difficult as it is necessary may be appreciated by noting the place Cavell finds in his work for the haunted and falling structures of Poe and the similarly bedeviled households of Hawthorne. In marked contrast to Thoreau and Emerson's verbal edifications, a house of Poe's construction is typically unlivable because it is unleavable. And it is unleavable because the inhabitant of such accommodations cannot get definitively behind him the dead accusing hand of some ghostly co-inhabitant whom in life he shunned or killed. Like the railroad of Thoreau—it riding us, not we it—a house of Poe's imagining is not a place to dwell or *sit* ("what is a house" asks Thoreau, "but a *sedes*, a seat?" (*Walden*, 55)), but something which (as the word *obsession* more or less says) crushingly and smotheringly sits *on* its builder or inmate. If Thoreau completes his edification by showing how to leave it "and advance confidently in the direction of his dreams" (*Walden*, 216), Poe's writing enacts the nightmare of our constructions going all to pieces on top of us because we cannot leave them alone even as they will not leave us alone.

Paradoxically, the way out of this maddened and imprisoned condition is to heed Thoreau's call to make "some progress toward settling in the world" (*Walden*, 58). But although the writer of *Walden* urges us to "drive a nail home and clinch it so faithfully that you can wake up in the night and think of your work with satisfaction [for "So will help you God, and so only"] (*Walden*, 221), he also counsels us to get on with the adventure of life by living "quite laxly and undefined in front, our outlines dim and misty on that side; as our shadows reveal an insensible perspiration toward the sun" (*Walden*, 216–17). The alternative to faithfully executed four-square performance is sloppy building and accounting practices, and to his chagrin Thoreau knows that such failures in construction and construal are fraught with ruinous spiritual and practical costs. In place of the condition of constant awakening, they keep in business the pathology of anxious wakefulness. They assure a life of penal servitude, with the spirit wastefully expended in the revenants of many unhappy returns. If you are ever so much as to enter into the possibility of saving your life by losing it, you first have to find that life. You have to settle where you live and what you live for. To "put down roots" is one valence or inclination of a Cavell given to speculations about our unending pilgrim or (im)migrant condition, but, like Thoreau's, his version of a truly great migration has little to do with far-flung exploration or plantation. As Cavell sees it, we are experimentally to put down roots not to find where we want to live but to find out "what wants to live in [us]" (*SW*, 157), what is necessarily of our condition and partiality. Similarly, Cavell's Emerson is out to settle what there is "enthusiastically" (*SW*, 136) to abandon himself to, what (as the prophets say) is from God, what he can commit his spirit to and not lose his breath into the bargain. This kind of transcendentalist takes philosophy's preoccupation with going up toward first principles and turns it into a "going on" that would first and last strive to settle what sun (which at the very end of *Walden* is called "but a morning star") toward which to expend and orient the per-spiring sweat of one's brow.

In response to the pieties customarily mouthed by his neighbors, Thoreau closes the portion of *Walden* most directly about the prompting depth, transparency and stillness of the pond with the exasperated rebuke of "Talk of heaven! ye disgrace earth" (*Walden*, 134). This is, with a vengeance, the calling to accounts of the American Jeremiad, but if Thoreau permits himself such outbreaks of wrath, it is not the only, or more pertinently, not the final expression or character he articulates for himself in *Walden*. Intimately connected with his pointing an accusing finger at his neighbors' disgraces is his urgent plea for, and perpetually renewed offer of, the vessels of grace they are defiling. The primary, central and most capacious of these vessels is the thing itself of Walden Pond. "Of all the characters I have known," Thoreau confides, "perhaps Walden wears best, and best preserves its purity . . . the same thought is welling up to its surface that was then [i.e. many years ago in his childhood]; it is the same liquid joy and happiness to itself and its

Maker, ay, and it *may* be to me . . . I see by its face that it is visited by the same reflection" (*Walden*, 130).

In bringing *The Senses of Walden* to a close, Cavell is clearly making it his business to bring his book about a book round to the same prompting grace of clarity and resolution as the place and book Thoreau made the business of his life for 2 years. In his account of his sojourn next to Walden Pond, he clearly wishes to be as salutary in his promptings: as the thing itself of the pond, that "earth's eye" and "gem of the first water" (*Walden*, 125, 121), which "its Maker . . . rounded with his hand, deepened and clarified in his thought, and in his will bequeathed to Concord" (*Walden*, 130); and as the book *Walden*, which Cavell calls the "boon" of Walden (Pond), "its writer cup[ping] it in his hand, see[ing] his reflection in it, and hold[ing] it out to us" (*SW*, 119). Like this water ever a joy to itself and its maker and like the humanly articulated "boon" of this book reflectively welling up into the stilled surface of its characters, Cavell would, in turn, have his book about this book be received as "gospel." He would bequeath it as a trenchantly sword-like testament which, for all its cuts of challenge and rebuke, does finally and positively resolve into its faithfully steadfast character as both a witness to, and a provider of, the living waters of renewal, a bearer of that kind of insistently local news which is both inspiringly good and solidly trustworthy. If Cavell's writing enacts its subject, then faith or confident trust is not just one of this writing's doctrinal tenets. It is, more pertinently, the spiritual boon or viaticum this writing directs its reader's way. It is (as in Emerson's *Self-Reliance*) the breath Cavell emits, or (as in Thoreau) the fragrance he wafts to those he would take into his confidence (*Walden*, 52). The "act and calling" of the writing is a gift of the spirit which Cavell would have each of his readers, by turns, hear in the wind "and carry it express" (*Walden*, 11) . . . if only that reader have the ears to hear it and let it address his or her condition.

Thoreau's spiritual economy would "revise" an old story of ours about finding by losing, saving by spending, settling by voyaging (and voyaging by settling). For Cavell, this revision of mythology finds expression in a picture of the human self as the ceaseless *activity* of being beside yourself in a sane sense (*SW*, 104). One side to the self is the auditor or "spectator" (*SW*, 108). It would make transparently clear how the other side, the "indweller," is getting expressed or distorted, how one's circumstances have or have not "grown from within outward, out of the necessities and character of the indweller, who is the only builder" (*SW*, 106). This Thoreavian variation on what Cavell calls Wittgenstein's "voice of correctness" would provide scrupulous audits of our accounts, would seek to get things settled, to get them back (says Thoreau) "on track." But this voice of correctness is driven to the audit of our condition not as to an end in itself but as to a continually renewed calling on us to turn our investigations and pursuits around "the fixed point of our real need" (*Investigations*, §108), and so find the footing necessary to "leaping free of enforced speech, so succeeding it" (*TN*, 118). And from each new leaping and departure, a new settlement, and so on, in a ring of neighborly giving and receiving that sustains a self constituted out of the vital outreach of the "indweller" and the judicious jot-and-tittle scrutiny of the "spectator." Not taking sides, Cavell sides Wittgenstein's old-country "language of life" with Emerson's new-world "life of language" and thus finds (and founds) himself. For him, Emerson's reiterated witnessing to the "life of language" is always about the never completed labor of making good on Wittgenstein's promised homeland of our ordinary grammar by showing how, as found and turned here in the west, this ordinary now and always provides the footing by which we might succeed in stepping lively on our transport, "ready to die out of nature, and be born again into this new, yet unapproachable America I have found in the West" (*EL*, 485).

Taking steps to put a confident end to endgames

At the entrance to *The Senses of Walden*, Cavell places an epigraph from Martin Luther that seems to announce and indeed sacralize the high stakes he is placing on Thoreau as a philosopher of our losses and our findings. Undoubtedly placed there in view of what Cavell will see Thoreau making of the restorative "boon" of Walden Pond, the epigraph reads: "For all our life should be baptism, and the fulfilling of the sign, or sacrament of baptism; we have been set free from all else and wholly given over to baptism alone, that is, to death and resurrection. This glorious liberty of ours and this understanding of baptism have been carried captive in our day."[18] For the Reformation, the understanding of this glorious liberty was located in the Word Crucified and Risen as recounted in (*sola*) *scriptura*; for Cavell's Emerson, the saving word is to be found in a westward dissemination calling for an "abandonment of and to language and the world" (*IQ*, 175). If these understandings of deliverance seem either too submissively orthodox or too wildly antinomian, it would be well, at the outset, to recall the stern accounting Cavell brings to the well-worn text of Jesus dying for our sins: "redemption [is impossible] so long as . . . we think that an event near 2,000 years ago relieves us of responsibility rather than nails us to it—so long, that is, as we live in magic instead of faith" (*MW*, 162). The responsibility of faithfully assuming your gloriously redemptive liberty is indeed a responsibility, and it is never over and done with. Rather, it is always (and only) at hand with each step in a called for "redemption of language" (*SW*, 92) that successively presents us with all the makings of the either/or of a dumps or a budding ecstasy. The love of wisdom wafting Cavell's way from Thoreau attracts in him the summarizing idea of baptismal rebirth, but by this very act or passion of attraction, such a redemptive possibility "carried captive in our day" is itself drawn "handsomely" into a transfiguring conversation with the "problematic of the day, the everyday, the near, the low, the common, in conjunction with what they [i.e. Thoreau and Emerson] call speaking of necessaries, and speaking with necessity" (*TN*, 81). And this near and this common—this "argument of the ordinary"—is, as Cavell repeatedly emphasizes, here present in *every* word of this writing, which is constantly bringing the "heaven under our feet" (*SW*, 101, quoting *Walden*, 187) up to the light cast there from "a sense of the intimacy of words with the world, or of intimacy lost" (*IQ*, 170). If we are nowadays still to live only for the death and resurrection of baptism, we are now to be released or abandoned to an understanding of ourselves as called toward a new testament of covenantal attunement (and covenantal backsliding) which Cavell finds it in himself to propose as the scriptural basis for a "theology of reading" (*T*, 53).

If this still sounds like the untransfigured return of an only barely repressed Christian culture, then listen to Cavell on the threadbare question of *King Lear* as a Christian play. With manifest zeal, he redirects the titles and predicates of divinity away from the empyrean gods and toward the same earth where Thoreau found heaven under our feet: "All appeals to Gods are distractions or excuses, because the imagination uses them to wish for complete, for final solutions, when what is needed is at hand, or nowhere. But isn't this what Christ meant? . . . [in *King Lear* Cordelia's] grace is shown by the absence in her of any unearthly experiences; she is the only good character whose attention is wholly on earth, on the person nearest her" (*MW*, 302). As the friend and prophet of our finitude and with Emerson as his Virgil of the ordinary, Cavell would discredit all final solutions and, like Emerson, "direct his work against every finality" (*CH*, xvii). At close to the dawn of his writing career, Cavell is already calling for an end to the regnant idea and story of our ends as we have come to know and gather them under the rubric of Eschatology: "the somewhere all explanations end" (*IQ*, 134). In a 1964 essay on Beckett's *Endgame*, entitled "Ending the Waiting Game," Cavell writes that "what Hamm sees is that salvation lies in the ending of endgames, the final renunciation of all final solutions. The greatest endgame is eschatology, the idea that the last things on earth will have an order and a justification, a sense. That is what we hoped for, against hope, that was what salvation would look like. Now we are to know that salvation lies in reversing the story, in ending the story of the end, dismantling Eschatology" (*MW*, 149). Contrary to the conventional wisdom about Beckett and his works, Cavell represents this virtuoso of going on and failing to go on not as dead set on the tired modernist routine of "protesting one's emptiness" but as being about the very different business "of *seeing* what one is filled with" (*MW*, 156). *Endgame* shows us as so "meaning our lives up" (*MW*, 145) that only if these sophisticated scales fall from the eyes, can we come into the kingdom of a great but ordinary vision: "Then the angel may appear, then nature, then things, then others, then, if ever, the fullness of time; then, if ever the achievement of the ordinary, the faith to be plain, or not to be" (*MW*, 156). As indicated by its parallelism with *the faith to be plain* and *the achievement of the ordinary*, the "fullness of time" here so devoutly wished is not the end-time of various Christian fundamentalisms (and various Christian sophistications). Instead, Cavell makes this Biblical phrase of consummation point to the full taking on of this present edge of time—this *kairos*—as found in the near, the low, the common, the everyday. Cavell's "ordinary" is both the scene of our dereliction and the only site and occasion of our possibilities. If the quotidian is an apparent endgame decline unto death, calling for an inquest or autopsy, it is also our cue to decline, as we turn in spirited and lively origination toward an augury of the ordinary that would be in quest of the everyday not as a given but as a calling, a prize, and a task.

If there is about all this not a little of the "questionable tone of moral urgency" (*CH*, 46) Cavell finds and cheers in Emerson, it is something that only gets amplified in Cavell's subsequent essays and "lectures after Emerson after Wittgenstein." Contracted from these two and also from Heidegger, this air of what I want to call prophecy or annunciation proceeds from (and is accounted for) by the thought "that a certain relation to words (as an allegory of my relation to my life) is inseparable from a certain moral-like relation to thinking" (*CH*, 46) because to get (as Heidegger says) on the way of thinking is to labor in the hope of, as it were, coming to full term with each of the conceptions we find vouchsafed to us in our form of life. This hope is that words will "mean deeply" not by virtue of the in-gathered ambiguities and patterns of the verbal icon but by way of (as Cavell says of some words of Shakespeare) taking on "a spiritual instant or passage for which only these words discover release, in which they mean deeply not because they mean many things but because they mean one thing completely" (*MW*, 269).

The fullness of time and term Cavell prays for apropos Beckett is precisely not "the somewhere all explanations end." And it is, polemically, not such "(false) absences" (*IQ*, 174) as the Transcendental Signified set up by deconstruction so as to set off and assure the obvious rightness of its own bravely disillusioned look into the *mise en abyme* of endless deferral.

In aversion as much from this absolutism of deferral as from its twin of arrival and final solution, Cavell's call is for each of us utterly specific sayers and hearers and hearsayers to stay the course of that defining human activity in which, time after time and step by step, one essays to "see an explanation to its end somewhere" (*IQ*, 134). "Call this," writes Cavell, "the establishing of thinking as knowing how to go on, being on the way, onward and onward. At each step, or level, explanation comes to an end; there is no level to which all explanations come, at which all end" (*TN*, 116). As against some eschatological Somewhere as the Purpose in which all other purposes do (or do not) find their end and peace, Cavell would take on "the hard Nietzschean alternative" to nihilism: namely, the task of "purposely undoing, reevaluating all the purposes we have known, re-locating the gravity of purpose itself" (*MW*, 150)—relocating it, *exempli gratia*, to the words here at hand as they carry on what Cavell would announce as an incessantly present "[struggle] between the hope and the despair of writing and reading redemptively" (*IQ*, 25).

The drive toward the dismantling of Eschatology—a drive, similar to Chekov's effort "to squeeze/His slave's blood out and waken the free man"[19]—complements Cavell's participation in contemporary philosophy's more widely trumpeted animus against foundationalism. It is as if among the characters of what certainly looks like it is straining toward the characters of a great apocalypse, neither Alpha nor Omega has any place or standing. And so we readers after Cavell and after Emerson find ourselves back with them as on a stair at the outset of "Experience" (or at the outset of (what is called) experience). We find ourselves addressed by an opening interrogative sentence as to where we find ourselves "in a series of which we do not know the extremes, and believe that it has none" (*EL*, 327). The sequence of words thus opening themselves up to us in this essay is a series of steps out to get us on our own way in the progress (or success(ion)) of a life that each step of the way is "always to be found [and] always at the risk of loss" (*IQ*, 132).

Because this lover of wisdom finds his own philosophical footing in Emerson's character of "wisdom" as "to finish the moment, to find the journey's end in every step of the road," he can, as writer and philosopher, do no other but contract the fervor of the "moral or religious demand" he witnesses in Wittgenstein, Heidegger and Emerson, not as "the subject of a *separate* study . . . call it Ethics" (*TN*, 41), but as a pervasive yeast-like presence and agency, calling on its readers to attend to these words, to which they are presently abandoned and in which they might yet find themselves. Picked out like all of his human *semblables* to be both the patient bearer of the law and the spirited bringer of that law's impishly protean character, Cavell would be about his philosophical business like the Emerson after and beside whom he would be next in the vineyard. By and on the way of his words, he would let rise the intuitive leaven of what he has it at heart to say, and so take steps to deliver into the hands of his reader the promise of a new birth of our glorious liberty, not here effected once and for all but now confidently to be found "in every word, with every breath" (*C*, 55).

2

Reading Romanticism

"Where perfection—or nearness to it—is imagined
Not in the aiming but the opening hand."[1]

Seamus Heaney

In the introduction to *In Quest of the Ordinary,* Stanley Cavell is very explicit about when and how he found himself gravitating toward romanticism. "As I was trying to follow the last part, part 4, of my book *The Claim of Reason* to a moment of conclusion," he writes, "my progress kept being deflected by outbreaks of romantic texts—a quatrain from Blake, Wordsworth's Boy of Winander, Coleridge's Ode on Dejection, *Frankenstein,* a division in Emerson's 'Transcendentalism,' a passage from *Walden.* After completing the manuscript, I would from time to time ask myself for some account of this interference. What is philosophy for me, or what has it begun showing itself to be, that it should call for, and call for these, romantic orientations or transgressions?" (*IQ,* x). We have Cavell's own written word for it, then, that he turned his philosopher's eye and ear to romanticism when this underunacknowledged piece of him began to be heard as a restive confederacy of voices clamoring for an account of themselves, and *a fortiori* for an account or reading of the one in whose written expression they were buried or lodged.

Cavell calls these romantic outbreaks "interferences" and "transgressions," but also governing "orientations" toward his acknowledgement of an interest in and perhaps a silent melancholy about "our everyday condition" (*IQ,* 9) as a death-dealing alienation, which he hears variously called by Thoreau *quiet* desperation, by Emerson *silent* melancholy, by Coleridge dejection, and by Wordsworth despondency and torpor. All of these summary indictments of what these writers understood themselves to be contending with speak of a loss or suffocation of voice—what Coleridge represents in "Ode to Dejection" as "the smothering weight [on his] breast." And they all look forward to Cavell's declaration that as his reading of romanticism turned into its reading of him, he found that his philosophy was calling for a romanticism in quest "of the (of my) (ordinary) (human) voice" (*IQ,* 26).

In regard to these interrelated issues of a threatened human self and a stifled human voice, Cavell will eventually acknowledge that "[he keeps] coming back to aspects of the idea that the having of a language is an allegory of the having of a self."[2] Not surprisingly for an "ordinary language" philosopher, he comes to feel that a human self is an identity we acquire in ways that are parallel to and even constituted by language acquisition. Cavell's interest in language acquisition is coeval with his interest in Wittgenstein, and it has persistently hovered over two passages from *Philosophical Investigations*: the book's extended opening quotation from Augustine's *Confessions*, where the older Augustine conjectures how his infant self must have learned Latin by attending to the words and gestures of his elders; and (further on in the *Investigations*) what Cavell calls Wittgenstein's recurrent "scene of instruction" between a relative neophyte in the language and some older hand as they arrive at any place where (as Wittgenstein puts it) the "explanation" of a concept "comes to an end" and there is put to the test the attunement of elder and tyro on the import, range, and force of this concept.

Despite all the criticism Cavell and Wittgenstein direct at Augustine's picture of language acquisition, it has its interest for them in that it focuses attention on the undeniable but complicated fact that any individual say in a language (granting its possibility) cannot come into its own without its others and precursors in the language. Anyone with a future in a language, like the young Augustine emerging from infancy, is by the words of others called upon to respond to these words, pick up on them and so start negotiating the baby steps of learning to talk, which can ideally lead to, as we say, one's own say or voice in things. But the great danger of this fact about a language—that it is a form of life inherited and passed on, not a machine replicated to code—is that, instead of becoming competently dexterous masters of a language, we will instead turn into incuriously rote parrots of those performances of it we have happened to hear, with the not fully human result that we will turn, as Thoreau derisively puts it, into "a race of tit-men, and soar but little higher in our intellectual flights than the columns of the daily paper" (*Walden*, 72). Hence, Cavell's Emersonian insistence that maturation into a voice of one's own is a singular attainment, one that has to be won over and over "in every word, with every breath."

The danger of acquiring no signature voice of one's own and in effect forfeiting one's right to be counted one of the species ἔχον λόγον is implicit in Emerson's persistently expressed "chagrin with the way the world is given to use words" (*CH*, 65). In "Self-Reliance," Emerson writes, "[Man] dares not say 'I think,' 'I am,' but quotes some saint or sage." The brevity of this notwithstanding, it is representative of Emerson in that it casts his constant call for self-reliance in terms of the opposed speech acts of saying and quoting. Paradoxically, Cavell hears Emerson quoting the Cartesian insight "that I exist only if I think" but credits his individual but routinely unrecognized voice in the history of philosophy as taking this Cartesian nugget one strikingly original step further into a call on his readers, more quoters than sayers, to (as Cavell puts it) "stop quoting and start saying something, [start finding] their voices, apart from which they do not know they exist, and hence 'have' signatures" (*AP*, 121). In the light or acoustic of this Emersonian turn on Descartes' *cogito* as the last best hope for our human existence, the "having" of a language depends on finding your own *voice* by letting the "'I' into [your] thinking" (*IQ*, 108). This is the most urgent of imperatives for anyone haunted, as Cavell is, by the possibility that "none of my actions and thoughts are [or seem] mine—as if, if I am not a ghost, I am, I would like to say, *worked*, from inside or outside" (*IQ*, 110, Cavell's emphasis). Cavell goes on to say that not only do we thus claim our human existence by getting the "I" into our thinking, we also thereby create our own individual human existence in a feat of self-authoring that does not begin with "the dust of the ground and magic breath . . . [but rather with] an uncreated human being and the power of thinking" (*IQ*, 111), which at each individual site of the human is continually sustaining itself in a circuitry of tuning in and sounding out that must necessarily find its place and make (or not make) its difference in the company and at the provocation of one's others. Cavell acknowledges that this might seem "nothing more than the by now fully discredited romantic picture of the author or artist as incomprehensibly original, as a world-creating and self-creating genius" (*IQ*, 110), but he seems confident both that he can effectively demystify the apparent extravagance of this picture into the plausible and necessary work of ego-formation, and that the details of the picture add up to something very different from solipsism, given the crucial place it reserves for a world of others, both human and non-human.

But the notion of self-authoring (to which I will return) is not the only or even the major stumbling block on Cavell's way to romanticism. This distinction belongs to animism, the concept around which Cavell organizes the one chapter of *In Quest of the Ordinary* directly concerned with English romantic poetry and made up largely of readings of Coleridge's "Rhyme of the Ancient Mariner," and Wordsworth's "Immortality Ode." In this chapter, entitled "Texts of Recovery: (Coleridge, Wordsworth, Heidegger . . .)," Cavell initially expresses considerable misgiving about a romantic animism that seems to take it for granted that we live in the presence of Wordsworth's "speaking earth," and that "there is a life and death of the world dependent on what we make of it" (*IQ*, 68). From this opening ambivalence, however, Cavell's engagement with Coleridge and Wordsworth works its way toward the emergence of a desire for a reconceived animism that philosophy need not disown. To get clear this turn in Cavell's thought, it is necessary to appreciate how forcefully he heard his own dissatisfaction with the supposed Kantian settlement of skepticism echoed in Coleridge's contention (in *Biographia*

Literaria) that the aftermath of Kant's domineering response to the scandal of skepticism had left us with a world of objects not only "dead [and] fixed" (*IQ*, 44), but killed by our own hand's wielding of the categories of understanding to the exclusion of the "thing in itself." From here and with an admitted bending of chronology, Cavell came to see Coleridge's later Kantian preoccupations already at work in the earlier "Rhyme of the Ancient Mariner," understood by him as "an enactment . . . of skepticism's casual step to the path of intellectual numbness, and then of the voyage back to (or toward) life, pictured as the domestic" (*TN*, 57).

In Cavell's hardly idiosyncratic reading of the Kantian settlement of skepticism, it instituted an unbreachable line of divorcement between appearances and what they were the appearances of. This line, defining modern philosophical skepticism and featured in *In Quest*'s subtitle of *Lines of Skepticism and Romanticism*, has such an iconic place in Cavell's imagination that he chooses to preview his reading of "The Ancient Mariner" with a prolegomenon to the effect that he "must appeal to the experience of those who have tried to explain Kant's work . . . I mean to that moment at which, quite inevitably, one pictures its architectonic by actually drawing a line or circle, closing off the region of the thing in itself" (*IQ*, 47). He thus insists on this actual line of instruction so as in some measure to smooth his reader's way toward a boldly idiosyncratic reading of the poem, which, while it keeps the slaughtered albatross steadily in view as decisive for the mariner's fate, takes what is commonly deemed the mariner's gratuitously perverse killing of this bird of good omen as not his original sin or transgression but the fated consequence of his all too "casual" repudiation of the ordinary as it is allegorized in his ship's having (in the poem's marginal gloss) "passed the line and been driven to the cold Country"—the latter, for Cavell, a topography of the rigidly frozen mindlessness one is headed for when one seeks to sublime the logic of our language beyond the terms or "lines" of "the forms of life which grow language" (*CR*, 170).

The unresponsive mindlessness specific to this kind of "philosophical preoccupation" (*MW*, 238) promises (false) generalizing ascents only to leave us foundered in the "disabling sublimizings" (*TN*, 55) which provoke Wittgenstein's "relentless project to . . . de-sublimize thought" (*TN*, 71). A usefully simple example of this project is what Wittgenstein has to say on the language game of *games*. To the easy and purportedly logical assumption that card games, board games and athletic games *must* possess some one thing (a logical entity professionally known as a universal) common to them all, a voice in the *Investigations* fairly shouts back, "Don't think, but look!" (*Investigations*, §66). Look at how we competent users of the language cast the net of the word *game* so confidently, widely and methodically not because of one essential feature common to all its applications, but because, in our form of life, the word has extended itself along a weave of "family resemblances" much as "in spinning a thread we twist fibre on fibre. And the strength of the thread does not reside in the fact that some one fibre runs through its whole length, but in the overlapping of many fibers" (*Investigations*, §67). One desired result of such a grammatical investigation is to bring up to the light the tissues of relation that constitute the schema or *holdings* of a word; one major obstacle to pursuing or even seeing the point of such a working out of how "*Essence* is expressed by grammar" (*Investigations*, §371, Wittgenstein's emphasis) is the preconceived and specifically philosophical idea that such tissues of relation are only various wrappers behind each of which there lurks the unalloyed prize of the one common thing that justifies their one common name.

Subliming thought's self-bewitchment toward a latter end of impasse and loss of progress is worked out in a powerfully compressed metaphor in Remark 107 of the *Investigations*:

> The more narrowly we examine actual language, the sharper becomes the conflict between it and our requirement. (For the crystalline purity of logic was, of course, not a *result of investigation*: it was a requirement.) The conflict becomes intolerable; the requirement is now in danger of becoming empty. We have got on to slippery ice where there is no friction and so in a certain sense the conditions are ideal, but also, just because of that, we are unable to walk. We want to walk: then [Cavell's translation, for the significance of which see *TN*, 55] we need *friction*. Back to the rough ground!

Wittgenstein refigures the transcendence of our crystalline "requirement" for "a *super*-order between—so to speak—*super*-concepts" (*Investigations* §97) into ice underfoot so as to bring out how the drive toward sublimity must, if successful on its own terms, disable that "taking steps" (with, by, and from every word) which Cavell understands any meaningful progress in thinking to call for. Any words of ours that we would let fly upward to the dictates of "our requirement" are, writes Cavell, "just because of that in danger of becoming empty" (*TN*, 56). Impressed into such service, they are in danger of declining into "frozen slides of the motion of our ordinary words, becoming the language of no one, unspeakable moments which refuse the value of the experience of ordinary words, their shared memories" (*TN*, 64). This language of no one seeks an epistemological utopia (etymologically, a nowhere) where in wish and fantasy "the connection between my claims of knowledge and the objects upon which [they fall . . . would occur] without my intervention, apart from my agreements" (*CR*, 351–2).

Cavell positions this avoidance of the human as all too human because "we understandably do not like our concepts to be based on what matters to us . . . it makes our language seem unstable and the instability seems to mean what I have expressed as my being responsible for whatever stability our criteria may have, and I do not want this responsibility; it mars my wish for sublimity" (*CH*, 92). Having found that we have all too "casually" pledged our epistemological allegiance to the raised banner of sublimity, we fall into the grip of feeling that to do their work our words must not be *our* words. Kicking against the pricks of these poor things of our own, we try to "unleash" them "from our criteria . . . to unleash our voices from them." We seek to "abdicate such responsibility as we have over" them (*CH*, 22). We seek to empty our words of ourselves.

To get this tangled drama of avoidance perspicuously clear, Cavell repeatedly stages the play of the mind in the act of finding that its own regnant idea of intellectual rigor is driving it toward a scene of self-recognition where the ghostly selections of its "requirement" are to see themselves as blindly devoted to emptiness. In the trenchant accents of a Greek chorus, Cavell concludes "in a word" that "the motive to skepticism" is "this emptiness itself. Anything short of the ideal is arbitrary, artificial, language at its most mediocre. I must empty out my contribution to words, so that language itself, as if beyond me, exclusively takes over the responsibility for meaning" (*TN*, 56). Placed in this philosophical or epistemological context, Cavell's mariner becomes a representative talking, thinking human being, who has become "enchanted by a way of thinking" (*IQ*, 47), which drives him toward a condition of icy emptiness, fixation and loss of progress "not through ignorance . . . but through a refusal of knowledge, a denial, or a repression of knowledge, say even a killing of it" (*IQ*, 51).

With his insistence on the blatant animism and pathetic fallacy of the albatross loving the mariner ("the bird . . . loved the man/Who shot him with his bow"), Cavell seeks an opening up of the possibility that this love is both the antithesis of the cold country and the condition for the mariner's murderous response to it, understood as "the denial of some *claim* upon him" (*IQ*, 56). This framing of the story as one of claim and denial is one Cavell proposes in extension of both his account of Lear as a father who cannot bear, and so must (a)void his daughter's love, and of *The Claim of Reason*'s brief that this claim of reason is to be found and owned up to in the "ordinary," as it is laid out before us in the everyday agreements by which we call things as we do in "countings" of them, which, in turn and *ab ovo*, depend on their counting for us.

Cavell tempers this strikingly original reading of "The Ancient Mariner" with the timely reminder that it is not incompatible with "the familiar reading" of the poem "as an allegory of the Fall" (*IQ*, 48). Happily conceding that an interpretation of the Eden story is "a romantic's birthright, not to say obligation" (*IQ*, 48), he presents himself as meeting this obligation with a reading of the poem that leans heavily on what the Fall is itself an allegory of. Going back to *Genesis*, he stresses that "the explicit temptation of Eden is to knowledge" and thus to "a denial that as we stand, we know" (*IQ*, 49). Furthermore, the consequence of our first parents' bent toward the original Cavellian misstep of "disowning knowledge" is their coming to "know their nakedness," a turn of events and phrasing whose "oddity" Cavell underlines and interprets as their all too human exposure to the vulnerability of a human knowledge constituted by a "natural language" characteristically "[marked] by its capacity to repudiate itself, to find arbitrary, or merely conventional, the lines laid down for its words by our agreement in criteria," this a repudiation of (our) ordinary (language) which "drives" or "forces" the repudiator to "another definite, as it were, frozen structure" (*IQ*, 48). Cavell's mariner, then, is an Everyman ἔχων λόγον, who has all but inevitably been tempted by a picture of knowing as "a harmony, a concord, a union, a transparence, a governance, a power—against which our actual successes in knowing, and being known, are poor things" (*CR*, 440). Since, as Cavell repeatedly says, there is nothing more human than just these aspirations leading to just these disappointments and repudiations, he (and not he alone) is inclined to think of this so-called Fall of Man as the Rise of the Human (*IQ*, 51).

One might put Cavell's re-seeing of the Fall in the "Ancient Mariner" this way. Into the ear of Eve (which, being interpreted, is (Form of) Life), the Adversary seductively whispers, "As you stand, you know nothing. Authentically to enter into your rightful condition as beings who know, you must cross the line and become as gods." This allegorizes our diurnally reiterated moment of transgressing the lines laid down by our language games, where the first step is "casual . . . always already taken" (*IQ*, 48), but once taken, gathering a momentum such that those launched on its way find themselves as if "driven" toward a frozen emptiness far beyond the lines of human condition. "So speaks serpentine infinity," Cavell concludes, because "the beginning of skepticism is the insinuation of absence, of a line, or limitation, hence the creation of want, or desire; the creation, as I have put it, of the interpretation of metaphysical finitude as intellectual lack" (*IQ*, 51).

With his emphasis on how the mariner never definitively gets behind him his defining experience of the cold country, Cavell leaves it open that this wandering loner, doomed to the continual repetition of his traumatic experience, is never truly "recovered to the world of men," with the consequence that "the country to which he returns (our world) *remains* dramatized, diagrammed, by the cold country he has survived" (*IQ*, 62, Cavell's emphasis).

To Cavell, this suggests that literary or "romantic" explorers of skepticism are not so much interested in arguing their readers out of a skeptical position as in *showing* that reader that "this vision expresses the way you are living now" (*IQ*, 44) in what Coleridge's "Ode to Dejection" calls an "inanimate cold world," which you have let slip into the "shroud" of a winding sheet. For one so addressed on the actuality of our "living our skepticism," the pertinent response will not be philosophical argument or refutation. It will be "the reconstruction or resettlement of the everyday" (*IQ*, 176), a project which Thoreau's edification of *Walden* most thoroughly exemplifies for Cavell, but which he sees animating anything he would confidently call a romantic "text of recovery."

Integral to both Coleridge's and Cavell's sense of a world gone dead on our watch is how, historically, this horror provoked its counterpart in a romantic poetry that sought to "give the world back, . . . bring it back, as to life" (*IQ*, 45). But the price of what has since Whitehead[3] been routinely called the romantic reaction is precisely the kind of animism which an old school of anthropology virtually defined as the primitive, and which has enjoyed a persistent after-life in its literary co-conspirator of the "pathetic fallacy," which some now very old (and programmatically anti-romantic) "new critics" ruled out of line for its attribution of a feeling life and speaking tongue to everything under the sun. If, then, Cavell was inclined to say "thanks for nothing" to the Kantian settlement of skepticism, to the romantic response to this settlement, at least a piece of him was inclined to say "No thanks for everything" (*IQ*, 53).

Drawn to the English romantic poets but pulled up short by their manifest allegiance to the questionable idea of animism with all its "superstitious, discredited mysteries" (*IQ*, 45), Cavell finds himself further drawn toward "a reconception of the subject" (*MW*, 84), modeled on the self-styled "therapies" of Wittgenstein whose goal of "perspicuous representation" requires an unremitting philosophical vigilance about how we impose conceptions on our experience which then impose on us. In this particular instance of *animism*, Cavell will eventually conclude that he found something attractive and haunting in romanticism that "philosophy may poorly call animism,"[4] but the general cast (or play) of Cavell's mind in this regard was already evident at the time of his opening toward romanticism when he expressly refused any direct answer to a query about the romantics' master-tone of the imagination with "I don't want to use the concept of imagination as a way of not having to think."[5] What, more positively, Cavell endlessly finds himself having to think about is (his) *experience*, a concept in whose etymological root of a "going *through* [*per*]" he discovers not what academic philosophy routinely "soberizes" (*IQ*, 59) into the sense impressions of experience but the "romanticized" stuff of *peril* or *experiment*.

That Cavell had been in fact and for some time drawn toward something essential to him that could be and had been called animism is already evident in his unguarded appreciation of the breathing human "character" Thoreau finds in Walden Pond. It also shows up in the reading of *Othello* with which *The Claim of Reason* concludes.

This reading understands the domestic tragedy of Othello and Desdemona as a working out of the calamitous consequences of "other-minds" skepticism when (as Othello says and Cavell emphasizes) one's world is staked on the one beloved other, so that with her gone chaos is indeed come again. It further claims that the play replicates the "logic, emotion and scene" (*CR*, 483–4) of a material-object skepticism, back to which Cavell then turns with the suggestion that in lived human experience this variety of skepticism (which, as Cavell insists and Hume concedes, is so "cold, strained, and ridiculous" that it "cannot be lived") may derive from the "other-minds" variety and not as is commonly thought, vice-versa. The consequence that Cavell draws from this reordering of the ontogeny of our skepticisms is not trivial. For if it dawns on you that material-object skepticism's painstaking analysis toward an air-tight conclusion about the inaccessibility of the "thing-in-itself" both expresses and hides a prior and very much "lived" other-minds skepticism, it may further occur to you that the supposedly more basic material-object skepticism cannot so much as get off the ground without a whiff of the jealously fearful suspicion that one's trust in an external world has not been well placed; this is a mistrusting of where we find ourselves which implies an attitude toward the world as something in some way capable of conversing or communicating with us, and so in some way capable of lying to us or betraying us.

At approximately the same time as Cavell was drawing *The Claim of Reason* to its close with his reading of *Othello*, he was also finishing his *Pursuits of Happiness* on the comedy of remarriage, a genre he ventured to invent and organize around the chances for a day-by-day recuperation of marital intimacy in what John Milton called "a meet and happy conversation," brought up to date in the spirited dialogue of the couples in these early Hollywood talkies. Now in his encounter with romanticism and in specific response to the position of the wedding guest as the audience of one for what the mariner has it at heart to say, Cavell projects these movies' exploration of marital intimacy out into the wider but also more individual task and possibility of us each and all called to an "intimacy at large" with the world, where "the expression" of this and our other "intimacies now exists only in the search for expression, not in [institutional] assurances of it" (*IQ*, 65), and where it is poetry that is charged with this search for the performative expression of such intimacies that have to obtain between the human and the world if there is to be any human or world to be found there at all.

To a Cavell tempted to call "The Ancient Mariner" an "*Antithalamion*," the mariner's interrupting eye and incantatory voice constrain the would-be wedding guest to the hearing out, instead, of this tale about (Cavell is hardly alone in saying) "letting yourself be loved devotedly and reciprocating the devotion (as if love were a ring)" (*IQ*, 65)—the kind of ring that would be a fitting icon for Wordsworth's self-described "spousal verse" of mind and nature. Cavell concludes that if this "intimacy at large" of the human and the world is "the poem's hope for and its recommendation of the intimacy with the world that poetry (or what is to become of poetry) seeks, then it will not be expected that we can yet say whether this projects a new animism, a truer one, or whether the concept of animism will fall away, as if outgrown" (*IQ*, 65).

In Cavell's reading of the "Ancient Mariner," the poem commences with a disowning of knowledge and drives on toward a chilling evisceration of the human. In counterpoint with this loss at sea, Cavell hears Wordsworth's "Immortality Ode" as a piece tuned in the key of a *nativity* or *natality* ode calling for a (re)birth of the human with the complementary proclamation, as in Milton's "Ode on the Morning of Christ's Nativity," that all the "old oracles are fled" (*IQ*, 73). Precisely because this "text of recovery" acknowledges that the hour of splendor in the grass is gone, it would find a way of letting time lapse toward the possibility of "a newborn Day" (*IQ*, 75), where the initial "visionary gleam" is said not to fade *out* but "*into* the light of common day." By the light of this interpretation, the poem describes not the vision's loss but its migration toward the low and near under our feet, a migration that amounts to a happier disillusionment in which "the vision is preserved in the way it is forgone" (*IQ*, 75). Consequently, when the "Immortality Ode" speaks of our birth as "a sleep and a forgetting," this is to be taken "not (not merely, at any rate) as a description of a past event, indeed of the first event, in our biographies; but equally as a statement about the conditions of human birth, of the birth of the human, one that we, as we stand, might still suffer, sometimes called a second birth; a statement about [alluding to what Wordsworth called *The Prelude*] the growth of the human mind after childhood" (*IQ*, 73).

That our childhood abandons us does not mean that the only remaining way for us to recall or participate in it is to dead-end ourselves into a "sack of nostalgia" (*IQ*, 74). Nor does it mean that we are to let go of childhood in a "lapse of memory" (*IQ*, 74). Rather, the abandonment of our childhood—its leaving us and our leaving it—proposes a "success of forgoing" (*IQ*, 74), an *activity* of "bearing childhood as gone, as having become what we are, sharing our fate" (*IQ*, 73–4). One's childhood is gone, and one is left here bearing it on this edge of time and called to acknowledge it. Condemned thus to the fact and meaning of *this* childhood—sentenced to "being the odd one one is, one's having that to recollect and imitate that one has" (*IQ*, 75)—one is called away, as said, from any forlorn effort to get even for this, and called onward toward such "mornings of mourning" as would lead one to accept the verdict of reality and time, and so refit oneself for life precisely as the odd or individuated one one has become.

This is how Cavell's reading of the "Immortality Ode" ends. It opened, as said, on the rather different note of discontent with a poetry that addresses flowers and listens to what (in Patrick Kavanagh's colloquially ebullient phrase) "every blooming thing"[6] from "Fountains, Meadows, Hills, and Groves" down to "the pansy at my feet" has to say for itself. After that inauspicious opening, Cavell's reading, as it were, starts over again from where the poem itself starts: in a world bereft of its original splendor, a world no longer in full bloom and no longer speaking to us or making an impression on us. From there, Cavell finds his way clear to capitalize on Coleridge's insight that his friend's poetic power was grounded on his "intimacy with the very spirit which gives the physionomic *expression* to all the works of nature" (*IQ*, 72, emphasis added), and from there to go on to some of his most excited prose to the effect that Wordsworth's "construction of the ordinary" would "replace the ordinary in the light" in which we see and live it as "a world of death, to which we are dead," replace it in a manner such that this apparently successful "bringing back of the world, as to life" would call on its readers in turn, and only by their individual turns, to replace this world of death to which we are dead "with freedom ("heaven-born freedom'); and with lively origination, or say birth; with interest" (*IQ*, 75), the interest analogously called out and enacted when, from the depths of his misery and fixation, Coleridge's ancient mariner finds it in his heart to "bless the water snakes unawares" and so make at least a start toward "[accepting] his participation as a living being with whatever is alive" (*IQ*, 61).

If the ordinary in the light in which we routinely live it has become the "life-in-death" dominating the middle regions of the "Rhyme of the Ancient Mariner," then Cavell hears Wordsworth calling for a transfiguring of this ordinary with that "interest" (*IQ*, 75) which Wordsworth so uncommonly interested himself in, and which Cavell computes as analogous with Thoreau and Emerson's equally alarmed appeals for us "to take an interest in our lives,"[7] as if the open secret shared by these nineteenth-century sages and watchmen is that our condition is such that "nothing (now) makes an impression on us" (*TN*, 92), because we have succumbed to a death-like "torpor" where, in Wordsworth's diagnosis, our craving for "gross and violent stimulants"[8] constitutes an exact and numbingly redundant set of symptoms for how, as he says in a famous sonnet "For this, for everything, we are out of tune;/It moves us not." For Cavell, the "drama of concepts" (*IQ*, 37) played out in the "Immortality Ode" commences from an aggrieved sense of abandonment in a world gone dead, and goes on to a call for "interest," the latter a turning toward what, amid all the glacial debris of our life, still remains charged with attraction for us, its call on us the sign and promise of our "heaven-born freedom." In short, the newer and truer animism that an appreciative Cavell finds Wordsworth to be in quest of would replace our own construction of a "world of death" with the spirited receptions and responses of our own animated and animating interest, vouchsafed in what further on in his philosophical progress Cavell will call those experiences of "perfect pitch" that range "from ones amounting to conversions down to small but lucid attestations that the world holds a blessing in store [like that the ice-foundered mariner found 'unawares' in the water snakes], that one is, in Emerson's and Nietzsche's image [for blessedly 'autonomous powers of perception'] taking steps, walking on, on one's own" (*AP*, 47).

Remembering *In Quest of the Ordinary*'s punning play on a coroner's "inquest" and the more stereotypically romantic sense of a chivalric quest, one might think of this specifically English Romantic region of *In Quest of the Ordinary* as similarly in quest of an animism that would be an essential and constitutive part of the ordinary in that it would give an alarming account of our numbed reception of the world so as to prepare the way for replacing it with *interest*. It is as if, having let his title announce his own quest of the ordinary and having enlisted some romantic writers in this venture, Cavell found himself losing the heart for it in the face of the romantics' dubious animism, and then further found himself turning less to the recounting than to the *performing* of how he warmed to this "questionable" concept: how he came to see it as in need of rescue from the frozen reception and understanding it had fallen into, and then how, through his passionately aroused interest in some representative romantic texts not just freighted with animism but powered by it, he thawed the concept out into a dilating flood of new light on how it might be a peculiarly modern and post-Kantian predicament that, time after time, we have to find our way back to the life's breath of a world gone dead by our own murderously suffocating constructions of it. In any case, by the time Cavell has reached the climax of this performative sequence, he is unrestrainedly lifting his voice up in appreciative gratitude for a Wordsworthian version of animism closely tied to Cavell's (and Wordsworth's[9]) own master-tone of the "interest," to which our world-wording "concepts . . . [give] expression" (*Philosophical Investigations*, §570).

Early and late, Cavell reminds himself that we count (i.e. conceptualize) only what counts for us. But what if the world-historical "torpor" so fervently deplored in the Preface to *Lyrical Ballads* has so little abated that this American philosophical voice come to full flower in the late twentieth century has just cause to fear that nothing any longer counts for us, that "nothing (now) makes an impression on us" (*TN*, 92)? Then the one revivifying thing needed for our condition and world would be the "interest" whose use and placement in this same preface (Cavell testifies) "absolutely went through [him]."[10]

Of breath and stone in Cavell

The reconceived animism of interest that Cavell finds in Wordsworth and would make his own is on extravagant display in the companion volumes of *A Pitch of Philosophy* and *Philosophical Passages*, published almost a decade after *In Quest of the Ordinary*. Gone in these books is any diffidence about animism, as with positive abandon Cavell brings the signifiers of *wind, air, breath* and *spirit* to his master theme of the human voice as the local but ever volatile habitation of Nietzsche's "sacred Yes" and Emerson's "sacred affirmative" (*SW*, 133). In these two books, Cavell resorts to figures of air and breath in even the most casual and offhand remarks. Acknowledging his long delay in commenting on Derrida's reading of John Austin, for example, he explains that the public controversy between Derrida and John Searle on this question launched the whole thing "into a life of its own, more than filling the air in which an intervention of my own, recounting my sense of Austin's voice, might have found room to breathe" (*AP*, 58). It is worth recalling also that the originally projected title for the Jerusalem-Harvard Lectures that form the core of *A Pitch of Philosophy* was "Trades of Philosophy," a title dropped, says Cavell, because "the concept of trades failed to invoke the wind it names" (*AP*, ix). (Looking forward to my exposition of the commanding place in his thinking that Cavell will find for the interrelated necessities of human breath and the globally enclosing atmosphere of our planet, I will here simply and no doubt prematurely assert that this late-flowering imagery of wind, air, breath and spirit cannot be just metaphorical flourish or rhetorical embellishment. Just as the lines from Richard Wilbur constituting the epigraph to this book deem us incapable of speaking of the "rose of our love" without the existence of real roses, so apparently does Cavell need these tenuous and intimately related realities of breath and air to bring up to the light what he thinks about the defining human activity of thinking.)

If our body-temperature "breath made words" (*PP*, 25) is the sign of, and the *way* toward, a voice and life of one's own, it finds its Satanic adversary in the unresponsiveness of stone. That a life-or-death psychomachia between unyielding stone and breathing human life figures importantly in Shakespeare's *The Winter's Tale* will go a long way toward explaining why a reading of that play concludes the series of public lectures on romanticism constituting the bulk of *In Quest of the Ordinary*. Uncontroversially in *The Winter's Tale*, a Hermione (as if) turned to stone symbolizes or concretizes the coldly annihilating fury of a Leontes, who on the threshold of her return to him will redemptively find it in himself to voice the heartfelt *mea culpa* of "does not the stone rebuke me?/For being more stone than it?" (V.ii.36–7). And still earlier, in *The Claim of Reason*'s reading of *Othello*, the matter of stone (of the alabaster or marmoreal variety) is also put into prominent play. At the climax of Iago's seduction of him, Othello swears by an (oddly) "*marble* heaven" that he will stand firm against any blandishments from his wife, and in thus vaunting his makeover into stone he in effect dedicates himself to (writes Cavell) the "turning of Desdemona into stone" (*CR*, 489), a contagion of petrification come to its fulfillment on the other, breathing, side of this marriage in the manner of Desdemona's slaying by suffocation, a whispered suggestion of Iago, which an enflamed Othello pounces on with the exclamation, "Good, good! The justice of it pleases, very good!"

To suggest how central and pressing the Either/Or of breath and stone is for Cavell, I propose now to go back to a place in Part One of *The Claim of Reason*, where the opposed imagery of stone and breath is, while not exactly prominent, strikingly placed. My purpose is to suggest how the necessity of (some kind of) animism to our human, talking form of life was a formatively early and powerfully "obscure prompting" of Cavell's (*WV*, 162). Given the profundities and obscurities of the matter, it will take a while for this to become clear.[11]

We already have had occasion to note that the point of Wittgenstein's signature "grammatical investigations" was to bring back to mind what we "say" about an object of investigation so as, in case after case, to establish "the position of an 'object' in our system of concepts" (*CR*, 76). Here, I would like to draw attention to how, after having thus made his case for the necessity of grammatical investigations in the case of material-object skepticism, Cavell moves on to "subjective" or other-minds skepticism and its textbook example of the *pain* of others. As it happens, his opening example in this new stage of his argument is John Keats confessing that in his tour of Scotland the "misery" of Robert Burns hung like a "dead weight on the nimbleness" of his pen and spirits (*CR*, 82). Singling out Keats's reaction to Burns as something like a "best case" of knowing the pain of another, Cavell then makes what is for him the cardinal grammatical point that response is as integral to the grammar of what *pain* is (called) as *sit* is to *chair*. To know what a "chair" is (called) is to know, among other pieces and possibilities of its grammar, that *this* is what we call to "*sit* on a chair." Similarly, to know what "pain" is (called) is to know, among other pieces of its grammar, that it is something that calls for response. That the pain of others "calls us out" is indeed so "matter of course" (Wittgenstein's *selbstverständlich*) that the all too common stinting of response in the face of it is itself counted as a kind of response, that of the heart, not of flesh, but of stone. Given our frequent and quite ordinary successes in knowing the pain of others, Cavell asks whether the philosopher's virtually preordained conclusion that "outward" criteria cannot reach the "pain itself" will "seem" something "I impose on these matters; that I am the philosophical problem" (*CR*, 83). To which talk of seeming, Cavell trenchantly responds, "I am [the problem]. It is in me that the circuit of communication is cut; I am the stone on which the wheel breaks." Even if I and all those with whom I share a language have well-established criteria for the psychological state of pain—like what we call winces or cries *of* pain—these criteria (so goes the drill) are only "outer." They no more provide access to the inner life of the other than the sense-data of a chair deliver the thing itself. In the face of this, Cavell admits that "there is something [criteria] do not do [and] it can seem the essential." They may be the necessary instruments for our wording and knowing of the world, but they cannot do our thinking and responding for us: "*I* have to know what they are for. *I* have to accept them, use them" (emphasis added). But (Cavell ruefully adds) this requirement of our individual use of our criteria will "make my use of them seem arbitrary, private."

But then, as already noted, Cavell recuperatively reminds himself of the background against which "[Wittgensteinian or "grammatical"] criteria do their work and even make sense." Specifically, Cavell's internal memorandum to a piece of himself in danger of succumbing to a terminal disappointment with criteria gathers and itemizes the following from Wittgenstein: his flatly obvious observation that "only of a **living** human being and what resembles (behaves like) a **living** human can one say it has sensations and consciousness" (*Investigations*, §281); his grounding imperative that "what has to be accepted, the given, is . . . forms of **life**" (*Investigations*, 226); his wondering question as to "what gives us *so much as the idea* that **living** beings, things, can feel?" (*Investigations*, §283, Wittgenstein's emphasis); his quasi-Blakean proverb that "the human body is the best picture of the human soul" (*Investigations*, 178). As indicated by the bold type, the thread running through all these reminders is (forms of) **life**: that hardly arbitrary or static "whirl of organism" (*MW*, 52; *CH*, 81), to which we all are as commonly fated as each one of us is particularly fated to a unique body of one's own. Cavell's grounding insight and claim here is that, unlike the identifying criteria by which John Austin could surgically distinguish a mistake from an accident, "there are not human criteria which apprise me, or which make any move toward telling me why I take it, among all the things I encounter on the surface of the earth or in its waters or its sky, that some of them have feeling; that some of them 'resemble' or 'behave like' human beings or human bodies;

or that some exhibit (forms of) life—unless the *fact that* human beings apply psychological concepts to certain things and not to others is such a criterion" (*CR*, 83, Cavell's emphasis).

For Cavell, the apparent arbitrariness with which we do in fact, and with a naturally arrived at unanimity, single out certain things as living beings has many consequences. It leads him, as already said, to stress, against a common picture of the later Wittgenstein that the *Investigations*' appeals to the ordinary are not set on refuting skepticism. Rather, this book's remarks and reminders provide a perspicuous representation of our relation to the world and our others in it that all but insures the emergence of skepticism. For our grammatical criteria for what the most ordinary things, occurrences, and emotions are (called) are always and only just that: ours. If one takes this fact in a certain spirit, our "imposed" criteria must seem not to block skepticism (as Austin thought his criteria could) but to call for it. But in quick succession to this acknowledgment of how disappointing criteria can seem, there dawns for Cavell the more inviting aspect of this situation to the effect that if we are indeed called to a thinking and wording of the world, "what has to be accepted, the given, is . . . forms of life" (*Investigations*, 226). The world and our others in it are, before all else, to be acknowledged from a posture of reception, whose distinction from knowing or "grasping" can be clarified by Wittengenstein's pointed remark that "my attitude toward him is toward a soul. I am not of the *opinion* that he has a soul" (*Investigations*, p. 178, Wittgenstein's emphasis). Or in other words of Wittgenstein: "This is simply what I do. (*So handle ich eben.*)" (§217).

In the skeptical recital of how we cannot possibly know the pain of others, I become the stone on which the wheel breaks when I make it a point of misplaced intellectual honor not to accept the given of any given human body as a "home of my concepts of the human soul." And thus "to withhold, or hedge, our concepts of psychological states from a given creature [human or animal], on the ground that our criteria cannot reach to the inner life of the creature, is . . . to withhold myself, to reject my response to anything as a living being" (*CR*, 83). One caught in the grip of this kind of rejectionism is so far from accepting the human body as the best picture of the human soul that, to the perverse contrary, he or she "blanks" the very idea of the body as expressive, the very idea, Cavell writes, of "anything as *having a body*" (*CR*, 83, Cavell's emphasis). For such a mere spectator or observer of the other, there is "nothing the body is *of*. It does not go beyond itself, it expresses nothing; it does not so much as behave. There is no body left to manifest consciousness (or unconsciousness). It is not dead, but *inanimate*" (*CR*, 84, first emphasis Cavell's, second mine). The ghost has been so completely suctioned out of the machine that it is not so much that we cannot get to *him* but rather that there is now nothing of the right (breathing) human kind to get to. "The most *anything* inside it could do (e.g. something we choose to call 'nerves' or 'muscles') is to *run* or *work* the thing, move it around" (*CR*, 84, Cavell's emphases).

In not accepting one's human other "as a home" for such ordinary psychological concepts as *expectation, fear, joy* or *horror*, the signs and criteria for these *états d'âme* go dead. They lose the wind in their sails and come to a dead stop far off from their home port. This is what becomes of our most ordinary psychological concepts when, on whatever grounds, I find myself rejecting my response to anything as a living being. And as has been copiously recorded in both ancient and contemporary historical cases of rejecting the humanity of a different race or ethnicity, this disowning of what Cavell calls "my responsibility (responsiveness) in the existence of others" (*CR*, 86) will inevitably recoil back upon the disowner. Voiding your human other into (at best) a marvelously contrived automaton entails the fearful symmetry that what you do to this other, you do to yourself. About this stinting of the human by what we do or do not do with such words as *pain* or *anger*, *remorse* or *sympathy*, Cavell is very graphic and visceral. It is not just, he writes, that these dead signs and criteria "can't get past his body to *him*." They, he adds, "can't even reach as far as *my* body." They become "word-shells ... stuck behind the tongue or at the back of the mind," and "merely working them out loud doesn't breath life into them. Words have no carry. It is like trying to throw a feather; for some things, breath is better than strength; stronger" (*CR*, 84). The other's call on me as a fellow member of the human form of life is "not exactly that I have to *put* the other's life there; and not exactly that I have to *leave* it there either. I (have to) *respond* to it, or refuse to respond. It calls upon me. It calls me out. I have to acknowledge it. I am as fated to that as I am to my body; it is natural to me" (*CR*, 84, all Cavell's emphases).

To the figuratively packed and highly wrought language of "It is like trying to throw a feather; for some things, breath is better than strength; stronger," a markedly more slack and even awkward writer adds, "this is also something I meant by saying that voicing my criteria has to have the force of 'call.'" Cavell is here referring to the conclusion of the first chapter of *The Claim of Reason*, where, on the way to standing up for what he calls our "separate counts and out-calls of phenomena," he demurs from the common judgment that Wittgenstein's view of language makes it "too public and does not do justice to the control I have over what I say" and instead confesses to his "wonder" at how Wittgenstein can arrive at what Cavell too acknowledges as a "completed and unshakable edifice of shared language" by way of "such apparently fragile and intimate moments—private moments—as our separate counts and out-calls of phenomena, which are after all hardly more than our interpretations of what occurs, and with no assurances of conventions to back them up" (*CR*, 36). Our criteria for what the many things and events of our world are (called) do constitute themselves into an "edifice of shared language," but as with the dead and stuck "word-shells" in need of some warmly fluent human breath to bear them on to their world-wording work, Cavell insists that by themselves the criteria are dead. They must be voiced or "called out" by individual users of the language. Without the continual calling out of these responses, there would not be so much as the possibility of raising an edifice of shared language up from off the ground (of human interest) on which it stands.

Cavell's rehearsal of the misgiving that if *I* have to use criteria, they must be only private and arbitrary is meant to bring into sharper focus the bedrock acknowledgment that for criteria to work at all there must be in place a shared form of life and language and in prospect the ongoing naming of nameables in our "separate counts and outcalls of phenomena." Far from being arbitrary, our individual voicing of criteria is positioned by Cavell as indispensable to the very possibility of human knowledge understood as the "human capacity for applying the concepts of a language to the things of a world" (*CR*, 17). Try to dispense with the out-calls of individual human agency and you reverse the second-creation fable of Deucalion and Pyrrha. You turn humans into the stones on which any possible cycle of communication breaks, as (in Cavell's remarkable image) the human voice-box becomes a dead-zone of word-shells "stuck behind the tongue and at the back of the mind," where the only way out from thus choking on words of no carry, reach or pith is not the muscle that would try to throw a feather but one's own breath of life, because "for some things breath is better than strength, stronger."

To the already noted axiom of Cavell's that in our constructions or wordings of the world we count only what counts for us, we can now add (or more forcefully emphasize) his corollary that for this wording of the world to happen, I have to count not only in the transitive sense of doing the counting and "out-calling" of things, concepts and events. I must also count, intransitively. I must matter. This picture of language does not simply allow for some peripheral owning of one's words. It dictates a particularly insistent "owning" of them in the sense of a continually renewed pressure to own up to such words as we each let loose from what the Greeks called the ἕρκος ὀδόντων: the fence, hedge or line of the teeth. We are called by our nature to "have a say in what we mean" because, as early as *The Senses of Walden*, Cavell had settled on a quasi-Kantian deduction of the necessary a priori "conditions of language as such," which uncovered that while the meanings of our shared words are ungainsayably there before us, it is also to be acknowledged that in our lives with them these "words and their orderings are meant by human beings" so that "the saying of something when and as it is said is as significant as the meaning and ordering of the words" (*SW*, 34). A necessary article, then, in what Emerson's "Fate" calls the "dictation" of language is that we each are called upon to contribute our own say or voice to its ever re-forming constitution. Not that we cannot seek a way of evading this dictation. But if you evade it by failing to count, you yourself will not count or matter. You will be turning yourself into a specimen of the "man [who] dares not say 'I think', 'I am.'" In a recurring image of Cavell's—one he signally applies to Hamlet—you will not be in the world but merely haunt it.

In Cavell's brief and openly tentative essay on *Hamlet* (unchanged in the updated 2003 edition of *Disowning Knowledge*), he speculates that the title-character's predicament anticipates Emerson's charge that we each and all have to claim or "prove" our human existence. Entitled "Hamlet's Burden of Proof," the essay sees the revenge at the rot-infested heart of the play as "the destroyer of human identity" (*DK*, 188), a claim we have already heard in Cavell's reading of Wordsworth's "Immortality Ode." Similarly in *Hamlet*, Cavell hears the paternal ghost's call for revenge as an interdicting of his son's "enacting his own existence" (*DK*, 189). The haunting demands of the ghost force the odd, particular one Hamlet (and everyone else) is to try to make things come out even for a ghostly father who thus preemptively blocks him from "the taking of his [own] place in the world" (*DK*, 189), and so turns him into one of the multitudes already, as it were, spoken for. The predicament of a Hamlet, whose mother rather too glibly asks why the death of his father "seems . . . so particular with" (I.ii.75) him is that, lacking advancement in the world, he can only haunt it. Until perhaps the last act, he cannot with any conviction say of his world, "let [it] be" my field of action (V.ii.226).

The self and where it finds itself

An anxiety about one's, from the beginning, only haunting the world draws Cavell on to thinking of "the (my) (ordinary) (human) voice" and its performative proof of one's human existence as something more to be attained than recovered; and the same anxiety pulls him back to the venerable philosophical question of the human soul, albeit with a new found confidence that "we need [no] more out of the concept of the soul here than as a term for a subject's subjectivity, a thing possessed of mentality or mindedness or moodedness, one whose actions, as Heidegger roughly put it (making something of the German *Handlung* in his way), are ways of handling things (something Charlie Chaplin knew as well as Heidegger is not to happen on an assembly line)."[12] Along with this change in philosophical emphasis and direction comes a related change in philosophical style. For unlike the brisk precisions with which John Austin on "what we say when" directed Cavell to the lost track of the human voice, later Cavell typically writes of an attainment of voice in a more densely figurative manner, previewed in the passage from *The Claim of Reason* on which I have been dwelling, and coming to one of its more unexpected arrivals in the declaration (in both *A Pitch of Philosophy* and *Philosophical Passages*) that it is through "the *pawn* of voice"—as differentiated from, say, the expenditure or the play or the management or the ministry of voice—that my words become mine in "a success of forging" (*IQ*, 74) that forms me into an authentic member of the animal species ἔχον λόγον.

Cavell lets it be understood that had he not as a boy helped out in his father's pawn-shop, this metaphor would never have so much as occurred to him. Coming from a philosopher who will eventually insist on the autobiographical dimension of his philosophy, this can hardly count as an admission of metaphorical whim. On the contrary, Cavell would undoubtedly call the figure's occurrence to him a given of his condition, something fated to happen. Be that as it may, another more manifestly public condition for Cavell's here settling on the metaphor of the pawn is the grammatical fact that the term is the correlative of his master-tone of *redemption*. One pawns one's watch in the hope of eventually redeeming it. In addition, since it is internal to the idea of pawning that it begins with an act of (provisional) abandonment, the idea recalls and, as it were, reimagines Cavell's earlier call for "an abandonment of and to language and the world" (*IQ*, 175).

Having sighted the agency and even the authoring of the human self in "the (my) (ordinary) (human) voice," Cavell eventually found that he no longer could put off letting Jacques Derrida become one of his more significant others, an other of the Continental tradition in philosophy who contemporaneously with Cavell's career had stigmatized the same human voice of Cavell's championing as something like the scene of the crime for countless illusions about self-presence and countless denials of *différence*. But despite Cavell and Derrida's starkly divergent assessments of the human voice, Cavell had, since almost the moment of Derrida's arrival on the scene less of American philosophy than of American literary studies, been periodically apprised of some evident similarities between his and Derrida's thought. To these provocations and suggestions, Cavell replied only briefly and uneasily (most of it in the pages of *In Quest of the Ordinary*), and it was not until the second chapter of *A Pitch of Philosophy* that he would directly engage Derrida on the "interacting themes of voice, writing and philosophy" (*AP*, 61) as they had been worked out (or worked over) decades earlier in Derrida's

Limited Inc., a volume containing Derrida's original response to John Austin in *Signature Évènement Contexte* as well as the ensuing pyrotechnics of his long reply to John Searle's dismissive review of that response. Beginning from at least *The Senses of Walden*, Cavell had always insisted on something very much like Derrida's fundamental insight that by the very fact of their emission, the words we broadcast into the air bear the rupturing mark of a *différence*, by the grammatological necessities of which our spoken no less than our written words are (contrary to Plato's *Phaedrus*) abandoned by us into the endlessly orphaned and unsponsored proliferations of discourse. But if Cavell cannot in good conscience reject outright a picture of our words as both always already there before us and as, what's more, distanced from us in the very act of saying them, he does (to use a master-tone of Derrida's) *supplement* this with a further remarking of an (often) frayed or strained attachment to our words, where there is no end of either abandonment or attachment because not only are one's words abandoned by the self from which they issue but this self is (Cavell stresses) "abandoned to them, in them" (*PP*, 103). As the ancient Greek commonplace of ἔπεα πτερόεντα puts it, my words are indeed "winged words," but Cavell emphatically adds, they "fly from me *and* stick to me" (*AP*, 123, Cavell's emphasis), as if "the price of having once spoken, or remarked, taken something as remarkable (worth noting, yours to note, about which to make an ado) is to have spoken forever. . . . to have taken on the responsibility for speaking further, the unending responsibility of responsiveness, of answerability, to make yourself intelligible" (*PP*, 65). In Austin's more sober figure of the written signature playing such a prominent role in "*Signature Évènement Contexte*," our "saying of something when and as it [is] said" (*SW*, 34) is "tethered" to that one of us who turned the common fund of our shared words into this specific utterance.

That we can each attain a signature voice to which we are abandoned (and which in finest voice enacts "an abandonment of and to language and the world") does not mean that any one of us is capable of "having" a language, if by this is meant the fantasy of a "private language," which Wittgenstein constantly discredits as an impossible fool's gold because, in Cavell's trenchant declaration, "my language is the language of others, or else it is not a language" (*PP*, 101). But if it is axiomatic for ordinary-language philosophy that we cannot own a language, we do have the run of it in an individual and individuating "lease of voice" (*AP*, 129). This prospect of a voice of one's own called out into performance by the possibilities of a commonly shared language does not entail a violent or supercilious exempting of oneself from human condition. On the contrary, it requires a receptive bearing of this condition, this given of what we "say together," that should school us in the inane folly of "imitatively declaring one's uniqueness" and turn us instead toward the humbler hope of "originally declaring one's commonness" (*IQ*, 132). This hope is central to Cavell's philosophy, and it finds perhaps its most densely metaphorical expression in his two interlocking claims about the words out of our mouths: that we are each and all "abandoned to them, in them" (*PP*, 103); and that "I recognize [these] words as mine when I see that I have to forgo them to use them. Pawn them and redeem them to own them" (*PP*, 103). As one's watch or guitar is abandoned to a pawnbroker in the hope of its redemption, so in this recounting of our human, talking form of life our uttered or written words are consigned to a public forum where, whatever influence they may or may not there exert, it is only "in recognizing *this* abandonment to my words . . . [that] I *know* my voice, *recognize* my words (no different from yours) as mine" (*PP*, 65, Cavell's emphases).

According to this figurative use of what daily rests pledged as to value and suspended as to use in a pawn shop, the commonly shared words that are the elements out of which any would-be individual voice composes itself are valuables whose use consists in a forgoing of them in view of redeeming them and making them (again) one's own. For Cavell, in short, the pawning of our words is as much the most called for use of them as the sowing of them is the most profitable use of those seeds which are such a prominent figure for words in both *Walden* and in the gospels' parable of the sower.

Within Cavell's work as a whole, there has been a long preparation for this "having" of a voice (and hence a self) that paradoxically depends on the outing or "othering" that is, as it were, internal to the very idea of human utterance. In *The Claim of Reason*, for example, Cavell's tracking of the great Wittgensteinian theme of "how false views of the inner and outer produce and sustain one another" (*CR*, 329) leads him to the conclusion that "knowing oneself is the capacity, as I wish to put it, for placing-oneself-in-the-world" (*CR*, 108). (Since outside the context of the argument in which it is embedded this characterization of self-knowledge may not be immediately transparent, I will much too quickly sketch Cavell's major and strikingly ordinary example. When I spill milk, I would appear to know (Cavell writes) that "*that* circumstance [what a hyper-objective observer might call "flat" or ground-level milk] *is* (counts as) *what* I did"; I would appear to know that just that small and transitory event or object in the world, just "*that* (the spilt milk)" counts as, is "what *I* did" (*CR*, 108, all Cavell's emphases, except the last).) This "placing-oneself-in-the world" with its interchange between the "inner" of the self and the "outer" of this self's history and circumstances is something which the much later *Philosophical Passages* is manifestly recalling when it lets the sharply turned accents of "Pawn them and redeem them to own them" spring the further question, "What does that say, otherwise (that is, allegorically), about having a self, that is about putting myself into the world, and receiving it from there?" (*PP*, 103).

Even the strikingly original metaphor of the "pawn of voice" had been long prepared both in Cavell's life and in his philosophy. His fascination with a discourse of economics was already evident in his manifest wonder at, and scrupulous recording of, how precisely as a book about writing and expression, *Walden* is (like the Bible with its laying up of treasures, wages of sins and pearls of great price) saturated with the terms of value and exchange. And the specific question of the paradoxical owning of our words through releasing them was subsequently there in the call of *In Quest of the Ordinary* for an "inheritance of language, an owning of words, which does not remove them from circulation but rather returns them, as to life" (*IQ*, 114). And so when Cavell began to claim autobiography as a necessary part of philosophy, pawning—the life's work of his immigrant father—was just waiting to become, like Emerson's "low, near and common . . . [that] we would really know the meaning of," a conspicuously humble and gritty term of the "economy," which, at Thoreau's prompting, Cavell had long identified with philosophy. It was just waiting to become Cavell's home-made inflection of Austin's "our word is our bond," a commonplace about the pledged value of our words that Cavell had already uncommonly glossed with the observation that our every utterance is a promise, as if the saying of a word were the giving of our word (*AP*, 182).

Whether one sees our words as the bonds or pawns of ordinary language, either figure speaks of them as somehow lost to us and in need of redemption, a truth of Cavell's condition that was brought home to him with the force of a conversion when in response to John Austin's relentlessly superficial questioning of "what we would say when," he became ruefully convinced of his own feeble hold on the words of his own language, and by the same stroke "found his own philosophical voice or the track of it" in our ordinary language as a vast network of agreements in what things are (called), which neither he nor anyone else can ever have any recollection of having signed on to, but which all of us are called upon to acknowledge as the precious word-by-word creation of an intelligible world for which we are endlessly answerable or responsible.

Cavell's persistent efforts to see and (re)mark his way clear to how the having of a self requires a posture of openness, whose *ne plus ultra* of a "placing-of-oneself-in-the-world" would be "an abandonment of and to language and the world," provokes him into recalling for purposes of amendment his earlier claim about how differently Heidegger and Emerson conceive the human task of "putting myself into the world, and receiving it from there" (*PP*, 103). Formerly, Cavell had felt obligated to write that for Emerson "the task of the human being . . . [was] *contrary to Heidegger's discovery of it*, not to learn how to dwell but to learn how to leave, to learn abandonment" (*PP*, 103, emphasis added). Now, listening again to himself on these two immeasurably significant voices in his philosophical life, Cavell amends his former polarizing assessment of Emerson and Heidegger into the suggestion that "this [Emersonian] having by giving (or spending, as Thoreau sees it)" (*PP*, 103) is no more contrary to Heideggerean dwelling than Thoreau's resolution to spend himself on the works and days of Walden is to his determination, by just this venture, "to make some progress toward settling in the world" (*Walden*, 58).

At this point in *Philosophical Passages* Cavell goes on to remark, with extravagance aforethought, that the paradoxical "having" or gaining of a self by spending it "is allegorized in every syllable that escapes you" (*PP*, 103). This is perhaps a too abrupt descent from the vast reaches of an entire world to the pin-point locality and fleeting tenuousness of our individually voiced syllables. In addition, Cavell's use of "allegorized" might well strike one as an empty flourish, smacking too much of both jargon and "literariness." But this allegorizing stroke (leaning heavily on the word's origin in the common Greek word for "other") issues naturally from what has become one of Cavell's most confidently held and far-reaching philosophical convictions, namely, that "othering" is at the heart and origin of significant human utterance because "having a self" (or a soul or subjectivity or mindedness) is an unending process of "putting myself into the world, and receiving it from there?" (*PP*, 103). So for all its apparent air of gratuitous flourish, Cavell's stroke of "allegorized" has gathered into itself a great deal of philosophical energy, as has his glancing reference to how we always understand "otherwise," always see and "say otherwise (that is, allegorically)" (*PP*, 103).

But in what I would offer as yet another instance of Cavell staying with Wittgenstein but going on with Emerson, the specific "place" to which Cavell allegorizes this thought about "putting myself into the world, and receiving it from there" (*PP*, 103) is not something like, say, the "asphodel that greeny flower" and "what is found there" of William Carlos Williams, or that Shakespearean time of year when the trees have become bare, ruined choirs where late the sweet birds sang. It is the ins and outs of our breath made words. And the provocation toward just this way of speaking "otherwise (that is, allegorically)" about where we find ourselves could only have resounded so tellingly in Cavell's ear (I am contending) after he had come to terms with romantic animism. Only after he had turned that stone of offense into a cornerstone of his thinking could his second pass through

Emerson's "Fate"—in "Emerson's Constitutional Amending: Reading Fate" (in *Philosophical Passages*)—have discovered that the whole of this essay on "thinking as the exchange of fate for freedom" was compressed into Emerson's indisputable (but apparently pointless) claim that "we should be crushed by the atmosphere but for the reaction of the air within the body" (*EL*, 954). In this second of Cavell's published passes through "Fate," in other words, we have a record of how there eventually dawned on him a new aspect to Emerson's trying out of the old knots of freedom and necessity, in which, as we shall see, the human voice giving expression to the uniquely embodied person in which it finds itself discloses itself as the nodal point of the defining human exchange between fate and freedom, a disclosure this that led to Cavell's manifestly astonished finding that "since the breath . . . is an ancient image of the soul or self . . .what is happening, on my reading of 'Fate,' is that the self is identified as what is breathed in and out" (*PP*, 103).

The reading of "Fate" performed by Cavell's "Constitutional Amending" is not, as said, his first. That appeared in *In Quest of the Ordinary* and dealt with only a handful of sentences, from which, as detailed in my first chapter, Cavell teased out what (as indicated by its punning use of *character*) is the mostly grammatological claim that "our antagonism to fate to which we are fated, and in which our freedom resides, is as a struggle with the language we emit, of our character with itself" (*IQ*, 40). In his later, more globally ambitious and more, as it were, breathy and animated reading of "Fate," Cavell does not revise his earlier assessment of the essay as "perhaps Emerson's principal statement about the defining human condition of freedom" (*PP*, 14), nor does he voice any second thoughts about the linguistic turn he brings to the two Kantian standpoints of necessity and freedom. Very much to the contrary, this proponent of "knowing oneself [as] the capacity. . . . for placing-oneself-in-the-world" (*CR*, 108) takes his thinking of Emerson on thinking "in every word, with every breath" even further into the world by abandoning himself to an extravagantly literal emphasis on the barometric fact, both comprehensively global in scope and insistently individual in experience, that each one of us bears the weight of our planet's entire atmosphere (its "breath-sphere), and yet bears *up* under this pressure and may, nay must, turn it to one's own account by "[making] one's breath words in order not to suffocate in the plenum of air" (*PP*, 25).

For all its remarkableness, this emphasis on the literal pneumatic ins and outs of the human, talking form of life is not something about Emerson's "Fate" that Cavell has, as it were, pulled out of thin air. It is of the essence— part of the essential character or grammar—of an essay literally humming with expressions like: "certain ideas are in the air"; "the truth is in the air"; "the benefactors of the race" are "part of our air, our breath." In short,

Emerson's essay gives off a pervasive air of us all as but creatures of the air whose distinctive capacity for *understanding* "encodes a way of standing toward the world, of bearing up under and countering its pressure."[13]

Cavell's (re)reading of "Fate" comes to its own pressure point of emphasis and release in the following trio of Emersonian sentences: "If the Universe have these savage accidents, our atoms are savage in resistance. We should be crushed by the atmosphere but for the reaction of the air within the body.... If there be omnipotence in the stroke, there is omnipotence in the recoil." With the second sentence, the interchange between the atmospheric plenum and our individual portions of the sustaining air becomes explicit as Cavell turns the factual given of a would-be crushing atmosphere into a comprehensive figure for his finding that "the ideas that are in the air are our life's breath; they become our words; slavery [the pre-Civil War American reality of 'Fate'] is supported by some of them and might have crushed the rest of them; uncrushed, they live in opposition" (*PP*, 25). A remnant of "uncrushed" but highly pressured (say, stressed or agonized) ideas witnesses to what is ours to bear. But, like the suffering-into-truth aspiration of tragedy, this "tragic essay" (*PP*, 33) would go one recuperative step further. It postulates an unguarded reception of the Universe and all its "savage accidents" such that its answering retort back into the (our) air is itself endowed with a universal and god-like "omnipotence," equal and opposite to the incoming stroke. The recoiling strokes consequent upon a stripped and unlidded reception of a universe of savage accidents will not themselves be accidental. To the contrary, they will bear the plenary power and authority of what Kant sought in the *universal* voice and what Cavell seeks as the "neutrality" of the "philosophical authorship."

This intense focus on our self-creating thinking as a matter of our "[making our] breath words" might seem counter to Cavell's earlier appreciations of Thoreau and Emerson as specifically *writers* of an American scripture, shunning this forever talking America and opting instead for a "reserved and select expression" that Thoreau would "notch on his stick" and Emerson on the lintel of his door post. But, as Cavell himself notes, this early and continuing emphasis on the constitutions of writing thinks of them as, from the outset, constructed in the service of something picked up out of the air. The writer of *Walden*, for example, would "hear what's in the wind and carry it express" (*Walden*, 11) into the preserving expression of the book itself of *Walden*. The prize and point of the book's "select expression" is what is found there in the wind, with Thoreau recommending and practicing a writing where "the volatile truth of our words should continually betray the inadequacy of the residual statement [and where their] truth is instantly *translated* [and] its literal monument alone remains" (*Walden*, 217). While this radiant gist of self-reflexive writing admits that even the best in this lettered kind are inadequate remainders of the chemistry that fired them in the first place, Cavell receives (and Thoreau means) its trenchantly ringing clauses not as a counsel of writerly despair but as a bracing reminder both about what should be the animating incentive of one's written expression and about what must, in the nature of the human talking form of life, be both the actualizing and the constraining instruments of any wordsmith in the business of hearing what's in the wind and carrying it express.

At the other terminus in this constant rendering and receiving of the volatile truth of our words is how writing, as the maturing of thought—what Thoreau calls its "flower and fruit"—is, by its nature, fated to "[wafting] some fragrance" from writer to reader (*Walden*, 52). While the animating spirit of such writing is instantly spirited away with more than a suggestion of *translation's* theological meaning of conveyance to heaven without death, back on earth it suffers a more common, linguistic translation into *literal* monuments, which are, in turn and at their coming to term, ordained to give off an air and odor that would "express our faith and piety" in such words as "are not definite [but are] significant and fragrant like frankincense to superior natures" (*Walden*, 217), such superior natures, I would like to say, as the perfectionist "next self" Cavell hears Emerson constantly trying to pen into his essays as a "city or constitution of words" bent on "the achieving of a promise of expression that can attract the good stranger to enter the precincts of its city of words" (*CH*, 7). (The "city of words" trope is not Cavell's invention. It comes from the ninth book of Plato's *Republic* (592a) where the dialogue characterizes the just city just now so thoroughly talked through or up as a "city of words," a polis ἐν λόγοις κειμένη.)

Even when Thoreau roundly disparages the spoken tongue as "commonly transitory, a sound, a tongue, a dialect merely, almost brutish, and [learned] unconsciously, like the brutes of our mothers" (*Walden*, 68), his aversive laying up of his treasure in the father tongue is, both in him and in Cavell's account of him, an investment whose promised return would be the reclaimed *speech* (*SW*, 34) of a nation. The steps taken into the father tongue are, in short, the necessary way by which to bring what we do with words up to the light of consciousness so as to answer the endless call on us "to keep faith at once with the mother and the father, to unite them, and to have the word born in us" (*SW*, 16).

Behind Cavell's placing of the self-authoring act of human thinking in the incessant ins and outs by which we "make our breath words" stands his conviction that the understanding and wording of the things of a world requires the Wittgensteinian *seeing* of them *as* something else, this a fundamental sense of where our words come from that has obvious family resemblances with common claims about the root-and-branch metaphoricity (and hence deferral) of all language. I would venture to suggest that Cavell's distinction in this line of thought lies in his hard won conviction that the very existence of a human self capable of language and metaphor is fundamentally dependent on that self's need and "capacity. . . . for placing-itself-in-the -world" (*CR*, 108), this a conviction of Cavell's that he factors out into the related claims that we each come into a world that is both all new and all other to us and always already worded, that our coming to have just there a language and a voice is an *allegory* of our coming to have just there a self (*PP*, 103), and "that the 'having' of a self is being the *other* to one's self, calling upon it with the words of *others*" (*PP*,102, emphases added). This relentless emphasis on our human subjectivity or mindedness as necessarily related to whatever, at different stages of its development, it finds to be some other speaking to it is both rooted in, and provoked by, Cavell's early and specifically historical claim that at least from the romantics onward "subjectivity [had become] the route back to our conviction in [the encompassing given or 'other' of] reality" (*WV*, 22). Not unlike the proponents of the pervasive metaphoricity of language, so persuasively playing on the root meaning of μετά as *next* or *after* or *beyond*, a Cavell, chagrined at the plight of the "modern [human]subject" so manifestly inept at the placing of itself in the world and thus so routinely afflicted with a nagging sense of "lostness [and] exile" (*PDAT*, 206), finds himself playing with abandon on the ἄλλος and the *outer* lodged respectively in *allegory* and *utterance* and just there—in the othering or outing of utterance—finding the treasure of those "things of air" that are the individual "outcalls" of "the (my) (ordinary) (human) voice" as it responds to all the "whirl of organism" that is the world as we find it. According to Emerson's description of each of us as "a stupendous antagonism, a dragging together of the poles of the Universe" (*EL*, 953), we are, as said, such creatures as whose thinking capacities come into their own as an *understanding* that "encodes a way of standing toward the world, of bearing up under and countering its pressure." Our founding charter as the species ἔχον λόγον is not only to bear reality and bring it to term but also to counter it with our aversively turned attraction toward such perfectionist thinking and "upbuilding" of the human (*EL*, 67) as Emerson deems the "main enterprise of the world for splendor [and] extent."

One happy consequence of this way we have of being concomitantly called to know who we are and where we find ourselves and also what we might yet more authentically become is that it provides not just the possibility but the requirement that the writer committing himself to the "father tongue" must still keep faith with the mother tongue of our first origins and hence strive toward a standard of expression, conceived by Thoreau as a "Realometer" and founded on the conviction that "be it life or death, we crave only reality."

In the concluding pages of "Where I Lived and What I Lived For," Thoreau puts it to his reader that "if you stand right fronting and face to face to a fact, you will see the sun glimmer on both its surfaces, as if it were a cimeter, and feel its sweet edge dividing you through the heart and marrow, and so you will happily conclude your mortal career" (*Walden*, 66), he is obviously thinking of his own life as a writer who is not out to "suppose a case but [to] take the case that is; to travel the only path I can" (*Walden*, 220). Armed with this insight, Cavell helpfully sees Thoreau's Biblical image of the word as sword (*Hebrews*, 4.12; *Revelations*, 1.16, 2.16) as his figure for his self-imposed injunction that his "sentences must at each point come to an edge. He has at all times to know simultaneously the detail of what is happening, and what it means to him that it happens only so" (*SW*, 44). (This craving for reality does not dismiss (our) imagination. It calls for it, understood as "our capacity for images, *and for the meaning or phenomenology of our images*—of dawn and day and night, of lower and higher, of straight and curved, hot and cold, freezing and melting and moulting, of birds and squirrels and snakes and frogs, of houses and bodies of water and words, of growth and decay, of mother and father" (*SW*, 103, emphasis added).)

If as readers we let ourselves be penetrated by any sharply honed words directly addressing our condition and placement in the world, we may be able to see not just the fact of "the first stalk of a returning plant asserting itself with patches of snow still holding their ground" but also the intimation of that fact that, as Thoreau puts it, "so our human life but dies down to its root, and still puts forth its green blade to eternity" (*SW*, 44). Father and mother [we can call them meaning and fact, Cavell says] will be united and "the word . . . [re]born" in us when by dint of such incisiveness and an answering impressionability, we will have to put a stop to our "mortal career," by which Thoreau, ever the wisecracking wordsmith, means our fatally careening loss of control over, and interest in, the ordinary of our own life and our only world.

When Cavell directs his allegorizing thought "about putting myself into the world, and receiving it from there," he is relentlessly holding onto and staying with one of "the brutest of brute facts" (*SW*, 16): namely, the ambiguous gift or weight of the air we breathe. If this air did not unremittingly go on happening to us, we would be dead in minutes; if, on the other hand, it encountered no resistance from the vital air within us, we would all be crushed into non-entity. To these most basic of basic facts, Cavell after Emerson gives the extravagantly concentrated attention befitting something even more "given" than what Cavell notes as the *necessary* "first level [of] literal or historical sense" (*SW*, 16). And with an equally methodical extravagance, he moves on from the detail of what in his and any human life always is and must be happening to "what it means to him that it happens only so" (*SW*, 44). He moves on toward a confidently entertained picture of any member of the human life form (whose nature it is to be social) as not a drop in the sea of existence, or a cog in the wheel of the way things run, or a voiceless marionette mouthing the words of some Grand Puppeteer or Ventriloquist (often identified as Language or Fate), but, to the contrary, a member in potentially good standing of the ζῷον ἔχον λόγον, called upon to take steps toward "[having] a say in what we mean" by making his or her "breath words in order not to suffocate in the plenum of air" (*PP*, 24).

The note of "*extra-vagance*" that I have been ringing the changes on is (as so emphasized and segmented by Thoreau) not unrelated to the dynamics of a fashioning and animating of the self by "becoming other [or *extra*] to yourself," and is to Thoreau not a solipsistic failure of discipline but his variation on the Emersonian standard of an "abandonment of and to language and the world," what his own very individual idiom calls that distinctive excellence of any writing that would "wander far enough beyond the narrow limits of my daily experience, so as to be adequate to the truth of which I have been convinced . . . [and so] lay the foundations of a true expression" (*Walden*, 216). Such a true and even (to use an Emersonian word) cheering expression arises from a Wordsworthian "intimacy with the very spirit which gives the physionomic *expression* to all the works of nature." As we have seen, it is a similarly true and inviting expression that Thoreau sees in the "thought" and "expression," perpetually "welling up to the surface" of Walden Pond. This pond is "the landscape's most beautiful and expressive feature . . . [the]earth's eye, looking into which the beholder measures the depth of his own nature" (*Walden*, 125), But perhaps even more tellingly, that "gem of the first water" exemplarily represents to its rapt beholder an unseen depth of responsiveness and impressionability made evident in every minutest ripple with which its surface "betrays the spirit that is in the air" so that even in freezing cold when "I may perceive no difference in the weather, it does. Who would have expected so large and cold and thick-skinned a thing to be so sensitive?" "Yet," and critically at the ice-splitting approach of spring, "it has its law to which it thunders obedience when it should as surely as the buds expand in the spring" (*Walden*, 201).

Wordsworth stroking out on his own

Cavell's conviction that we acquire a language and a world together is clearly part of what draws him to the English romantics, but in his hardly eccentric account of these poets, they do not stop at making the sheer existence or phenomenality of the world dependent on us. They project "a life and death of the world dependent on what we make of it" (*IQ*, 68). Although this way of symbiotically binding a living language, self and world together may at first seem a fantasy of the imperially anthropomorphizing self, Cavell constantly insists that it characteristically begins in a scene of devastation, figured in comprehensive backdrops like the empty glacial spaces of "The Rhyme of the Ancient Mariner" and clinically diagnosed by Wordsworth as that world-historical "torpor," expressing a "denial of the existence, hence of the value, of the world" and originating in an individual refusal to "take your existence upon you . . . to enact it" (*DK*, 187).

This account of something about romanticism, which Cavell will eventually claim has been "miscalled animism by philosophy" (*PDAT*, 266), points me in the direction of an early moment in *The Prelude*, which concretely shows how some form of animism was, as it were, "naturally" present at the creation of the poem's autobiographical subject. The double-edged incentive driving this and my other readings of Wordsworth is to show that Cavell's understanding of the apparent "craziness" (*IQ*, 55) of Wordsworth's animism as "interest" is justified by the details of Wordsworth's poetry and has the effect of turning that poetry into a more "reasonable, or say convivial companion at the table" (*IQ*, 153) of his interests or of any human interests, and also to show that, conversely, the poetry of Wordsworth can, according to the reading-as-being-read ratio, illuminate the hiding places of Cavell's power as a philosopher. It can bring up to the light what in his thinking through of things was attracted to a body of poetry, never after *In Quest of the Ordinary* provoking any further readings from him, but still (I suspect and claim) having its obscurely prompting way with him along what Emerson calls the "road power keeps," which is quite other than "the turnpikes of choice and will, namely, the subterranean and invisible tunnels and channels of life" (*EL*, 482).

From its very beginnings, *The Prelude* is conspicuously animistic in its many scenes of self-recollection and self-emergence. The poem opens with Wordsworth expressing his gratitude to the gentle breeze that "greets" him at his deliverance from a prison-like city. This breeze first provokes in him an exultant "I breathe again" and then the justly famous "corresponding mild creative breeze" from which the whole of *The Prelude* gets under way. Especially when one recalls that Wordsworth is inflecting Milton's Holy Spirit (itself a Christian inflecting of both the muse of classical epic and the *ruach* of Hebrew Scripture) as the *sine qua non* of epic composition, one cannot help but sense that, in all seriousness, Wordsworth is here awarding primacy of agency to a wind which is "messenger" and "friend" to him, which (in the 1850 version) is on a "mission," and which in both 1850 and 1805 is said to be very actively engaged in a "ministry." Since it is in response "to all this speaking earth" that Wordsworth comes out with his own outcalls of "his breath made words," one seems forced to conclude that Wordsworth's self-defining poetic activity as a maker of "breathings for incommunicable powers" (3.188) comes after, is indeed the gift of, the speaking earth he finds himself interested in and in conversation with. To explore how an animism of a certain, reasonable kind is, as it were, present at the creation of Wordsworth's self and of his world, I would like to turn now, in necessarily extended quotation, to the first fully developed scene in this "heroic argument" about the growth of a poet's mind: namely the boat-stealing episode of *The Prelude*'s first book.

> One summer evening—surely I was led by her ["Nature"]—
> I went alone into a shepherd's boat,
> A skiff that to a willow-tree was tied
> Within a rocky cave, its usual home.
> . . .
> No sooner had I sight of this small skiff,
> Discovered thus by unexpected chance,
> Than I unloosed her tether and embarked.
> The moon was up, the lake was shining clear
> Among the hoary mountains; from the shore,
> I pushed, and struck the oars, and struck again
> In cadence, and my little boat moved on
> Even like a man who moves with stately step
> Though bent on speed. It was an act of stealth
> And troubled pleasure. Nor without the voice
> Of mountain-echoes did my boat move on,
> Leaving behind her still on either side
> Small circles glittering idly in the moon,
> Until they melted all into one track
> Of sparkling light. A rocky steep uprose
> Above the cavern of the willow-tree,
> And now, as suited one who proudly rowed
> With his best skill, I fixed a steady view
> Upon the top of that same craggy ridge,
> The bound of the horizon—for behind
> Was nothing but the stars and the grey sky.
> She was an elfin pinnace; lustily
> I dipped my oars into the silent lake,
> And as I rose upon the stroke my boat
> Went heaving through the water like a swan—
> When from behind that craggy steep, till then

> The bound of the horizon, a huge cliff,
> As if with voluntary power instinct,
> Upreared its head. I struck, and struck again,
> And, growing still in stature, the huge cliff
> Rose up between me and the stars, and still
> With measured motion, like a living thing
> Strode after me. With trembling hands I turned
> And through the silent water stole my way
> Back to the cavern of the willow-tree.
> There, in her mooring-place, I left my bark
> And through the meadows homeward went with grave
> And serious thoughts. (1.372–417)

With "an act of stealth/And troubled pleasure" and not "without the voice/ Of mountain echoes," the boy of this enduring memory transgresses the lines of *meum et tuum* with a shepherd's boat. But then when his gleeful mastery of his "elfin pinnace" takes him out beyond the boat's sheltering cave, he is forced into a 180-degree turn by the overbearing presence of a "huge cliff" which, because of the mountainous setting and the backward-rowing oarsman's enlarging perspective from cave to open water, seems to "rise up" against him, "stride" after him and thunder at him: "No. Thou shalt not steal." As abruptly powerful an effect as this has on the boy, the poet Wordsworth provides a glide-path up to its startling animism not only by its opening reference to the "voice of mountain echoes" but also by earlier and briefer intimations of his former self as, in one season, a poacher of woodcock snares and, in another, a pillager of eggs from ravens' nests.[14] On the former autumnal occasion "when the deed was done," the boy "heard among the solitary hills/Low breathings coming after me" (1.330). And about the latter springtime episode, he remembers "with what strange utterance did the loud dry sky/Blow through my ears" (1.348–9).

To young Wordsworth, the world speaks directly and pointedly, and in this first strictly autobiographical movement of *The Prelude*, the massive minerality of this cliff has the last authoritative word when "as if with voluntary power instinct" it "rose up between me and the stars, and still/With measured motion, like a living thing/Strode after me," when, as it were, the living thing of the crag seemed to go beyond talking the talk of singling-out utterance, and started, terrifyingly, walking the walk of arraignment.

To gauge accurately what Wordsworth is saying here about the "seedtime of his soul," one has to first acknowledge that it is altogether natural that this member of "a race of real children . . . wanton, fresh" (5.436–7) should on occasion kick over the traces and go in for some mildly transgressive behavior.

This, I submit, is all that is meant by the first words of the episode claiming that the doer of the deed was "surely . . . led by her [i.e. the 'Nature' of the preceding verse-paragraph]." It's a warm summer night; he's a red-blooded North of England lad and the boat's there for the taking. On his spirited own, he will test his skill and daring with it. And altogether natural that the boy's testing of limits will provoke the push-back of a cliff face seemingly endowed with watching eyes and a prosecutorial mien, especially when the boy's previous egg-pilfering put him in the extremely exposed and manifestly unforgettable position of "[hanging]/Above the raven's nest, by knots of grass/ And half-inch fissures in the slippery rock/But ill sustained, and almost, as it seemed,/Suspended by the blast which blew amain,/Shouldering the naked crag" (341–6). But along with this, I trust, reasonable recuperation of this childhood scene of projecting one's guilt onto outward things, one has also to acknowledge that a persistent treasuring of this sense of a world all alive to one and one to it and its "ministry of fear" might seem the thing of a child best put aside by the man. It might appear, if not outright mad, then at the very least a childish thought for an imagined infancy of the world more vulnerable than ours to "the superstitious, discredited mysteries of animism" (*IQ*, 45). And yet it seems that as neither boy nor man can Wordsworth do any other than report the *fact* that to the impressionability of his youthful mind the great mass of the striding mountain, on good and sufficient grounds, *appeared* to be coming after him, and his adult judgment that, for all its obvious mistaking of the inanimate for the animate, this experience was the vouchsafing to him of a very personal care and ministry. Wordsworth will persist in attributing to this experience an inestimable worth because it was among the first remembered instances in his life of what in the "blest the infant babe" conjecture of *The Prelude*, he will call "the first/Poetic spirit of our human life," which "abated and suppressed" in most grown-ups, remains in some, proudly, and "through every change of growth or of decay/ Preeminent till death" (2.275–80).

Cavell seems to sense that the flagrant animism of this and other scenes from Wordsworth's life is no longer as controversial or embarrassing as it perhaps should be because of what he acknowledges as its brilliant psychological recuperation by critics like Geoffrey Hartman and Harold Bloom. The gist of this still powerful critical tradition is that in Wordsworth there is a never finally resolved interchange between Nature and human consciousness, and that although Wordsworth himself explicitly calls his work a "spousal verse" in praise of the continuous rendering and receiving of mind and external world, some of his most powerful poetry—most signally for Hartman his account (in *Prelude*, 6) of being surprised and overtaken by his own god-like power of imagination—show a poet for whom the mind, when most worthy of itself, gathers itself broodingly around such memorably charged "spots of time" as the boat stealing episode, the gift of whose "efficacious spirit" is that in them "we have had deepest feeling that the mind/Is lord and master, and that outward sense/Is but the obedient servant of her will" (11.268–72). If outward things seem endowed with respiring life and meaning, it is a life and meaning that have been put there by the lord and master of (a) human imagination. In this quasi-Blakean view of Wordsworth, his "Nature" is but the echoing mirror into which his imagination displaces its glory, a glory that obscures its sole imaginative begetter just as surely as His Creation obscures the Biblical Creator or (as in Wordsworth's day) the long expanse of the Nile still effectively hid the source from which it annually poured down its life-giving flood to fertilize the whole Egyptian plain.[15]

As this rough summary suggests, the preferred terms of criticism in this tradition are "consciousness" and "nature." Bloom, for example, asserts that "the central spiritual problem of Romanticism is the difficult relation between nature and consciousness" (*IQ*, 45). But Cavell confesses that he is almost as uneasy with this line of romanticist criticism as he is indebted to it. For him, "consciousness" has too much unmanageable post-Kantian baggage (*IQ*, 45), not to mention that "nature," with its drift toward the material likes of rocks and stones and trees and away from the desires and drives natural to any form of life, might not be the best of globalizing terms for "all the whirl of organism that Wittgenstein calls 'forms of life'" (*MW*, 52), especially when Cavell finds congenially ready to hand in both the Wittgenstein of his constant study and the Heidegger of his frequent citing the alternative global concept of *World*. And so Cavell reframes this joining with each other of the human and where that human finds itself as not the face-off of consciousness and nature, but the turning to and away from one another of knowledge and world where, as said, knowledge is understood as the "human capacity for applying the concepts of a language to the things of a world" (*CR*, 17).

It was Cavell's dissatisfaction with this still vital line of romanticist criticism that provided the immediate occasion for the following clarification of his philosophical outlook, already quoted in my opening chapter:

> As Wittgenstein more or less puts [it]: the issue is not to explain how grammar and criteria allow us to relate language to the world but to determine what language relates the world to be. This is not well expressed as the priority of mind over reality or of self over world (as among others, [Harold] Bloom expresses it). It is better put as the priority of grammar – the thing Kant calls conditions of possibility (of experience and of objects), the thing Wittgenstein calls possibilities of phenomena – *over both what we call mind and what we call the world*. (*CT*, 97, emphasis added)

This very economically saves the intuition of a "might of souls" that is searching for expression both in Wordsworth's own "mind as lord and master" and in Bloom's "priority . . . of self over world," not to mention Cavell's early remark that "subjectivity has become the route back to our conviction in reality" (*WV*, 22). But while retaining this sense of the mind's power as extending all the way to "a life and death of the world dependent on what we make of it," it still leaves space—the same coextensive space—for a complementary Wordsworthian intuition about the pressing weight and life of things. His eye fixed firmly on the priority of Wittgensteinian "grammar" to both mind and world, Cavell can accept (as far as it goes) the now common picture of language as "[coming] to be hooked onto or emitted into the world" (*AP*, 116), but he characteristically puts in a more emphatic word for "a reverse direction, in which the world calls for words, an intuition that words are . . . world-bound, that the world to be experienced, is to be answered, that this is what words are for" (*AP*, 116). It is, in short, in response to the world in which we find ourselves that we come "to individuate things and name, settle on nameables . . . determine what *counts* as instances of our concepts, this thing as a table, this as a chair, this other as a human, that other as a god" (*IQ*, 86).

To return now to the boy in the boat-stealing episode, he does not name the cliff a sternly just god or a super-ego or his conscience, but that is the kind of huge and mighty form (to be named later) that the cliff assumes in his imagination and precisely why its apparently impending mass persists in Wordsworth's adult memory as an unforgettable spot of time speaking to him of something greater than himself and having authority over him. Inhabiting a region before the use and reach of moral discourse, the boy does not yet deal in such namings and conceptualizations, but by the agency of just such images as this cliff striding after him he is being readied for them. The distinction is essential for an appreciation of what is, as Wittgenstein might say, *off* about any reading of this spot of time that would take it as just the case of an impressionable boy projecting the "inner" reality of his guilt onto the "outward" thing of the cliff. This reading is undeniable as far as it goes, but in its trading on how "we allow false views of the inner and outer [to] produce and sustain one another" (*CR*, 329), it does not go far enough because it too quickly skims over the "secular mysteries" of "the depth to which an ordinary life requires expression, and the surface of ordinary means through which that life *must*, if it will, express itself" (*WV*, 180, emphasis added), express itself in (or more precisely on the way to) concepts which do not remind us of "something antecedently known" but are instead in the business of "instituting knowledge, reconceiving, reconstituting knowledge, along with the world" (*IQ*, 86). At this liminal stage in the boy's development, he has undoubtedly been the beneficiary of some moral instruction and example, but the only moral "innerness" he has to his own credit at this point is a vague unease, which itself latches on to the "low breathings" of the winds "coming after [him]" as its local but volatile habitation.

The taking and returning of the boat is a thoroughly contingent event. It might not have happened at all, or it might have run its course in a thoroughly forgettable manner. But it did happen to Wordsworth and it stayed with him in memory as happening just so in perceived fact and just so in looming significance, because the event brought on a self-recognition, in which he was (to put it mildly) interested, and by which he was authoritatively singled out for a rebuke that obliged him to turn himself around. In the ominously moving incumbency of the cliff, there was provided to the young Wordsworth a strikingly vivid and sharply limned image for what was then only beginning to make all the difference in and to him. The way the cliff entered into him for good was his first step onward to a less "dim and undetermined sense" (419) of what could no longer hold its fire as the previously "unknown mode of being" (420) of this emerging "moral agent, judging between good/And evil not as for the mind's delight/But for her safety, as one who was to *act*." (8.668–70, Wordsworth's emphasis). The influence of Milton is everywhere in Wordsworth's *Prelude*, not least in this opening memory which uncannily naturalizes "man's first disobedience" into a founding event more pertinently called not the fall of man but the rise or birth of the human.

From his first steps or strokes out toward an unknown and distinctively human mode of being just beginning to take hold and grow in him, Wordsworth finds that anything of any moment or interest happening to him seeks projection or "placement" in outward things. The volatile reality stirring in the boy as a result of the cliff's interdicting of his glad animal spirits finds a lasting residual statement in just that image of the cliff and all the circumstances of perspective and horizon that made it appear to move just when and as it did. In that boy on that boat, something was quickening toward expression, but at this stage of the boy's development the expression is not yet ready to settle into words like *limitation* or *finitude* or *transgression*. Rather it seals itself hieroglyphically in the remembered picture of this event, an event pushed toward crisis by the boy's own transgressive hand and climaxing in the come-back of the cliff, striding after him "as if with voluntary power instinct."

This opening picture in the growth of a poet's mind portrays the "outer" as necessarily present at the creation of an "inner," variously named by Cavell privacy, subjectivity, mindedness or soul, and here remembered by Wordsworth in its larval state in progress toward that point not where he would but where he *had to* stand single in relation to his world if he was ever to become a poet "making breathings for incommunicable power." I am quoting from the remarkable *ars poetica* that emerges out of Wordsworth first self-conscious contendings with his "animistic" proclivities. Early in the Cambridge book of *The Prelude*, he confesses that as a university freshman, newly separated from the "sublime shapes" of the Lake District with which he had been so "conversant," he found his mind becoming strangely "busier in itself than heretofore" as

> To every natural form, rock, fruit or flower,
> Even the loose stones that cover the highway,
> I gave a moral life – I saw them feel,
> Or linked them to some feeling. The great mass
> Lay bedded in a quickening soul, and all
> That I beheld respired with inward meaning. (3.124–9)

What immediately follows upon this confession is still unabashedly but not quite unapologetically animistic. Suspecting that all this must in "these tutored days" (154) seem strange, Wordsworth immediately addresses an anticipated charge of madness. The imaginative ways of his youth were, he says, natural to the "poets of old time" and to "the first men, Earth's first inhabitants" (152–3), and they constitute madness only if it is mad to be "wakeful even as waters are/To the sky's motions" (135–6), evidence of derangement only if it is a loss of control to be as responsively "obedient as a lute/That waits upon the touches of the winds" (137–8).

But then as he settles into a more tranquil style of recollection, Wordsworth leaves off defending himself, and confidently turns to Coleridge with his *ars poetica*, central to which is his claim that this "madness" is of the divinely creative kind so routinely and (for the most part) honorifically ascribed to poets:

> And here, O friend, have I retraced my life
> Up to an eminence, and told a tale
> Of matters which not falsely I may call
> The glory of my youth. Of genius, power
> Creation, and divinity itself,
> I have been speaking, for my theme has been
> What passed within me. Not of outward things
> Done visibly for other minds – words, signs
> Symbols or actions – but of my own heart
> Have I been speaking, and my youthful mind.
> O heavens, how awful is the might of souls,
> And what they do within themselves while yet
> The yoke of earth is new to them, the world

> Nothing but a wild field where they were sown.
> This is in truth heroic argument,
> And genuine prowess – which I wished to touch,
> With hand however weak – but in the main
> It lies far hidden from the reach of words.
> Points have we all of us within our souls
> Where all stand single; this I feel, and make
> Breathings for incommunicable powers.
> Yet each man is a memory to himself,
> And, therefore, now that I must quit this theme,
> I am not heartless; for there's not a man
> That lives who hath not had his god-like hours,
> And knows not what majesty sway we have
> As natural beings in the strength of Nature. (168–94)

The recollection of *The Prelude* turns the advent of a mind "busier in itself than heretofore" into a self-recognition in which the young Wordsworth was "as if awakened, summoned, rouzed, constrained" (3.109). Not only was he drawn out of his slumbers concerning what "passed within him." He was also, with a newly awakening interest, drawn or "constrained" to the fact and experience of his imaginative powers.

What the 270-line preamble to *The Prelude* records as the poem's backdoor genesis as autobiography—that subject choosing Wordsworth rather than he choosing it—reprises this event of the uprooted freshman directing a more focused and self-conscious attention to what passed within him as that "genuine prowess," whose origin is the "point . . . we all of us [have] within our souls/Where all stand single," that point issuing for Wordsworth into his utterly individual (re)countings and out-callings of anything remembered to have (in various formulations) spoken to him or respired with inward meaning, or been the making of him, or the forging of binding vows for him. In separation from his native ground, the young Wordsworth turns (back) to the great power of his "youthful mind," but not without some suspicion that this young man's mind then coming to full self-consciousness might be written off as pathological. And at the heart of the dubiousness is not the way the adult poet speaks of his work as "makings" or "breathings." While perhaps not the description of poetry that would come most readily to mind, this does ground the term in its etymology of "making" even as it stresses its aspect as "song" and vocal performance. For even these "tutored days" this is not that difficult to assimilate. But what may be harder to countenance is what appears to be the adult ratification of an adolescent animism where everything under the sun, not excluding the "loose stones of the highway" seemed to feel, breathe, speak and inspire. ("No thanks for everything" indeed.)

Noting that "making breathings for incommunicable powers" is a baffling statement, the editors of the *The Prelude 1799, 1805, 1850* suggest that these "'breathings' are perhaps the poet's own inadequate attempts to communicate the incommunicable."[16] This is undeniable, but it is perhaps little more than the undeniability of the tautological. More importantly, the note seems to be in thrall to the assumptions of an unexamined representational thinking. It seems to assume that the incommunicables in question are objects of consciousness, whereas what Wordsworth says his poetic breathings are breathings *for* (as opposed to *of*) are not objects but *"powers."* Although it can be artificially induced and sustained by what we call respirators, our breathing is a power each one of us has to execute (if that is the right word) on his or her individual own. It is, unmysteriously, an incommunicable power, its incommunicability one of those "very general facts of *human* nature" (*CR*, 110) like talking and walking, sitting and standing, sleeping, and drinking water, which in Cavell's thoroughly traditional vision of human condition extend all the way on to whatever dramas of peril, responsibility, and opportunity can be found pertinent to all the gospel and country songs about some lonesome valley you've got to walk by yourself. With the hardly idiosyncratic use of breathing as a figure for his power and acts of expression, Wordsworth drives home the point that the "made" (i.e. the poetic) breathings of his words are his alone because they issue from a point of origin where he (but he no more than anyone else) cannot but stand and breathe single. In Cavell's terminology, the incommunicable power that Wordsworth is making breathings for is his counting and recounting of what the things and occurrences of his life are (called), a power that he "conjectures" all the way back to "verily . . . the first/Poetic spirit of our human life" (*Prelude*, 2.275–6), by which "the infant babe" is drawn toward the composing of its own mind and world. Strikingly direct and apodictic about the self- and world-creating "might of souls," Wordsworth boldly informs his reader that his recounting of his life is about nothing less than "genius, power, creation . . . and "divinity itself." (This run of synonymous appositions ending with "divinity itself" strongly suggests a single, as it were, monotheistic *power*, usually (for the romantics) called Imagination. It suggests that one is to take Wordsworth's "incommunicable powers" as what classicists call a poetic plural or—very appropriately for this heroic argument climaxing on the "image of a majestic intellect"—a plural of majesty.)

With its chiasmic tracing of the individual human soul and the form of life it shares with all its human others, the bald statement that "*Points* have we *all* of us within our souls/Where *all* stand *single*" acknowledges that

Wordsworth's portion of "genuine prowess" and "genius"—his spark of this divinity, called genius by Emerson—is also operative in each and every one of us when we answer the call for our individual countings and outcalls of what occurs to us. And just as Wordsworth does not claim a god-like creativity for himself alone, neither does he lament its incommunicability. Instead, he glories in it as "in the main far hidden from the reach of words," but nonetheless capable of issuing into self-expressive breathings that can in turn provoke in receptive readers a corresponding acknowledgment both of the remembered experience of one's own god-like hours and of the loadstar weight of such hours in the committing of one's self to this "genuine (i.e. this inborn or native) power" of lively origination by which a human life may be indeed said to count. I take it as a measure of the continuity between the simpler Wordsworth of *Lyrical Ballads* and the Miltonic sublime of his *Prelude* that in his sensitive reading of early Wordsworth David Bromwich comes to the conclusion that our poet's master theme or subject was "the unexchangeability of human things,"[17] with the consequence that the prize Wordsworth constantly found himself in quest of was, in the phrasing of Hannah Arendt invoked by Bromwich, "the single voice of one unexchangeable person."[18] Such a stance toward human condition, writes Bromwich, led Wordsworth to be "always interested in people who continue to be themselves, who insist on themselves"[19] no matter the freight of custom, the grief of loss or the upheavals of history. Early and late, high style and low, this way of being in the world characteristically led Wordsworth into a poetry that would be not so much a vehicle for his thoughts and feelings as an exploration of "the conditions in which all thought and feeling emerge"[20] into endlessly different human configurations.

To this end of the emergence and resolution of one unique human subjectivity into its own unique lineaments, the boat stealing passage is fraught with lines and the crossing of lines, with bearings and course changes and points of reference and guiding stars and moorings. It first posits a "rocky steep" or "craggy ridge" as the "horizon" for the events it is to recount, and then represents the young protagonist as exuberantly proud of the skill that lets him put the ridge's most salient crag to good nautical use as (in the clarifying 1850 version) a "fixed" point of reference to keep his course toward a "chosen point" as efficiently straight and "unswerving" as possible (*1850*, 368–9). But then this *ad hoc* load-star of the scene's initial horizon becomes a very diminished, irrelevant and even invisible thing when from "behind [its] craggy steep, till then/The bound of the horizon," the second cliff "towers" up into view and comes "between [the boy] and the stars." The boy first acted as if his *circum-stances* (whatever to the farthest horizon rings him round or stands over against him) were "nothing but the stars and the grey sky," but he soon learns otherwise, as his own actions provoke the entrance of a new actor on this scene, one making an apparently unappealable claim to these skies. Moreover, to make this threatening cliff disappear the boy must row back toward it. In order to silence its authoritative voice of interdiction, he must enlist his skill as an oarsman in the service of his new role as a prodigal son returning to the house of his father. He must himself complete a course of instruction running from an opening delusion of mastery where the sky's the limit and all is permitted to what, in a related context, Wordsworth calls the "correction of my desires" (*Prelude*, 11.374), and he himself must work toward the completion of this course of instruction by means of the same craft that got him into hot water and with just such strokes of return as require the turning of his unguarded, say his trusting, back to what has been so thunderously calling him to account for his free-booting behavior.

Presented with this passage's blurred cross-hatchings of both literal and moral lines laid down and crossed and reasserting themselves, a reader might well find it as difficult to see the play of the literal bounds and checks as to appreciate the figurative force and moral implications of all these apparently (just) matter-of-fact limits and horizons. The difficulty stems from what is indeed the passage's blurring of the literal and the moral-figurative—say the vehicle and the tenor—into one another, but this is an effect neither of a failure to make things clear nor of a crafted strategy. It is the tact of a poet faithfully remembering what were his felt and experienced impressions at this liminal stage on his way toward a fully developed life within the life-lines and life-markers of all those forms of (human) life like *hope* and *pride* and *daring* and *conscience* and (the knowledge of one's) mortal limits, whose only home is the human soul.

As traumatizing as Wordsworth's nocturnal encounter with the cliff was, he will eventually and ever after think of it as a "ministry" because what he found there was a self-generated authority larger than himself and illustrative of the good fortune that for him "the passions that build up our human soul" were "[intertwined] not with the mean and vulgar works of man/But with high objects, with enduring things" (1.433–6). And there is more of the natural in this coming to terms with the cliff than the simple fact that it is a comparatively enduring part of the "nature" to be found everywhere in the Lake District. For from an impulse to that impulse acted upon to a judgment of that action received and a correction initiated, the entire narrative leading up to the cliff traces a very natural course of some (human) actions and some reactions from a world, which, for example, will in response to some new positioning of a human self offer new perspectives and put new pressures on that self. It was the nature of the boy's glad animal spirits that led him to be so free and easy with another's boat, and subsequently it was his eager testing of limits that, by the laws of perspective, first provoked the come-back of the cliff and then the voluntarily initiated course correction. Unlike such all too human depositories of authority as abusive parents or intolerant inquisitors or the "Blind Authority [of the pedagogue] beating with his staff/The child that might have led him" (3.640-1), nothing here has either the look or the sound of the arbitrary or the imposed. On the contrary, the cliff commands the boy's actions and reactions with the authority of a revelation of just what the young Wordsworth was getting himself into and must, at his age, begin to own up to.

Young Wordsworth saw in this cliff some thing (some *thing*) he "would fain call master" (*Lear*, I.iv.29). He counted it as a commanding authority because its suddenly threatening appearance spoke directly to his condition on that specific occasion. The animated play of *that* cliff was the thing that caught the conscience of *that* impressionable boy. Eventually this speaking earth will call on any member of the form of life ἔχον λόγον to respond in our self-defining coin of words. But before that, the world converses with us in (to quote Thoreau again) "the language which all things and events speak without metaphor, which alone is copious and standard" (*Walden*, 75). To a soul not yet ready for words of a certain significant character, the world communicates memorably concrete images possessed of a "haecceity [or] sheer that-ness" (*WV*, 117) that must, in Wordsworth's words, remain "far hidden from the reach of words."

This is an openly animist intuition about the human ascent to self-expression (and so self-authoring), for which Cavell finds further philosophical ratification in the "possible philosophy of romanticism" he detects in the later Heidegger of 'The Thing'" (*IQ*, 66). Placing this essay in the post-Kantian tradition of Continental philosophy, Cavell sees it turning Kant's Copernican Revolution upside down, or inside out. For if Kant taught "that in order for there to be a world of objects of knowledge for us, a thing must satisfy the conditions ... of human knowledge," Heidegger counters that "in order for us to recognize ourselves as mortal we [who are (Heidegger writes) 'in the strict sense of the German word *bedingt* ... the be-thinged, the conditioned ones'] must satisfy the conditions of there being things of the world" (*IQ*, 66). Heidegger's countering of representational thinking with a call for a thinking in the business of "letting things encounter us" (*PDAT*, 266) is, to Cavell's ear, an echo of Emerson's discovery (in "Experience") that precisely because his mourning self "can't *get* it [the world] nearer me," "he must accept the world's nearing itself to him" (emphasis added). He must open himself out to the "acceptance of a certain revised form of life (philosophy may poorly call it animism) outside himself, outside any human power" (*PDAT*, 266).

"Patience, patience"

Convinced that the handsome in our condition is our reception of the things of a world, Cavell is clearly impressed by Heidegger's teasing out of "the etymological entwining of thinking" not only with that simplest of all words, *thing*, but also "with the word for thanking." For Cavell, this is a congenial "unfolding of ideas in which a certain progress of thinking is understood as a form of thanking, and originally a thanking for the gift of thinking, which means for the reception of being human" (*SW*, 132). He welcomes these Heideggerean thoughts about *was heisst Denken* as a ratification of Emerson's "all I know is reception" and his "power of affirmation or . . . weakness for it." But such thoughts may all too easily seem to owe their affirmative power to a willful denial of what the reputedly Panglossian Emerson himself calls the "rude and ferocious" way of a Providence or Nature that "will not mind drowning a man or a woman; but swallows your ship like a grain of dust" (*EL*, 945).

But a more perspicuous acknowledgment of the necessary role which an often devastating nature or actuality plays in the upbuilding of a thoughtfully receptive mind is the major achievement of Cavell's second, insistently animistic reading of what he calls the "tragic essay" of "Fate." In this re-reading of "perhaps Emerson's principal statement about the condition of human freedom" (*PP*, 14), Cavell not only welcomes all the discourse of breath and spirit previously unnoticed by him, but also makes an extravagant ado about it. In particular, he hears the essay's three sentences about the plenum of air and the recoiling breath of our "outcallings" as something like what Walden Pond—that "earth's eye, looking into which the beholder measures the depth of his own nature"—was to the book and place of Walden: the entirety of Emerson's thinking about thinking not condensed into a drop but spirited away into our breath made words.

While continuing to stand by his claim that "Fate," written only a decade before the Civil War, is addressing our capacity for thought and so *a fortiori* addressing the "condition of human freedom" (*PP*, 14), Cavell now also claims that, despite all the apparent non-appearance to the contrary, the essay does acknowledge the clear, absolute and pressing scandal of the slavery made the law of the land by the American Constitution. But at the risk of seeming to blame the most immediate victims of this abomination, "Fate" performs its labor of "constitutional amending" not, says Cavell, polemically but philosophically. For when this tragic essay urges every human "victim of his [or her] fate" to "rally on his [or her] relation to the *Universe*" and leave "the demon who suffers, [and] take sides with the deity who secures *universal* benefit by his pain" (emphases added), the "deity" thus so fervently called for is the thinking that seeks the necessary and universal truths of human condition, by, as Emerson wittily puts it, "taking sides" with the universe in that "neutrality" of "philosophical authorship" which to Cavell is "the single process with two names of Emerson's aversive thinking": the "converting" or "turning around" of the actual, and the "transfiguring" (*CH*, 36) of that actual's onslaught of "savage accidents" into the responses of an intellect which, in its disdain for the "crowing about liberty by slaves," is set instead on telling all and asserting nothing.

This is an attitude toward the "odious facts" of life and the world as we find them that has a long history, during much of which it attracted the name of *theodicy*. Defined by the dictionary as "the vindication of God's goodness and justice in the face of the existence of evil," it is an attitude that constitutes a major portion of Wordsworth's inheritance of a Milton whose avowed purpose in *Paradise Lost* was to *just*ify—to make right—the manifestly punishing ways of God to man. If the adversarial Satan of *Paradise Lost* is condemned to an eternity of turning all good into ill, its exemplary hero is ordained to take upon himself all our ill and "[turn it] to good, more wonderful/Than that which by Creation first brought forth/Light out of darkness (XII.471-3). Similarly, Wordsworth at the outset of *The Prelude* gives explicit expression to his confidence that he has recuperated all "the terrors [and] miseries" of his most troubled years into a needed "ministry of fear" laboring toward "the calm existence that is mine when I/Am worthy of myself" and eliciting from him the affirmative cry of "Praise to the end/Thanks likewise for the means!" (I.355-62), this a doxology echoed in the poem's closing testimony that all of its recounting of its subject of "genius, power,/Creation, and "divinity itself" (III.171-2) is "in the end/All gratulant if rightly understood" (XIII.384-5).

Nowadays, theodicy is as suspect a concept as animism. Nonetheless, it can still illuminate what Cavell-honored moderns like Nietzsche and romantics like Emerson and Wordsworth are on to in their calls for a sacred affirmative, which, if it is not to be just so much talk, must found itself on a full and accurate accounting of one's losses and griefs. It is in the spirit of the theodicist, for example, that Cavell hears in *Walden*'s conclusion on "the sun [as] but a morning star" (*Walden*, 223) a punning reference to the dying down to the root of that *mourning*, which can alone make practical the book's recommendation for living in "infinite expectation of the dawn" (*Walden*, 61). And in Cavell's own case, this unapologetically grand narrative of finding one's gain in one's losses—seen by him as shaping romantic works into both books of losses and texts of recovery—finds its specifically philosophical beginnings in his early commitment to Wittgenstein's axiom that in the discovery that "I do not know my way about" there dawns the path toward perspicuous representation, and earlier and more intimately still to his experience of finding his philosophical voice "or the track of it" when the teaching of John Austin made it clear to him that he had only a feeble hold on even the most ordinary words of his native language.

The excited tone of Cavell's rereading of "Fate" suggests that precisely with this new reading of it he better "[got] the hang of" (*MW*, 85) his own convictions about our "need to recognize perdition in order to find ourselves" (*PDAT*, 221), and that this began to happen when he found it newly remarkable and significant that this Emersonian essay on the human "knot intrinsicate" (*Antony and Cleopatra*, V.ii.304) of freedom and necessity deploys an exquisitely sustained imagery of breath that very perspicuously represents both our fatedness to all that is inescapably bearing down on us *and* that oppressive fate's provocation of our individual responses to it not in the manner of a robot, slave or empty bag, but in the style of one by definition ἔχων λόγον and so in aspiration capable of being aversively abandoned to "the world I [thankfully] think." In heightened tones of praise for Emerson's philosophical efforts in a dark time of American slavery, Cavell expresses his thoughtful gratitude for the long delayed dawning of a new face or aspect to his abiding philosophical anguish over our life in and with the actual language of an actual world, which, although it is repeatedly found to be one massive savaging and debasing of human condition, nonetheless remains the only ground from which to spring an arch back toward recovery since, as Cavell had already explicitly claimed, the "actual is the womb, contains the terms, of the eventual. . . . The ordinary has, and alone has, the power to move the ordinary, to leave the human habitat habitable, the same transfigured" (*TN*, 46–7).

By its very nature as an act of thinking that would speak with necessity of the weight and force of what sets it off, any recoiling stroke with which our "Fate understands itself" must be a turning from "the words of ordinary life (hence the present forms of our life) that now repel thought, disgust it" (*PP*, 14). But even though "the world I think" will thus be continually found aversively turning from the actual world, it must of necessity be also turned to that actuality of "savage accidents," which, precisely as the accidents befalling it, it must "converse" with but need not and must not favor with the predicate of necessity. For in the "stupendous antagonism" of the human, it is the "world I think" that is charged with "[knowing] the value and law of the discrepance" (*EL*, 492) between itself and the weight of a sad and dark time, with the consequence (continues Cavell) that "the world I think," no matter how much occluded by the actual world, is not gone and so not to be mourned. Rather, it is to be borne in the attitude toward (our) history that Emerson calls for in his "Patience patience, we will win at the last" (*EL*, 492), a *cri de coeur* and encouragement that Cavell understands not as a piece of wistful cheerleading but as an acknowledgment of the "demand upon Emerson's writing, and his readers, to let the pain of his thought, theirs, collect itself" (*PP*, 31), like a charge, which if maintained instead of, say "bled" or dissipated, might, at the last, disburse itself into such flashes of light(e)ning as what Seamus Heaney calls "a phenomenal instant" of alleviation and illumination when "the spirit flares . . . /The good thief in us harking to the promise,"[21] the promise, I am suggesting, of the "[perfectionist] world I think."

Contrary to the high-end intellectual rumor that the language speaks us, Emerson's picture of our life within our language represents the individual breather of words as where the "outcalling" action of thinking and speaking occurs and where human freedom is claimed. Emerson's picture does indeed require the constraining conditions of world and language with which any individual voice in the language must contend, but by the same stroke with which it thus obviates the schoolboy notion of our freedom as "a single exception [where] one fantastical will would prevail over the law of things . . . as if a child's hand could pull down the sun (*EL*, 967), it also affirms that the thoughtfully recoiling strokes with which we each may apply the words of a language to the things of a world need not be some merely private or arbitrary assertion. Indisputably, our ham-fisted wieldings of language are *almost* universally of just this "because-I-say-so" variety so repellent to "the world I think." But a thinking able to stand its ground in an unguarded and "maintained" reception of a "*universe* of savage accidents" will itself attain to the universal.

The recoiling stroke of thinking is the other, mastering, side or phase of a subjection or obedient "listening" to the world variously hit off by Emerson and Cavell as *impressionability, reception, obedience,* or *acknowledgement* (and by Wordsworth as wise passiveness). Cavell's most extravagant phrasing for this optimally human way of being in the world has it becoming, as said, a wildly extravagant "abandonment of and to language and the world." Compared to the sober tones of *acknowledgement* or *obedience, abandonment* recommends itself to Cavell because of its perilous and even melodramatic sense of a casting off into threatening wastes or crushing depths, where the recoiling strokes of aversive thinking take on the air of what a tragic protagonist is fated to undergo, albeit with a decided bias or attraction (at the last) toward the kind of hope intimated in *Oedipus at Colonus* and only suggested at the end of *King Lear* when, in the accents of a chorus, Kent glimpses the possibility of some serious and unflattering speech now that "the weight of this sad time we must obey/Speak what we feel not what we ought to say."

From the outset of its title of "Emerson's Constitutional Amending," Cavell's second reading of "Fate" has Emerson, moving (in the legislative sense of the term) to amend the slave-holding Constitution that purportedly binds these United States into a Union but really, conspiratorially, sustains a house divided. With this reading, Cavell sets his supposedly genteel precursor deep in the troubled and blood-soaked grain of his native land, delivered by its own hand into bondage and thus provoking or giving birth to the voice of this New World Jeremiah who, Cavell repeatedly insists, found thinking for America. This dynamic of a recoiling response to the patiently borne weight of a slavish and polluted time is so reminiscent of tragedy's drive toward the suffering into the truth of πάθει μάθος that I for one cannot help but suspect that it was something like this abbreviated formula for the hard won hope of tragedy that led Cavell into his startling identification of "Fate" as a "tragic essay" (*PP*, 33), its "pent prophetic prose" not describing or explaining the thinking with which we claim our freedom but rather (in Cavell's explicit claim) working like drama so as to *enact* its thinking as the withstanding of a fate which is first and always to be borne but which may yet be gathered into the charge or incubation of such words as would, in the Thoreauvian ideal, directly address our presently enslaved condition so as to turn that condition around into the cry and attaining of freedom.

In the course of unpacking Emerson's claim that "if there be omnipotence in the stroke, there is omnipotence in the recoil," Cavell declares, "Every word is a word spoken *again*, or against again. There would be no words otherwise" (*PP*, 25). These two sentences are both brisk in delivery and "pent" in signification. They deploy only the most ordinary words in order to compose a philosopher's apriori analytic statement about something internal to (what we call) words. The sentences' mix of the eccentric and the ordinary all but demands a second reading or hearing of them, in which their propositional content may suddenly appear uncannily obvious and logically necessary, given that a set of vocables cannot become a word except through its constant recurrence and reception as indeed a word. And since (Cavell continues) the recoil of thinking word-by-word has "been expressed at any time only by breathers of words, mortals, their strokes may be given now, and may gather together now – in a recoiling – *all the power of world-creating words*" (*PP*, 25, emphasis added). Thus does Cavell return without any reservation to what in *In Quest of the Ordinary* he at least initially called the "questionable idea" of an animism that makes the life and death of the world dependent on what we "breathers of words" make of it (*IQ*, 68). But this animism is in play not only at the human pole of this interchange. It is also present, and domineeringly so, at the other pole of "a certain revised form of life (philosophy may poorly call it animism) outside [any human self], outside any human power" (*PDAT*,

266). For the human subject most apt to strike it rich in the power of world-creating words is the one "most imbued with the *spirit* of the time" (*PP*, 30) the one most "impressionable" in his or her bearing of the plenum of air surrounding us and bearing down on us.

Without exception, each of us is born into a world and a linguistically turned form of life that were both there before us. Speaking for all of us, Cavell writes, "I do not make the world" and the things into which it endlessly gathers and differentiates itself. Neither do "I," he continues, "systematize the language in which the thing differs from all other things of the world. I testify to both, acknowledge my need of both" (*PDAT*, 244). Like the Augustine invoked at the inception of the *Investigations*, we must each take our first and endlessly succeeding steps into our world and form of life by "being the other to one's self, calling upon it with the words of others" (*PP*, 102) and in the event finding oneself called upon to respond in one's own voice to what's in the wind of this encompassing reality that romanticism characteristically calls nature and Thoreau the "language which all things and events speak without metaphor, which alone is copious and standard" (*Walden*, 75).

3

A Wordsworthian Calling of Thinking

"*Every man has to learn the points of compass again as often as he awakes, whether from sleep or any abstraction.*"

Henry David Thoreau[1]

"*Further, it is the language of men who speak of what they do not understand; who talk of Poetry as of a matter of amusement and idle pleasure; who will converse with us as gravely about a taste for Poetry, as they express it, as if it were a thing as indifferent as a taste for rope-dancing, or Frontenac or Sherry. Aristotle, I have been told, has said, that Poetry is the most philosophical of all writing: it is so: its object is truth, not individual and local, but general and operative; not standing upon external testimony, but carried alive into the heart by passion; truth which is its own testimony, which gives competence and confidence to the tribunal to which it appeals, and receives them from the same tribunal. Poetry is the image of man and nature.*"

William Wordsworth[2]

Stanley Cavell strikingly characterizes the work of the English romantics as "conceptual investigations."[3] With one stroke, this aligns the romantics with the author of *Philosophical Investigations* and seems to run counter to the still dominant reception of romanticism as a movement given to the "spontaneous overflow of powerful feeling" or (in Byron's image) the "lava" of the imagination. I say "seems" because if Cavell would inherit the English romantics as exemplary practitioners of a thinking carried out "in every word and with every breath," he does so only in conjunction with his deepening conviction that our conceptual constructions are, in the nature of things, called out of us by what we as a form of life have found ourselves "partial" or "attracted" to. As important and necessary as conceptual or "grammatical" investigations remain for Cavell, their distinctive philosophical point is that through their beginnings in a "stopping to think . . . as if to let our needs recognize what they need" (*CH*, 20), they open the way toward what a severe Wittgenstein calls the "fixed point of our real need," a fervent Cavell "the exits of desire."

An analysis of the non-rational incentives to English romantic poetry was a major contribution of Jerome McGann's *The Romantic Ideology*, a book that for all its brevity may rightly be considered an example of what Cavell calls "philosophical criticism": that is, "a mode of criticism [that] can be thought of as the world of a particular work [or of a particular culture] brought to consciousness of itself" (*MW*, 313). The culture brought to light in McGann's book was less romantic literature itself than its professionalization in a literary academy, given to "an uncritical absorption of Romanticism's own self-representations,"[4] and thus endlessly replicating a German ideology that evades real material contradictions by displacing them into a supposedly independent world of Ideas. McGann is not, of course, indebted to Cavell for his emphasis on the incentives to romantic discourse. That distinction belongs to the Marx of *The German Ideology*, alluded to in McGann's title. But struck by the centrality of *incentive* in both Cavell's appreciation and McGann's critique of romanticism, I have found it remarkable to what different spheres they assign the incentive to the same cultural event, exposed by the one as a hardly disinterested ideological formation, but taken to heart by the other as a compelling reading of himself and his quest after the "neutrality" of "philosophical authorship," in which the stakes seem to be nothing less than the possibility of the human and the experienced reality of the world in which this human form of life finds itself.

Both McGann and Cavell interrogate romantic discourse with a "*cui bono?*" about just who stands to benefit from the typical romantic representation of our experience. Situating the human exclusively within the horizon of history, McGann argues that the interests of a regnantly emerging class could not but lead these poets into their artful "dramas of displacement and idealization."[5] But in Cavell's differently pitched interest in the "natural history" of our human "form of *life*" (*TN*, 42–3, Cavell's emphasis), the interest in question is not (or not just) that of some "horizontally" or ethnographically different human group, but rather the biological or "vertical" differentiation of the form of life of us human talkers, including Austrian, Brit, or American, but excluding plants and animals. The interest Cavell pursues is not something to be exposed; it is something to be revealed and made manifest. In striking contrast, McGann's demystifying account of romantic poetry has it neither pursuing nor delivering any true line of thinking. Whether this so-called thinking's adequacy to the world is conceived as a grasping or a receiving of it, it is not thinking at all. It is ideology, thinking's most intimate and most effectively distorting mimic.

For the exposition of this openly suspicious account of romantic discourse as little more than the forced but unacknowledged march of ideology, Marjorie Levinson's account of "Tintern Abbey" has become a model of clarity. According to Levinson, Wordsworth's "textual procedures transform lived contradiction into the appearance of aesthetic complexity."[6] They contrive to overlook fissure, scandal and impasse so as to secure the insight of "heterocosmic affirmation"[7] and the satisfactions of "achieved form."[8] If the burden of this position is that professional students of romantic literature must be more guarded against the seductive constructions of their subject, then Cavell's counter example from the neighboring discipline of philosophy is that of a thinker finding himself unguardedly drawn toward romantic texts when, against the grain of his own professional commitments, he hears them directly addressing his condition, as if they knew where to find him and how to find him out.

Almost from the beginnings of his philosophical life, Cavell was, as we have seen, committed to reading Wittgenstein as an "inheritor of the task of Kant's transcendental logic, namely to demonstrate, or articulate, the a priori fit of the categories of human understanding with the objects of human understanding, that is, with objects" (*TN*, 80), but an inheritor who would lead the world-disclosing authority of Kantian condition back home to the ordinary or "everyday" (*TN*, 33) use of words. Eventually, Cavell comes to testify that this Wittgensteinian appeal to the everyday "home" (*TN*, 32) of our every word was "counting on" something more satisfyingly worked out in the look and sound of Emerson and Thoreau's prose as it addresses the broadly romantic "problematic of the day, the everyday, the near, the low, the common" (*TN*, 81) with nothing more fundamental to "go on" than the "writer's faith" (*SW*, 104) that (in Cavell's constant emphasis) our *every word* bespeaks "some intimacy between language and world" (*TN*, 81). Or some "intimacy lost" (*T*, 33), in which our "terms as [our] conditions" (*IQ*, 27) might be received as not just the constituters (as opposed to the limiters) of our access to the world (*CH*, 22), but as messengers bearing news of what counts for us as a form of life.

According to Cavell, the philosophy of ordinary language might just as well be called "the philosophy of *metaphysical* language" (*AP*, 6) because Wittgenstein's goal of "clearing up the ground of language on which we stand" requires the dismantling of an entire edifice of philosophical construction (*Investigations*, §118), internal to which is the compulsion to "sublime the logic of our language" (*Investigations*, §38) and, in the event, deaden us to the world delivered to us in our terms and conditions. Such a deadening or numbing to human condition is what Cavell saw in the Antarctic wastes and fixities of Coleridge's "Ancient Mariner," represented by him as, in effect, an uncanny anticipation of the way Wittgenstein pictures a mind bent on "a *super*-order between so to speak *super*-concepts" (*Investigations*, §38) as bound and determined to land itself on a coldly fixating plane of ice where there is absolutely no footing.

To Cavell, then, the English romantic poets are practitioners of conceptual investigations not because they are attracted to the be-all and end-all of some fixed (and fixating) noumenal essence but because, time after time and case by case, they are called to an urgently practical and never finally concluded *finding* of one's self in the way we have come to word the world as we do. Again, *Walden* is a pertinent example. To Cavell, this is a book whose edification would put the manifestly distracted minds and even more scattered wills of its readers on the spot. It would call on its neighbors and readers "who are said to live in New England" to get (back) on track by exposing themselves to this writing's exemplarily different way of settling or "repeopling" the woods (and the words) of this new world. A romanticism that is thus "in quest of the ordinary" is not out to force an intellectual fix. As epitomized in Wordsworth's "wise passiveness" and emblematized in Cavell's emphasis on the openly receptive hand of acknowledgment, it is turned outward to the conditions of our human experience, waiting for it to be declared in these conditions where we find ourselves—what, not as stasis but as a stance or standpoint, is our position or interest in all this.

In short and as said, our attunements expressed through our criteria bear witness to what has mattered to us, what we have found *worth* saying. How we count indicates what counts for us; and by this directive or route, Cavell would affiliate the writers he directly and philosophically inherits with modern prophets and romantics like Rousseau, endlessly preaching that we have fouled our own nest not by ignorance but by alienation, not, that is, by some blank deficit of knowledge but by the creation and pursuit of a pack of false necessities, in whose tumultuously raised cry we have become hounded strangers to ourselves, every one his own albatross, and so every one called to his own redemption. No wonder, then, that the academic tent of meeting Cavell says he would be most at home in something called the "Department of Redeeming,"[9] a nomadic institutional address where a philosopher like him could one day teach romantic literature as "texts of recovery" and another give more or less straight *Ethics 303* lectures on how the rational basis of moral argument consists not in any as yet unrealized purchase on universally demonstrable truths but in methods whose point and aim is "a knowledge of our own position, of where we stand; in short to a knowledge and definition of ourselves" (*CR*, 312), and thus to a sorely needed remaking of ourselves. The specifically romantic agenda of this Department of Redeeming would be, as Cavell resolves, "to find what degrees of freedom we have in this condition [of bondage to emptiness and false necessities], to show that it is at once needless yet somehow, because of that, all but necessary, inescapable, to subject its presentation of necessities to diagnosis, in order to find truer necessities" (*IQ*, 9). This "romantic quest which [Cavell] is happy to join" is in the business of recovering what William Blake calls in several places "the lineaments of gratified desire," as these will be endlessly articulated by whatever, according to the economics and esthetics of speech, we have found worth saying.

Marjorie Levinson finds little of either worth or direction in what Wordsworth finds worth saying. For her, Wordsworth is a writer who, through spousal fairy tales of communion, would "restore continuity to a socially and psychically fractured existence,"[10] so that where there was "[deadlock] at the practical level,"[11] or "unworkable, unspeakable loss, there is [the supplement of] redemptive, figural definition."[12] Unlike Cavell rallying with full-throated allegiance to what he welcomes as a romanticism in quest of the ordinary, she enters the lists in order to "compel a tired organic apparatus to reveal its fabulous fusions."[13] Surprisingly, however, these two diametrically opposed stances toward Wordsworth share some noteworthy features. Whether it is conceived as thinking or ideology, the act of mind and expression in question begins in being at a loss, in not knowing one's way about. It begins in what Levinson variously names *fissure*, *impasse*, *deadlock*, *fracture*. Furthermore, both accounts bear down relentlessly on the *interest* driving Wordsworth on to just what he does and does not note. But, of course, the interest Levinson sets her sights on is something to be smoked out as perniciously private and bent on the avoidance or "overlooking" of the public realities of deadlock and fracture, while the interest that Cavell's thinking is in quest of is precisely and explicitly not that which he as well as anyone else knows any powerful group can fix into privileged place as the supposedly objective and disinterested report of the ways things necessarily are. It is instead that portion of human interest or incentive that arises, as Cavell puts it, from "the human fix itself" (*CR*, 110), from those "forms of life which are normal to any group of creatures we call human, any group about which we will say, for example, that they *have* a past to which they respond, or a geographical environment which they manipulate or exploit in certain ways for certain humanly comprehensible motives" (*CR*, 111, Cavell's emphasis). The interest Cavell is interested in is that true Promethean fire which, according to Shelley's *Prometheus Unbound*, "gave man speech, and speech created thought,/Which is the measure of the Universe (II.iv.72-3). The interest Levinson is interested in is something very different, something to be pilloried as an evasive exercise in "fabulous fusions."

The "resolution" into which Cavell happily but demandingly sees *Walden* crystallizing shares with Levinson's "fabulous fusions" the sense of a scatter of elements here buckling into definition and integrity, but this sameness in difference (the difference between, say, working through an *ambivalence* and clarifying an *ambiguity*) suggests why it is so difficult to keep steadily in mind the world of difference between them. Levinson can talk the characteristic romantic act of recollection and ingathering down (or up) into an apparatus for manufacturing fabulous fusions because, all her claims to the practical notwithstanding, she overintellectualizes this deeply practical act. Her framing of these things is just made for holding up to scorn an imposed and totalizing intellectual coherence, which, it should go without saying, is manifestly inadequate to the dense and complicated play of historical happenstance and contradiction it would presume to master or explain. By way of contrast, Cavell describes his route to romanticism as the eventual finding that his life in philosophy was calling on these romantic others not for clear and distanced certainties to appease the mind and conveniently obviate action, but for a series of testaments to the kind of quest falling to the lot of any of us who at any time might find him or herself newly awakened to the need for a clearance onward toward autonomous acts turned around the axis of our real need, find ourselves called on for a here-I-stand resolution about just what, in the acknowledgment of pervasive dereliction and ruin, we and our energies are to be in the service of. In the terms of Wordsworth (invoked in Cavell's first book), Cavell finds in romanticism not some idealizing opium of the dispossessed, but one sternly challenging exemplar after another about what one is to do when one finds that it is just our human fate to have become "A moral agent, judging between good/And evil not as for the mind's delight/ But for her safety, one who was to *act*." (Cavell quoting Wordsworth (1805 *Prelude*, 8.668–70) in *MW*, 314; Wordsworth's emphasis).

Cavell's coming to romanticism as the still persistently present cultural place perhaps most exemplarily in quest of a recovery of and to the track of our desire does not deliver us from historical mischance. It nails us to it. In particular, it nails us to our fate as each a specimen of the "modern subject," of which (Cavell will eventually say) the *Investigations* are a portrait, hit off in strokes of (in Cavell's clinical diagnosis) *lostness, exile, devastation, strangeness, disappointment, perverseness, sickness, torment* and *fear of suffocation* (*PDAT*, 206). The good of such a nailing to our condition is that from it alone can there be unfolded into a cleared space of acknowledgment not only the found and given [*vorgefunden, gegebenen*][14] terms or conditions of our social realities and histories, but also the found and given terms or conditions of our human, talking form of life which, having been called to and charged with, we have manifestly not lived up to. In contrast with this resolutely practical (and rebuking) picture of what romanticism would be about, the account given of it in New-Historicism is not, for all its talk of Praxis, practical enough. It turns struggles for conviction about courses of action into instances of what Cavell memorably calls "meaning our lives up" (*MW*, 145). It pictures romanticism as blindly and hopelessly driven toward "a transcendental displacement of human desire"[15] when, in Cavell's reading of the same cultural project, the imperative is to put together "constitutions of words," in which, by the passage "from an Intuition of what counts to a Tuition of how to recount it" (*TN*, 102), desire would be found and released in a mode of writing where every word is placed and constellated with others of its kind so as to bear witness to what we as a form of life have found needed the telling, what we have found worth the candle of remarking and conceptualizing.

A spot of Wordsworthian time

To be myself practical about all that depends on this turning of our inquiry from the panoptic coherence of a theory of our lives to the utterly specific imperatives of acknowledgment and resolution, I turn to some practical criticism of one of the two official spots of time in Book 11 of *The Prelude* (1805). That spot of time is what is usually called the "gibbet mast" episode (a naming of it which I will be contesting). With my reading of this passage (*Prelude*, 11.278–327) I hope to show that this representatively powerful stretch of Wordsworth's writing, though untouched by any of Cavell's direct attention, nonetheless *answers* to his thinking with effects and yields of disclosure, which have been unavailable to and indeed blocked by our current professional investments. What Wordsworth's autobiographical account of a little boy lost in northern England most generally answers to (and casts light back on) is Cavell's intuition that the incentive of this autobiographical/ romantic/lyrical writing is toward a constitution of words, which would somehow be both "[an account] book of our losses" and "a text of recovery," as if an autopsy performed on the actual ordinary remaining to us after all our casual slaughters of the everyday could, at the last, come to count as the first step on the way of an auguring quest, not dead set on flying *up* above the track of where we find ourselves, but instead turned to the business of "going *on*" (*SW*, 136; *CH*, 10) with an ordinary that unendingly comes round to us in a thinking, that is now to be (re)pictured and (re)born as a staying of the course of whatever attractions we find, upon investigation, to have been apportioned to us as the near and the common.

(My claim that this segment of Wordsworth's writing *answers* to Cavell's intuition about what this kind of writing is for might be more practically, say testably, entered by saying that the episode yields up something of the character of its mystery and the mystery of its character to such "master-tone" tuitions of Cavell's own writing as *character* and [secular] *mysteries* themselves, and also [to give only a partial list]: *abandonment, finding, losing, way, bottom, ground, casual, casualty, going on, down, up, steps, lasting, hand, reading, writing, standing, thinking, re-membering, empty, death, (re)birth, exposed, near, common, low, high, ordinary, interest.*)

The first spot of time finds a 5-year-old Wordsworth in the tutelary company of an adult. Accompanied by "honest James," this child, whose hand can scarcely "hold a bridle," rides into the hills, becomes separated from his "encourager and guide," loses his increasingly fearful and stumbling way, and with mounting panic comes to the remains of a murderer's gibbet. This memorial of mortally inflicted and capitally atoned violence strikes terror in the boy, but once arrived at the "bottom" it marks, he does not dwell on it. No sooner is he brought to a standstill before the gibbet than he "forthwith" applies himself to "reascending the bare Common" where he sees the spot of time proper: a "naked pool" set starkly beneath the hills; a "beacon" high above on a summit; and in between a young woman carrying water in a pitcher.

And here the narrative ends, seemingly in the middle of things. Wordsworth manifestly found his way home and lived to tell the tale. But the narrative gap about how precisely this rescue came to pass indicates that, however this little boy lost was in fact found, Wordsworth's recollection is set on substituting for any empirical, matter-of-fact finding of him the memorably lasting sight of what, when thus lost, he saw before him: the "visionary dreariness" that "invested" the pool, girl and beacon. The complex of pool, girl and beacon reflects the boy's present condition back to him. It finds him out. It pictures the way he has just now discovered things to be with him: a 5-year old far from home and "by some mischance" separated from his adult guide and protector. The indefiniteness of "by some mischance" is, again, remarkably incomplete reporting, but it very economically renders the effect of abruptness with which the boy is in a twinkling plunged back into a totally stripped and unsponsored childhood. For it is in a far different mood that Wordsworth remembers this boy starting out on his excursion into the hills. Manfully astride his horse, the boy was then nothing if not cocky. Running on "proud hopes," he was already riding for a fall into the condition of an unaccommodated foundling, fearfully alone and abandoned to the elements.

Within the boy's nascent semiotic capacities, the naked pool "[lying] beneath the hills" captures the stricken condition of one abruptly overwhelmed and profoundly exposed: the condition of a Jobean infant *redivivus*, who has to suffer again, and with full awareness, the experience of coming naked into the world. By itself, the pool starkly presents what is here to be dealt with; it measures the depths from which this boy seeks deliverance. But in conjunction with the memory's other two elements, it also points the way out of these depths. Along with the sighting of the water-bearing girl, the pool points upward to the hard labor of effecting such deliverance by taking steps on one's own—steps, which, in succession to the girl's difficult but persistent progress, would orient themselves by the preeminently stationed beacon, the latter a stand-in for the protectively commanding presence of the lost "encourager and guide." Clearly, it is the distraught and disoriented mind of the child that has, as it were, come upon (or invented) these three *données* of pool, girl and beacon into the synthesis of their mutually sustaining saliency. As disoriented as it is—or precisely *because* it has been so abruptly knocked off its high horse—this mind is indeed "lord and master . . . outward sense/ But the obedient servant of her will."

(Historically, Penrith Beacon was one of several housings for the signal fires that, in times past, might at short notice flare up along the edgy border between England and Scotland. Seeing the beacon in this light, we might think of it as calling the embattled girl and the lost boy to arms. Or, elaborating a figure from Alan Liu, one might say that the beacon "supervises" their moves.[16] The humbly pedestrian complement of this aerial perspective is that of a young traveler on the moor coming to the alarmed acknowledgment that he has lost his way there and must now look up to the beacon as a telling landmark by which to recover his bearings.)

Reticent about just how the boy came to be separated from James, the narrative is Wordsworthianly prolix about the boy's "dismounting" his horse and going "down" the rough and stony moor to a "bottom." All this apparent finickiness about the ups and downs of this experience will insistently have its say because this story's semiotic matrix is a stripped and Joseph-like abandonment to the pit or the depths, a spatially structured matrix whose draw time no more than space is allowed to escape. Scholarship has established that the Penrith execution dates from no more than 8 years before Wordsworth's boyhood encounter with it.[17] But Wordsworth's confusion of this relatively recent scene with the grimly gibbeted remains of an execution carried out a century earlier at Hawkshead leads him to paint a distinctly different picture. Wordsworth does not simply, and misleadingly, state that the initial inscription on this mound occurred "in times long past." With a sensitive subjection of his syntax and verse rhythm to the perspective of a young boy, the poet presents this recurrent act of inscription as if the push toward it is issuing from some archaic origin, as "still from year to year/ By superstition of the neighborhood/The grass is cleared away; and to this hour/The letters are all fresh and visible." (The last line-and-a-half describes a counter movement out and up into the clarified resolution of written characters. As such, this writing about writing anticipates the saliently raised "pre-eminence" of the beacon.) Arrived at more than one kind of "bottom," the boy is understandably spooked by all the terrors compacted into the letters of the murderer's name. So he confronts these characters as if they were coming after him from a deep backward and abysm of time. This is not factually the case, but it is powerfully true to the boy's experience of this scene of guilt and harsh retributive justice.

In perhaps the finest historicizing of Wordsworth's work, James Chandler has shown how the spots of time enact a "disciplining" of the poet's mind, a correction of that mind's course antithetically provoked by its obstinately entertained delusion about the "freedom of the individual mind," unmoored from any limiting conditions of place and history.[18] Chandler positions Wordsworth's struggle for this mental discipline between the French Ideologues' exclusive reliance on the individual intellect's "private stock of reason"[19] and Edmund Burke's counter championing of the prescriptive "prejudices" encoded into England's unwritten constitution of itself. Building on Chandler's demonstration that the drama of this long poem is a drama about thinking and specifically about the fantasy of a privatized thought, I would like to propose that, whatever immediate demons of French Ideologues and French Revolutions Wordsworth may have been wrestling with in Book 11 of the 1805 *Prelude*, his passage through this crisis in the growth of his mind finds its fullest—say its most philosophical or most thoughtful—accounting in Cavell's diagnosis of the all too human phenomenon of "the desire for thought, running out of control" (*TN*, 54) as it seeks to "sublime the logic of our language" (*Investigations*, §38) beyond the finitude of those forms of life which "grow language" (*CR*, 170). I propose, that is, to set the mental traveling of *The Prelude*—its repeated passages of error and return—against the background of the forms and practices of "correction," called for by what Cavell, following Wittgenstein, seeks to flush out into the open as the *fantasy* of a private language, the fantasy of a way of saying and thinking that could disown our attunements in forms of life and still pretend to be called thinking and not an empty mindlessness.

As Chandler points out, Wordsworth's expressly philosophical approach to the spots of time of Book 11 replays the plot of loss initiating the composition of *The Prelude* as a whole. In both passes through this master plot, the writer acknowledges that precisely as a function of claiming an absolute independence of life or intellect, he has lost his way, come to a standstill, not knowing which way to turn. So when, after a series of false starts in Book 1, the writer of *The Prelude* gives out with the grievous question "was it for this" [that I was granted the life to be exemplified in the spots of time], Chandler is surely right to affirm that the "this" referring to Wordsworth's loss of progress "is precisely the situation over which poetry triumphs to come into being."[20] But an aspect of this impasse to which Chandler gives insufficient weight is the great Wordsworthian theme of *interest*. For the difficulties *The Prelude* negotiates at its outset dramatize the dispiriting loss of progress attendant on that lack of true interest, deftly emblematized by Wordsworth in the hectically irresolute catalogue of aborted poetic projects, with which he puts paid to one of the more potentially numbing requirements of the epic genre.

The Prelude, then, only gets its subject underway when the writer's deficit of interest dialectically provokes its counter of reanimating memories of childhood. Further along in Wordsworth's journey, when this chronicler of himself finds himself bewitched by "some charm of logic" that makes "an emptiness/[Fall] on the historian's page, and even on that/Of poets," (11.90–2), it is a logic-induced emptiness which creates the gravity well, along which the newly stalled Wordsworth finds himself drawn toward the spots of time as features of himself and his history, which he finds he must now own up to if he is ever to get *back* on the way of his thinking and writing. From first to last, then, *The Prelude* is interested in that "going on" or "taking steps" which, for Cavell, constitutes thinking. Here at the decisive turning point in the poem's heroic action, it shows its representatively lost author confidently recovering his bearings and again getting on his way against all in "your philosophy" that would stall, fixate or suffocate his inclination to take an interest in, and so give thought to, his life.

Chandler represents Wordsworth's turnaround as a matter of his now appreciating as "mysteries of passion" (11.84) what formerly, as a self-divided English *philosophe* or ideologue, he dismissed as groundless prejudices from "the weak being of the past" (10.823). The Cavellian idea of receiving words and the forms of life these words articulate—epitomized for him in Emerson's "all I know is reception"—does not contradict this reading of a poet temporarily severed from his roots but then restored to his native English stock of thinking. On the contrary, Cavell's repeated emphasis on the human as a species whose nature is custom or "the social" is profoundly receptive to the idea of "second nature" invoked in the title of Chandler's book. But when Cavell refers to custom as "second nature," we may be confident that, unlike most new-historicists and post-structuralists, he is not putting *nature* under erasure as just an empty counter to get something pertinent said about the real thing of custom or convention. Quite the contrary. For, as already mentioned, Cavell follows Wittgenstein in stressing that our "forms of life" grow out of our *natural* circumstances and responses. He argues that this key Wittgensteinian term is not only, or even mainly, about the "horizontal" differences between, say, French and English. It is also and most originally in Wittgenstein, about the "vertical" differences in "natural history" between the human life form and, for example, that lion about whom Wittgenstein famously observes that if he could talk we couldn't understand him (*Investigations*, p. 223).

Reminding ourselves of the necessary agreements or attunements that condition a form of life should make dawn an aspect of Wordsworth's work as not beating what might all too easily be construed as a know-nothing retreat into Burkean *pre-judice* but as being (as I would like to put it) progressively about the very different business of bringing us all back, with interest, to those common *judgments*, which, as encoded into the language of the ordinary, are always already indicative of the natural attractions and authentic necessities of the life form of us talkers. (I am preceded here by Charles Altieri's trenchant assertion that Wordsworth is "not a poet of nature but *the* poet of philosophical grammar," but the way I hear Cavell, Wittgenstein and Wordsworth in conversation with one another, it strikes me that precisely *because* Wordsworth is the poet of philosophical grammar, he must also be a poet of (our) nature, writing, in Paul Fry's finely allusive title, "the poetry of what we are.")[21]

To the degree that Wordsworth the young ideologue worked to cut himself off from the form-of-life "background against which our criteria do their work, even make sense" (*CR*, 83), he found himself driven toward a forced and disabling repression of forms of life. This is Wordsworth's autobiographical way of finding himself in the position of one of those astonished casualties of philosophy, whom Wittgenstein was forever trying to get simply to see their loss of progress so that he could then call them back to the "language-game which is [a word's] original home" (*Investigations*, §116). Detoured into "your philosophy" and become sharply aware of its not affording satisfaction or progress, Wordsworth found himself, in Cavell's phrase and emphasis, "*having to remember*" (*MW*, 314) a tale of first loss when he first became unsettlingly at home with *loss*, on terms of familiarity with it.

Although the 5-year old's abrupt plunge into a condition of being lost and disoriented strikes considerable traumatic power, it cannot by itself account for the incident's manifest staying power. For that, the gathering idea or term of *loss* is needed. Limned at the "twilight of rememberable life" (1799 *Prelude*, 1.298), this child, prompted by very real stumblings and terrors, found himself *conceptually* ready (as, by contrast, a newly weaned infant would not be conceptually ready) to have something happen to him that he himself could count as being lost. So in Wordsworth's present enterprise of remembering his adult self as lost to and in philosophy, Wordsworth is drawn back *to* this archaic history as something to be drawn *on* as the founding scene of loss deposited in his memory bank. On this spot of personally hallowed time and ground, there arises for Wordsworth not so much the fact of loss as his initiation into the publicly expressed and exposed *condition* of loss—what on the ground of our agreements in forms of life we "say together" (as the word *con-dition* says) so as to make answer to this calling out of *loss* everything from losing your keys or your place or your balance, to whatever we may still be able to mean by a lost soul or a lost generation.

In *The Prelude*, Wordsworth would give an account of himself by thinking through his budget of experience. What his accounting of that experience comes to is that he is lost or abandoned. That what he is preeminently exposed to is his mortality becomes clear in the second spot of time, centered on the sudden death of his father.[22] There, the 13-year old becomes an actual, say an officially counted, orphan. In the first spot of time, a still younger Wordsworth temporarily, but with strikingly abrupt force, suffers the fate of a foundling. Both spots are emblems of unaccomodated humanity; they both "stand for [Wordsworth's] humanity" (*IQ*, 114) as subject to mortality not as a contingent event but as a necessary condition of what we are—what, by the nature of our natality and finitude, we are ineluctably exposed to. If the conviction of loss is the recurring occasion for taking thought about oneself— if it is "the incentive to thinking"—then this taking thought must remain faithful to the condition of its own existence and action. In the language which the 1850 *Prelude* offers in summary of the Snowdon vision, the "naked pool" is a ground of "sense" that will conduct toward a pertinently "ideal form" of accounting only if that pool of human condition is fully assumed or taken on, only if it is from this, and only this, experience that one draws the figures to enter into one's account.[23] (As Cavell has already been quoted as saying apropos his master-theme of acknowledgment: only the "actual" is the "womb, contains the terms, of the eventual . . . Wittgenstein's insight is that the ordinary has, and alone has, the power to move the ordinary, to leave the human habitat habitable, the same transfigured" (*TN*, 46–7).)

Since to Wordsworth, no less than to Cavell, nothing is more "actual" than our losses and our disappointments, both of his recovering spots of time rise up before the blocked progress of his autobiography as radical scenes of loss and abandonment. They reach the Wordsworth writing about the "imagination, how impaired and how restored" just where he finds himself: lost in and to "your philosophy." Both spots rehearse what Cavell kerygmatically announces in Thoreau as that "morning of mourning, [that] dawning of grief" (*T*, 54) which (in Cavell's reading of Freud) is the one thing endlessly needed to refit our fixated selves for life and progress in the world.

Wordsworth's recounting of his founding experience of loss carries a recuperative power because at the iconically condensed finding of himself in the verticality of pool, girl and beacon, there rings out as internal to this condition a call to go on beyond where he is in the taking of steps toward the finding and recovering of himself. For the constellation of pool, girl and beacon is not simply what the boy is (called); this reading or calling out of the boy also provocatively calls its subject out to an answerable style of response, to his own upright show of character. This is most striking in the embattled gait and bearing of the girl. Her progress up the wind-swept hill epitomizes the boy's own exposed condition, but her bearing of herself also counts as an example calling on him to take steps of his own—steps which cannot but be taken on his own but also steps which can do no better than take their bearings from the perspicuously raised up standard of a public beacon, newly urgent and pertinent to this untraveled traveler suddenly finding himself at sea. This spot of time provides a concrete autobiographical instance, then, of what Cavell finds the "Intimations Ode" to be calling for from us adults: that is, a "recovering from the loss of childhood by recovering something of, or in, childhood (in particular, recovering its forms of recovery)" (*IQ*, 73).

The girl is the element in the spot exerting the strongest draw on Wordsworth's interest and attention. Once James has fallen out of view, she is the only (other) living human here, and the only component of the memory that was of just that day. When "long afterwards" the young man Wordsworth "roamed about/In daily presence of this scene," the beacon and pool were still there, but the girl was long gone. There, for Wordsworth, for that one specular moment, she then moved on into her own life, while the adult who would compose *The Prelude* found himself, as it were, stuck with her, like a fate. Unlike the pool or the beacon, the girl makes Wordsworth *have* to remember her. Her presence to him circa 1776 was as ephemeral (and as powerful) as the wind, but the boy who saw her that day persistently found himself having to remember her bearing of water, as if the travail she experienced in that aversive posture toward the forces of wind and gravity constituted an intimate double or other to him, something that was not yet finished with him, something that had more to say to him or bring forth about him.

If this "girl who bore a pitcher on her head/And seemed with difficult steps to force her way/Against the blowing wind" forms the human gravitational center of this spot of time, then it is truly remarkable how neglected and virtually unthought of she is in contemporary critical discourse. Typical of such neglect is the way a sophisticated reader like Alan Liu will make this spot of time crucial in his account of Wordsworth's poetry, but barely mention the girl. Her only appearance in his lengthy book is short, parenthetical, and dismissive: she is a "relic" of "Maryology," a piece of "religiosity" in what Liu routinely names the "gibbet mast scene."[24] There are exceptions—notably Thomas Weiskel and Jonathan Wordsworth[25]—but most professional readers of this scene fall in line with Jonathan Bishop's influential assertion that the girl, pool and beacon are only "accidental concomitants" of the gibbet.[26]

Both in Wordsworth's first recollecting of the spot and in his repetition of how he would need colors and words unknown to man to paint it right, it is the girl who holds climactic pride of place in series with the pool and the beacon. And while the second mentions of the beacon and pool are just deictically abbreviated repetitions, such is not the case for the girl. Her second time around, she has matured into the "woman," but even more significantly the entire second mention of her is performed with a measureable quantum of variation, the effect of which is that the apparent redundancy of "the woman, and her garments vexed and tossed/By the strong wind" comes across not as fewer words and diminished information value but as an increment of *concentration*, a concentration of emphasis just made for the subject/author's gathering of his attention toward that one positional spot within the spot, occupied by the figure of the girl.

Although I am claiming that it is new light on Wordsworth to see the pitcher-bearing girl as a figure for his writing, it is not as though contemporary criticism has not repeatedly read what it calls the gibbet mast scene as self-reflexive of the writing in which it occurs. But this noting of self-reflexivity has been fixated on the "unknown hand's" recurrent engraving of the murderer's name into monumental letters. J. Douglas Kneale's *Monumental Writing: Aspects of Rhetoric in Wordsworth's Poetry* gives the most thoroughly single-minded expression to this approach.[27] For Kneale, the murderer's "literary remains" underwrite a "posthumous text" which, in recognition of "the proleptic displacement of a life by letters," "gives and takes away a life in letters."[28] Such readings of absence (which New-Historicists like Levinson have inherited)[29] gather conviction and often claim their origins in Paul De Man's contention that all of Wordsworth's autobiographical poetry is epitaphic "even if it obliges us to imagine a tombstone large enough to hold the entire *Prelude*."[30]

In the same spirit as De Man, Alan Liu proposes as the "paradigm for Wordsworth's" poetry Frances Ferguson's identification of the epitaph as "the epitome of poetic language."[31] In her eye-opening reading of Wordsworth's "Essay on Epitaphs," Ferguson found both the subject and the title of her book in Wordsworth's alarmed diagnosis of a "counter-spirit [in language], unremittingly and noiselessly at work to derange, to subvert, to lay waste, to vitiate, and to dissolve."[32] With these words, Wordsworth is targeting less the mind's way of getting in its own way with its penchant for subliming the logic of our language than the historically specific annoyance of the artificial poetic diction of eighteenth-century poetry. But I would not quarrel with anyone raising Wordsworth's counter-spirit to the generalizing power of a vulnerability internal to language as such, and almost inevitably vexing its own creation. I would only add that Wordsworth on the counter-spirit in language can be heard another way, a way more attuned to Wordsworth's countering call for a language that would be as naturally sustaining and as quietly efficacious as "the power of gravitation or the air we breathe."[33] Particularly since Wordsworth's counter-spirit acts so as to bring on such precisely emptying effects as *wasting* and *vitiating*, it can be heard as what, with his ear to the ground and the wind, Cavell repeatedly insists is the fact that we do, for the most part and largely because of a lack of interest, talk and write not so much inaccurately as emptily—in "*inane* phraseology"—and so must be (repeatedly) called back to the "real language of men," this a call for the effective heeding of which (as Cavell says expressly to De Man) "it does not help to picture language as being turned from the world (say troped) unless you know how to picture it as owed to the world and given to it" (*T*, 48).

By itself, the anonymous hand behind the monumental letters could indeed suggest how our words can be turned from life, becoming what we have seen Cavell deploring as "the language of no one" in what Cavell repeatedly arraigns as "your philosophy" or "the desire for thought running out of control." But if this is so, then the writing of this epitaph characterizes only what the writing in which it is exhibited (say, gibbeted) is out to effect a recovery *from*. Seen as a figure for your philosophy's death-dealing inscription of itself into an (ordinary) human life, this plot of ground does, as we say, have Wordsworth's name on it. Its monumental letters knew just where to find Wordsworth as he came to that crossroads in the recounting of his life, when he was set on the conventionally "philosophical" task of making our words conform to the requirement of a subliming logic. But this is hardly what, at the last, Wordsworth would be about with his words. On the contrary, it is, as James Chandler says of the initial impasse out of which *The Prelude* grew, "the situation over which poetry triumphs to come into being."[34] The analogy between Wittgenstein and Wordsworth strikes me as patent. In the growth of Wordsworth's mind, the turning (back) to the true thinking of what he calls Imagination (and Wittgenstein calls perspicuous representation) begins in the same experience of loss at which Wittgenstein spotted the beginnings of a philosophical problem. "A philosophical problem," writes Wittgenstein, "has the form: 'I don't know my way about'" (*Investigations*, §123). To find yourself abandoned in the way "your philosophy" has of inflicting loss is therewith to experience the "incentive to thinking" (*CH*, 19–20) and to experience it in such a way and on such occasions that what we call thinking will have to be reconceived as a reception or acknowledgment of the conditions for our knowing or saying anything at all—something Cavell sees exemplified in what he calls Emerson's "abandonment of and to language, and the world" (*IQ*, 175). A condition of abandonment not only brings on the incentive to thinking; it also keeps one persistently on the way of this thinking.

Received in the light of the way Cavell both trusts and distrusts the ways in which we are given to use our words, the monumental letters found next to the gibbet need not mark some absolute end-game of language. Instead, they may be more concretely taken as there placed by this writing so as themselves to place just where Wordsworth found himself when he subjected this language of ours to your philosophy's emptying and deadening work, murdering to dissect. In aversion to this possibility of our words for the death-in-life of a terminal and lived emptiness, Wordsworth would have his autobiographical writing exemplify how the "mystery of words" (*Prelude*, 5.621) can also make "breathings for invisible powers" (3.187). He would, that is, give himself over to what Thoreau calls the "volatile truth" of our words, which "is instantly translated" out and up from the "literal monument" of their inadequately "residual statement" (*SW*, 27; *Walden*, 217).

In Wordsworth's first spot of time, the "volatile truth" of our words makes its appropriately fleeting appearance when, confronted with the dead letter of the monumental epitaph, the boy is "forthwith" (I will put it) *translated* toward an active taking of steps which draw near to their finding end in a hieratic female figure, the emphatically aversive dynamism of whose posture—vexed, tossed and uphill in a strong wind—suggests the difficult task of delivering up the volatile life of our words—words which, it bears repeating, are always calling for just this maieutic labor of bringing them (back) to (our) life, because we are always turning this rumored bread of life into stones, as with perfect symmetry we "refuse the value of the experience of ordinary words" (*TN*, 64) and force on them a "frozen emptiness of sublimity" (*TN*, 56).

The pitcher-bearing woman is both preserved in, and quickening of, Wordsworth the rememberer. As housed in his memory, she has drawn the water forth and would bring it home. Her labors are at first, or at bottom, just the ordinary "woman's work" of the day, but over the course of Wordsworth's remembered life with this laboring image, its travail comes to be powerfully amplified into intimations of the womanly burden and mystery of bearing a child. The woman exhibits a bearing and carriage, which (as I have tried to suggest) draws to itself such terms as *labor, travail* and *delivery*. She resonates with the issue of life and generativity, resonates that issue all the way out toward the endless human task of conceiving and bearing our humanity.

I trust I am not alone in sensing the interlocked importance of the fact that this figure is a woman and that her bearing is what I would characterize as hieratic. But I fear that I may find myself quite alone when I suggest as a possible key to this ceremonious collapsing of the sacred and the reproductive the "Biblical type-scene" of the young woman thankfully found at a well which is, writes Robert Alter, "obviously a symbol of fertility."[35] But bear with me.

In the type-scene Alter defines, the woman at the well is not just any woman. Like Isaac's Rebecca, she is the future betrothed, the beloved and necessary medium for accomplishing the promise of an elect human generation. I would put my intuition (or fantasy) about this Biblical type-scene's pertinence to Wordsworth this way: In and through this woman's persistence as that which most profoundly names him—this woman as in effect *his* type-scene—Wordsworth finds that he has become imaginatively wedded to her. And the here delivered fruit of this imaginative union is the way the poet's letting the image of the woman call upon him calls him back to that calling, which Shakespeare has one of his characters call a laboring in the mind (*A Midsummer Night's Dream*, V.i.73). As remembered in *The Prelude*, then, the girl becomes the heraldic *mise en abyme* not for the static and spatial form of this work but for what, time after time, is calling for the work of this form and its kind. The pitcher-bearing woman intimates what, on and by the way of this writing, has been found to be this writing's incentive. She announces what all along has been calling *The Prelude* out into its character as a self-naming, self-recuperating constitution of words.

A picture of Wordsworth laboring to give articulated birth to himself in letters bears a striking resemblance to what Cavell will have to say about Emerson's writing as a representative corpus or "constitution" out to show its "partiality" toward the task of giving birth to the human and the social.[36] Briefly, Cavell's "This New Yet Unapproachable America" receives Emerson's "Experience" as a work of mourning for the author's son and namesake, dead at five. Cavell's intuition about the work of mourning performed by "Experience" is that it labors to bear up under the edict of Waldo's terminal separation by bringing forth on this continent and for these shores a body or constitution of words, within which the quickening life and promise of Waldo (and so the promise of "this new, yet unapproachable America") would be kept, buried or guarded (the latter the root of tuition). According to Cavell, the essay has an "idea of itself as pregnant" (*TN*, 103), which leads to "Emerson's imagining his giving birth somehow as a man" (*TN*, 104) as if "coming to terms were a coming to term" (*TN*, 21). So in the course of reading the famously aphoristic and fragmentary essays of this writer who (Cavell insists) founded thinking for America, we find ourselves being counseled to "*bear* with these distractions, with this coetaneous growth of the parts, they will one day be *members*, and obey one will" (*TN*, 100; first emphasis mine, second Emerson's). For reading Emerson—coming to terms with him—is a process in which, as Cavell puts it, " 'parts' become 'members' . . . a process in which remembering (a name for philosophy's work) is given its origin in dismemberment" (*TN*, 21).

Remembering my own (but surely not just my own) sense of *The Prelude* as beginning in fragmentary snapshots of unbidden memory and building itself up into an explicit claim to epic representativeness, I conceive the progress of Wordsworth's epic poem as having or requiring a gestation like Emerson's embryonic development toward his "constitution of words." *The Prelude* gets on the way of its progress only when its author/subject finds himself at a loss in that distraction and dismemberment of purpose, which is the self-reproaching referent of the poem's initiating cry, "Was it for this?" And from there, the poem is a work in progress of remembering, where the composing of a self out of these *disiecta membra* is not, as said, undertaken for the sake of constructing a theory about oneself, but in the spirit of "seeking to know what you are made of and cultivating the thing you are meant to do" (*CH*, 7).

As set on the way from the pool to the beacon, the woman bearing some ordinary waters of life becomes a Wordsworthian figure of desire or a figure of Wordsworthian desire, and specifically a figure of his desire for taking thought—for giving an account (of himself), for re-membering himself. Like Emerson in "Self-Reliance," this memorably persistent double of Wordsworth "stands for humanity" (*IQ*, 114). But if she stands for what "The American Scholar" calls Man Thinking, then she stands up for the inflection of this thinking toward its feminine or patient matrix from within which we might find it in ourselves to "stop to think (say not for action but for passion), as if to let our needs recognize what they need" (*CH*, 20). She offers a picture of thinking and coming to our senses which is, one might say, literally "unknown to *man*" (emphasis added). But if this woman "more near" stands for our humanity in and as she can stand or bear it, she also stands for it in the way her own upright and uphill bearing calls on a representatively human Wordsworth to take a correspondently upright and thinking stand toward his experience of being lost and cast down. She calls on him to take steps of his own so as to find his own way home—*home* as in Wittgenstein's "the home of a concept."

In the one-half-tone-off oddity of Emerson's phrase, "the mysteries of human condition," Cavell hears the finding that our life is had only on condition, and that we are thus, each and all, called to be as receptive to the condition(s) in which our histories, social and natural, have left us, as the "naked pool" of the first spot is, *exempli gratia*, open to all the atmospheric and climatological givens it finds itself embedded in and at the mercy of. Wordsworth's "naked pool" suggests the necessary but forbidding aspect of the great Cavellian master-tone of acknowledgment. The other, more inviting, aspect of this master-tone shines down from the border beacon as a figure for the lights afforded by the terms and conditions of the (our) ordinary (language). A literal landmark to both the woman and the boy, the beacon supervises the space in which that boy lost himself and then found himself in the laboriously wayfaring figure of the woman. It articulates the "bare common" where *in principio* the boy found himself at a loss and with his work cut out for him. If a literal landmark is what the boy then made of this communally edified structure, this boy's life clearly did not end with its 5-year-old impressions of the complex of beacon, pool, and woman. Further on, when the grown man stands ready to remember himself as lost to and in "your philosophy," the persistently remembered beacon stands ready to become the "lost guide" of the ordinary, an ordinary which would command and deliver what alone can provide the criterial signposts by which we initiates into a form of life may get ourselves back on the way of a thinking, acknowledged to be over rough and "logically" untidy ground, but, for all that, endlessly attractive, not just because it affords our life-form a needed friction and orientation, but more basically, because it holds out the promise that, with any and every word, we might find ourselves stepping on our transport to the track and release of our desire.

What is found to count as the type of a majestic intellect

I have kept largely in reserve the most sustained New-Historical reading of Wordsworth, a reading which, as it happens, places the spots of time at the origin of the work of Wordsworth's art. In his *Wordsworth: The Sense of History*, Alan Liu would have it that when the matter of the French Revolution opened the author of the 13-book *Prelude* to the invasive other of history, it brought on a flood whose cresting in Books 9 and 10 antithetically provoked or "[made] possible the intensity of the poem's [programmatically evasive] lyrical self-consciousness in Books 11–13."[37] But Book 13's "decisive close ... on a crescendo of impersonal Mind is unconvincing based on everything the poet has so far told us about his shifting sense of self."[38] So the 13-book mobilization of Wordsworth's poem must preveniently represent its author/subject as "corrected," a task assigned to the spots of time.

Liu rightly emphasizes the "It" resounding throughout Wordsworth's claim of access (atop Snowdon) to an impersonally imperial intellect, and brilliantly shows how this impersonality (Cavell and Emerson's "neutrality") counts as the answer to the poem's initiating question, "Was it for this?" The experience of this life was not, Liu hears Wordsworth claiming, granted for the distracted personal maunderings of the first part of Book 1. It was granted for *this*, for this access to an authoritative claim on [in Kant's terms] a universal, objective and necessary Reason, which, in antithesis to the imperial power of Napoleon and in acknowledgement of Wordsworth's draw toward the ordinary, is not "simple empire [but] the empire of the simple."[39]

But to Liu, Wordsworth manages this speciously evasive recuperation by a tactical retreat into "simple autobiography," the latter derisively equated with "Revelation" and marking the transformation of history into personal history, and French empire into the mind's empire."[40] As with Marjorie Levinson's strictures on Wordsworth's "fabulous fusions," this justifiable insistence on the autobiographical in Wordsworth reads like a virtual transcription of Cavell on the relations of language, mind and subjectivity ... but again with all the values reversed. For to a Cavell who would eventually try his hand at autobiography on expressly philosophical grounds, the "methods of Wittgenstein and Austin demand a systematic engagement with the autobiographical" (*AP*, 6) because on questions of "what we should say when?" these philosophers knew that they had no better authority than their own lives. In Cavell's pithy phrasing, these are thinkers who must always be "laying their bodies on the philosophical line, and living to tell the tale" (*APP*, 10).[41]

According to Liu, Book 11 of *The Prelude* performs an autobiographical "correction [of desires]" whose achievement in and by the spots of time represents the Archimedean point on which Wordsworth turns his empire of the mind toward its closure on the "It" of the necessary, the universal and the objective. Liu has legitimately enough taken this phrasing of a "correction of desires" from the second spot of time, and I would like to listen to that Wordsworthian phrasing with, as it were, Wittgensteinian ears. For the "*correction*" of those of us (essentially, all of us) who are *out*, *away*, or *astray* is, as already conveyed in these pages, incessantly called for in both Cavell and Wittgenstein's philosophical practice. A Cavell alive to both the manner and content of Wittgenstein's standing order back to our language games as "the home of a concept" speaks of this tonality in the *Investigations* as its "voice of correctness" (*TN*, 38). The correctness in question, however, is not coming down from any power superior to the individual masters of a language. Instead, the kind of correction endlessly in force (or at play) in Wittgenstein and Cavell is one dictated by the network of *our* criteria, on which I, but I no more than anyone else, am the authority.

What, at Cavell's Wittgensteinian leading, I am trying to get open is the seriousness, depth and, comprehensiveness of Wordsworth's call for a wise passiveness, as that appeal looks toward Cavell's "argument of the ordinary" and its ultimately disclosed imperative of a plenary abandonment of and to language and the world. As with Emerson's reiterated cry for the "patience, patience" of one sitting at the feet of the common as at the feet of his guru or master (*SW*, 147), the wise passiveness of Wordsworth preeminently draws him on to "the light of things" ("Tables Turned"), but being the plenary acknowledgment it aspires to be, it cannot be true to itself if it represses that Thoreauvian craving for a reality, which the reputedly too cheery Emerson tells us is beset with "savage accidents" and has in its "interiors" much of "the forms of the shark . . . [and] the sea-wolf," this a look into the abyss, which resonates profoundly with the climactic and the egregiously neglected feature of the "perfect image of a mighty mind" which Wordsworth claims to find atop Snowdon: namely, that vision's close on the booming Atlantic concavities of a "deep and gloomy breathing-place through which/Mounted the roar of waters, torrents, streams/Innumerable, roaring with one voice."

The 14 lines devoted to this oceanic "breathing-place" (*Prelude*, 13.57) constitute the climax to what Wordsworth saw and heard that night, as opposed to his often eloquent but sometimes stumbling after-the-fact efforts to explain what exactly was found there of the mind and its "perfection." And yet, with the exceptions of Joshua Wilner and Simon Jarvis, this climactic passage has attracted very little sustained attention.[42] By Liu, it is only once mentioned, only in passing, and very heavily wrapped up in his book's driving thesis about Wordsworth's flight from history.[43] More surprisingly still, when Liu does directly deal with the Snowdon passage and quote it at length, he leaves out these climactic lines entirely. "Here is the Snowdon experience in my selection," he writes, and then proceeds to quote in full how this mountain climber in quest of some sublime mountain glory finds himself enclosed in a thick coastal fog until, in time and because he is trudging upward "with forehead bent/Earthward, *as if in opposition set/Against an enemy*" (Liu's emphasis), the ground suddenly appears to brighten at his feet

> And with a step or two seemed brighter still;
> Nor had I time to ask the cause of this,
> For instantly a light upon the turf
> Fell like a flash. I looked about, and lo,
> The moon stood naked in the heavens at height
> Immense above my head. (13.37–42)

From here the extended quotation continues until both man and moon can masterfully look down upon a huge "sea of mist" punctuated by neighboring summits and itself differentiating itself into such apparently solid features of this rugged coast as "headlands, tongues and promontory shapes," as they "shoot themselves" into "the Sea, the real Sea, that seem'd/To dwindle, and *give up its majesty,/Usurp'd upon as far as sight could reach*" (13.50–51).

That is the last of what Liu quotes here, and the concluding emphases are his own. Here are the immediately following lines, omitted in his selection:

> Meanwhile, the moon looked down upon this shew
> In single glory, and we stood, the mist
> Touching our very feet; and from the shore
> At distance not the third part of a mile
> Was a blue chasm, a fracture in the vapour,
> A deep and gloomy breathing-place, through which
> Mounted the roar of waters, torrents, streams
> Innumerable, roaring with one voice.
> The universal spectacle throughout
> Was shaped for admiration and delight,
> Grand in itself alone, but in that breach
> Through which the homeless voice of waters rose,
> That dark deep thoroughfare, had Nature lodged
> The soul, the imagination of the whole. (13.52–65)

This boomingly heard "fracture" turns the eye and ear of Wordsworth's mountain-top epiphany back down below sea-level toward the roar of ocean as the closing stroke in this "perfect image of a mighty mind" (13.690). The perfection of mind figured in the full-orbed moon looking "down upon this shew/In single glory" is, clearly, clarity, Wittgenstein's perspicuous representation. But as the succinct French of a *fausse idée claire* suggests, clarity by itself hardly suffices. Even to be so much as adequate, the mind needs to be attentive. It needs to take in, and take on, the puzzling events and experiences provoking it into its distinctive action of working things out and making sense of them. And to advance from adequate to mighty, the mind must be capaciously receptive. It must incessantly test and enact its readiness for a responsive hearing of the "whole whirl of organism" that is our world and histories as we find them. It is the necessary and often perilous experiencing of this "whirl of organism" that is encoded into the sonically enchafed flood on which Wordsworth concludes his description of what in the 1850 version of *The Prelude* he will call this "type of a majestic intellect" (14.67).

Articulating what provokes and *animates* thinking, this finishing stroke to Wordsworth's character of thinking is as necessary to it as a short left-to-right horizontal line at the base of a single vertical would be to the penning of the "L" initiating *Liberation*. Leave it out and you are left with the "I" of the "tyrannical"[44] *Imperium* into which Liu has turned Wordsworth's "type of a majestic intellect." In plainer terms, Liu's reading crops out the "deep and gloomy breathing-place" of roaring waters at the base of the mountain and so ends up with a violently redacted and, as we say, top-down picture of a "totalitarian" intellect.[45] I grant the obvious: that the "naked" and "sovereign" moon, reached only after a long trek up through impenetrable fog, is for Wordsworth a treasured icon of hard-earned intelligibility and even of the "peace" that Wittgenstein proposed as the goal of his philosophical practice. But this icon can be characterized as bent on reading "out of court" both "everyday reality" and "the collective agon of absence—of the loss, dispossession, becoming—that is history"[46] only if one fails to give any hearing to the breach of waters Wordsworth has placed after the moon as its polarizing other of becoming. Behind what one is tempted to call this willful blindness is the prior one of not seeing that the fog through which Wordsworth lumbers his way up to the (prospect of the) moon is as much the path to it as an obstacle on its way. For that fog recalls the enveloping atmospheric condition, called (by Keats) Wordsworth's being "in a mist"[47] and by Wittgenstein that "being at a loss" that gets one on the way toward the clarity-achieving thinking signified in the heavenly station and luminous glory of the moon.

The two major constituents of Wordsworth's found image of a majestic intellect are the full moon at "height immense" and the breach's noisy welter, the two facing one another from either end of a vertical axis. And these two "huge and mighty forms" are emphatically not divorced from one another. Very much to the contrary, the light of the moon is said to "feed" on the depths of the breach, and its explicitly stated connection to the breach attracts an even stronger and more pregnant metaphor in the 1850 version's picture of a "mind ... that broods/Over the dark abyss."[48] For in line with Cavell's very Wordsworthian intuition that the "world calls for words," the mind's attainment of clarity is figured here as if it were constantly being born out of streams innumerable of experience breaching into the "voice of waters," where (Wordsworth continues and concludes) "Nature/Lodged the [animating] *soul*, the imagination of the whole" (emphasis and gloss added), lodged what in its further imagining as a "dark deep thoroughfare" is acknowledged as the necessary way or transit, say birth canal, toward the moon's realm of heavenly light.

The direction from which this thunderous ocean chasm reaches the climber atop Snowdon is the opposite from that of Emerson's airborne savageries raining down on any human agent both the material and the incentive for one's opposing strokes of intellect. But these extremities meet semiotically in that *altitudo* that can denote either atmospheric heights or primordial depths, and, more importantly, the dynamics of the interchange between world and human agent are the same for both. Just as Emerson, in Cavell's recounting of him, "encodes" understanding as our distinctively human "way of standing toward the world, of bearing up under and countering its pressure" (*E*, 244), so Wordsworth's climactic turning of his attention back down to the mounting roar of waters inflects reception or wise passiveness toward its aspect as one's nakedness before a world, which day by day is to be borne as just this riddled and riddling whirl of rift, loss and fracture.

The "Intimations Ode" has a pansy telling oft-told tales, and the *Prelude*'s boat-stealing episode a mountain crag endowed with weighty accents of interdiction. But the "fixed, abysmal, gloomy, breathing-place" (1850 *Prelude*, 14.58) neighboring Mount Snowdon projects an even deeper and more pervasive animism, one more or less explicitly declared in the passage's concluding paradox that "in that breach/Through which the *homeless* voice of waters rose/... had Nature *lodged*/The soul, the imagination of the whole," a statement of the case that seems to transpose the divine voice of creation breathing over the waters of the deep into a human voice of self- and world-creation, which as itself an issue of this deep, is, in turn and in the nature of things human, called upon to turn back (with animating interest) to its own origins in its own experience.

This is a picture of the mind in action that betrays a marked family resemblance with Emerson's "all I know is reception" and with Cavell's related intuition that it is the endless becoming of the world that calls for words and thought. That Wordsworth's vision of a majestic intellect does indeed represent the world as so *calling* for words is initially signaled by the fact that although this primordial breach is introduced visually as a "blue chasm," it is thereafter exclusively represented as an auditory phenomenon, in sharp contrast to the "silent light" (1850 *Prelude*, 14.73) of a moon that is all and only visibility. Like those "low breathings" (1.330) and "strange utterances" blowing through" Wordsworth's young ears (1.348-9) at the dawn of his remembered life, the breach at the base of the Snowdon vision is something predominantly (and just short of overwhelmingly) *heard*. And as with Sausurre's influential account of phonetic *différence* as the generator of meaning and signification, this breathing place "roaring with one voice" could not so much as begin to articulate itself into things capable of being significantly heard or read, were it not beforehand a place of *différence*, a place differentiating itself into such inflections and disturbances of the air as may be extended beyond phonetics to the fact and weight in a human life of such occurrences of the unexpected and the untoward as are paralleled in literal reading by narrative gaps asking to be filled or catachrestic signs appealing for their intelligible recuperation.

But if, as Cavell insists, your assigned reading as a member of the species ἔχον λόγον is of what is before you in widest commonality spread, then *différence* will assault you with ruptures and falling offs that smack less of the ink and lamp of textual catachresis than of real and historically lived disappointment, dereliction and dismay, what in specific reference to the "breach" or "rift" of the ocean, Simon Jarvis calls the "shock of the real," when breaking through the comfortable fabric of habit and routine it is experienced as "a cut, a gap, a 'chasm' or 'breach.'"[49] In Jarvis's reading of the complete sound-and-light spectacle of Snowdon, what Wordsworth finds ungainsayably next to the mountain is the "the Sea, the real Sea," an emphatic phrasing which (Jarvis adds) "tells us what to take for figure and what to read by the letter. The sea of mist is a figure at whose edge the literal sea can be seen."[50] In my similar but less visual reading of it, the breaching of the real sea into a Biblical roar of waters is "the place of the remarkable, the place of everything we find "worth noting, [ours] to note, about which to make an ado" (*PP*, 65). Both readings dwell on this breathing place as, pointedly and crucially, opened up and, as it were, discovered by all "the terrors [and] miseries" recollected in the *Prelude*, but by just that writing and recollection held to lead to the same kind of "soul-humanizing" benefit which (in "Elegiac Stanzas") attends the "deep distress" brought on by the death-at-sea onslaught of "the light'ning, the fierce wind, and trampling waves." Both readings are variations on the "idea of [specifically human] growth" as "a process in which remembering (a name for philosophy's work) is given its origin in dismemberment" (*TN*, 21). They both take Wordsworth at his world-affirming word when he says that in that "fixed, abysmal, gloomy, breathing-place" (1850 *Prelude*, 14.58), "Nature [had] lodged/The soul, the imagination of the whole," for, as Jarvis writes, "*Imagination* is imagined here as what is indubitably real and lived in experience, as what we experience when the 'universe of death' or 'counter-spirit' to which we become comfortably habituated is interrupted. Imagination happens to us at that instant when we are brought emphatically to affirm that we live."[51] Wordsworth's picture of the origins of a mind fated to thought and language is one where in the (punctually recurring) beginning is not the (partial) word but the primal event of a breaching or natality to be taken "[not merely] as a description of a past event, indeed of the first event, in our biographies; but equally as a statement about the conditions of human birth, of the birth of the human . . . a statement about the growth of the human mind after childhood" (*IQ*, 73), this a growth so cut through and driven onward by the necessities of "parting . . . departure, dividing, branching, grafting, flowering, shearing, issuing, delivering, breeding: separation, parturition" (*IQ*, 88) that it draws out of Cavell the wild and quasi-Derridean surmise that "life no less than death . . . [appears to be] a condition and process of dissevering" (*IQ*, 89).

Even if Wordsworth had not explicitly named the rift or breach the animating "soul and imagination of the whole," it would still be clear that he grants it a primacy in the life of the mind, corresponding to its climactic place in the narrative. This is a claim about the primordial position of this breaching/breathing place of experience that is starkly different from Liu's closing summation that "Snowdon, then, is a vision of poetic Imagination that has 'usurped' upon the world,"[52] a judgment that seems to find its justification in the lines (quoted emphatically by Liu) that refer to "the Sea, the real Sea, that seem'd/To dwindle, and *give up its majesty,/Usurp'd upon as far as sight could reach*," never mind either that these lines, so differently read by Jarvis, speak of seeming rather than being or that in this acoustically busy place a usurpation limited to "as far as the sight could reach" might not be the end of the story. Nonetheless, Liu's emphasis on the political character of Wordsworth's vision is justifiable. The passage bristles with words like *sovereign, contest, usurpation* and *majesty*, a vocabulary prepared and, as it were, neighbored by all the literal ups and downs the episode contains to only a slightly lesser degree than the first official spot of time. Take, for example, the already emphasized detail about Wordsworth's going *up* the mountain "with forehead bent/Earthward, *as if in opposition set/Against an enemy.*" This not only frames Wordsworth's literal ascent as a contest as to what will be master and what mastered. It also suggests the mutual implication of these ups and downs as they are here gathered into one human body scaling the mountain but, precisely because of that ambition, constrained into an emphatically *earthward* stance. In order to sustain this complexity and not reduce it to the misleading "either/or" question of what is to be up and what down, what master and what slave, I would begin responding to it with Emerson's paradox that "one who has more obedience than I masters me, though he should not lift a finger" (*EL*, 272), an aphorism that Cavell takes to be about "reading" the world with the attentive responsiveness which he will eventually call simply the capacity for listening (*IQ*, 116). For a Cavell listening thus to one of his masters, the mastery he himself seeks is the other face of obedience or listening. But the moon that Wordsworth sees from atop Snowdon has struck so many common readers of it as such a splendidly ideal and isolated symbol of intellectual mastery (and so many professional readers of it as therefore a thoroughly suspicious icon of the same) that it fairly cries out for a turning of the "obedience-is-mastery" paradox around into its equally true and telling inverse that mastery is obedience, here worked out in the imagery of "the clear presence of the full-orbed Moon/[looking down] from her sovereign elevation" (1805 *Prelude*, 14.53–4) dialectically feeding on and brooding over its polarized other of that "fixed, abysmal, gloomy breathing-place–/[from which] Mounted the roar of waters, torrents, streams/Innumerable" (1850 *Prelude*, 14.58–60).

In the light of this, I trust, quickly recuperated paradox of the mastery to be attained by listening and its manifest pertinence to Wordsworth's image of a mighty mind or majestic intellect, I would amend Liu's made-for-ridicule "imperium of the simple" into Cavell's argument (for the sovereignty) of the ordinary. Let dawn on you this aspect of the "simple" and of the character of the "empire" this "simple" calls for, and you might come to see that, far from being the arbitrary totalitarianism that Liu makes of it, Wordsworth's "type of a majestic intellect" proposes a *constitutional* monarchy in the Emersonian sense of seeing that only as right and sovereign which is after my (our) own constitution. Or, put otherwise, the majesty here come finally into its own is that which Emerson sees set in train when "we hear eagerly every thought and word quoted from an intellectual man . . . [so that] in his presence, our own mind is roused to activity, and we forget very fast what he says, much more interested in the new play of our own thought than in any thought of his. 'Tis the majesty into which we have suddenly mounted, the impersonality, the scorn of egotisms, the sphere of laws, that engage us" (*EL*, 955).

In stark contrast to Liu's brief against a supposedly rigged tribunal of Wordsworthian mind peremptorily "throwing out of court" both "everyday reality" and "the history of agony,"[53] such a constitutional sovereignty is constrained to give the last and deciding word to the twinned actualities of historical mischance and everyday human condition. In an elegant continuation of the court-room imagery attending his imagery of imperium and ukase, Liu supports this particular indictment of Wordsworth with what he apparently takes to be some self-incriminating words out of the accused's own mouth: "the mind is to herself/Witness and judge" (*Prelude*, 12.368-9).[54] One way to get a purchase on how pertinent the insights of ordinary language philosophy are to this charge is to point out that these eight words of Wordsworth's constitute a succinctly accurate description of perhaps the most fundamental axiom of that philosophy: namely, that on these matters of human condition, I am indeed the evidence, and the judge and jury . . . but I no more than anyone else.

But granting Wordsworth's notional allegiance to a wise passiveness, where is the mind's capacity for receptivity or listening to be specifically found or heard in the Miltonic sublimities and chthonic noise of the Snowdon episode? To address this question, I return to something which I agree with Liu is worth emphasizing in Wordsworth's recounting: the way he describes himself as negotiating the mountain "with forehead bent/Earthward, as if in opposition set/Against an enemy." The combative set of his head is of a semiotic piece with Wordsworth's "panting" breath and "eager pace, and no less eager thoughts." It powerfully suggests what Wordsworth often deprecates in himself and others as the very unhandsome condition of "spirits" hectically "on the stretch" (*Prelude*, 4.324). The Emersonally aversive counter to this particular spirit on the stretch is poetically performed in the next several lines which, in turn, come immediately before Wordsworth is struck with the light of the moon "like a flash" upon the turf. These lines go like this:

> Thus might we wear perhaps an hour away,
> Ascending at loose distance each from each
> And I as chanced the foremost of the band (13.33–35)

Pedestrian and prosy Wordsworth could hardly get more pedestrian and prosy than this. But listen again for what may be clearly (and only) *heard* in these lines. Pick up on their semiotic matrix of a relaxation or "looseness" that is the precise opposite of that head bent earthward as if in opposition set against an enemy. Hear that looseness in a first line where the grammatically indefinite *"an* hour" is furthered loosened by the *perhaps* and the modal *might*, and the *as chanced* of the next line. These conspicuously ordinary and unremarkable lines *perform* the relaxed receptivity that allows this eagerly panting seeker of the sublime to be surprised and brought up into a light, which, not insignificantly for the argument of the ordinary, he first finds "at his feet" and on the "ground."

I find confirmation for reading this as an image of the handsomely receptive aspect of our condition as opposed to a mode of "Western conceptualizing" for which the clutching human hand emblematizes a "kind of sublimized violence" (*CH*, 39) in some lines from the Snowdon ascent that seem so blandly and pointlessly matter-of-fact that I know I will be accused of over-reading them. But there the lines are, coming to the not inconsiderable count of six. Wordsworth has sunk "silently" into "commerce with [his] private thoughts" and "nothing [was then] either seen or heard the while/Which took me from my musings"

>   save that once
> The shepherd's cur did to his own great joy
> Unearth a hedgehog in the mountain-crags,
> Round which he made barking turbulent.
> This small adventure – for even such it seemed
> In that wild place and at the dead of night –
> Being over and forgotten, on we wound
> In silence as before. With forehead bent . . . (22–9)

The aggressive drive to unearth something, the yelping noise of it all, and the strong suggestion that notwithstanding all the "barkings turbulent" and "teasing" round the "coiled-up prey" (1850 *Prelude*, 14.23–4), none of this currish behavior ever eventuates into anything like a "kill" are all set against the thus violated silence and the forthcoming event of reception in which Wordsworth is surprised by a gift of light not violently unearthed by him, but rather coming to him and laid at his feet, all of which seems to illustrate what Cavell was already saying early in his career, that "it is the thing we [humans] do not know that can save us ... what theology knew as grace" (*MW*, 325–6), what Wordsworth reveres as wise passiveness and Emerson condenses into "All I know is reception" (*EL*, 491).

That New Historicist criticism is blind to the "power in passiveness" so prominent in Cavell may be illustrated by Liu's commentary on a Charles Le Brun depiction of Mary Magdalen, Wordsworth's two-line misreading of which he makes into something of a visual frontispiece for his thesis about the *Prelude*'s programmatic "transform" of the sublime of Revolutionary history into a false lyrical beauty. The two lines from Wordsworth catch this Revolutionary tourist in the act of gravitating to the beauty of the Magdalen while turning from the rubble of the Bastille. Liu's analysis of the painting is a finely discriminating act of art criticism, and deftly woven into the larger fabric of his argument. He is clearly right to call Wordsworth's rendering of the painting a misreading.[55] Doubtless influenced by what a Magdalene penitently weeping at Jesus's feet is expected to be doing, Wordsworth depicts her as sorrowing, when she is clearly not in sorrow but caught up in some ecstatic rapture. This Magdalen "is not in the aspect of sentimental sorrow, but in the act of being dramatically ravished or violently transported."[56] Given all the fine things Liu has to say about the painting and about Wordsworth's (mis)appropriation of it, I find myself at a loss at how grossly or roughly *Liu* misreads it. In only one example of an extremely violent language, he calls the experience the Magdalen is undergoing "a rape of beauty by the sublime."[57] But a rapture is not a rape. The attitude given expression in the Magdalen's face is one of rapt openness, and her visual intertext is the obedient virgin of the Annunciation receiving the Word delivered to her and standing ready to bring it to full term. By contrast, Liu sounds like he is talking about a Ledaean body out of Yeats and frighteningly "caressed/By the dark webs, her nape caught in his bill." But when Yeats wrote this in a poem originally entitled "Annunciation," he at least knew that he was envisioning a way of generating worlds that was the precise opposite of the attitude of reception enshrined in the traditional Annunciation scene and its derivatives.

LeBrun's Magdalen is an emblem of wise passiveness. Prototypically a "heart that watches and receives," her attractiveness to Wordsworth (and the point of her enraptured beauty's stark juxtaposition to the violence of Revolutionary thought and practice) is that she herself is so alive and responsive to what (to quote Thoreau again) rightly and strongly attracts her. In its fervently active and eroticized posture of reception, the painting may be thought of as an icon for what Cavell calls that handsome/attractive/receptive part of our condition as a "stopping to think (say not for action but for passion), as if to let our needs recognize what they need" (*CH*, 20). To New-Historicist work with its pervasive air of power and violence, such pictures of the mind as radically receptive will appear soft-headed or wishful. But the investigations of Wittgenstein and Cavell, I am claiming, make dawn an aspect of this radical receptivity, which demands intellectual rigor and contests just who in these regions of knowing and thinking and acknowledging may be in the grip of the deepest and most disabling fantasy. What Liu derides in Wordsworth as a specious "empire of the simple" is, in Cavell and Wordsworth, a mastery granted only to those having great obedience, stillness, or waiting, only to those willing to let the words of their experience and the experience of their words make an impression on them and so tell them all they know.

To the New-Historicist charge that all such wise passiveness before, or patient reception of, or stilled listening to, the things of a world amounts to the historically evasive nullity of the "mind without action,"[58] I would here note that this is something Cavell addresses in his reading of *Macbeth*. Entering into a direct conversation with the Renaissance variety of New Historicism, Cavell there strives to get open the question of just what is to count as *history* and to that end offers Emerson's "History" as an uncanny anticipation "of the spirit of the [French] Annales' historians' disdain for great events, their pursuit of the uneventful, a pursuit requiring an altered sense of time and change, an interpretation of what I call the ordinary or the everyday" (*DK*, 225). Thinking both of Liu's rather large assumption that Wordsworth just could not get off the subject of the celebrity First Consul and Emperor, and also of his (Liu's) Edict of Nullification against Nature ("*There is no nature*... 'nature' [as opposed to a tree] I have never set axe to"),[59] I would draw particular attention to Cavell's quoting of Emerson on how he is "ashamed to see what a shallow village tale our so-called History is ... What does Rome know of rat and lizard? What are Olympiads and Consulates to these neighboring systems of being?" (*EL*, 256). These neighboring systems of being, which have, on the one (global) hand, been called nature or world, and on the other hand, the "human fix itself" of "those forms of life which are natural to any group of creatures we call human, any group about which we will say, for example they *have* a past" (*CR*, 110, 111, Cavell's emphasis). These precisely and necessarily neighboring systems of being can be heard clamoring for their acknowledgment in a romanticism that has found its "self-appointed mission" to be one whose "stakes appear sometimes as the loss or gain of our common human nature, sometimes as the loss or gain of nature itself, as if the world were no more than one's own" (*IQ*, 43). This is a statement of the case and the point of English romantic poetry which resonates powerfully with Simon Jarvis's concluding picture of Wordsworth as a poet "whose verse fights tooth and lung" against a "technical philosophy" where both "subject and object have been hallowed out by disenchantment" into "these nothings which we are supposedly to accept as the very substance of our lives: the phenomenalized object, the evacuated subject; the total then made of this no-subject and no-object."[60] Jarvis gives us a philosophically technical account of the historically specific way Cavell's "perverse . . . modern subject" (*PDAT*, 206) has dead-ended itself into the apparently terminal emptiness both of itself and of its world. Coming as it, uncannily, does from (mostly) the Continental side of our philosophical present, this double-edged account of where we presently find ourselves might render us more ready to enter into the spirit of the "abashed" surmise provoked in Cavell by a mourning Emerson on the opening to him of the "life of life": the surmise, namely, that we may "have not only to conclude that we are not beyond the demands of romanticism, but . . . to hope that the demands of romanticism are not beyond us" (*TN*, 114).

4

Bursting from a Congregated Might of Vapors: Desire, Expression and Motive in Shelley

"And the green lizard, and the golden snake
Like unimpeded flames, out of their trance awake."

Adonais, 161–2

"The only right is what is after my constitution, the
only wrong what is against it."

Emerson, "Self-Reliance"

"Didactic poetry is my abhorrence," Shelley writes trenchantly in the preface to *Prometheus Unbound*. He elaborates that what he has instead set out do in this work is to "create beautiful idealisms of moral excellence" that will give expression to "the *yes* [the heart] breathes" (*Prometheus Unbound*, III.iv, 150, Shelley's emphasis) and draw the human mind to "love, admire [and] trust,"[1] what it finds there. This is, in miniature, a manifesto of the perfectionist writing defined by Stanley Cavell as a "city" or "constitution" of words drawn toward "the achieving of an expression public enough to show its disdain for, its refusal to participate fully in, the shameful state of current society, or rather to participate by showing society its shame, and at the same time the achieving of a promise of expression that can attract the good stranger to enter the precincts of its city of words" (*CH*, 7).

Another and more conventionally philosophical affinity between Cavell and this English romantic poet only a few times mentioned by him is that much of the latter's considerable output in prose is concerned with Cavell's starting point in the epistemological preoccupations of modern Western philosophy.[2] This interest eventuated in the philosophical idealism of Shelley's "intellectual system," and it often pervades his poetry in a very self-conscious manner. It, for example, stands behind his advisory to the readers of *Prometheus Unbound* that the work they are about to read uses an imagery "unusual in modern poetry" but (Shelley adds) ubiquitous in Dante,

Shakespeare and the ancient Greeks: namely, an imagery "drawn from the operations of the human mind, or from those external actions by which they are expressed" (*NS*, 207).

Shelley's interest in what and how we know anything at all eventually induced him to place a "burning fountain" (*Adonais*, 339) of desire in the same conceptually generative position as Emerson's "genius" and Cavell's "interest." Attracted early to the *Alma Venus Genetrix* of Lucretius and later to Dante's Beatrice, he went on to create a body of work in the English tongue, whose every word (so I will be contending) echoes Cavell's unorthodox claim that perhaps the "most thoughtful" act of thinking is "to let true need, say desire, be manifest and be obeyed" (*TN*, 45).

Although for both Shelley and Cavell the one thing clamoring to be unbound and let happen as the truth of our condition is the Promethean fire of desire, they both find provocation, sustenance and ratification in the high culture of (mostly) the West, which Cavell constantly calls over praised and undervalued.[3] For while Wordsworth often appears to be taking pains to conceal his considerable learning, Shelley is constantly putting himself forth as a *docta poeta*. Even as the iconoclastic revolutionary in him senses that he and his contemporaries are on the verge of "some unimagined change in our social condition or the opinions which cement it" (*NS*, 208), he would still have the highest ranges of his poetry find its footing in such of his self-appointed precursors as Aeschylus, Dante, and Milton. Similarly for Cavell, the roll call of his many interests includes not only movies and this "new yet unapproachable America [Emerson] found here in the West," but many of the most imposing and venerable monuments of Western intellect and their way of making unavoidable "the question . . . whether there is to be a shareable high culture native to these shores, and whether we should want one, making our own claim to verge on that pitch of the life of the mind" (*T*, vii).

As detailed in my account of how Cavell read (and was read by) romanticism, his sense of where the highest pitch of the life of the mind comes from and what it must be about is in no small part the result of the conviction eventually wrested out of him that his philosophy was calling for romanticism. That conviction led him on to a newly received Emerson (and Thoreau) where an exemplary human perfection was endlessly seeking its local but volatile habitation in the capacity of the writer's "breath made words" to become a prophetic tongue of fire which, in revealing its inventor's gift for staying attuned both to the breath of a culture and the breath of a world or "nature," could incriminatingly show its contemporaries the darkening and descending way they were pursuing, while not, as it were, staying put with it but instead responding to it in the aversive recoil of lively origination. To Cavell and Emerson, then, "the great man"—whom

"Emerson's understanding of the origination of philosophy as a feminine capacity ... seems to divine [to be] a woman"—is "the man most imbued with the spirit of the time." He is that most "impressionable man" (*PP*, 30) who in a dark time must, like Shelley's Prometheus among the gods, be "as a nerve o'er which do creep/The else unfelt oppressions of this earth" (*Julian and Maddalo*, 449–50). In Shelley, what corresponds to this picture of where our soul or mindedness comes from and of the tragic magnanimity to which it may aspire (and of the madness it courts) is his constant turning of a British-empiricist vocabulary about the "operations" of the human mind into the provoking effects of what the preface to *Prometheus Unbound* famously refers to as the spirit of the age.[4]

That Shelley's talk of the spirit of the age is not just a rhetorical flourish confined to the preface of *Prometheus Unbound* is made clear by a first act where the agonized title-character is the scene of a psychomachia waged between his furies and his "ministering spirits,"[5] and where both of these two contestants for Prometheus's ear and voice are "air-born shapes" (I.807) whose instruments of either torture or succor are not mainly but *solely* the words of their suggestions and counsels. As the act opens, the noxiously damning *fiat* of Jupiter is tyrannically in place. Eventually it will be globally represented as the "dim and dank and grey . . . atmosphere of human thought" (I.676–7). Earlier, it is spelled out in excruciating detail by what Jupiter's furies assert to be the necessary state and predetermined history of the form of life which Prometheus has gifted with language. Countering this attitude toward where we find ourselves are the ministering spirits as they eventually come to Prometheus with the news and promise of a new day in the "atmosphere *we* breathe," (676, emphasis added) which is (they declare) like that gathering season in the affairs of humankind when "buds grow red when snow-storms flee/From spring gathering up beneath,/Whose mild winds shake, the elder brake/And the wandering herdsmen know/That the white-thorn soon will blow" (790–5).

This quick review of the linguistically turned imagery of wind, breath and atmosphere in the first act of *Prometheus Unbound* can only suggest the thoroughness with which both its poetry and its imitated action work out its prefatory remarks about the spirit of the age and its impressionable reception.[6] To demonstrate the continued prominence of this master-tone in three of Shelley's most mature and confidently assured poetic achievements will be a major task of the two following chapters. For now, I will limit myself to saying: *first*, that a *prima facie* case for Shelley's corpus as throughout replete with an imagery of breath and voice may be found in such master-strokes of the critical tradition as Donald Reiman's insistence on the "unique position in Shelley's symbolic universe [of] the wind, which in its wilder manifestations as 'storm,' 'tempest,' or 'whirlwind' was Shelley's symbol of Necessity," or Earl Wasserman's privileging of Shelley's figure of the "breathing earth" as the animating spirit of the whole of *Prometheus Unbound*, or Geoffrey Hartman's complementary proposal of a more proactive "politics of the spirit" as the means by which Shelley would pursue his "passion for reforming the world"[7]; and *secondly*, that the significance and effectual "Power/Girt round with weakness" (*Adonais*, 281–2) of this circuitry of atmospheric pressure and human voice informs the small but immeasurably pivotal role (in Act II of *Prometheus Unbound*) of the not *muta* but *invisa persona* named Echo, to John Milton the "queen of parley" (*Comus*, 241), to John Hollander the "regent of discourse" (17), and to Francis Bacon "a thing not substantial but only a voice; or if it be of the more exact and delicate kind, *Syringa*—when the words and voices are regulated and modulated by numbers, whether poetical or oratorical."[8]

In Shelley's relentlessly self-reflexive poetry, what is typically found coming into existence at the cue of "living winds" from the "golden Eastern air" (*Epipsychidion*, 516–17) are not just the literal "buds" that "grow red . . . / From spring gathering up beneath" but also the metaphorical "flowers of poesy," which like the bell-shaped productions of Shelley's "Sensitive Plant" have each their own kind of "sound, and odour, and beam" (93). Repeatedly, Shelley metonymically concentrates the season of Flora into the literal flowers of spring while simultaneously troping them into what at the time was the still widely current commonplace of the "flowers of poesy." The main warrants for this complex claim about Shelley's bent for troping literal flowers into both poetry and the promise of rebirth are the mind-numbing ubiquity of the one trope in our culture at large and the strategically placed frequency of the other in Shelley's work. For the moment, I will offer just one opening example of the latter. Many more will follow.

"Hymn to Intellectual Beauty" is, as Judith Chernaik has authoritatively declared, a poem in which (along with "Mont Blanc") Shelley "formulates for the first time in his own voice the themes that are to dominate his major work."[9] At its narrative climax, the hymn's titular deity benignly overshadows its autobiographical protagonist just as he is "musing deeply" on our painful human "lot" at "that sweet time when winds are wooing/All vital things that wake to bring/News of buds and blossomings" (55–90). With its climactic event thus set at the advent of spring and in an enabling mood of human brooding, the hymn can then seamlessly pass from the theophany of the enveloping deity to the poetic "calling" it effects in the "passive youth" because the seductive "wooing" of the winds toward the good "news" of buds and blossomings is so clearly a metaphor for how when Shelley was indeed captivated by "the beautiful which exists in thought, action or person not . . . [his] own" (*NS*, 517), he found himself called on to carry that beauty express into such of his own "flowers of thought" (*Epipsychidion*, 384) as this very hymn to the "awful Loveliness" (71) of Intellectual Beauty. But if this is the founding moment of Shelley's poetry, it would seem to play all too easily into the common criticism that this poetry and its author are all too delicately and passively in flight from the "actual" and all too easily given to an excessively florid style. In response to this criticism, it should first be noted that in his many returns to this scene of his poetic initiation, Shelley invariably makes its human weather and setting a season of profound loss and anguish. Time after time, anything coming to a Shelleyan protagonist as "A Metaphor" of the harmonized natalities of "Spring and Youth and Morning" (*Epipsychidion*, 120) comes to him out of a devastating winter of the world. With the caveat, then, that Shelley's signature enactment of the human heart flying in impassioned service to the "accent unwithstood" ("Masque of Anarchy," 145) of the attractively beautiful is almost always the coming of a "spring cradled in tempests" (*Prometheus*, II.i.6), I want for the moment to concentrate on the way Shelley, as an exceptionally pure example of the perfectionist writer "directed less to restraining the bad than to releasing the good" (*CH*, 18), would with the majority, but not necessarily the best or most trenchant, of his words exemplarily enact a burning fire of attraction toward, *exempli gratia*, the Asia of *Prometheus Unbound*, fervently addressed as "the life of life" whose "lips enkindle/With their love the breath between them" (II.v.48–9).

One of Shelley's more succinct and manifestly self-reflexive representations of a bursting out of the fires of desire and creation toward "the beautiful in thought, action or person not our own" is the much invoked passage from *A Defence of Poetry*, where "the mind in creation" is likened to "a fading coal which some invisible influence, like an inconstant wind, awakens to transitory brightness" (*NS*, 531). Contrary to the received reading of this as about what the "Defence" only later gets to—the "process of fading and decline which begins prior to composition"[10]—here, the fading of the coal is here only its initially dimmed condition out from which some unseen influence "like an inconstant wind" calls it forth into radiant brightness. With an exquisite irony, Shelley's fading coal has become so drenched in cultural rumor and academic commonplace that we have let its initial attribute of *fading* drown out its quickening progress toward the enflamed act (or passion) of *awakening* predicated of it. This Shelleyan image for a mind caught up in the activity of τὸ ποιεῖν directs our attention not to some ostensibly static object like a hunk of coal or a seed or a not yet blossoming flower, but to that object's recurrently at-hand possibility of bursting forth into new flame, life or bloom.

The resuscitation of Shelley's fading coal is only one instance of a characteristically self-reflexive romantic preoccupation with (what is called) inspiration and may more mundanely be thought of as the incentive consequent upon attraction. Nowhere cited by Cavell, it nonetheless illuminates why he would eventually hear his philosophy calling for a romantic poetry, which "[takes] its own possibility as its subject" (*IQ*, 66) as it both calls for and enacts a wise passiveness which (Cavell will eventually insist) requires a ground-breaking rethinking of *impression* not as "a uniform physical process [the process of sense impression so common and fundamental in Locke, Hume and Kant] but [as] a mark of intellectual or spiritual achievement, an occurrence not to a tabula rasa, as something at the beginning, as it were, of the possession of a mind, but an occurrence to the rarely impressionable, causing as it were a *flowering of mentality*" (*PP*, 97, emphasis added).

Cavell's "flowering of mentality" refers to the same event of the "mind in creation" that Shelley figures as "a fading coal" awakening to transitory brightness. Both figures bank on a mindful impressionability that will lead to a bursting out of expression, which is not at all willed but hardly listless. What becomes of Shelley's fading coal is only one of his figurings of a truth borne in upon him by his experience as a poet: namely, that "poetry is not a power to be exercised according to the determinations of the will ... [as if one could] say, 'I will compose poetry'" (*NS*, 531). This is a conviction about the passively received and ultimately ungraspable origins of our flowering islands of mindfulness that early in his career Cavell began thinking his way through along a path which began with his initial chagrin at Kant's denial of the possibility of intellectual intuition (*SW*, 129ff), eventually yielded to his joy upon hearing the challenge posed to this axiom by Emerson's "All I know is reception," and finally turned into his reconceiving of "impressionability" as "a mark of intellectual or spiritual achievement," given expression in flowerings of mentality.

Cavell and Shelley's use of the same flower metaphor for the most handsome aspect of our distinctively thoughtful condition suggests that they are of one mind about the one most fundamental "operation of the human mind." This is a suggestion made only stronger by the textual fact that Shelley has embedded his fading coal in an extended discourse of flowers that leads up to his use of the coal's resuscitation as a figure for the "mind in creation" and from there complexly branches out into the accomplished "bloom and odor" of all the many individual flowerings of this mental nature.

The fading coal occurs in a paragraph whose first two sentences are a crisply delivered statement of its major claim: "Poetry is indeed something divine. It is at once the center and circumference of knowledge; it is that which comprehends all science, and that to which all science must be referred." This accords with Shelley's "intellectual system," and like his more notorious claim about poets as the unacknowledged legislators of the world, it gives that system a linguistic turn, similar to Cavell's understanding of our [poetically generated] terms as our Kantian conditions for knowing anything at all. After these two opening sentences, the paragraph ramifies into an extended imagery of roots and blossomings:

> It [i.e. poetry] is at the same time the root and blossom of all other systems of thought: it is that from which all spring, and that which adorns all; and that which, if blighted, denies the fruit and the seed, and withholds from the barren world the nourishment and the succession of the scions of the tree of life. It is the perfect and consummate surface and bloom of things; it is as the odour and the colour of the rose to the texture of the elements which compose it, as the form and the splendour of unfaded beauty to the secrets of anatomy and corruption. (*NS*, 531)

After the simple but startling claim of its first sentence, which several paragraphs later will be reprised and condensed into "that bold and true word of Tasso—*Non merita nome di creatore, se non Iddio ed il Poeta*" (*NS*, 533), every subsequent move in this passage plays into a complicated language game, whose goal is to make good on the predication of a "divine" creativity to poetry, recalling Wordsworth's insistence that to speak of what passed within him is to speak about nothing less than "genius, power, creation... and divinity itself." Shelley first appropriates for his poetic calling the venerable image of the divine creator as a circle whose center is everywhere and circumference nowhere and then brings this common geometrical figure for divine omnipresence and omnipotence back down to earth so as to bring out the spatial metaphors and epistemological bearings of the subsequent "comprehend" and "refer." As *circumference* generates *comprehends*, so *center* generates *referred*. It restores this ostensibly abstract word to its precise place in the definition of a circle as the locus of all points on a single plane equidistant from any given point, to which they are all carried back, or *re-ferred*. With such moves, Shelley is not advancing the common and unexceptional claim that poetry too is a form of knowledge. He is claiming or (perhaps with William Blake) re-claiming for poetry and language a world-forming power of creation.

But as sweeping as this claim is, Shelley is at this point only getting started. For after these opening sallies claiming for poetry the creative power of the godhead, he proceeds to model center and circumference into the three-dimensionality of "root" and "blossom," into both the deep-down genesis from which all things "spring" and the exfoliating charms of bloom and adornment. And from there, this highly poetic prose accumulates into a vigorously realized picture of poetry as that on which alone depends either the sterility or the flourishing of all our systems of thought with all their many ways of counting and recounting what things are (called). The passage negotiates its way through a large and varied cast of geometric, horticultural, and theological figures, but it clearly gives pride of place to the flower trope as it folds and gathers the others into itself, and then finds itself expanded into that which "if blighted, denies the fruit and the seed, and withholds from the barren world the nourishment and successions of the scions of the tree of life." Shelley is here openly saying what Cavell had, as it were, to unearth as the claim also of Coleridge and Wordsworth: i.e. that there is a life and death of the world dependent on what poetry makes of it (*IQ*, 68).

Immediately after this brief for poetry as omni-creating and so "indeed something divine," the *Defence* recalls the essay's opening cardinal distinction between τὸ ποιεῖν and the instrumental "reasoning" of τὸ λογιζεῖν, and remarks that, unlike the latter, poetry is not "a power to be exerted according to the determinations of the will." This is the claim about the receptivity of the "mind in creation" that the figure of the fading coal brought back to flaming life illustrates. But then after this figure has done its work as a more fervent and instantaneous variant of spring bursting into flower, the passage quickly modulates back into a lushly attractive language of flowers, in which poetry is a "power" that "arises from within, like the color of a flower which fades and changes, [so that in a variation on the theme of the fleeting and 'inconstant wind' blowing where it lists] the conscious portions of our natures are unprophetic either of its approach or its departure." The flower image that had earlier expanded into the all-encompassing tree of life thus finds its way back to the necessarily individual expressions of "the gardener Fancy . . . / Who breeding flowers will never breed the same" (Keats, "Ode to Psyche," 62–3). It finds its way back to the "odour and colour of the rose [which is] to the texture of the elements that compose it as the form and splendour of unfaded beauty to the secrets of anatomy and corruption." To the attentive reader who can still remember that throughout this passage we have been reading about the flowers of *poesy*, this "perfect and consummate surface and bloom of things" is to be recovered for human affirmation and guidance in such flowers of perfectionist thought and poesy as, for example, "Lines Written among the Euganean Hills," a poem that climactically announces that "in the deep wide sea of Misery" it itself would be one of the treasured "flowering islands" of human accomplishment that it has been singing, that it itself would, by the "light and smell" of its own "breathing and shining," bid fair to attract the "polluting multitude" to its precincts so that "they, not it, would change. . . . and the world grow young again." (350–73)[11]

Besides the bursting forth of flowers and the flaming up of an apparently burnt-out coal, the "mind in creation" attracts a number of other representations in Shelley's poetry. One of the more frequently invoked is lightning's discharge of an atmospherically gathered electrical energy. The image figures powerfully in Shelley's account of what a creatively responsive reader like himself might (as we say) get out of Dante. In a highly condensed language owing much to the endlessly recurring natalities of Dionysos and the legendary phoenix, Shelley says of Dante's "very words" that they "are instinct with spirit; each is as a spark, a burning atom of inextinguishable thought; and many yet lie covered in the ashes of their birth, and pregnant with a lightning which has yet found no conductor" (*NS*, 528). Just as the inconstant wind may bring a fading coal back to flaming life, so here a reader's previously torpid receptors and "conductors" may, at any moment, be surprised by such words as were initially "instinct" and are still "pregnant" with a spirit, which however often it may (and in a sense must) bury itself in the ashes of the dead letter may still be brought back to life when in its guise as a literal monument to some "burning atom" of thought, it finds an apt "conductor" in any one of its readers.

Shelley's picture of all the literal monuments of our "minds in creation" routinely left for dead in our numbed reception of them speaks of a death in our lives and a life in our morbidities that finds one of its most telling expressions when Shelley's "Ode to the West Wind" first invokes the divinely overpowering wind of its title as inextricably both "Destroyer and Preserver," and then goes on to speak of the words of this very poem as, in the end, oriented toward the rebirth of Spring and troped into the same sparks and ashes as Shelley's praise of Dante. The ode ends with an "unextinguished hearth" of "ashes and sparks" that are explicitly identified as the poet's own "words among mankind." The ashes own up to Shelley's sensible fear that his words will elicit no adequate response. The sparks project his hope that, in time, the wind will blow the ashes into verbal sparks (and seeds) of thought for a still obdurately "unawakened earth." This desire for a reawakened earth comes, of course, just before the famous rhetorical question—"If Winter comes, can Spring be far behind?—but it is also the climax to an explicitly aspirational movement that commenced with the speaker's fervently delivered prayer that the 'spirit fierce' of this wind [be]/My spirit" and "through my lips" here turn into the "trumpet of prophecy" that he would have his words among mankind become.

Just this bare sketch of what the ode makes of the west wind would be sufficient to establish what I am hardly alone in arguing: that is, that the poem is pervasively self-reflexive, that it is about nothing so much as Shelley himself and the breath of his being as a poet. What I wish further to draw attention to, besides the sheer magnitude of Shelley's prophetic ambition, is the gathering and recoiling aerodynamics of what he here prays for: namely, that the words of just this ode might channel the devastating "breath of autumn's being" so that the "spirit fierce" of this wind [would be]/My spirit" and "through my lips" the "trumpet of prophecy." This, I submit, is an uncanny anticipation of Emerson on the savage strokes of the universe and the human recoil of our breath made words.

As I have shown elsewhere at more length,[12] the possibility of the poem's initially destroying wind being thus so propitiously gathered into the aversive response of its own utterly individual speech-act was embedded in the poem itself when it initially represented the wind as violently driving the "winged seeds" into "their dark wintry bed where they lie cold and low,

> Each like a corpse within its grave until
> Thine azure sister of the Spring shall blow
> Her clarion o'er the dreaming earth, and fill
> (Driving sweet buds like flocks to feed in air)
> With living hues and odours plain and hill.

The self-contained pastoral image, enclosed in an ostensibly awkward parenthesis and flanked on the one hand by "each like a corpse within its grave" and on the other by the "living hues and odors" of flowers, details the blowing of the myriad flowers which the "blowing" of the clarion wind of spring will awaken into being. With this parenthesis, a Shelley alive to the traditional figurings of words as winged and words as seeds not only is making the clarion wind of spring call on the dreaming earth of winter to arise and express itself anew in vernally answerable flowers of thought. He is also preparing the way for the closing trumpet of prophecy and to that end already exploiting the equivalence of pastor and poet so prominent in the pastoral elegiacs of *Adonais*. He is, in short, making this destroying and preserving wind of continual rebirth the guiding and animating force that might alone shepherd these "words among mankind" toward the not to be withstood accent of prophecy. Given the writerly wit with which Shelley embeds the winged potentialities of not dead but only sleeping (or dormant) seeds into his discourse of "destroyer" autumn, one can be sure that this urbane poet knew exactly what he was doing when he makes siblings of the slave-driving force of the autumnal wind and his beautifully azure sister "driving" her flock of sweet buds up into the feeding (i.e. the pasturing) air. He was using the related concepts of consanguinity and conspiracy in order to drive home his hard earned lesson that any would-be instrument of prophecy would be only a tinkling cymbal of wishful thinking, if its callings for rebirth were not grounded on its full and present taking on of the west wind and all its destroying power. ("The actual is the womb, contains the terms, of the eventual. . . . The ordinary has, and alone has, the power to move the ordinary, to leave the human habitat habitable, the same transfigured" (*TN*, 46–7).)

Fire, ardor, tinder-box impressionability. These are all readily acknowledged characteristics of a poet, who was also given to a politics and poetry of the spirit that required both his listening to "the *yes* the heart breaths" and his sounding out of his own response to that sacred affirmative with his "own breath made words" through "passion-parted lips" (*Prometheus Unbound*, II.i.74). Shelley is, in short, a Pentecostal writer along the demythologizing lines of Michel Serres.[13] Not only does he make fire-bearing Prometheus the mythic alter ego of his (agonized) best self, he also repeatedly has the winds of spring play the role of the dynamic bearer of heat and the provoker of more and still more fiercely awakening life, as when, in *Adonais*'s particularly exuberant discourse of Spring, the poet known to his friends as Bysshe and nicknamed the snake/*biscia* (*NS*, 475) finds yet another emblem of the season of Flora in "the green lizard and the golden snake" leaping toward the newly attractive heat of the vernal sun "like unimprisoned flames out of their trance awak[ing]" (161–2).

With its express assimilation to suddenly sprung or unimprisoned flames, the leaping of the green lizard and golden snake into their vernal liveliness gives expression to a considerably more energetic or pardlike "mind in creation" than either Flora called out into her "living hues and odours" or a fading coal recalled to brightness. As already suggested by Shelley's praise for Dante's words as deadened atoms of inextinguishable thought still instinct with spirit and "pregnant with a *lightning* which has yet found no conductor," the major figure for the vigor and promptitude of Shelley's "pardlike spirit beautiful and swift" (*Adonais*, 280) is what the preface to his *Prometheus Unbound* confidently names the spirit of an ostensible age of despair where "even now the cloud of mind its discharging its collected lightning" (*NS*, 208).

Evidence for the prominence of lightning in Shelley's work can be found literally everywhere in that work. One particularly telling example is how in "The Cloud," it plays the major, specifically the "piloting" role in a poem where the literal atmospheric phenomenon of its title is "an analogue of the Mind" and its entire narrative "the life-cycle of a human soul."[14] But of even more moment perhaps than the visual nature and effect of lightning is the characteristic *action* of unbonding or *bursting* that it shares with a fading coal or an ice-bound flower breaking out into flame or bloom. Bursting is also the finally anticipated fate of the political and social horror so succinctly set forth in "England in 1819," a sonnet where the spondaic accumulations of one disgrace and injustice after another are imagined to be pressing down like "graves from which a glorious Phantom may"—on the turn from one line of verse to the next—"Burst, to illumine our tempestuous day." Here lightning is the implied metaphor for the hope to be wrested out of a dark time. Shelley's signature "Ode to the West Wind" is more explicit. In its second and straightforwardly Maenadic section, we find both the visual of lightning and its characteristic action of bursting. Kenned into sudden "fire and heat," the lightning there awaited is deemed to be gathering in the noxious and apparently rock solid atmosphere of a storm which, for just that reason, can be invoked with prophetic confidence as a "congregated might/Of vapours, from whose solid atmosphere/Black rain and fire and heat will again *burst*."

In meteorology, lightning is the flashing out of electrically charged air; in the Greek pantheon, it is the intimidating scepter of Jupiter that *Prometheus Unbound* will eventually have turned against a tyrant who mistakenly thinks that he is the one and only wielder of the lightning bolts of "the thought/ Which pierces this dim Universe with light" (II.iv, 40–1) This all too common case of intellectual pride running before a fall is the imitated mental action of the opening scene of Act III, an action which the subsequent scene defines in joyful retrospect as the tyrant reaping the "whirlwind" of his own oppressions and so playing the part of an imperiously high-flying eagle come to grief in a "bursting cloud" that blinds him with its "white lightning" and "baffles" him with its "thunder." This second scene of Act III, in other words, takes pains to make it clear in word after word that the scene immediately preceding it was a concrete dramatization of the hoped for gathering of Jupiter's "atmosphere of thought" toward that breaking point when, as in the words of the play's preface, "the cloud of mind" would become so unbearably saturated with Jupiter that it had to seek release by "discharging its collected lightning" and hastening on to "some unimagined change in our social condition or the opinions which cement it."

For sufficient reasons having to do with Shelley's conviction in the moral necessity of "reaping what you sow," this example and numerous others in his work have something of the air of an impersonal world-historical process to predetermined destiny holding its way. But this one-sided impression needs correction in view of the preface's complex but reasonably straightforward assertion that, according to the polarized dynamics of the spirit of the age, "a Poet, is the combined product of such internal powers as modify the nature of others, and of such external influences as excite and sustain these powers; he is not one but both" (*NS*, 208). Acknowledging that both human individual and human artist must alike be "creators and creations of their age," Shelley turns to a common nineteenth-century distinction between the spirit of an age and the "forms in which [this spirit] has manifested itself" in order to stress that an adequately human response to the spirit of the age manifests itself not in the easily assumed forms and fashions of the times but in the provoked eruption of the "uncommunicated lightning of [each individual's] own mind" (*NS*, 207).

As different as Shelley and Wordsworth undoubtedly are, the one's "*uncommunicated* lightning" and the other's "breathings for *incommunicable* powers" (*Prelude*, 3.188) face in opposite directions from that same crucial point where each is convinced the self stands single and must count and live up to what Emerson pregnantly calls the "significance of the individual" (*EL*, 943). With the breathings he makes for his incommunicable powers, Wordsworth endeavors (in Shelley's phrase) "to touch the enchanted chord" in his readers and provoke in them the memory of their "own godlike hours." By the "calling out" of, in each case, an individual mind, that individual subjectivity is called upon to acknowledge that what at the bidding of this other is being asked of it is the "uncommunicated lightning" of its own incommunicable powers.

Wordsworth's sense of his poetry as the "making" of whispered or intimated "breathings for incommunicable powers" is tonally or atmospherically very different from Shelley's presentation of his (and others') poetic output as the flashing out of an uncommunicated lightning. To be sure, each of these poets has his different moods. Shelley can be diffident and skeptical, Wordsworth can be unruly. But for the latter, typically the sky of mind opens out "with gentlest visitation," while for the former the cloud of mind bursts out in lightning bolts of telling self-recognition, constraining the poet to ride (in Emerson's figure) these words that are the "horses of his thought" through a "flight" that would be "swifter than fire/... [drinking] the hot speed of desire" (*Prometheus Unbound*, II.iv.4–5). This is not one among several major features of Shelley's writing. It is the major feature of that writing, and in my judgment it draws Shelley closer than even Wordsworth to a philosopher for whom "the most forbearing [and "most thoughtful"] act of thinking" would be "to let true need, say desire, be manifest and obeyed" (*TN*, 45). I say this in spite of the suspicion that for many Cavell's like-mindedness with Shelley might not redound to the credit of either. It might make more compelling the familiar criticism, frequently applied to both Shelley and Emerson, that our poet avoids dealing with what he himself singled out as "sad realities." For our philosopher, it might raise the objection that he rather too airily slides past the obvious distinction between needs and desires. But surely after all his years of sustaining his own "pitch of philosophy" by staying with Wittgenstein and going on with Emerson, Cavell is not deaf to the difference between Wittgenstein's call to reorient our investigations around the "fixed point of our real need" and Emerson's differently inflected call to take that only as right which is after one's own constitution. Indeed, as Cavell's placing of "true need" and "desire" in apposition with one another suggests, he is more than commonly alive to the fact that the convergence of need and desire is definitive of perfectionist writing from as early as Plato's *Republic* (Cavell's lengthily itemized model for the features of a perfectionist city of words (*CH*, 6–7)) where the just life is found to be also the happy or gratified life. Shelley's fervently desired convergence of need and desire is manifest in his many strictures on what he calls the "education of error" which is our "whole [actual] life" (*NS*, 507) as it goes on creating tyrannously false needs, that will not cease to attract and ensnare until their self-destructive consequences have wised us up to them and made manifest and constraining what at the outset of the accursed world of *Prometheus Unbound*, for example, is the not yet totally extinguished attraction of Prometheus toward Asia as his Dantean "Amor che muove il sol e l'altre stelle."

The fervor with which Shelley cherishes the uncommunicated lightning of his own mind draws him on toward, as it were, time-lapsing the blowing of flowers (of the mind) into a "bursting," to match and keep pace with the speed and promptitude[15] of his own "pardlike spirit." Such a complex of metaphors indicates how much more than either Wordsworth or Coleridge, Shelley and the other younger romantics lived (and wrote) up to the poetic character of the "rich-haired son of the morning" articulated by Collins and emphasized by Harold Bloom.[16] With pointed reference to Wordsworth, this is a distinction of fire and intensity which Shelley puckishly insists upon in his *Peter Bell the Third*. After much sincere praise for the work of Peter/Wordsworth in "[making] alive/The things it wrought on [and]/Wakening a sort of thought in sense" (310–12), Shelley evidently feels constrained to add the following qualification:

> But from the first 'twas Peter's drift
>   To be a kind of moral eunuch
> He touched the hem of Nature's shift,
>   Felt faint—and never dared uplift
> The closest, all-concealing tunic. (311–17)

Whatever may be the proportion of mischievous malice in this send-up of Wordsworth, it reveals not only Shelley's impatience with the perceived repressions of his poetic forebear, but also how he, by contrast, gloried in a tameless, swift and proud constitution that "had gazed on Nature's naked loveliness," but with the acknowledgment that, in the nature of things human, he had done so "Actaeon-like" (*Adonais*, 274–6) and thus suffered an aftermath of "his own thoughts" turned into "raging hounds" pursuing "their father and their prey," even as again and again this pursuer pursued would find himself bursting back out with the "Hope [that] creates/From its own wreck the thing it contemplated" (*Prometheus Unbound*, V.573–4).

This picture of Shelley positioning himself at a καιρὸς of agonistic bearing and recoil where he abandons himself to what Cavell calls "passionate utterance" (*PDAT*, 155–91) is not confined to the celebrated self-portrait of *Adonais*. As I have suggested, it can also be found both in the succinct compass of "England in 1819" and in the expansive recounting of Jupiter's downfall in Act III of *Prometheus Unbound*. And (as a final and signature example) it can be found at the very center of "Ode to the West Wind" where a voice, living in acknowledged subjection to the death-dealing breath of autumn's being and to all appearances sealed within "the dome of a vast sepulchre/Vaulted with all thy congregated might/Of vapours," nonetheless solicits from nothing other than that oppressively "solid atmosphere/[from which] Black rain and fire and heat will burst" that it in turn and at the place where he must stand single become the uncommunicated lightning of his own mind.

5

"The Breath Whose Might I Have Invoked in Song": *Epipsychidion* and *Adonais*

> "It is not what the erotic writers [Hellenistic pastoralists like Theocritus and Moschus] have, but what they have not, in which their imperfection consists. It is not inasmuch as they were Poets, but inasmuch as they were not Poets, that they can be considered with any plausibility as connected with the corruption of their age. Had that corruption availed so as to extinguish in them the sensibility to pleasure, passion and natural scenery, which is imputed to them as an imperfection, the last triumph of evil would have been achieved. For the end of social corruption is to destroy all sensibility to pleasure; and therefore it is corruption. It begins at the imagination and the intellect as at the core, and distributes itself thence as a paralyzing venom, through the affections into the very appetites, until all become a torpid mass in which sense hardly survives. At the approach of such a period, Poetry ever addresses itself to those faculties which are the last to be destroyed, and its voice is heard, like the footsteps of Astraea, departing from the world. Poetry ever communicates all the pleasure which men are capable of receiving: it is ever still the light of life; the source of whatever of beautiful, or generous, or true can have place in an evil time."
>
> Shelley, Defense of Poetry (NS, 521–2)

> "*E io a lui: 'I' mi son un che, quando Amor mi spira, noto, e a quel modo ch'e' ditta dentro vo significando.*'"
>
> Purgatorio, 24.52–4[1]

Both the initial predicament and the closing turn of *Epipsychidion* have a long history in Shelley's vocation as a writer. Not for the first time does the writer of this poem, widely judged to be "essentially about the role of poetry as the most appropriate object of human desires" (*NS*, 391), find himself in hot pursuit of the incentive to his own poetic constructions, and not for the first time does he, at quest's end, acknowledge that what thus draws him on is never definitively grasped and secured. This incentive flees from him as quickly as it comes to him, and the "winged words" with which the poet strives to note its effects are, in the end, felt to be "chains of lead" dragging down yet one more "fiery flight" toward "love's rare Universe" (588–90). The incentive to the writing of *Epipsychidion* is a vision called "Emily"; but this vision is as provocatively fleeting as the shadow of Intellectual Beauty at the beginning of Shelley's mature writing life, or at its end the evanescent presence-in-absence of the morning star, which no sooner makes its entrance as "the shape all light" in *The Triumph of Life* than it slips back out of sight like "a light from Heaven whose half extinguished beam/Through the sick day in which we wake to weep/Glimmers forever sought, forever lost" (429–31). Inscripted into a similar astronomical language of *worlds*, *stars*, and *comets*, the vision of Emily becomes the true sun of the speaker, her endowment of "magnetic might" drawing the "central heart" of "this world of *me*" so powerfully toward her that even when she is lost in "the night which closed on her" (242) she continues to transmit commanding news of herself, as evidenced by just this course of verses set on erecting a literal monument to her compelling attractiveness.

Flowering paradises, infernal roots

In its introductory "advertisement," the "editor" of *Epipsychidion* informs its readers that its author "[died] at Florence" just as he was preparing to set sail with Emily for their island paradise. With this distancing move, Shelley identifies *Epipsychidion* as a testament, that genre of writing penned in the prospect of one's death and intent on handing down what one has found worthy to be held dear by one's survivors. Once the writer/protagonist of *Epipsychidion* becomes "sandalled with plumes of fire" and keyed toward Emily as "the loadstar of [his] one desire" (218–19), he is manifestly bent on testifying to nothing else but the urgency of a calling, which, in the words of the *Defence*, would set itself the task of "redeem[ing] from decay the visitations of the divinity in man" (*NS*, 532). But *only* the visitations, for although the traces of such redemptive work is what the poem would leave in the keeping of its readers, it does not claim to have *accomplished* a definitive verbal recuperation of the divinity it would, by these words, make hauntingly (re)appear. Because these poor things of our words are "weak/ The glory they transfuse with fitting truth to speak" (*Adonais*, 467-8), the final speech-act of *Epipsychidion* acknowledges that its own animating spirit must eventually give the slip to the harness of its own verbal constructions. But if these constructions are, at poem's end, deemed foot-dragging clogs to one's flights of fire, there is no help for it. The poem's breathlessly questing speaker presents himself as without any choice in pursuing the divinity he adores even unto the last expended breath of his being. He is so *captus amore* that it is simply not in him to refrain from losing his breath in the service of the deity whose fleeting presence has been so fatally and peremptorily made known to him.

A perfectionist writer who thinks in verse, Shelley would have *Epipsychidion* pursue the task and track of his thinking along a spirited run of heroic couplets straining to breathe attractive life into what these thoughts have found to count as the rightful god of his thinking and talking form of life. From the "oscuro e pauroso baratro" (*NS*, 392) of the grimly forbidding actual, the poem raises up a splendidly perfectionist world, which Shelley knows, as well as Emerson, is not "the world I converse with in the city and in the farms [but] the world I *think*" (*EL*, 491). If we are trenchantly informed that the words of "neither prayer nor verse could dissipate/The night which closed on [the vision of Emily]" (241-2), we are just as emphatically told that neither could such words "*uncreate*/That world within this Chaos, mine and me,/Of which she was the veiled Divinity,/The world I say of *thoughts* that worshipped her" (242-5, emphasis added).

About the ardent verbal quest it has embarked on, the poem is programmatically self-conscious. At the outset, its writerly protagonist launches a "denominative assault"[2] on the "idol of my thought" (268), addressing the latter as (a partial list) a *benediction*, a *star*, a *glory*, a *delight*, a *refuge*, a "violet-shrouded grave of Woe" (69). But it is not very long before the writer of these words himself acknowledges that in thus "measur[ing]/ The world of fancies seeking one like [Emily]," he has "[found]—alas! my own infirmity" (70-71). Reminiscent of the secular mysteries brought into play by "the distance between the depth to which an ordinary human life requires expression and the surface of ordinary means through which that life must, if it will, express itself" (*WV*, 180), this opening *tour de faiblesse* is matched by the closing acknowledgment of ultimate failure already quoted. In between, there fall the adumbrating words and lines that articulate themselves into a progress poem that would, with the breathing of these words, adore, serve and (vainly) strive to make appear the goddess of its idolatry. With its title invoking the ancient genre of the epithalamion, the poem inflects that genre's joyful progress toward a bridal chamber into such consummations and progenies as are pertinent to a *psyche*—a word (Shelley knew) rooted in the common Greek verb for breathing. Clearly a discourse of desire, *Epipsychidion* is also bent on giving expression to its own desire of discourse, its pursuit of Echo, whose reception as a summarizing figure for discourse John Hollander has brilliantly documented as a commonplace of the poetic traditions into which Shelley habitually inscribed himself.[3] The poem represents the *vita nuova* of its protagonist as beginning only when upon the acknowledgment of Emily as a presence not to be put by he "went forth, with hope and fear/And every gentle passion sick to death,/Feeding my course with expectation's breath" (246-8).

Epipsychidion's initial figure for the aporetic divine service it performs is the aromatic flower or bouquet. "This song," the speaker vows to Emily at the outset, "shall be thy rose: its petals pale/Are dead indeed, my adored Nightingale/But soft and fragrant is the faded blossom,/And it has no thorn left to wound thy bosom" (9-12), and so "In my heart's temple I suspend to thee/These votive wreathes of withered memory" (3-4). The first of the poem's many descriptions of itself, this opening gesture of floral dedication identifies the poem it launches as both a book of (withering) losses and a text of recovery. The poem knows itself both to arise from out the house of mourning and to be passionately bent on making its weave (or course or garland) of words into one sustained speech act of votive force and optative mood. And then at approximately its midpoint when the poem turns from history to expectation and to the *boat* or *barca* waiting on a fair wind toward its flowering island of heart's desire, the speaker makes a point of recalling his earlier floral figure for his present venture and so prays Emily that she "Scorn not these flowers of thought, the fading birth/Which from its heart of hearts that plant [i.e. himself] puts forth" (384-5).

These are, it bears emphasizing, poetic flowers of thought. They are, in addition, breathings of adoration, petition and dedication modeled on such pagan and High Church services as use fired incense and heavily scented flowers to send a pleasing odor of praise up to one's grievously distanced Lord or Donna:

> Warm fragrance seems to fall from her light dress,
> And her loose hair; and where some heavy tress
> The air of her own speed has disentwined,
> The sweetness seems to satiate the faint wind;
> And in the soul a wild odour is felt,
> Beyond the sense, like fiery dews that melt
> Into the bosom of a frozen bud. (105-11)

These lines climax on the individual soul's transfiguring reception of the sweet and "fiery dews" that save it from a killing frost; they contrive to turn into one garland of evocation the mix of Promethean fire and refreshing moisture needed to release a buried potentiality of the soul from the chills and droughts threatening to nip it in the bud.

The poetic service of *Epipsychidion* catches fire from the "divine brightness" (77–8) of an Emily addressed as "Thou Mirror/In whom, as in the splendour of the Sun,/All shapes look glorious which thou gazest on!/Aye even the dim words which obscure thee now/Flash, lightning-like, with unaccustomed glow" (30–4). If the writer of these lines figures the beginnings of his new life as the baptism by both water and fire packed into "fiery dews," he quickly modulates this self-presentation into the intimately related image of his once dim words now pulsing toward the radiant fullness of a votive flower, whose expense of sweet fragrance either lives or dies depending on the warm light and moisture showering down on it from Emily:

> I pray thee that thou blot from this sad song
> All of its much mortality and wrong,
> With those clear drops, which start like sacred dew
> From the twin lights thy sweet soul darkens through,
> Weeping, till sorrow becomes ecstasy:
> Then smile on it, so that it may not die. (35–40)

As is appropriate for a man penning his testament, this self-styled "passive Earth,/This world of love, this *me*" (346, Shelley's emphasis) is already thinking of himself not as a man still walking the earth under the blue Italian sky, but as the verbal construction we know as *Shelley* and commonly find in the selections of poetic flora called anthologies, the *Shelley* who as a poetry-producing form of life would by these words give testifying expression to how "the intense, the deep, the imperishable/Not mine but me" (390–1) has been "led into light" (75), and grown into these "flowers of thought, the fading birth/Which from its heart of hearts that plant puts forth/Whose fruit, made perfect by thy sunny eyes,/Will be as of the trees of Paradise" (384–8).

For now, however, the protagonist of *Epipsychidion* finds himself not in Paradise but only *in via* toward that imagined land of heart's desire. In a word, he finds himself in Purgatory. One of the more obvious ways in which *Epipsychidion* signals this is its often deplored advocacy of "free love" (147–89). As has long been recognized, the sentiment and some of the very wording of these confessional (i.e. creedal) lines derive from a moment of reflection in Canto 15 of the *Purgatorio*, when Dante pauses in his ascent up the mountain so that Virgil can provide him with some corrective instruction about the most fitting object of human desire.[4] As he warms to his pedagogical role, Virgil insists that the economy of the spirit differs radically from the zero-sum game according to which material goods are produced and distributed. In contrast to the latter "where/if there is company each part is smaller,"[5] the exchanges and contestings of the spirit are such that the more its goods and gifts circulate, the more they abound. Both the audacity of Shelley's claims and their too literal reception by those not taking him at his word that *Epipsychidion* represents an "*idealized* history of my life and feelings"[6] have obscured how with his virtual quoting of some conspicuously reasoned thoughts from Dante, this poetic inheritor of the *Commedia* intimates that he is similarly in quest of a purgatorially refined desire. Launched along a refining path of spiritual progress, the speaker of *Epipsychidion* is here stopping to take thought for human desire, and in that effort he is enlisting Dante as, so to speak, his Virgil.

In Shelley's appropriation of Dante, it is not just love that extends and replenishes itself according to an economy of the spirit. So do understanding and imagination. The "Understanding grows bright,/Gazing on many truths" (162–3). And "Imagination" is interested in all of God's plenty as

> from earth and sky,
> And from the depths of human phantasy,
> As from a thousand prisms and mirrors [it] fills
> The Universe with glorious beams, and kills
> Error, the worm, with many a sun-like arrow
> Of its reverberated lightning" (164–9).

This description of an imaginative power distinguishing itself by the worm-quelling feats of the Pythian Apollo is so dazzling and multi-faceted that one might easily forget that for this defender and practitioner of poetry the preeminent instruments of the imagination—its mirrors, arrows, beams and reverberating strokes of lightning—are those commonly circulating things we call words. And the circulation of our words is, I would contend, the human activity where Virgil's economy of the spirit is still both most ordinarily and most credibly at play. For as Wittgenstein and Cavell repeatedly point out, it is necessary to the fungible value of a language that it be *shared*. If as human subjects we are indeed subjected to the fate and chance of finding ourselves in a given field of verbal intercourse (and a given world or "whirl of organism"), then the more we each and all have this common stock of language at our authoritative command, the more of its good and profit will sustainingly circulate among us.

In his advocacy of "True Love" (160), the speaker of *Epipsychidion* not only receives as his own Dante's doctrine concerning the things of the spirit and their vitally reproductive circulation. He also proclaims that to the wise just this doctrine has been for ages both an "eternal" law and that refreshing well, access to whose proverbial depths of truth will set one free to pursue the work one is called to do:

> that deep well, whence sages draw
> The *unenvied* light of hope; the eternal law
> By which those live, to whom this world of life
> Is as a garden ravaged, and whose strife
> Tills for the promise of a later birth
> The wilderness of this Elysian earth" (184–9, emphasis added)

The emphasized *unenvied* draws very specifically on Virgil's tutorial on desire. For this discourse takes place on the terrace of Purgatory dedicated to the deadly sin of *Invidia*, the blinkered and all too commonly cherished way of counting another's gain as but yet one more item in the tally of one's own losses. In contrast to this construction of our life together as a zero-sum game, the *Purgatorio*'s economy of divine love would have it that "quantunque carità si stende/cresce sovr'essa l'etterna valore": the more the circle of charity extends itself the more on that basis or ground does it increase and multiply as the eternal good or value it is. For (in W. S. Merwin's translation) "the more they say 'ours' there, the more/good there is for each one, and the more/ charity is burning in that cloister."[7]

For Shelley, this possibility that human intercourse could become such a productively meet and happy conversation constituted a beautiful idealism of intellectual and moral excellence exquisitely pertinent to a writer so continuously galled by "that common, false, cold, hollow talk/Which makes the heart deny the *yes* it breathes" (*Prometheus Unbound*, III.iv.149–50). Shelley knew that his many evocations of a perfectionist social intercourse (such as *Prometheus*, III.iii.23–63) were only dreams. He explicitly says so in the preface of *Prometheus Unbound*. But he was quick to add both there and elsewhere that such visions of excellence could exert a real and commanding influence on his readers similar to that exerted upon him by Dante. Shelley's experience as a reader in perpetual conversation with the self-appointed others he crowned his "kings of thought" constituted no small part of what attracted him to one of the most persistent features of his writing: its tenacious inquiry into the possibilities of dissemination, flowering and harvest implicit in the human fact of language; or (to speak literally) into the possibilities of reception, promise, and consequence implicit in every word we let fall from our mouths or pens. In *Epipsychidion*, Shelley appeals to an always already lost but still (he trusts) recoverable ideal of verbal interchange in the context of his own laboring in verse and with extended reference to any other acknowledged or unacknowledged legislators of the Emersonian "world I think." His conception of the work ordained for those drawn like him to the dream of a more animated, thoughtful and fruitful style of human intercourse assumes both that the wilderness of the field they are called to labor in is always already a garden lost and that such as it deplorably is, it still holds out the promise of later Elysian flowerings.

In another one of *Epipsychidion*'s manifest acts of cultural critique, the agonistic strivings of the martyr are predicated of those whose "taste" of a "best philosophy" (213) makes them adept at turning a commonly hellish condition into a path toward glory. The speaker has been recounting how after his fleeting vision of Emily, he was haunted by her "voice" (201) as it resounded and breathed with a "harmony of truth" (216), which comes to him not only through the susurrus of the "whispering woods" (201) and from the "odours deep/Of flowers, which like lips murmuring in their sleep/ Of the sweet kisses which had lulled them there/Breathed but of *her* to the enamoured air" (201–5, Shelley's emphasis), but also from such cultural monuments as find a local habitation

> in the words
> Of antique verse and high romance,—in form,
> Sound, color—in whatever checks that Storm
> Which with the shattered present chokes the past;
> And in that best philosophy, whose taste
> Makes this cold common hell, our life, a doom
> As glorious as a fiery martyrdom. (209–15)

As they yoke together a choking cultural present and a gratefully received and intensely imagined world of "enamoured air" (205), these lines inflect the *Symposium*'s account of Eros's parentage in Penia (desolating want) and Poria (abundant wealth or resource), so prominent in *Prometheus Unbound* (in I.752–71),[8] toward a giving out of breathings whose fervent expressiveness is the dialectic counter to a stifling constriction of any formerly achieved expressions of a like-minded kind. The singer of *Epipsychidion* would have everything breathe of Emily. He will climactically imagine himself and his love catching a favoring wind toward their land of heart's desire. But this singer of "what he loves in dream" (*Prometheus Unbound*, IV.268) so devoutly wishes for such consummations largely as a function of how a shattered present is always threatening to take the wind out of his sails and choke off any animated cultural expression from him or any of his kindred spirits, living or dead. Shelley's entire career pursues the effort not only to make sense of all that has repeatedly caused the vessel of human life to run aground, but also to come up and give out with a recuperative saving of such grim appearances as would provide a motive not just for going on but for going on at that full tilt of witnessing, by which the martyr would make our "sorrow become ecstasy" (39).

Driven since at least "Hymn to Intellectual Beauty" both by what has lamentably become our attained actual condition and by what he trusts is our attainable perfectionist condition, Shelley strives toward recuperating even the saddest of realities into a credible warrant for persisting on the track of what he finds he cannot help but value. It is fitting, then, that the lines culminating on Emily as the "harmony of truth" will honor and recommend the same resolutely hopeful thinking through of things, which *Julian and Maddalo*, quoting Shakespeare, had already called "that true theory. . . /Which seeks a 'soul of goodness' in things ill" (203–4), and which *Epipsychidion* here analogously identifies as "that best philosophy" which strives to (re)envision the ravaged garden or wilderness of "this cold common hell, our life" as indeed a judgment on us, but "a doom as glorious as a fiery martyrdom." (Shelley could have found a congenial and confirming model for the martyr's agonistic transit to glory in the same canto of the *Purgatorio* that inspired his excursus on "free love." For the most striking *poetry* of this canto is its portrait of the first Christian martyr rising toward his heavenly crown in such exemplary witness that the more he is dragged to earth, stoned and vilified, the more zealously does he "make of his eyes gates open to heaven" (Merwin's translation).)

The characteristic Shelleyan work would be "A love in desolation masked" (*Adonais*, 251). It would be, in Cavell's terms, both a book of losses and a text of recovery. *Adonais*, for example, very succinctly represents the ways of Venus—which are our ways—as subjected to bloody earthly trials whose latter end is the precisely floral and "eternal" redemption succeeding to her passage out of a "secret Paradise" and subsequently down to a place—*our* place—of

> barbed tongues, and thoughts more sharp than they
> [that] Rent the soft Form they never could repel,
> Whose sacred blood, like the young tears of May,
> Paved with eternal flowers that undeserving way (209–16)

And Shelley discerns the same agonistic workings of desire as much in modern history as in Greek myth. In its hardly idiosyncratic recounting of Western poetry's modern revival, the *Defence*, for example, notes that when "Love became a religion," the poets, who were the "prophets" of this new religion ("Chivalry was its law"), were noteworthy for nothing so much as singing "the delight which is in the grief of Love" (*NS*, 525), and through that grief and delight "[celebrating] the dominion of love" (*NS*, 526). To Shelley, the still reigning prophet of this new religion was Dante representing his (new) life's work as growing out from the middle of the apparent dead end and "*selva oscura*" he had made of it. From there, pilgrim Dante was constrained to move on (in Shelley's words) to "his apotheosis of Beatrice in Paradise and the gradations of his own love and her loveliness, by which as by steps he feigns himself to have ascended to the throne of the Supreme Cause" (*NS*, 525–6). Shelley's praise of the *Paradiso* as "the most glorious imagination of modern poetry" (*NS*, 526) points toward *Epipsychidion* as his own poetic contribution in this kind. For in this poetic effort metaleptically "taking after" the *Commedia* (i.e. trying both to keep pace with it and to emulate it),[9] what is called God remains a Supreme Cause, but, as is virtually axiomatic for Shelley after "Hymn to Intellectual Beauty," the idea of godhead is here inflected toward something that might more aptly be called the Commanding Incentive, or Shelley's own "dominion of Love."

For Dante, the supreme (or scholastically "final") cause of his work comes to full communal flower in the *Paradiso*'s gathering of all the blessed into that image of an eternally possible natality which is "la rosa sempiterna,/che si digrada e dilata e redole/odor di lode al sole che sempre verna" (*Paradiso*, 30.124–6). (A lumbering and admittedly Shelleyan translation of these lines—one that has despaired of catching the way exfoliating petals, floral fragrance, musical scales, steps, and courses (of construction) all come to bear on the atom of thought which is *si digrada*—might go something like this: "the eternal rose that in rising measure opens, lifts and breathes its odor of praise to that true sun that perpetually springs into forever green life."). This sweetly breathing and *sempiterna* rose is the final flourish, home and peace which the *Paradiso* assigns to (in Shelley's words) this "perpetual hymn of everlasting Love." But nourishing the root of Dante's everlasting rose (one can imagine Shelley insisting) is the blood of a rent and wounded Venus, a blood which to be deemed "sacred" because it paves with "eternal flowers" our undeserving way. In short, the joyfully breathing splendor of the *Commedia*'s paradisal rose has its origin in the darkly rough soil of loss and perdition, the architectonic of Dante's poem representing itself as coming into the full run and flower of its expression only because of the earlier moment of profound crisis when its protagonist found himself rooted and stalled in the pinned-down middle of an individual life and thus driven on to his life's calling as the visionary recuperator and cultivator of **nostra** *vita* not as his private lookout but as the common business that human life itself is called to be about.

The art of finding yourself in an obscure forest

Loss as the radical incentive toward the writing of *Epipsychidion* has not gone unnoticed. In addressing its speaker's first experience of being abandoned by the vision of Emily, Stuart Sperry points out the significance of his then naming himself "a man with mighty loss dismayed" (229). "The phrase," writes Sperry, "marks the first and only appearance of the principal male noun within the poem ... as if the experience of loss the passage records were definitive, the initiation into adulthood, the mark of one's humanity, perhaps even the crucial determinant of the male ego or identity."[10] This is finely observed and expressed, but the dawning of dismay represents only the first step into the heart of loss. The recounting of the new life that is thereafter to be lived in the light of Emily's enchanting but quickly withdrawn smile will require almost a hundred more lines before its seed-time of loss can flower into the speaker's implicit but hardly veiled claim that the *Divina Commedia*'s inaugurating finding of salvation in loss captures the one most crucial point in his own spiritual biography when "at length into the *obscure Forest* came/ The Vision I had sought." (321–2, emphasis added). The path toward this mid-poem identification with a Dante finding himself in his own *selva oscura* illustrates what Thoreau calls the writer's defining work of "[keeping] faith with God by revising mythology" (*SW*, 113) in order to arrive at, in Wallace Stevens" phrase a "mythology of self" only possible by "being the other to one's self, calling upon it with the words of others" (*PP*, 102). For Dante is not the only "man of words" that the speaker of this poem will find standing for him and calling him out. He also lets call on his own history his own revised readings of such mythic "forms more real than living men" (*Prometheus Unbound*, I.748) as Narcissus, Actaeon and Endymion, all in the name of trying to call out the identity of "the intense, the deep, the imperishable/Not mine but me" (391–2).

Called out by the brightly beckoning "Being" of Emily, the writer of *Epipsychidion* reports that as a consequence of her almost immediately abandoning him, he was compelled to set out on a conspicuously aural pursuit of a "phantom" loveliness, eluding his grasp but nonetheless (an encouraging "voice" assures him) somehow "beside thee" (233) in the world. To this, the lightning-quick aftermath is: "Then I—'where?'—the world's echo answered 'where!'" (234). The line is clearly penned in open acknowledgment of its debt to the precious Ovidian turn of "[Narcissus] dixerat: 'ecquis adest?' et 'adest!' responderat Echo." (*Metamorphoses*, III.378) The line stamps the identity of Narcissus, the doomed pursuer of Echo, on an explicitly bereft speaker who then goes on to confess how in the ensuing "silence . . . [and] despair" of his Emily he was moved to question "every tongueless wind that flew/Over my tower of mourning, if it knew/Whither 'twas fled, this soul out of my soul" (236–8). As he thus abandons himself to the pursuit of this thing of air that is the soul out of his soul, this now openly "narcissistic" speaker hopes against hope that the object of his desire—vanished into the thin but resonant air—is somehow to be found in the feverishly questioned winds, which, though "tongueless," still return an echoing "where!" whose exclamatory pointing broaches the possibility that just such an obstinate questioning of this atmosphere of "enamoured air" the speaker now finds himself pursuing will, at the last, provide some pertinent news of his whereabouts and his wherefores.

In addressing Shelley's fundamental ethical stance, Carl Woodring has persuasively claimed that for Shelley the "precept of Jerusalem [to love thy neighbor as thyself] has the special meaning of . . . Narcissus finding his fullest self mirrored in the nymph Echo" (322).[11] Shelley's self-reflexive figure of Narcissus, I would add, also includes what Woodring calls the other, complementary Athenian "precept" about knowing yourself. For internal to Shelley's rehabilitation of Narcissus is the socializing of that figure into the reflective self-esteem of a form of (human) life, called by *Prometheus Unbound* "Man, oh, not men! . . ./Man, one harmonious Soul of many a soul" (*Prometheus*, IV.394, 400). The myth of Narcissus and Echo became so central in Shelley because the received Ovidian account of a beauty generally deemed to be culpably imprisoned in narrow self-regard called out to him for an intensified focus on those sweetly sad features of the myth that suggest an endless work of self-recuperation, whose two beckoning instruments of recovery are the reflection of a "world of thoughts" and the Echo of (our) *logos* or discourse.

"Feeding [his] course with expectation's breath" (248), the protagonist and writer of *Epipsychidion* is drawn toward what he hears resounding in the world along the lines of his desire and assuming the mythical form of Echo. Although this femininely conceived object of desire is represented as only fleetingly present, she nonetheless gives her pursuer reason to hope because on what he takes to be unimpeachable authority, she remains "beside" (233) him like the day-time morning star of Venus in poem after poem of Shelley's. The writing pursuant to this experience of loss seeks not so much to "*arrest*" (*NS*, 532) the visitations of its prime mover as to keep up its own end of the spirited conversation to be sustained between it and what is "[dimly to be seen] within our intellectual nature [as] a miniature as it were of our entire self, yet deprived of all that we condemn or despise, the ideal prototype of every thing excellent or lovely that we are capable of conceiving as belonging to the nature of man" (*NS*, 504). Explicitly named in "On Love" as the "soul *within* our soul," this "prototype" of all that we could think of as excellent and lovely is clearly a perfectionist image in elective affinity and gravitational alignment with "this soul *out* of my soul" (238, emphasis added) so ardently pursued not only in the Emily of *Epipsychidion* but also in (to name but one other instance) that "Life of Life" in *Prometheus Unbound* called Asia. When Thoreau is working his way through his analogously perfectionist image of the "next self," he traces a similarly charged polarity between (what we commonly call) the inner and the outer, between the *intus et in cute* (Persius, *Satire* 3, line 30) that Rousseau chose as the epigraph for his *Confessions*, and the whole world of creation in conversation with which such utterly single individualities would seek to find and place themselves. "Nearest to all things," Thoreau writes, "is that [indwelling] power which fashions their being. *Next* to us the grandest laws are continually being executed. *Next* to us is not the workman whom we have hired, with whom we love so well to talk, but the workman whose work we are" (*Walden*, 90, Thoreau's emphases). I am letting the allusions run freely here so as to suggest how much is packed into Earl Schulze's succinct formulation of what at this defining juncture of *Epipsychidion* Shelley is in quest of. "Shelley's quester," Schulze writes, "must learn to read himself, as if that were the same as reading the will of God,"[12] this a remark uncannily like Cavell's on our "subjectivity . . . [as] the route back to our conviction in reality" (*WV*, 22).

Essential to the way the protagonist of *Epipsychidion* begins as a (revised) Narcissus and turns into a Dante both lost and found in the dark wood of his life are the intervening links of identification he forges between himself and the figures of Actaeon and Endymion. Reporting on Mary's place in his life, Shelley casts himself as an Endymion to her gently lulling Diana. But as he now recounts this former edition of himself sealed in the gaze of the woman who once provided him some much needed peace, he confesses that the bed of repose he then made for himself was "a chaste, cold bed" (239) in which he was "laid asleep, spirit and limb" (295). These are hardly kind or even courteous words for one's "best Mary," but why Shelley now seems to feel (if not totally to acknowledge) that he had become caught in a chill nowhere of suspended animation will become more understandable in light of what the poem is doing with the immediately preceding allusion to Actaeon—clearly there, but, unlike the Endymion figure, neither explicitly named nor elaborately developed.

The figure of Actaeon slips unobtrusively into the progress of *Epipsychidion* when its first-person narrator finds himself reporting how as an immediate consequence of the absconding vision of Emily he then "rashly" sought "in many mortal forms . . . the shadow of that idol of my thought" (267–8) only to be caught up short when

> as a hunted deer that could not flee,
> I turned upon my thoughts, and stood at bay,
> Wounded and weak and panting. (272–4)

Actaeon, of course, plays a central, organizing role in the famous self-portrait of *Adonais*. Inscribed like a signature into the middle of Shelley's elegy, this hunter turned into the hunted crystallizes what Shelley's most accomplished biographer calls the defining "pursuit" of Shelley's life into a quest that, precisely because of its accesses of vision, finds itself consumed by the hounding cry of all the thoughts this life must own up to as (still) of its own begetting but now fiercely turned back on their "father and their prey."

Unlike the explicitly identified Actaeon of *Adonais*, the allusion to him in *Epipsychidion* is only passing and implicit, but one very profitably dwelt upon by several of the poem's most astute readers, most notably Schulze. Veiled in the demoting alias of a "hunted deer" (272), this all too human and *rational* animal—this ζῷον ἔχον λόγον—lives ineluctably in a world of thoughts, and what he says he did at this charged juncture of his spiritual autobiography is that "[I] turned upon my thoughts and stood at bay" (273). But these thoughtful and pressing realities of self are not then and there confronted. They are *kept* at bay. Precisely at the moment when a reckoning or accounting seems at hand, we get neither recognition-scene nor crisis worked through. We get a respite, not worthy (I am contending) of being called a "deliverance"

> When like a noon-day dawn, there shone again
> Deliverance. One stood on my path who seemed
> As like the glorious shape which I had dreamed [as the moon to the sun.]" (278–81)

The wife in this family romance quite literally interrupts her husband's calling as Actaeon. To the *Actaeon Interruptus* which she for the time being makes of him, she comes as a distinctively secondary and lunar helpmate, bearing only that reflected glory granted to a heavenly body whose "borrowed light" derives from the reigning sun of the speaker's life. To this vision and glory, she is "as is the Moon . . . to the eternal Sun" (279–80). This awkward attempt at praising Mary is a thicket of ambivalence. But no matter how ambivalently *and* genuinely Shelley gratefully remembers Mary as the comforter of his afflicted self, this pale and ardorless form of deliverance must strike anyone acquainted with Shelley's life and work as a bloodless negation of the kind of vision rooted in loss which he constantly bore witness to and saw played out on the Christian cross as well as in a spargasmatic Dionysos. This "noon-day dawn" provides such refuge as is to be gained from willfully pushing out of sight and mind the hounding "world of thoughts" which it is any would-be Actaeon's calling to have traumatically visited upon his impressionable self as "that world within this Chaos, mine and me/Of which she [Emily] was the veiled Divinity,/The world I say of thoughts that worshipped her" (243–5).[13]

Epipsychidion's skillfully choreographed glide from a hurriedly entered and dropped Actaeon to the lengthily dwelt upon still life of Shelley as Endymion exposes the latter as an attempt to dodge the consequences of one's own most persistently perfectionist thoughts. Try as Shelley might to praise the reigning planet of his marital life as "the Queen of Heaven's bright isles,/Who makes all beautiful on which she smiles" (281–2), the tones of spatial sequestration, emotional frigidity and suspended animation in which he hymns his sojourn in the cave of Mary cry out to be reheard as his unmanning metamorphosis into a human agent so "asleep in spirit and limb" as to be (he says) disowned by both life and death. "She hid me," this picture from a marriage says, "as the Moon may hide the night/From its own darkness, until all was bright/Between the heaven and earth of my calm mind" (287–9). But in the context of this would-be Actaeon spirited away to a cave of apparently endless and dreamless sleep, what does such unfailingly mild brightness suggest? What, in particular, does it mean to be hidden from one's own darkness, when this ostensible and no doubt fully intended compliment is coming from a poet who scarcely more than a year later will praise the "breath of darkness" as that alone which allows "the least of heaven's living eyes" to come into their due splendor (*The Triumph of Life*, 390–2).

The anesthetized Endymion of Mary's cave is grotesquely out of character both for the spirited poet who likened himself to an unleashed west wind, "tameless, and swift and proud," and for the man whose friends often remarked on the tensed aliveness and "promptitude" of his bearing. In "Ode to the West Wind," the summarizing word for this poet's signature action is *strive*. If not for the desolation that has befallen him, says this voice responding to a desolating voice out of the whirlwind, "I would ne'er have striven/As thus with thee in prayer in my sore need." So here in *Epipsychidion*, it bears remarking that in the high praise meted out to those "whose strife/Tills for the promise of a later birth/The wilderness of this Elysian earth," it is simply assumed that the genus of any specific life of promise is *strife*. For the tempest of strife is Shelley's element, the very air he breathes. And if Mary provided a temporary safe haven from it in one of its more unruly moods, that respite (so Shelley now recounts his experience) came at the cost of an almost complete emotional and spiritual shutdown, a breather to end all breathings. In that cave of apparently perpetual rest, Shelley's responsive powers lay dormant, and they came out of hiding only when the convulsing influence of the subsequent "planet of the hour" restored this "world of love, this *me*" to its element in storms "[shaking] the ocean of [his] sleep" and rescuing him from the stifling embrace of the "unawakend earth" so obstructively and unresponsively placed at the conclusion to "Ode to the West Wind."

Calling for thought, remembering its incentive

Shelley's account of his Endymion period tries rather unsuccessfully to practice what he preaches about seeking a "soul of goodness" in everything. A much more confident attempt at a similar transformation is the ardently expectant words with which the poem's protagonist calls for a disruptive Comet's return as "love's folding star" (374). Although this mercurial apparition left chaos in her wake, Shelley now seems disposed toward viewing her as a *felix culpa*, as just the kind of felicitously timed cataclysm that was needed to expose a version of himself now perceived to have been built upon illusion and avoidance.

The vicissitudes of Shelley's personal life have provoked a good deal of autobiographical decoding of *Epipsychidion*'s rather cumbersome astronomical machinery. Chief among these is still that of Kenneth Neil Cameron, proposed many years ago and still widely accepted.[14] For Cameron, the comet is Claire Claremont and the earlier passage about the "planet of the hour" and a subsequent "tempest" is resolvable into a one-to-one series of counters for such aftershocks of Shelley's calamitous first marriage to Harriet Westbrook as her suicide, and the succeeding fury of his sister-in-law making it her stormily vindictive business to deprive the surviving father of any legal standing in the life and upbringing of his children. Cameron's decoding of these lines is ingenious, but it clearly shows the strain of someone trying to reduce the semiosis of poetry to an encoded rehearsal of some discretely identifiable events and personalities. Far better, it seems to me, to take seriously Shelley's description of his poem as "like the *Vita Nuova* of Dante ... sufficiently intelligible to a certain class of readers without a matter-of-fact history of the circumstances to which it relates" (*NS*, 392). Far better, that is, to concentrate not on making the signified of each of this poem's many signifiers come clean in referential isolation from one another, but on tracking how its extravagantly tumbled out figures are throughout the poem striving to come to poetic terms with one another in the recounting of a life caught between numerous "planets[s] of the hour" and the one all-enfolding star of love.

The Planet/Tempest that "shook" the becalmed "Ocean" of Shelley's Endymionic "sleep" shares with the subsequently invoked Comet an attractiveness pregnant with ruinous effects. It is yet another figure for what the Comet also speaks of: the compelling force of an unruly erotic power "beautiful and fierce,/Who drew the heart of this frail Universe/Towards [its] own" (367–9) with devastating results. Despite the apparent bad end of such encounters, the speaker has no sooner mentioned the Comet than he is praying for her to come "floating" back into his and his poem's world as "love's folding star" (373–4).

This appeal for the all-gratulant return of the once rending Comet may, at this point in the poem, be insufficiently motivated, hardly compelling and not totally clear. But one thing about it is clear enough even at this stage. It is the characteristic turn of a perfectionist writer whose poetry has always been found "floating" the possibility that even at its most rending the experience of desire discloses a vitally necessary field of attraction, which is both the beginning of "this world of love, this *me*" and its end and harbor home. In a word, the speaker's expectant look toward the Comet's eventual transformation anticipates but does enact the performance of a credible theodicy for what Shelley consistently took to be the omnipresent god of love. It anticipates how, by these laborings in the mind, Shelley would justify (or make *right*) the ways of a God of love so manifestly wounding and crazing that the final and explicitly encouraging spirit of *Prometheus Unbound* can call it by such names as "monster" (I.778) and "Desolation" (772), a desolation consequent upon the "delicate thing" (772) which is the impressionable "heart" of "the best and gentlest" (775).

Building on René de Rougemont's insight that the poetic tradition into which Shelley so zealously inscribed himself transforms "the sufferings of love [into] a privileged mode of understanding,"[15] Angela Leighton has perceptively described *Epipsychidion* as a poem uneasily split into "two schizophrenic directions ... towards idealistic figurativeness on the one hand, and towards a 'matter-of-fact' life story on the other."[16] Despite his living in the wake of Rousseau as well as of Dante and Petrarch, Shelley still seeks to refine all he has suffered from desire into the most ethereal forms of courtly or divine love. Consequently, writes Leighton, this "centaur" of a poem calls for "a theory of the relation *between* figures and history, between literary play and literal reference."[17] For "on the one hand [*Epipsychidion*] may be read as a mythological expression of the forces of Love, Imagination or Grace. On the other hand, it may be read as a biographical allegory, in which the poet's sexual history is recounted in a decipherable meteorological imagery of women."[18] Demurring on either the possibility or the usefulness of any one-to-one referential deciphering of this poem, I would suggest that Stanley Cavell's late-blooming conviction that philosophy—*even* philosophy—demands "a systematic engagement with the autobiographical" (*AP*, 6) provides an illuminating perspective on how for Shelley as well, the transit toward what differing schools of thought would call a mystifying, idealistic, or explanatory myth of his sexual experience requires not the erasure or bracketing of such intimacies, but precisely the opposite. It requires an engagement with the conditions and givens of whatever one finds to have become of one's life and of one's desires in and for this life. It requires a re-membering of the traumas of desire that would re-see them as necessary articles or motions toward the ever-reforming constitution of "this world of love, this *me*."

Like a centaur, *Epipsychidion* exhibits from the waist up the ambition and something of the sound and look of Dante at his most exalted. But further down amid the mundanely roiling incentives to its composition, some portions of the poem have been deemed liable to Shelley's own strictures against the erotic poetry of the Hellenistic world. As for the Dantean half of this hybridic *monstrum*—a Latin word which besides meaning *hybrid* has the same root as *demonstration* and can denote a divine portent like the flaming hair of Aeneas's son in the second book of the *Aeneid*—that is sufficiently on display in many of the poem's moves and preoccupations, not least in the prayer that the once "convulsing" comet now float back into the poem's world as its folding star of love. By contrast, the poem's other more modern bias toward an embodied life of passionate attraction and repulsion directs attention to the opaquely clotted circumstantiality of such passages in this life as were dominated by the "planet of the hour" and its consequent tempest. Such passages pose peculiar and, in my judgment, not totally surmounted obstacles to the poem's manifest; but not untroubled faith in the "Italian Platonics"[19] of Dante and Petrarch. In any case, the result of these twinned ambitions is a recounting of Shelley's sexual history that has pleased few and disgusted many. That story seems to go something like this: the short-lived attractiveness of some "planet of the hour," for which the subsequent comet is a further and interpretively helpful figure, effected the fortunate disruption of the "miserable ease" (*Thus Spoke Zarathustra*, I.3) of the cave's moon-lit calm; that fiercely attractive force brought on a tempest of repressed desire so that, once quenched or sated, this shamefully indulged lust for the "planet of the hour" could prepare the ground (or waters) of (this) life for the earthquake of true and profound change by precipitating it into an emotional winter when "frost/crept o'er these waters, till from coast to coast/The moving billows of my being fell/Into a death of ice, immoveable" (313–16).

This cryptic confessional sequence featuring such Shelleyan master-tones as *tempest, frost, waters,* and *earthquake* tells of its passionate subject hardening toward an ice-cold limit of contraction, which retrospectively makes his settling into the role of Endymion look less like domestic tranquility than emotional torpor. What was initially represented as a needed stilling of the waters is now beginning to look like the drop in body-temperature associated with suspended animation and desperate clutchings after any signs of life. With this revised way of composing the experiences of his life, the now sufficiently distanced recounter of that life would represent himself as delivered from "the ocean of [his] sleep" and setting out on his way toward a newly awakened commitment to a more purely burning flame, whose animating spirit he trusts is the more enduring attractions of (in Leighton's words) "Love, Imagination or Grace."

Shelley's recuperation of the cataclysmic planet of the hour as a *felix culpa* depends on the profound value he placed on unleashing the lava of desire at the core of this "world of love, this *me*." In *Epipsychidion*, that desire will eventually come into its sharpest and purest focus when the speaker of the poem looks forward to how

> our lips
> With other eloquence than words, [will] eclipse
> The soul that burns between them, and the wells
> Which boil under our being's inmost cells,
> The fountains of our deepest life, shall be
> Confused in passion's golden purity,
> As mountain-springs under the morning Sun. (566–72)

The acoustically booming (and often politically inflected) analog of this fiercely purifying fire is what G. M. Matthews has copiously documented as the "volcano's voice" in Shelley: that is, his "breathing earth" in its most provoked mood "[steaming] up like inspiration,/Eloquent, oracular;/A volcano heard afar" ("The Masque of Anarchy" ll.361–3).[20] *Epipsychidion* closely associates the true Promethean fire of this volcanic voice with the specifically "magnetic might" of responsiveness which "this world of love, this *me*" finds the sun and moon darting "into its central heart" (348). That Shelley can thus speak of the uncharted (and "boiling") region of "our being's inmost cells" as expressing itself along the force lines of both volcanic eruption and planetary attraction allows him to claim that the volcano's voice in his life and work is called out into its perfectionist expression by nothing less than the attractive influence of heavenly bodies.

Coming to the recognition of himself as a "world of love," the speaker of the poem first looks longingly toward how the magnetic forces of sun and moon might "with alternate sway/Govern my sphere of being, night and day" (360–1) and become for him

> Twin Spheres of light who rule this passive Earth,
> This world of love, this *me*; and into birth
> Awaken all its fruits and flowers, and dart
> Magnetic might into its central heart;
> And lift its billows and its mists. (345–9)

There seems to be near universal agreement that the sun in this astronomical allegory refers to Emily and the moon to Mary. But the virtual emptiness of such personal referents should become evident once one realizes how clearly the juxtaposition of these two lights reprises the *Defence*'s opening account of what Shelley took to be his time's two disastrously embattled "classes of mental action" (*NS*, 510): τὸ ποιεῖν and τὸ λογιζεῖν, the mind's imaginings and its reasoning calculations. What the moon of *Epipsychidion* is here petitioned *not* to do is exactly what Shelley thought the misconceived "reason" of his time was doing to poetry. It is asked "not to [eclipse] a remoter light" (363) but to work toward the "one sweet end" (359) of their more perfect union. And just as Shelley's idea of the imagination would hardly have it rejecting the reasoned tuitions and crystallizations of its own seeking, so here the sun is implored to do its work while "not disdaining" the moon and its "borrowed might" (362).

With this envisaged collaboration of τὸ ποιεῖν and τὸ λογιζεῖν, the speaker would seem to have given a final cast to his astronomical machinery and set the course for his "sphere of being" (361). Having entrusted himself to the heavenly duumvirate of sun and moon, he will henceforth let his "sphere of being" be guided by them "through the shadow of the seasons three,/From Spring to Autumn's sere maturity," lighting it "into the Winter of the tomb,/Where it may ripen to a brighter bloom" (364–7). But precisely because these lines so roundly ring out with both the sound and sense of closure, they raise the question why, instead of his ending here, the speaker gives his final word and attention to the "Comet beautiful and fierce," why, in an apparent afterthought, he calls on this dynamism of "alternating attraction and repulsion" (371) to come back into this "azure heaven" not now to rend and wound but to the precisely opposite effect of "love's folding star."

Placed at the conclusion of the speaker's global accounting of the forces which he finds he is attracted to and would be ruled by, the comet draws such star billing that it in turn should draw a reader's attention to the obvious sign and wonder of its proposed transformation into the morning and evening star which Yeats called Shelley's star of infinite desire, and from there back still further to the textual fact that, although the properties of the sun and moon include the darting of their "magnetic might into the central heart" of this "passive earth," they are, true to our everyday experience of them, mainly "twin Spheres of *light*," their task to "*light*" the speaker on his earthly path of life (and death). That is what a regularly sustained alternation of reason and imagination can and will provide to the planet they shed their light on. But the speaker's immediately subsequent call for the initially disastrous comet to return as the folding star points beyond these co-regents of the mind to an "enamoured" impressionability without which the speaker could not be receptive to either sun or moon. And so into this exquisitely self-regulating world of the sun of τo ποιειν and the moon of τo λογιζειν, there is invited yet another heavenly light but more consequentially a differently conceived heavenly force—not that of light but that of attraction and repulsion—which the speaker evidently thinks is capable of being transformed into nothing less than what *Adonais* will soon call "that sustaining Love/Which through the web of being blindly wove . . . /Burns bright or dim, as each are mirrors of/ The fire for which all thirst" (481-5). Shelley's often tested but never shaken faith in a "Necessity . . . coincident with the law of love"[21] dictates not only that this *tertium quid* of desire be called back into the world of this progress poem but that it be there placed in the sovereign and governing position of that guiding "Vesper of our throng" (*Adonais*, 414) that is "love's folding star."

Reminiscent of the wisely passive *me* of Emersonian reception and Wordsworthian exhortation, "this passive earth/This world of love, this *me*" has as its most fundamental endowment not anything that it might have aggressively gotten or acquired, but whatever it has found to have been drawing it out toward the due sphericity of its own being and expression. (Shelley could be close to explicit about this. In the preface to his *Cenci*, he wrote that the "highest moral purpose" of dramatic art is the ultimately Socratic one of "teaching the human heart, *through its sympathies and antipathies*, the knowledge of itself" (*NS*, 142, emphasis added).) In the first, binary account of himself, the speaker committed the course of his life to an apparently unamendable co-regency of the sun of τò ποιε*ιν and the moon of τò λογιζε*ιν, and he called on these two classes of mental actions to adjust their differing claims on him. But in his succeeding triangulated accounting of where he finds himself, the "folding star of love" is both the one true cynosure and the one true caller of the game, because it is the figure for what the speaker fervently trusts are "our being's inmost cells/The fountains of our deepest life" (569-70).

In *Epipsychidion*'s final and thoroughly "enamoured" constitution of its protagonist's powers and possibilities, the twin lights of day and night need not be asked to make adjustments to each another. From the larger perspective of "the loftiest star of unascended Heaven/Pinnacled in the intense inane" (*Prometheus Unbound*, III.iv.203–4), these moods of the mind are seen as two differing responses in "mental action" to the one alluring call and motion with which "the glorious One" of Emily previously "*Floated* into the cavern where I lay/And called my Spirit" (366–8, emphasis added), called his spirit, I want to say, to "the most forbearing act of thinking (this may mean the most thoughtful) to let true need, say desire, be manifest and be obeyed" (*TN*, 45). The charged language of covenantal promise with which the speaker promises that "the living Sun will feed [the comet] from its urn/Of golden fire" (375–6) expresses the poem's desire, trust and pledge that an authentically vital imagination will bless and recuperate even the most brutish and rending of love's stings, even as by the same all-embracing dispensation the moon is now counseled to "veil her horn/In [the] last smiles [of the comet]" (376–7), because, be they ever so disruptive and unsettling, the attractions of love's folding star urge a greater claim than any such domesticated peace or intellectual closure as would shelter one from taking too keen an interest in one's own life and experience. This is why the "veiled Divinity" of this "world, I say, of thoughts that worshiped her" (244–5) answers not only to such expected invokings as "Thou Wonder, and thou Beauty" but also to "thou Terror" (29). For in its call onward toward its perfectionist vision, the Dantean *splendore* of Emily requires the destruction of all of her votary's standing arrangements and constructions. The poem recounts, and calls for, a radical conversion that does not shrink from flaming out into an imagery of self-immolation conveying the writer's conviction that it is only in the expending of one's life that one may find and save it.

With its call for the comet's return as "love's folding star," the verse of *Epipsychidion* lifts itself up into an extended figure of liturgical service, where "adoring Even and Morn/Will worship thee [the comet now turned evening *and* morning star] with incense of calm breath/And lights and shadows" (377–9). Recalling Wordsworth's "beauteous evening ... breathless with adoration," this turns the volatile "incense of calm breath" arising from the saturated air of morning and evening into a figure for how "the star of Death/And Birth is worshipped by those sisters wild/Called Hope and Fear" (379–81). Clearly identifiable as Venus in her two aspects as Lucifer and Vesper, this star and the breathings of hope and fear it draws up to it are what the speaker would have henceforth be the animating breath of his being, urging him "forth, with hope and fear ... into the wintry forest" (246–9) of a life where he would go on "feeding my course with expectation's breath" (248). In summary, we here witness a progression from the (mostly) conceptual or light-bearing dyad of the two classes of mental action to the very different dyad of a pronounced play of attraction and repulsion embodied in a personified Hope and Fear as these are, for better or worse, attuned to the Venus whose pervasive and characteristically bivalent appearance in Shelley's work as Lucifer and Vesper gives expression to his consuming philosophical and religious interest in our whence and whither, analogous to Cavell's abiding call for an acknowledgement of our finitude by taking on (and taking thought for) both one's mortality and one's "natality," defined by Cavell as "the condition of human birth, of the birth of the human, one that we, as we stand, might still suffer, sometimes called a second birth" (*IQ*, 73).

The sisters Hope and Fear worship the star of Death and Birth by "[piling] upon the heart... their offerings" (381–2), offerings which take the tenuous form of a sky-ascending "incense" giving expressive point and direction to this "sacrifice divine," for which "a World shall be the altar" (382–3). This world abandoning itself to its fiery self-immolation is the same subjectivity or mindfulness that previously identified itself as "this passive earth/This world of love, this me." But now this *me*, which only a moment ago was imagining itself as kept securely on track by the harmonized pulls of a remote moon and an even remoter sun, is gathering its attention inward toward the pulsing heart of its own most pressing hopes and fears. Our differently provoked and frequently crossed and perverted worlds of love can, to be sure, run amuck or become burnt out cases. Hearts can go wildly astray or can turn dry as summer dust. But it is the latter that is the great Shelleyan (and Wordsworthian) beast of torpor, an infernal condition of blocked or stifled responsiveness, whose nadir as recounted here is found, like the deepest pit of Dante's hell, in a rigid carapace of numbness when "the moving billows of my being fell/Into a death of ice immoveable" (315–16). To counter this reign of torpor, we have been granted a Promethean fire of responsiveness, which "gave man speech and speech created thought/Which is the measure of the Universe" (*Prometheus*, II.iv.72–3). This elemental fire can be variously received as an unsettling nuisance, a madly consuming fever, or a potentially refining fire. The speaker and protagonist of this poem is, at it were, religiously committed to the last of these proposed ways of receiving his life of desire, and guided by that confidence he here pilots his lover's discourse through all the forces and facts of his experience and toward his here nominating as the most comprehensive figure for his world, not the "organic form" of many romantics, nor the "text" favored by contemporary literary theorists, nor the "clock-work" of the deists, nor the *polis* of Socrates, but an altar of refining fire, its consuming cynosure of attention whatever action, purgatorially "beautiful and fierce," is upon that altar working itself out toward the consummation of such "a radiant death [or] fiery sepulchre" as would convert the entirety of this "cold common hell, our life" into "a doom/As glorious as a fiery martyrdom" (214–16). *Epipsychidion*'s manifest visual progress from the darkness of the *selva oscura* toward the attractive splendor of Emily can only happen at the prompting of its more fundamental turn from "a death of ice" toward the ardently responsive "*yes* the heart breathes." As if the open secret of the poem were that each stroke of revelation granted the human form of life by the sons and lesser retainers of light "burns bright or dim, as each are mirrors of/The fire for which all thirst" (*Adonais*, 484–5), as if in the beginning there was not the light of the *logos* but (a not unprecedented imagining) the burning fountain of *Venus Genetrix*.

This placeless heaven and its *genius loci*

The prayer of the speaker of *Epipsychidion* that the heavenly lights of sun and moon jointly light "the sphere of his being" into "the Winter of the tomb,/Where it may ripen to a brighter bloom" (366–7) voices the hope for the literary immortality, so commonly thought to be the driving force of *Adonais*. But there is more here and in *Adonais* than a shallow hankering to become famous and celebrated. Shelley is not *wishing* for fame. He is, rather, expressing his trust that his poetry deserves such an afterlife because it is of a character that any seasoned human intelligence would not willingly let die. His warrant for such a hope is that, as he said of some of his most valued precursors, his work "[has celebrated] the dominion of love, planting as it were trophies in the human mind of that sublimest victory over sensuality and force" (*NS*, 526). In more ordinary terms, he was both a persistent reader of his desires and a responsive steward of such words as might give expression to them. Since his words have given expression to the "deepest fountains of our life," he is confident that they are, as it were, already "an echo and a light unto eternity" (*Adonais*, 9).

A significant advance on the flowerings-of-mentality trope occurs shortly after this look forward to the "ripening" tomb and its yield of a "brighter bloom." The advance is the strikingly obvious one from flower to fruit in what the poet protagonist now expects of an Emily now addressed as his muse:

> Lady mine,
> Scorn not these flowers of thought, the fading birth
> Which from its heart of hearts that plant [me] puts forth
> Whose fruit, made perfect by thy sunny eyes,
> Will be as of the trees of Paradise (383–7)

These words pledge that henceforth the splendor of Emily's eyes will be the light within which the speaker's flowers of thought will labor toward a "perfect" maturation. They constitute a speech act of dedication and stem from their speaker's trust that the "fruit" of his laboring in just this light and spirit "will be as of the trees of Paradise." In view of the "favored place" (461) the poem now sets sail for, this closing turn on and advance from the earlier "votive wreathes of withered memory" (4) is not adequately characterized as yet one more expression of a hope deferred to the verdict of posterity. The first bid for literary immortality some twenty lines earlier did indeed look forward to a brighter bloom on the far side of the grave. But these further speech-acts of self-commissioning concentrate on the grounds for entertaining such hopes. They express the speaker's confidence that the hope of this work will be brought to fruition by and within its own textual character as an attractively achieved articulation of the heaven of heart's desire. The initial appearance of Emily called for flowerings of mentality. For the rounding out of that heavenly influence, she is now further imagined as the one guiding star for the course these words are to run from a budding "world of thought" to its maturation in such "literal" fruit as will constitute the perfectionist world he thinks.

The poem's long closing movement toward its imagined paradise combines a "locked-in" focus on the desired island and the sumptuousness of a lover's discourse detailing what as a "world of love" he has found to be of consuming attractiveness. Combining this sharp focus with a copiously abandoned praise-song, the speaker of *Epipsychidion* presents himself as a writer who has so completely given himself over to his perfectionist vision of Emily that he will and indeed must pursue this vision to its mature term, and so perhaps attain to the authority of one who knows thoroughly of what he speaks because, forsaking all others, he has followed this vision into the fully accomplished achievement of its character.

Emily's celebration as the one true and jealously excluding godhead can be better seen for what it is and is not by reviewing both the content and the form of her first appearance to the speaker. In what strikes me as a figure for Cavellian natality, Emily is first portrayed as granting the flourishing light and life of spring to a world beset with thorny obscurity and wintry death:

> At length, into the obscure Forest came
> The Vision I had sought through grief and shame.
> Athwart that wintry wilderness of thorns
> Flashed from her motion splendour like the Morn's,
> And from her presence life was radiated

[sic, i.e. the text here has a line-space, breaking up both a couplet and a sentence]
Through the grey earth and branches bare and dead;
So that her way was paved, and roofed above
With flowers as soft as thoughts of budding love. (321–8)

This account of Emily's initial appearance then gives her a voice as the "music from her respiration" (329) comes to dominate all other sounds so that even "the savage winds hung mute around" (332). Then, this music further transforms into Emily as rose, emitting not only her sweetly enchanting note but also the "odours warm and fresh [which] fall from her hair/Dissolving the dull cold in the frore air:/Soft as an Incarnation of the Sun/When light is changed to love" (335–6). And then, finally, this odor of benediction is said to have "floated into the cavern where [the speaker] lay" (337), and there to have "[called his] Spirit" according to a thermodynamics of Promethean fire in which "the dreaming clay/Was lifted by the thing that dreamed below/As smoke by fire" (338–40).

This picture of a quasi-Promethean ascent, its incentive fire but its expressive sign the rising smoke (or incense) of dream, is framed in both liturgical and thermodynamic terms. As it traces the lifting of a spirit on fire into the rising smoke of a whole or burnt offering, the picture pungently suggests all that would be required if the entire sphere of one's being were to be recreated in the light of Emily's radiantly smiling eyes. The majestically processional image of a long awaited Emily whose "way was paved, and roofed above/With flowers as soft as thoughts of budding love" (327–8) is also a vision penned in echoing homage to Cantos 30 and 31 of the *Purgatorio* where a similarly flower-encircled Beatrice finally vouchsafes the light of her eyes to Dante and so makes the heart's blood of his desire rise into a "novella fronda/puro e disposto a salire alle stelle" (*Purgatorio*, 33, 145). Closer to home, this staging of Emily's advent recalls the flower-strewing, bower-constructing effects of Love in Shelley's own work. As so often in this work, what is here represented as a simile for "flowers as soft as budding thoughts of love" is of the literal essence. For what answers to the vernal and matutinal light of Emily's eyes is this "world of thought," whose finest productions are those Cavellian "flowerings of mentality" (*PP*, 97) that Shelley so endlessly cultivated on and for "this passive Earth,/This world of love this *me*" (345–6).

As a spirit in the process of recounting its recreation in the light of Emily's redeeming eyes, the protagonist of *Epipsychidion* now declares that henceforth in this *vita nuova* he will labor exclusively in the light of those eyes and toward the articulated fullness of a new heaven and earth, whose air he will so attractively imagine that "every [corrupted] sprite beneath the moon" will be drawn toward it and will "repent its envy vain,/ And the earth grow young again" (*Euganean Hills*, 371–3). *Epipsychidion*'s vision is directed, then, not only to the Emily so strongly taking after Dante's Beatrice but also to the flowering island to whose shores it would transport her. As the poem draws to its conclusion, its *bella donna* and the *locus amoenus*, she is being urged to make her own converge into the one semiotic identity of the one true *topos* calling on its devoted followers to forsake all others and expend on it alone the entirety of the wind in their sails.

The poem's tracing of a highly refined literary imagination coming to itself in its commitment to the vision of Emily is further reinforced by the way the advent of this vision concludes with this testimony to the reality of his newly transfigured life:

> and in her beauty's glow
> I stood, and felt the dawn of my long night
> Was penetrating me with living light:
> I knew it was the Vision veiled from me
> So many years--that it was Emily. (340–4)

"I knew it was the Vision ... that it was Emily" rings down the visionary curtain on a life-changing epiphany that began 20 lines earlier with "At length, into the obscure Forest came/The Vision" (321–2). This is an example of what classicists call ring-composition. It is a way of finding your end in your beginning that gives a heightened and self-contained standing to, for example, the rich semiotic focusing performed by an epic simile. However much or little the term may have mattered to Shelley, he seems to have assimilated its music and here made it weave an enchanted circle around Emily as the one perfectionist vision the speaker is to tend and cultivate.

The form and function of this ring-composition also can cast a backward light on the poem's immediately preceding rhetorical unit, listing the series of dire, comet-like effects attendant on the planet of the hour (308–20). These thirteen lines are an extended *praeteritio*, the skeletal structure of which is: "[what then disastrously happened] ... these words conceal" (319). This remarking of a series of events by saying that they are going to be left unsaid acts as the negating complement to what will soon be inaugurating itself as the poem's affirmative focus on Emily and her island as the only topic which the poem now sees fit to spend the preciously refined breath of its words on. By way of this *praeteritio*, the speaker gives a minimal account of such crucial events in his life as must be given their place in the story but not, he insists, dwelt upon or cultivated. The explicitly given reason for this reticence is that "each [word] ... would be the key/Of staunchless tears" (319–20). But beyond this, the speaker is also anticipating how, with the triumphal coming of Emily, everything was so "penetrated" by her Orphean music that even "the savage winds hung mute around." The speaker's peremptory command—"weep not for me"—works to the same purpose as what *Prometheus Unbound* said of its agonistic "form of love" (I.763): that is, that in the light of its redeeming smile, all the stormy worst of our collective human life is turned to "recollected gladness."

Once the light of Emily comes to this poem's labyrinthine forest of false starts, sharp turns, densely tangled figuration and often clumsy astronomical machinery, its speaker shakes off his many verbal scatterings of awkwardness and self-consciousness and securely addresses both his nautical and discursive self to the island as the place destined for the dwelling of him and his love. The impression left on the reader of the poem's final extended *invitation au voyage* is not one of being addressed as, for example, the "stranger" of line 72, but rather one of overhearing the rapt expression of one so *captus amore* that nothing but the object of his desire exists or counts for him. (This effect is only heightened by the poem's self-consciously sophisticated conclusion on an *envoy* addressed to its own "weak verses." A reading of that envoy will be the final business of this chapter.) In sum and as already suggested, the vessel of poetry we know as *Epipsychidion* hits its stride and becomes gracefully yare only when it gives itself over entirely to the perfectionist vision of Emily and where it would take her.

"Peopled with sweet airs" (445), the destined island home of the speaker's imagination is steeped in its own self-generated atmosphere. It is "heavy with the scent" (447) of flowers that "dart their arrowy odour through the brain/'Till you might faint with that delicious pain./And every motion, odour, beam and tone/With that deep music is in unison" (451–4). These synesthetically harmonized "exhalations" are said either to "fall" from the sky or "rise" from the sea (470–1). But then in a mild but explicit correcting of this exclusive focus on the outer influences of sea or sky, we are brought back to the geothermal navel of this "calm circumference of bliss." We are reminded that

> Yet, like a buried lamp, a Soul no less
> Burns in the heart of this delicious isle,
> An atom of the Eternal, whose own smile
> Unfolds itself, and may be felt not seen
> O'er the grey rocks, blue waves, and forests green,
> Filling their bare and void interstices. (477–87)

These six lines strenuously gather together such Shelleyan master-tones as *soul, burn, heart, atom, eternal, delight, smile,* and *unfold*. But perhaps more suggestive than any of these is the not conventionally "poetic" *interstices*. The word echoes the *Defence*'s description of poetry as "[enlarging] the circumference of the imagination by replenishing it with thoughts of ever new delight, which have the power of attracting and assimilating to their own nature all other thoughts, and which form new intervals and interstices whose void for ever craves fresh food" (*NS*, 517). Aside from their literal repetition of the *Defence*, these "bare and void" (and so implicitly receptive) "interstices" also echo the way "Mont Blanc" closes on a *vacancy* calling out to the "human mind's imaginings." The indwelling source for the respiring life of the island is just such a human imagining, a burning atom of unextinguishable thought (*NS*, 528) that is the *genius loci* of this favored place, which (in Patrick Kavanagh's felicitous phrasing) is not a place at all but, as Seamus Heaney puts it, the "all idea" of a "placeless heaven,"[22] which Shelley has here imagined and textualized into a perfectionist *topos*, which, like Emily herself, is something *thought* and brought to term in and by the course of *Epipsychidion*.

But if after the island's exfoliating wonders we are, thus, called back to its *omphalos* of a burning atom of unextinguishable thought, this praise singer seemingly arrived at the center of this "world of love, this *me*" does not stop here. On the model of Blake's New Jerusalem, both a woman and a city, he moves on to the one structure on the island made for human habitation. Furthermore, this towering edifice comes to our attention trumpeted by the claim that upon this isle of earthly wonders, it is the greatest wonder of them all. The flower-breathing atmosphere of the island has been conjured up as something to take one's breath away. But then we are told that "the chief marvel of this wilderness" is this "pleasure-house" built "for delight."

Working on the assumption, which I share, that *Epipsychidion* is self-reflexive, J. Hillis Miller has read this tower that "overtops the woods" (487) as an emblem for the constructions of writing, and specifically for the (writing) work of *Epipsychidion*.[23] Having originally reared itself up into visible strokes of "antique and learned imagery" (498), the edification of this tower now finds itself covered with vines and ivy, punningly binding themselves (Miller points out) into "*volumes*" replete with their own supply of expressive imagery. Where before there had been lamps and images to illumine, now the succeeding or belated "parasite flowers" (502), standing for further work in this imaginative kind, carry on the work of illumination. And even when the chill of winter extinguishes these flowers, just that falling-off allows the heaven-sent splendors of day, moon and star to find their way through the "winter-woof of tracery" (504) and replace the lush abundance of the flowering season with the airy play of light and shadow cast by a remnant of vines and stems. Even in the wintry fall of this paradise, then, there is here a special providence, since it is precisely the seasonal demise of flower and leaf that gives time and makes space for the reception of such lights from on high as are allowed to "[work] mosaic on [the] Parian floors" (507).

As one of this writing's most fully developed images of what it is about and up against, the tower acknowledges the inevitable fading of all individual efforts in this kind, even as it attests to the ever reviving constitutional animus toward such perfectionist excellences as Shelley's work of the same name will call "a brighter Hellas [rearing] its mountains/From waves serener far" (1066-7). The all but spoken boast of the course of words that make up *Epipsychidion* is that the triumphs of clarifying, provoking and sustaining art to be found in "antique and learned imagery" do not just die away. They pass into other forms. As *Prometheus Unbound* puts it, they yield the stewardship of their "burning fountains" to further "voices and shadows" and "mediators" of "that best worship, love" (III.ii.57-9).

Even though this tower has been repeatedly and cogently identified as an image of art, it is also a "*wreck* of human art" (493). It is a ruin whose currently commanding appearance is most notable for the sense it gives off of its persistent and deeply ingrained origin in a force of nature that is

> as it were Titanic, in the heart
> Of Earth having assumed its form, then grown
> Out of the mountains, from the living stone,
> Lifting itself in caverns light and high. (494-7)

For literally millennia of artistic representation, such Titanic prodigies have been given a local habitation in the fiery and eruptive nature of volcanoes. Add to this the fact of ordinary (Ancient Greek) language that "Titan" comes from the verb τιταίνω—to stretch or strive—and you might find yourself irresistibly identifying this tower of art and language Titanically (i.e. Prometheanly) thrusting itself upward from the vicinity of the magna at the earth's core as yet another instance of the volcano's voice in Shelley. This voice is usually heard as the recurrent cry of revolution breaking out in an age "of irrepressible collective energy contained by repressive power."[24] As already noted, it often takes the form in Shelley of the volcanic eruption which both he, and Aeschylus before him, mythologized into the Jupiter-assaulting outbursts of Typhoon. Here on the flowering island of *Epipsychidion*, the style of Titanic expression is not insurrectionary rage but an affirmative upbuilding, rich with what G. M. Matthews notes is the "extreme fertility"[25] of volcanic fall-out, and here represented as seminally "lifting itself" up from the earth's core and into the stately form of the tower's capaciously airy lodgings of light.

Since this "chthonian tower"[26] comes to light and expression in a poem whose author has repeatedly characterized himself as a world or earth, we are, in effect, being asked to acknowledge this Titanic tower as the artistic issue of a creative force whose indwelling "plastic stress" (*Adonais*, 381) is here gathering itself into (1) this edification (of words), which is also (2) the offspring of a human and, *eo ipso*, striving form of life and (3) a nautical venture in what is to be made of the ocean of human experience on which we find ourselves always already launched. In other words and as if in illustration of its writer's faith that the Imagination must draw on "a thousand prisms and mirrors" (166), this edification of words replete with "antique and learned imagery" represents itself both as the biological issue of this "world of love, this *me*" and as the *barca* or vessel of a perfectionist discourse currently under full sail toward this edification "built for delight." By imagining its self-reflexive tower as "grown . . . from the living stone" with a volcanic force not to be withstood, the poem claims that a naturally rooted but routinely repressed necessity of (its) nature or constitution is piloting it toward the characterization of its own writing as a laboring into such an expression of the "*yes* [the heart] breathes" as can play a sustaining role in the continuously reforming edification of culture—a work of upbuilding or *Bildung*, which, as in the analog of Spenser's Garden of Adonis noted by Jerrold Hogle, is "eterne" only "in mutabilitie," and only "by succession made perpetuall."[27]

My sense of the tower as the site of an endlessly self-destroying and self-preserving constitution of perfectionist writing owes much to the work of Hugh Roberts, who has used ancient Lucretius and contemporary chaos theory to mount a brief but effective challenge to Hillis Miller's representation of *Epipsychidion*'s tower as an instancing of the deconstructionist understanding of the "linguistic moment," when language stops to give thought to its own status, limits and claims.[28] Roberts agrees with Miller that the "parasite flowers," flourishing and withering on the armature of the tower, do indeed figure the successions of art and/or language, but he disputes Miller's claim that on this picturing of language it is impossible for any truly new voice to spring out of what assumed to be the prison-house of language. "Shelley's cycles of creativity do not," Roberts writes, "debar him from genuine innovation—quite the opposite, as the image of the 'parasite flowers' makes clear. These flowers are not produced, as Miller's model would demand, from the remains of the ruined building; they have opportunistically occupied the space created by the erasure of the 'antique and learned imagery.' As such they represent an attempt not to 'start again' [Miller's futility-laced wording derived from DeMan] with ever the same material, but to start anew."[29]

Out of such interstices or vacancies as Shelley knew would always present themselves, there emerge new flowerings of mentality. But these interstices are only a necessary, not a sufficient condition for the individual "bursting" up either of new flowers of thought or new volcanic voices bearing the true, indwelling Promethean fire of Titanic genius and striving. The parasite flowers of mentality are as chthonic as the tower on which they bloom. As Thoreau might put it, they are our earth expressing itself not in volcanic lava but in these more common and varied floral forms (or events) that owe their brief but lovely lease on life to their seed breaking through the surface of the earth into just these natalities in place and on time for opening themselves out to the sun and shower that will, for a favored time, sustain their flourishing condition and illuminating function.

All this would seem to put these parasite flowers of mentality in a very admirable light. But Miller downgrades them not only for their supposed draw on a force or genius not their own but also for blocking our access to the world. For him, they are constantly "making a screen between sky and earth," a screen that "remains even in winter as a lattice of dried vines."[30] In response to this reading of *Epipsychidion*'s self-reflexive tower, I would first note an unacknowledged slippage in Miller's use of *screen*. In his second wintry usage of the term, it has to mean *filter*. But the summer flowers, illuminating "with dewy gems/The lampless halls" of the tower, do not *filter* any external sources of light. They completely block them out, but not to any grievous or privative effect, because at these recurring seasons in the tower's life as a trellis for flowers any outside light is as unneeded as it is excluded. For the poet's hand quickly turns these flowers so attractively adorning the tower inward toward its interior of "caverns light and high," for which, in season, these flowers alone provide not just sufficient but timely and preciously varied light. During such favored times, anything outside the tower is blocked while all within is splendidly and, as it were, naturally illuminated into an updated version of that "antique and learned" space of the *hortus conclusus* expressly made to be impervious to the assaults of any external despoiling or darkening (say serpentine) forces.

This is, I dare say, an image of what is not inaccurately described as Shelley's visionary and perfectionist art committed to "familiarizing" the imagination of its readers "with beautiful idealisms of moral excellence." With a "sound, and odour, and beam" (93) all their own, such summertime flowers of mentality are the work and glory of Keats' "gardener Fancy," who while "breeding flowers," specified as buds, bells and stars, "will never breed the same." So the tower's flowers, while indubitably parasitic are also strikingly original in, I would suggest, the sense and style of that original declaring of one's commonness which Cavell is continually in quest of, and which depends on the intertextuality of "being the other to one's self, calling upon it with the words of others."

In its aspect as what Northrop Frye would call the *mythos* of summer, *Epipsychidion*'s tower of art is a strikingly original reception and reconstruction of the venerable topos of the *hortus conclusus*, and a large part of its originality can be ascribed to how it is only for the time remaining of an Ionian summer that this tower/bower remains the closed-off space of a charmed and potentially charming circle. For this structure that is both a "wonder" and a "wreck" of art, the ostensibly odious facts of winter, decomposition, and withering are acknowledged, but with the remarkably positive slant that it is not, as Miller would have it, *even* in winter but *only* in winter that the tower's "winter woof of tracery" allows "the sky [to] peep" through it

> With Moon-light patches, or star atoms keen,
> Or fragments of the day's intense serene;—
> Working mosaic on their Parian floors. (505–7)

Although Miller's picture of the bine-stems of winter screening any incoming light and so creating a mosaic of shifting light and dark on the tower's marble floor is visually accurate, it does serious violence to the passage's manifest emphasis on the way this wintry season in the life of the world affords an *access* to previously occluded sources of light, and so recalls the emphatic claim of the *Defence* that the "sorrow, terror, anguish, [and] despair . . . are often the chosen expressions of an approximation to the highest good" (*NS*, 529). And while the thus vouchsafed "patches" of moonlight and "fragments" of day project a tracery of light and shadow, I, for one, do not know how "star atoms keen" can cast any shadow at all. Such pin-pricks of heavenly light either penetrate the tower or not, a fact emblematic of the passage's emphasis on how the wintry season—and *only* the wintry season—allows a host of heavenly lights to come into this previously enclosed and screened *out* space.

That Miller seems bound and determined to see a blocking or screening effect where there is infinitely more call to see multiple and cyclically sequenced apertures for the (filtered) access of heavenly light derives from the deconstructionist dogma that words block rather than constitute our access to the world, a deconstructionist article of faith that, as already noted, once prompted Cavell to say of Paul DeMan on language: "It does not help to picture language as being turned from the world (say troped [say screened and screening]) unless you know how to picture it as owed to the world and given to it" (*T*, 48). The danger of being stiflingly imprisoned in words and other "instruments of one's own creation" (*NS*, 507) is one of the most common of romanticism's understandings of what it is (perforce endlessly) about. Settle too much into any achieved ordering or naming of things, and it will indeed become what Kenneth Burke calls a "terministic screen,"[31] humbling reality to precept and making our pictures of where we find ourselves obfuscatingly conform to our form of life's previously codified accounts of what we are about. This is why Shelley constructs *Epipsychidion*'s tower of art and delight as a wonder and wreck of human art that will always be refashioning itself and its tuitions in obedience to whatever, in any present moment in the breath of a culture, compellingly finds its way into its precincts, whether these be winds of change, darts of love, rumors of war, shifting intimations of ambivalence, or needle-sharp shafts of guiding starlight.

As the death of the parasite flowers allows freshening winds of light to penetrate through the structure of the tower and into its interior, so repeatedly in Shelley the wintry seasons of discontent and the thorny agons of loss bring on the need and chance of seeing and telling things anew. This is why it is the "obscure forest" of his dismayed strivings that prompts Shelley's progress toward a vision of Emily and himself settling into this tower, which is to be maintained by "[fitting] up some chambers there/Looking towards the golden Eastern air,/And level with the living winds, which flow/Like waves above the living waves below" (515–18). You cannot clutch these living winds: they are "Heaven's free breath,/Which he who grasps can hold not" (400–1). But you can let yourself be inspired, stayed, and/or turned around by them. You can allow their currents of "golden Eastern air" to call out the responsive sap and thrust of such heliotropic flowers of art, mentality and language as, according to the "writer's faith" of Cavell's aspiration (*SW*, 104), do not screen out the world from us but word it into being there for us, but always with a rub on the ground or a catch in the voice betraying the "truth of skepticism," always, that is to say, with the never completely stifled doubt that since these words of ours are *only* ours, they can not satisfy the philosophical skeptic's demand for not just the appearance or the calling of a thing, but for the thing in itself, the Kantian *Ding an Sich*.

The constantly present threat of a linguistically turned skepticism, to which I have just alluded, looms large in the most philosophically sophisticated reading of *Epipsychidion*, Thomas Pfau's "Tropes of Desire; Figuring the 'Insufficient Void' of Self-Consciousness in Shelley's *Epipsychidion*." On the many occasions when Pfau draws attention to *Epipsychidion*'s pressing desire to "escape its own implications in the linguistic,"[32] he seems (like the comparably sophisticated Peter Sacks on the centrality of the same desire in *Adonais*)[33] to be operating on the still regnant axiom that words do not constitute our access to the world but block it. But if you come to what Pfau rightly calls Shelley's wrestlings with "the linguistic as [one's] irreducible and continuously elusive 'ground' of existence"[34] from the Cavellian understanding that "the drift toward skepticism is the *discovery* of the everyday, a discovery of exactly *what* it is that skepticism would deny" (*IQ*, 170, Cavell's emphases), you might find yourself prepared to reimagine a sense of *ground* not in need of scare quotes. You might find, with Cavell, Austin and Wittgenstein, that the ground we meet on is our shared language (to imagine which is to imagine a form of life), and you might then begin to suspect that precisely as one committed to the "writer's faith," Shelley is everywhere to be found struggling toward a trusting repose in such constructions of our language and form of life as show themselves to have been impressionably open to what's in the wind. You might come to see the well ventilated dwellings of Shelley's imagination as striving toward an unguarded welcoming of, and trusting commitment to that human "breath made words," which is our terms as our (Kantian) conditions (what we say together) and what together we so routinely and endemically misuse and misinherit, but not without the thereby accumulating potentiality of an aversive recoil into the exits of desire that has "been expressed at any time only by breathers of words, mortals, [so that] their strokes may be given now, and may gather together now—in a recoiling—all the power of world-creating words" (*PP*, 25).

From the lookout of the island's tower

> Earth and Ocean seem
> To sleep in one another's arms, and dream
> Of waves, flowers, clouds, woods, rocks and all that we
> *Read* in their smiles and *call* reality. (509–12, emphases added)

These at first luxuriantly panoramic lines rather jarringly conclude on a densely packed epistemological claim as to how, by way of the correlative activities of reading and calling, any one of us looking out from such a high keep of perfectionist writing might begin to "(re)read" and rearticulate the ground on which, and the currents within which, we find ourselves islanded. The lines' conspicuously epistemological finish echoes Shelley's "intellectual system," even as its closing on what we "call reality" recuperates the etymological and historical links running from *reor* (to judge, deem, or call) to *res* (the participial outcome of *reor*) and on to what is too often forgotten to be the belated philosophical (and some would say barbaric) neologisms of *realis* and *realitas*. The lines also reprise and condense similar moments of epistemological arrival in Shelley's poetry, such as that in *Prometheus Unbound* when the happily recovered mind is said to "[arise] bright/From the embrace of beauty" (III.iii.50–1) so that, "possessing and possest" (*Epipsychidion*, 549) by its enchantment, it may return the favor by casting on its at first dim "apparitions" of beauty "the gathered rays which are reality" (III.iii.49, 53).

In accord with the claims of a poetry that would give us (back) the life of the world, the smiling "heart" or "atom" or "soul" of this island has "unfold[ed] itself" into a tower built for delight and perspicuous overview, and the altering eye of this perfectionist construction of things has altered all around it into a picture of its emphatically thought or imagined world as a smiling repose of Earth and Ocean in one another's arms where the incessantly shifting encounter of human clay and experiential flux does not keep bitterly open a Promethean wound festering with the seawrack of history, but instead recurrently marks the liminal space of meeting necessary for the creation and furthering of all the successions of (what we would read as and call) reality. (In a later reprise of this figure, the smiling repose of an embracing earth and ocean will be raised to a passionately enamored pitch where (with a recalling of the foam or ἀφρός in *Aphrodite Andyomene*) "the pebble-paven shore/Under the quick, faint kisses of the sea/Trembles and sparkles as with ecstacy." (546–8).)

All this, I am well aware, can look very much like escapist fantasy and unchecked wish-fulfillment. But even while granting that the chambers of the tower anticipate nothing but fair and inviting weather as they face "level with the living winds, which flow/Like waves above the living waves below" (516–17), one should recall that arguably the most distinctive feature of *Epipsychidion* is (in the words of Angela Leighton already quoted) its two "directions . . . towards idealistic figurativeness on the one hand, and towards a 'matter-of-fact' [and overwhelmingly calamitous] life story on the other."[35] On the one hand, this poem signals its pedigree of idealistic figurativeness in such "antique and learned imagery" as the Greek *psyche*, Dante's Beatrice, the *locus amoenus*, the vessel and venture of poetry, and the flowers of poesy and rhetoric. But from another more clamorously demanding direction, the poem also originates in the everyday vicissitudes of the narrator's experience, and in his everyday taking of thought in and for this experience. These rough facts on the ground of his existence are, with a pressure not to be put by, what the speaker of this poem is trying to work his way through. The poetic production of his that we call *Epipsychidion* is the meeting of these two origins and provocations and the adjusting of their claims on one another. And although the poem arrives at a (re)inhabiting of an imagined island graced by nothing but salubrious winds, the greater part of its stormy progress toward this land of heart's desire is the story of just how, or indeed *if*, the "antique and learned imagery" so conspicuously decking the vessel of this poetry can still be successfully transported into modern predicaments, can still convey something of needed and pressing import for the course of a nineteenth-century life in which we may detect more than the beginnings of what Cavell (and not Cavell alone) calls the "modern [human] subject," more than commonly given to such maladies as (among others) soul sickness, lostness or exile, disappointment, and a fear of suffocation (*PDAT*, 206). This striving to make satisfying sense of one's experience through one's reception of some of the most persistently powerful images in our cultural inheritance is not adequately characterized as "schizophrenic."[36] It seems to me, rather, what any member of any given culture is called to do when, at whatever depth and for whatever stakes, she finds herself drawn toward assessing the world she was born into and is still voyaging through both for "the damage that was done/and the treasures that prevail."[37]

The treasures of a deep and copiously sophisticated literary inheritance are images in the fraught hold and animating soul of just about every passage of *Epipsychidion*. But if the reputedly actuality-shunning Shelley does indeed crave reality (as I am arguing), then these antique and learned imageries must be exposed to and severely tested by the often stormy air and troubled atmosphere of a post-Enlightenment man, who in describing himself as a "world of love" knew not only that "love far more than hate" had been "the cause of all sorts of mischief" for him (*Letters*, II.339), but also that to Rousseau and Dante this deceptively simple four-letter word meant two very different things and conjured up entire worlds of historical difference. That all of the tower's presumptively original "antique and learned imagery" is to be challenged and modified by the provoking force of what's in the living wind of one's own experience dictates that any standing representations of the tower must, over time, yield to further generations of light-bearing parasite flowers and ever newer plays of mosaic patterning on the structure's pavement. Consequently, *Epipsychidion*'s tower of delight and wonder of art is presented as a recurrently self-(re)constituting "wreck of human art," which will always be refashioning its appointments and specifications in obedience to the "all-sustaining air" (*Prometheus Unbound*, I.754; II.v.42)[38] of what's in the wind as the "spirit of the age"—both its heartening airs from heaven and its desolating blasts from hell. If from one point of view, the tower's exposure to the currents of influence in which it finds itself can invite a storm of pain, destruction and decay, from another perspective it bespeaks a prompt responsiveness to what is most immediately before one, a needed impressionability and native "genius" perhaps the greatest impediment to which is one's own long standing and potentially hidebound construction(s) of things. The creator of *Epipsychidion* is clearly a writer in possession of, and possessed by, the large and many-mansioned elaborations of "antique and learned imagery" on which he constantly finds himself dwelling and into which he repeatedly inscribes himself. But his own individually spirited and creative way of settling into the entailments of these elective affinities and attractions is to open their often mustily overpraised and undervalued standing in our culture to the ventilating rush and draw of his own personal experience. Shelley's is an art that would stay with (and be stayed by) what his poetic impressionability has found to be the commanding artistic triumphs of the past—Dante, Aeschylus, Shakespeare, Milton—but it is also an art addressed to (and provoked by) where at present it finds itself, an art which, to be true to its own calling, must stay open to what's in the wind, and must further stand prepared to carry the burden of these prompting motions of the spirit directly and, if need be, devastatingly into its own hitherto achieved construction of things.

Waging contention with their time's decay

Even though its occasion is untimely death, the authority of raw and clamoring experience does not seem to be anything that *Adonais* is very much interested in. The poem is so bookish and, in Shelley's own proud words, such a "highly wrought *piece of art*" (*Letters*, II.294, Shelley's emphases) that it has led as fine a reader of his life and work as Richard Holmes to the judgment that its style is all "mannerism and pomposity" and that "at best, Shelley produced the rhetoric of a funeral oration."[39] But just as the fervors of *Epipsychidion* accumulate into the structure of the tower, so too does the highly crafted panoply of *Adonais* find its fiercely burning incentive in what Stanley Cavell calls, with studied ordinariness, (human) interest. In its desire to take on the brute fact of Keats' corpse and spirit it away as a poetic *corpus* fit for "the abode where the Eternal are" (409), *Adonais* does indeed stress the achieved artifice of eternity. But while the poem works conspicuously hard at gathering everything it cares about into the enduring power of its own incisive expression, the navel of this performative tour de force—the navel of *even* this tour de force—is the abandoned fervor of interest driving it into its tightly woven and densely allusive textual fabric. Just as *Epipsychidion*'s tower erupts "as it were, Titanically," from its "known island-home" of desire (*Prometheus Unbound*, III.iii.43), so conversely for the monumental edification of *Adonais*. Cut these words and they will bleed. Open up their highly wrought performance of mourning and you will find the indwelling fire and incentive of their composition. The poem aspires to the condition of what it itself climactically pictures as "flame transformed to marble" (447).

Under its mantle of convention, *Adonais* performs a cultural critique, focused on the current state of language and poetry and pitched at the highest anagogical level of the gods and the nature and good of life itself. When, for example, *Adonais* claims that its title character is still very much and vitally with us, it is clearly considering *life* (and *death*) as a member of the select set of "emphatic concepts" that are "ineliminably, normative or evaluative as well as descriptive,"[40] and just as clearly it is bent on nudging its reader toward acknowledging this by means of nothing aside from such tightly coherent stanzas as the following:

> Peace, peace! He is not dead, he doth not sleep—
> He hath awakened from the dream of life—
> 'Tis we who, lost in stormy visions, keep
> With phantoms an unprofitable strife,
> And in mad trance, strike with our spirit's knife
> Invulnerable nothings. *We* decay
> Like corpses in a charnel; fear and grief
> Convulse us and consume us day by day,
> And cold hopes swarm like worms within our living clay. (343–51)

Naming where the mourners of Adonais remain the "dream of life," Shelley revitalizes this literary commonplace by drafting some lexical paradigms of "dream" (*visions, phantoms,* and *trance*) into a compactly forged syntagmatic relation with the waking pursuits of a generalized human endeavor.[41] The same poetic procedure is evident in the proposition that "*we* decay/Like corpses in a charnel" (348–9, Shelley's emphasis). The assertion gathers cogent force because the language continues to hold tightly together that has fear and grief "consume" us or "cold hopes swarm like worms within our living clay." In thus transposing "death" from the physical matter fit for a coroner's inquest to the many ways "that alone which knows" (177) may suffer unacknowledged death and casual (self)slaughter, Shelley turns the idea of the effectively vital away from the brute animations of clay and toward the Promethean spirit that "gave man speech, and speech created thought,/Which is the measure of the Universe" (II.iv.72–3). As he performs these turns on (what we call) *sleep* and *death*, Shelley in effect calls on the unawakened earth of his reader to see things this revised way and so be prepared, with one hand, to deliver a terminally rebuking death sentence on the reigning actuality of this world, while with the other (writing and reading) hand raising up another life among the ascendant kings of thought, those "splendours of the firmament of time/[which] may be eclipsed but are extinguished not."

The splendor in the firmament of English letters that is the most recent precursor of Shelley's *Adonais* is Milton's *Lycidas*, a poet and would-be pastor who prepared himself for the care of his flock only to be untimely drowned, his English charges consigned to hirelings who "grate on their scrannel Pipes of wretched straw," his sheep abandoned to an episcopacy of "blind mouths."

Like Milton before him, Shelley assigns to himself the role of a self-authorizing inheritor of both Athens and Jerusalem who would hold the backsliding England of his day to the fire of these still burning fountains of cultural origin and power. Writing to and about the pre-revolutionary England of 1638, Milton uses the genre's pastoral conventions to create an ideal of the good shepherd and to castigate the mitred realities of Stuart misrule, who are as harsh in song as they have been remiss in pastoral care. Almost two centuries further on, Shelley makes the slaughter of Keats epitomize the ruin that has once again been visited upon his "country's pride" by "the priest, the slave, and the liberticide" (30–2). English power ostracized Milton, and now it has murdered Keats, both of them poets and "godlike minds" (258) who "[redeemed] from decay the visitations of the divinity in man" (*NS*, 532).

From one side of eternity, *Adonais* reports the sad reality of a people falling short of its own cultural ideal. Toward the other side of this great rent in English fortune, the poem asserts that, despite such stiff-necked backsliding, the perfectionist ideal and its servants do abide, throned among the stars and thundering out of history. For "when lofty thought/Lifts a young heart above its mortal lair," these splendours of time do indeed (and in no very mysterious way) "live there/And move like winds of light on dark and stormy air" (392–6). But the business of bearing the word is not restricted to its stars. For when Chatterton, Sidney, and Lucan initiate Adonais into their house of literary fame, they are accompanied by "many more, whose names on Earth are dark/But whose transmitted effluence cannot die/So long as fire outlives the parent spark" (406–8). These "many more" include all the good citizens of the republic of letters, who in accord with Keats's conviction that "English ought to be kept up"[42] maintained it as a "vitally metaphorical language [marking] the before unapprehended relations of things" (*NS*, 482). When a language community inevitably proves less than totally attentive to this unending task, it disorganizes a vital system of relation into what John Wright's aptly calls "semantic entropy,"[43] the kind of windblown scattering of our own words that repeatedly draws from Cavell and Wittgenstein the lament that just as we so manifestly, casually and endlessly keep letting our words get away from us, so do we keep darkening ourselves to ourselves and end up not knowing either what we are made of or what we are called to do.

The all but inevitable drift of our (human, talking) form of life away from the spirit in which its "words and signs, the instruments of its own creation" (*NS*, 507) were framed constitutes perhaps the most authentically collective, daily and casual form of backsliding; and for its prophetic sign of contradiction Shelley designs *Adonais* as a perfectionist constitution of words meant to challenge and provoke the lumpishly powerful monolith of customary usage and mindless formula whose genotype is the words of prophecy and gospel as they have straggled away form a contextual life, "instinct with the most vital poetry" and become easy prey for institutional misrepresentation and co-optation. When referring to the post-Napoleonic peace of a vaunted age of "Restoration," for example, Shelley habitually names the crowned heads of this new world order "Anarchs." Onto the regnant powers of a world restored to (what *they* call) law and order, he fixes Milton's name for Chaos.[44] That is the literary and political background for why *Adonais* tropes an anonymous reviewer's shoddy treatment of Keats into yet another spectacle in a masque of English anarchy, where the sceptered isle is seen as less a nurse of heroes than as a lair for "unpastured dragons" who spill "their venom when [their] fangs o'erflow" (238, 330). By the performance of such highly wrought turns on some very common English materials, Shelley contrives to turn the polity of England into a culture for the "contagion of the world's slow stain" (356), an entropic brutishness against which the only St. George is the "one Spirit's plastic stress" as it

> Sweeps through the dull dense world, compelling there
> All new successions to the forms they wear;
> Torturing th' unwilling dross that checks its flight
> To its own likeness, as each mass may bear;
> And bursting in its beauty and its might
> From trees and beasts and men into the Heaven's light. (*Adonais*, 382–7)

To go along with the elegy's undermining and recasting of the "authorities" as conventionally understood, Shelley performs an inversely valorizing move for poets. Because they are the preeminent bearers of "the one Spirit's plastic stress," they also attract the predicates and prerogatives of majesty. The company Adonais will hereafter keep are the "kings of thought," his appointed station among them a previously "unascended majesty" (430, 412).

Uranian Venus' elegy within the elegy acts as a precipitating signal for the cortege of unnamed contemporary poets—Byron, Moore, Hunt, Shelley himself—who come weeping in another's fate their collective own. These poets figure more tangibly and act more publicly than the volatile wraiths of "Desires and Adorations, Winged Persuasions and veiled Destinies" (109–10) that gather mournfully around Keats's remains, but they do not represent the extreme of the tangible and public that the poem is reaching toward. More monumental than even the Byronic Pilgrim of Eternity with his "early but enduring monument" (266) is the constellation of departed poets who will eventually usher Adonais into their stellar company. In each instance of Sidney, Chatterton, and Lucan—the only explicitly named poets in *Adonais*—a posthumous name is the conclusion of a cultural process by which a man writing has become a monument of writing. For Keats/Adonais, this process is already under way in the imagining of *Adonais*. For when the Leigh Hunt figure leans over Keats "in mockery of monumental stone" (310), he crystallizes the tears of the muse into the attitude of a *Pietà*, summarizes them into a marble constant which is a memorial to Adonais' value and an earnest that his fellows will not willingly let such value die. Coming at the end of the funeral procession, the mute fixity of this mourner's gaze is only an apparent anticlimax to the extended keenings of the Shelleyan self-portrait. The grieving gaze of a maternal figure "who, gentlest of the wise,/Taught, loved, honored the departed one," solidifies into a monument of brass the poem's implicit assertion that grief from such mourners is a guarantee of sterling quality and a tender of enduring presence. In his death, Keats is, like Lucan, approved. He becomes solid, radiant and enduring, his work his monument.

Adonais is a progress poem in three movements, each successive throng sublimated into the increasingly glorious monumentality of the next. The volatile energies of Keats' inner life accumulate into a new poet on the contemporary scene, and the authentic arbiters of this scene then lift the corpus of this poet out of time and into the heaven of fame, Adonais set among the other Eternals but still originating in and composed of such impassioned breathings as his "Desires and Adorations, Winged Persuasions and veiled Destinies" (109–10). Immortality through the name is a very Hellenic notion, and it is with an Attic symmetry that Shelley couples the assured renown of Adonais with the denial of any name at all to his destroyer. The only place this "nameless worm" of a reviewer will have in the heaven of song is no place. He will be a "noteless blot on a remembered name" (327). The two starkly opposed destinies of Adonais and his destroyer flesh out the two epigraphs yoked together at the head of the elegy, the one looking toward the stellar and enduring worth of Adonais, the other visiting upon his earthly destroyer the punishment of verbal nonentity. To the question who could have been so brutal as to poison Bion, Shelley hears Moschus handing down the curt apodosis: εκφυγεν ωδάν: he has been expunged from this song. The other side of this poetic coin of retribution is that until the Future dares forget the Past, Adonais will be an "echo and a light unto eternity" (9). He will have a place in the canon of letters such that later generations may reverse the cultural process by which he became a star in the constellation of English letters. With Adonais's name as an abiding bequest to posterity, the work behind that name will draw its readers inward toward the fellowship with essence to be found in its animating Desires and Adorations, Persuasions and veiled Destines.

But before the finalities of death and posthumous reputation, there is the passion of earthly existence to be undergone by those who "yet live, treading the thorny road,/Which leads, through toil and hate, to Fame's serene abode" (44–5). Before the Leigh Hunt figure can serenely enact the monumental aspect of grieving Urania, the Shelleyan self-portrait must make her portion of tearful grief and flowering witness his own. He must represent his own course along this "rugged way" as continually breaking out into showers of "sacred blood" falling down on the field of human endeavor "like the young tears of May/[that] Paved with eternal flowers that undeserving way" (215–16).

Bringing up the rear of Adonais's poetic mourners, this figure is not a publicly known quantity like Byron or Hunt. Approaching "midst others of less note" (271), he is of obscure or nonexistent renown. But the vibrating thyrsus he holds in his hand identifies him as an avatar of Dionysos, that recurrently undone and rekindled force of life whose power breaks forth from the necessities of death and dismemberment. A study in polarity, the subject of the self-portrait is "a Love in desolation masked, a Power/Girt round with weakness." Previously, the poem has articulated two starkly opposed and separately clear types of the poetic character: the catastrophically sensitive Adonais and the cavalierly strong Byron/Pythian, one the victim of snakes, the other their queller. The self-portrait fuses these two possibilities into a single grieving poet, who bears such powerful witness precisely because he has suffered an unguardedly sudden and profoundly wounding impression of the unattained attractiveness of the life he finds himself in pursuit of:

> he, as I guess,
> Had gazed on Nature's naked loveliness,
> Actaeon-like, and now he fled astray
> With feeble steps o'er the world's wilderness,
> And his own thoughts, along that rugged way,
> Pursued like raging hounds, their father and their prey. (274–9)

So to be pursued by a cry of ineluctably remembered thoughts marks this Actaeon of the mind as identical in reflective kind to the protagonist of *Epipsychidion*, who could not "uncreate" the world of his thoughts that worshipped Emily. And so, with a self-identifying pun, the maker of *Adonais* binds (and crowns) the head of this sacrificial victim of "lofty thought" (392) with "pansies [*pensées*, thoughts] overblown/And faded violets, white, and pied, and blue." This self-portrait articulates perhaps the most complexly powerful of the many self-identifying or "signature" moments in Shelley's corpus. In it, the maker of this "highly wrought" work represents the grounds for his own implicit claim to a royal standing in the firmament of thought as his sustained living and writing in martyred witness to the world of "Nature's naked loveliness" he thinks, cannot but remember, and would (re)compose in his "partial moan" (298).

The subject of *Adonais* is human culture, its scope the long vista of recorded history, and its animus an apparently unquenchable faith that when the season for monumentality finally comes round, any surviving trash will be swept into the dust bin while whatever of the truly worthy has weathered the vicissitudes of time will be raised up into a heaven of fame. The climax of the poem is a variation on the theme of spiritual election, and a retelling of the ascent to higher realms that inaugurates Canto II of Dante's *Paradiso* with the advisory to its readers that "O voi che siete in piccioletta barca,/ desiderosi d'ascoltar, sequiti/dietro al mio legno che cantando varca,/tornate a riveder le vostri liti: non vi mettete in pelago" ("You in the small craft, with your eager ears following my vessel as it makes its passage out in song, don't lose sight of the shore, don't risk going too far out" (my translation).) Drawn toward the "Soul of Adonais like a star," the vessel of Shelley's poetry now arrives at a similarly self-distinguishing recognition as it commences leaving the "trembling throng/Whose souls were never to the tempest given" and orienting its course toward the psychopompic "Vesper of our throng," the latter's "inmost" positioning beyond the veil recalling the Jerusalem Temple that harbored the invisibly commanding power of Adonai-Elohim.

Visually inaccessible behind this "inmost veil," the radiant energy of Adonais nonetheless has a powerfully attractive effect on anyone drawn into the sphere of its magnetic force. In the manner of a guiding star and with the attractive action of a planetary force, this "Soul of Adonais" draws the voyager onward in his consuming thirst for the "Light whose smile kindles the universe":

> Burning through the inmost veil of Heaven,
> The soul of Adonais, like a star,
> Beacons from the abode where the Eternal are. (493–5)

In the terms of an established Shelleyan iconography of the heavens and the earth, this veil stands for the daytime blue of the earth's atmosphere blocking out the stars.[45] But perhaps even more to the point than this meteorological picture is the image of the apocalyptically rent temple veil, and in particular the strikingly revelatory and spargasmatic moment, when (as the tenth chapter of *Hebrews* glosses it) the expiration of Jesus brought on an outpouring of the spirit from his crucified flesh such that his followers might "enter into the holiest of the temple by the blood of Jesus ... through the veil, that is to say, his flesh."

This veil-piercing, flesh-consuming drive toward some innermost holy of holies models a characteristic Shelleyan climax, where skies previously imagined as a veil are "riven" so that the "last clouds of cold mortality" may be consumed by "the fire for which all thirst" (491, 485–6). In giving this rich and multilayered complex of imagery a much needed linguistic turn, Peter Sacks has persuasively argued that the "last clouds" of cold mortality figure the poem's own medium of language, and that consequently the poem's drive beyond this "interposition"[46] of a necessarily veiling language is caught in the act of pursuing an "antitextual flight,"[47] whose objective is an apocalyptic rending of the very fabric of language on which its own possibilities of expression depend. Beyond the veil in Jerusalem's holy of holies there is placed what its builders thought of as the deep, imageless and unnamable truth. Here in Shelley's secularizing address to a similarly omnipotent unnamable, what burns beyond the veil is a stellar "fire," for which all are said to "thirst" in direct proportion to how, in both reflection and bearing, they allow themselves to become the ardent mirrors of this fire in whose beginning they would find their consuming end.

This certainly seems to have left the great cloud of (unknowing) words behind. But instead of seeing *Adonais* as thus singularly driven to the renunciation of words, I would propose that because *Adonais* is a constitution of words drawn so finally but aporetically toward the fire that is driving it on to its own verbal construction, it may be just as accurately described as a work of art in flight *toward* rather than away from its textual condition(s). To Cavell, as we have seen, the thinking with and through every word is "at its most complete, as it were—a partial act" (*CH*, 42), and the most composed or considered of our words will be inclined toward bringing this "partiality" up to the light, inclined toward revealing their incentive to being so formed and let out into the breath of the culture. Where Cavell positions *partiality*, *Adonais* descries a "fire for which all thirst," and around that originary navel of incentive there should come to mind the recurrent Shelleyan picture—radiantly prominent in the "Life of Life" lyric in *Prometheus Unbound* III—which has a burning fountain, called the "Life of Life," sequestered beyond the veil (of Life) but also "transfusing" a sense of itself *through* and, as it were, *in* or *on* the screen of that veil. On this view of what words are and what they are for, it is through the literal evidence of its own construction(s) that *Adonais* projects and, as it were, embodies its drive toward the highly articulated expression that it is on its way toward becoming. The words through which *Adonais* constitutes itself announce that in their beginning of passion-parted lips is their end of a consuming fire of the mind, but this same tightly composed verbal fabric also underscores that it and its kind can alone mark out the path toward what, in the nature of things, will only be a Pisgah or an aporetic view of what is drawing the poem's only begetter on to this highly wrought performance of artistic witness.

The rub or (Shelleyan) clog, however, is that precisely because we (and Shelley) are ineluctably dealing in a language of our own making, we are constitutionally unable to repress the thought that, be it fancy or be it plain, this or any other possible fabric of our language can be little more than an elaborately imposed fabrication. Enter again Stanley Cavell's late arriving epiphany that "the drift toward [this specifically linguistic] skepticism is the *discovery* of the everyday, a discovery of exactly *what* it is that skepticism would deny" (*IQ*, 70, Cavell's emphases): that is, the thought-creating speech which is the measure of the universe; or (in Cavell's more, as it were, self-centered expression) "that your expressions in fact express you, that they are yours, that you are in them. . . . [that] your body, and the body of your expressions [are] you, you on earth, all there will ever *be* of you" (*CR*, 383, Cavell's emphasis). Explicitly acknowledged and problematized in Shelley's prose, this radical mistrust of our words persistently cuts through the ineluctably verbal texture of his poetry. *Adonais*, for example, unburdens itself of a deeply ingrained linguistic skepticism when immediately before its veil-rending conclusion it laments that the things, culminating in "statues, music, words," which it has been taking up and composing "are weak/The glory they transfuse with fitting truth to speak" (467–8). And *Epipsychidion* strikes a similar note when, turning on its own winged words and endeavoring to "pierce/Into the height of love's rare Universe," it calls them "chains of lead around [the soul's] flight of fire." Both of these expressions of linguistic skepticism hold close to climactic place in their respective verbal performances, and both clearly seem to imagine that our words are not up to the tasks they assign themselves. But as an alternative to this now thoroughly conventional wisdom about the inadequacy of our words, I would again invoke the picture of language (including a picture of its inadequacy) which Thoreau offers in the final run of writerly self-reflection he penned for the concluding chapter of *Walden*: "The volatile truth of our words should continually betray the inadequacy of the residual statement. Their truth is instantly *translated*; its literal monument alone remains" (*Walden*, 217, Thoreau's emphasis). Despite the deprecating language of "residual statement" and "literal monument," these two sentences clearly and explicitly attribute "truth" to our words. Whatever the nature of this truth may turn out to be, it is "encoded" in our words. In a darker idiom, it is there "impounded" or "sepulchred." Being "volatile," however, this impounded truth can and will be spirited away beyond any casing it might for the moment find itself lodged in. It is its fate to be always, in Thoreau's underscored word, *translated*. For a language to *be* a language, it has to be circulated and *borne* (the radical sense of *fero, ferre, tuli, latus*) back and forth among its users. Even as the life's breath of our words transpires into articulate expression, it is always already in transit beyond itself. The fate of our every word is what Shakespeare saw as that of jokes. They thrive only in the ear of the hearer (*Love's Labor's Lost*, V.ii.844). In his *Defence of Poetry*, Shelley's earnestly serious variation on this is that the latter (but not premeditated) end of a poet-nightingale's singing in darkness "to cheer his own solitude" may be to touch the "enchanted chord" in an auditor and there to strike up and "reanimate . . . the cold, the sleeping, the buried image" (*NS*, 532). For Shelley as for Thoreau, then, the volatile truth of our words is to be found in their calling out of what, if allowed transit to the "caves of the spirit" of our others, will re-sound from some deep but previously muted chord of that other's own constitution. What Shelley offers to and requires of any soul he finds himself in conversation with is not instruction. It is, as Emerson so trenchantly puts it, provocation.

Thoreau's account of our life with and in language can admit the deprecating characterization of our written words as "residual statement"—not to mention the astringent exactitude of "literal monument"—because, by the lights and bearings of this account, the composition of our words is not saddled with the impossible task of making their volatile truth stay put at one permanent residence or in one fixed formula. Instead, the truth with which our words are fraught is designed to be instantly translated when and as it draws out a second (and seconding) flame at another responsively struck subject-position in our human and talking form of life. Beginning in intuitions of what counts or matters for us and driven toward a recounting of these (call them (as *Adonais* calls them) desires, adorations and persuasions), our constitutions of words do in one sense leave their animating drives behind them. In the most successful deeds of writing, inspiration is indeed on its way toward transforming itself into (only) a literal monument. But in another sense, these constitutions of words are pitched toward the happy return of their animating desires. In the radical sense of guardians or stewards, they act as preserving "tuitions" of what they have been charged with. Through the achieved steps of their word-by-word expression, they call out to such readers as might find themselves in the character of this writing, readers like Shelley reading Dante's words and finding himself becoming the "conductor" of the "lightning" and "spirit" with which these "burning atoms of inextinguishable thought" remain "instinct" and "pregnant" even as they "lie covered in the ashes of their birth" (*NS*, 528).

Thoreau's picture of language accounts for the breathless and fiery self-consumptions of the verbal medium at the end of both *Epipsychidion* and

Adonais, but it does so in a way that retains the value and the necessity of casting words together in a fashion as scrupulously exact as Shelley strove to make the writing ventures of his Italian period. So much depends on the literal monument. To it is consigned the charge and chance of receiving, preserving and propagating the vital air and breath of our shared condition. The best in this kind are, indeed, but shadows and things of air. But if one patiently lets the character of this perfectionist writing read one, one might eventually discover and appreciate the "hands of perfect skill" (*NS*, 479) that Shelley imagined his Miranda bringing to her guitar so as to make its otherwise mute wood sing out so finely and attractively. Just as (writes Thoreau) "the finest qualities of our nature, like the bloom of fruits, can be preserved only by the most delicate handling" (*Walden*, 3), just so the excellences of our "next self" can come to no due sphericity of fruition in hands that have not been sensitively receptive to such neighboring and "living winds" of light as within which they might find their own most telling measure, voice and self.

Thoreau's metaphorically packed thought about (it bears emphasizing) an *ideal* of human expression is uncannily similar to Shelley's more prosaically expressed sense of τὸ ποιεῖν as engaged in an unending dialectic between the spirit of our forms and those forms in which the one spirit's plastic stress strives to preserve for the adverting mind some trace of its consuming incentive to just such a performance (*NS*, 207). The performance of τὸ ποιεῖν, which we call *Adonais*, sets out to inscribe yet one more literal monument to what its author would asymptotically approach as "the secret strength of things/Which governs thought and to the infinite dome/Of heaven is as a law" (*Mont Blanc*, 139–41). Internal to such acts of inscription is a trusting abandonment of oneself to whatever "volatile truth of our words" prompted them into their standing as the literally preserving monuments they have become. By this account of our life with and in language, the volatile forces at work in the best of our "residual" words are such that, drawn on by their "volatile truth, we talkers, readers and writers of these words endlessly take after them and are just as endlessly left with them, we in their keeping and they in ours.

The perfectionist constitution of our words—called by Shelley τὸ ποιεῖν— is not the screening and imprisoning impediment of our (debased) language as usual. On the contrary, it is in one called-for instance after another a performing of the human, understood as a clearance, transit or ferry (i.e. πόρος) onward to what one has it at heart to say in a releasing and offering of one's own breath made words as perhaps, at the last, the sounding out of where others of one's kind may find themselves. Like Thoreau, a Shelley, praised by Wordsworth as the best of poets in "workmanship of style,"[48] does not merely grant that the volatile force of our words does not *reside* in the residual statement. He insists on it. He insists that the way such volatile reagents as a writer's "Desires and Adorations,/[and]Winged Persuasions" (109–10) settle down into words on the page will and should continually "*betray*" the inadequacy of these articulated forms. It is, as it were, internal to the self-surpassing nature of the words that we share with one another in literary art that their volatile truth is, all along and *de ovo*, meant to be spirited away into literal monuments, and at the extremes of an axiomatic Eternity of the spirit, to be "lifted up" (Thoreau immediately goes on to say) "like fragrant and significant . . . frankincense to superior natures" (*Walden*, 217): superior natures cast not in the self-abasing image of our conventionally distanced deities, but in the human image divine of our own "next self."

To summarize: Shelley conceives *Epipsychidion*'s tower of art and delight as a recurrently self-(re)constructing "wreck of human art," which will always be refashioning itself and its tuitions in obedience to whatever, in the present moment of our experience and our culture, compellingly finds its way into its impressionable precincts. This interplay between the provocations of the present moment and what Yeats will call monuments of unaging intellect is the main business of *Adonais*. Closer to home and as strikingly set forth in the poem's self-portrait, this pastoral elegy is about nothing so much as the hope and possibility of its author's staying the course of being responsively present to his own life and calling, and by precisely that route staying in quest of being "gathered to the kings of thought/Who waged contention with their time's decay/And are of the past all that cannot pass away." The "plastic stress" of art which *Adonais* both sings and executes would, by its own responsive and shaping words, contend with its time's decay so as to spring an arch out beyond a corrupt and broken world and toward (in its own final phrase and destination) the "Abode where the Eternal are."

Flame transformed to marble

The "plastic stress" of *Adonais* comes to full term and flower in the poem's final approach toward the pyramid of Gaius Cestius, dominating the Protestant Cemetery in Rome. By the time the poem's speaker has arrived at this imperial monument, he has assumed the role of a passionately discriminating cicerone of noteworthy human work, and in that spirit and with the memorializing pyramid in immediate prospect, he urges his readers to allow the "Spirit of the spot" (438) to lead them on through this simultaneous *paradise, grave, city* and *wilderness* until their "footsteps" come to "a slope of green access/ Where, like an infant's smile, over the dead/A light of laughing flowers along the grass is spread" (439–41). The strategically chosen wording of this remarkably sunny graveyard poetry reprises such master-tones of the poem as a (leading) *spirit*, a (beguiling) *light*, and the (attractively) *spreading* effluence of flowers, even as (along with the subsequent stanza) it gives sweetly sad expression to Shelley's grief for his young son here laid to rest. In asking its readers to "pass" (438) over this place where one of its author's most intimate hopes and attachments has "gone before" (470), the poem is counseling them to take the necessary steps along what is not only a valley of dry bones but also a gently rising "slope of green access." For after this gradual ascent along the green earth, the time for apocalypse is evidently at hand when this flowering embankment so happily fitted to human steps and condition abruptly gives way to a vaulting pyramid whose kenning as "flame transformed to marble" converts the false etymology of *pyramid* (supposedly from the πύρ at the root of a funeral pyre)[49] into some true poetry about whatever might be meant by a monument or tongue of fire. The guiding and gathering progress of this pastoral elegy traces a *via negativa* through this funereal body of death so that at the genre's conventional turn toward consolation, it may suddenly become apocalyptic in pitch and direction, a turn whose point about the flame of desire is made even sharper by its contrast with the way the cemetery's "grey walls moulder around" as "dull Time/Feeds" on them "like slow fire upon a hoary brand" (442-3). For while this low-grade process of oxidation—what Robert Frost caught as life's "slow, smokeless burning of decay"— here gnaws at the edges of mortal things and acknowledges our situatedness in a "camp of death" (449), it also effectively foils and, in more than one sense, "sets off" the monumentally upward thrust of fire that Shelley's poetry makes visually dominate all the realities, dreams and polarities of the Eternal City that he makes both a city and a grave, both a wilderness and a paradise.

    Led by this cicerone of the spirit, the reader of *Adonais* arrives at a point in the poem's progress, which is spatially the center of its spiritual dig into this Roman site and temporally its climactic arrival at the last seen (as opposed to speculated or desired) object of its Roman pilgrimage. The poem takes on an obscure Roman potentate's bid for pharaonic immortality and with a poet's license and the plastic stress of its spirit stretched to the top of its bent, it "makes" the stones of the self-aggrandizing monument of this "keen pyramid" over into its own "wedge sublime" of *pyr*-fire zealously athirst for a correspondingly aflame em*pyr*ean, that has accrued all the value and force of Dante's final good and *summum bonum*. Here, fire does not creep and skulk its way toward general dissolution. On the contrary, it forcefully springs upward along its natural orientation *ad astra*. In a word, it is unbound into an exit or exodus of desire.

    This flame/pyramid rushes up toward the empyrean with the intensely narrowing thrust and point of a shaft of thought that is itself about the fervent incentive to such thoughts as commence in a fire of the mind and will seek expression in an incisive monument of writing. If a slowly mortifying combustion wears away the walled perimeter of this camp of death, further on into its mysteries of corruption one comes upon—and is implicitly bid to follow—a "wedge sublime" of fire, which, although circumscribed and conditioned by the slow fire of dull Time, will always be dialectically sparked into the kind of "quickening life" (164) out to hone itself into a penetrating expression for the pent-up force of its own most consuming desires. This sharply tapering and ardently aspiring figure springs from about as *"altus"* (i.e. both deep and exalted) a place in Shelley's imagination as one can imagine. Its dynamically rendered "wedge sublime" clearly recalls two closely related perennials in the garden of Shelley's poetry: *first*, the pyramid (or more often the *cone*) of night, as when in the last act of *Prometheus Unbound* a transfigured Earth finds himself "spin[ning] beneath my pyramid of night/ Which points into the Heavens dreaming delight" (IV, 444–5), and *second* (and not unrelated), the morning star's fadeout along the ascendant path of the nocturnal cone in which this star's "intense lamp" is seen "narrow[ing]/ In the white dawn clear" ("To A Sky-Lark," 23-4) and thus articulating the gravity well of its rushing path toward the third sphere of Venus, the same path onto which the closing Vesper of *Adonais* beckons its speaker.[50]

Rounding out *Adonais*'s appropriation of the Pentecostal tongue of fire is its equally spirited deployment of such images as the breath of our being or the wind in our sails. At the poem's climax, its speaker would face into the "breath whose might I have invoked in song" (487) and boldly claim that in now descending on him, this powerful breath is drawing him on and up. Where like a "low wind [whistling] near ... Adonais calls," there this wanderer over earth's "rugged ways" (278) of desire would betake himself and his "spirit's bark" (279). On the strength of this favoring wind, he would ascend into "Realms where the air we breathe is Love" (*Prometheus Unbound*, II.v.95), knowing all the while that the endlessly expanding circumference for this attractively enamored field of air must continuously replenish itself by reiterated delvings into what Shelley's poetry variously calls the "breathing earth," or the "central heart" of this world of *me*, or "the *yes* the heart breathes," or "the wells/Which boil under our being's inmost cells,/The fountains of our deepest life" (568-9).

Adonais may seem more set on leaving behind the deepest and most fiercely burning well-springs of our earthly life than the *Epipsychidion* from which I have just quoted. While, at day's close, *Epipsychidion* withdraws into the consuming passion of the lovers' cave, the pastoral elegy concludes its expected transit toward consolation with an apocalyptic ascent toward a new heaven but perhaps not a new earth. It still seems to me, however, that some readers of *Adonais*—most notably and influentially Earl Wasserman—have imposed on *Adonais* too sharp a dividing line between the motions of chthonic vitality and those of a heavenly enduring spirit. The "flame transformed to marble" of the pyramid does not come out of nowhere. It is provoked by what its author finds in the world before him in such commonly recurring but uncommonly imagined and worded events as "the green lizard and the golden snake" leaping toward the newly attractive heat of the vernal sun "like unimprisoned flames out of their trance awak[ing]" (161–2). More to the point, the similarly bursting and vaulting "wedge sublime" of the pyramid has all along been gestating in a poem out of whose lines it finally breaches into its ascendant majesty, and the last thoroughly natural and mortal preparation for the launching of this "flame transformed to marble" is the flowery incline of the cemetery leading up to it both topographically and textually. This gently pitched slope of a newly flowering plane of "green access" still paints a picture of our human life as a camp of death, but a picture now so transfigured that it can make (preeminent) space and give (climactic) time for that life's inclination toward the endless renewal that comes of being "pitched in Heaven's smile" (449). By the lights of this transfigured scene, we creatures of a day can further acknowledge that on the gravity-conditioned way of our sojourning, we have also found ourselves to be drawn toward the bright pavilion of "Heaven's smile," drawn to it by the same translating instinct of "life's sacred thirst" as will quite "naturally" draw our steps toward the "light of laughing flowers" so invitingly spread out along the gradient of the cemetery ground "like an infant's smile over the dead."

Since *Adonais* has been authoritatively judged to be coldly mannered and pompous, it would be well to remind ourselves not only that the poem makes the pomp of its climactic Roman pyramid originate in flame but also that fire burns throughout its entire frame. The pyramid's monumentality signals the lapidary finish the elegy clearly aims at, and that quality undoubtedly contributes to a common suspicion that this highly wrought work of art might be too polished, too anemically civilized and devoid of life. But at the other pole of the transfiguring transit from flame to marble, the fire of desire claims its both primordial and climactic place in the story. For fire is quite literally to be found everywhere in this poem: in its title character's explicitly announced Alpha and Omega in a "burning fountain" (339); in its partiality for the language of "kindling" as in the "kindling buds" (137) of spring or in the play of Adonais's imagination "from kindling brain to brain" (78); in its inaugural emphasis on the "frost" (3) that binds the dear head of Adonais, chills the "enamoured breath" (15) of his voice and draws from "their burning bed/[the] fiery tears" of his mother (21–2); in an ending that has the soul of Adonais "burning" like a star, this an ending to the reading of which, furthermore, one is asked to bring the full thermal force and energy of the immediately preceding stanza's skillfully overdetermined pyrotechnics where we are referred to a "light whose smile kindles the universe," where the benediction in the curse of life is something never to be "quenched" (therefore a thirst or fire ever burning), where the habit of being for *all* things great and small is to "burn" as each may mirror a "fire" for which they all "thirst," and in whose "beams" they are each and all "consumed."

Fire also burns through the Shelleyan self-portrait, the poem's most extended and concentrated exploration of poetic creation and reception. There is no deficit of implicit "banked" fires in this figure's initial designation as a "pard-like" spirit, and some quite explicit fire in the "killing sun smil[ing] brightly" on his cheek where "the life can burn in blood, even while the heart may break" (288). But, beyond these local reserves and outbreaks of fire, the self-portrait's major and encompassing way of presenting the thermodynamics of creation and reception is its already mentioned identification with the figure of Dionysos and his attendant Maenads. As Marcel Détienne has exhaustively demonstrated, Bacchus in his cups and Dionysos spurting life-spilling and life-seeding blood are two names for the one divinely "vital humor" of "liquid fire" to be found in both blood and wine.[51] As detailed by Détienne, the primordial force of this still unextinguished burning fountain of a deity finds its human home in the "internal maenad" of the "heart muscle," as it spontaneously keeps "leaping within"[52] and announcing itself as a "power that draws from itself and by itself to liberate its energy, suddenly with volcanic violence."[53] In the self-portrait of *Adonais*, Shelley's abiding sense of the titanically or Prometheanly expressive function of poetry finds a similarly everyday grounding in the "ever-beating heart" (294), that central organ of the human body previously elevated by *Prometheus Unbound* to the "awful throne of patient power/In the wise heart [from which Love springs]" (IV.557–60).

Shelley makes Dionysos the god he follows and into whose mysteries he would initiate himself, because this godhead, circulating in the likeness of the secret strength of things and bearing "the breath and blood of distant lands" ("Mont Blanc," 124) is so committed to an endless reception that (as Détienne reports) it required a temple memorializing one of its appearances to be every year stripped of its roof and so laid bare to the "ciel ouvert."[54] As already emphasized, the same yes-breathing desire to let the atmosphere one finds oneself in unleash both its worst and its best against one is the breath of Shelley's being as a writer who, in his prose, reported standing in rapt admiration before the "upaithric" (*Letters*, I.73) temples of Magna Graecia, and, in his poetry, repeatedly constructed such self-reflexive edifications of words as the tower of *Epipsychidion*, open to all weathers but, from first to last, "built for delight" and so "looking toward the golden Eastern air,/And level with the living winds." [55]

Behind Shelley's picture of himself as a fellow poet in mourning for Adonais and bearing the thyrsus as a pledge of that mourning, there, of course, lies the self-fashioning hand at work on just this self-representation. That hand could all too easily be pictured as but the receiving end of a transmission of "patient power" from Dionysos to a modern poet out to load every rift of his personal experience with the ratifying ore of Greek myth. But such a picture would be too one-sidedly mechanical. For, as Wittgenstein writes of words on a page, so with a cultural symbol like the Dionysian thyrsus. By itself, it is dead. To become again alive, it needs to be animated by the breath and blood of one's own experience. Any human hand that finds itself in reception of Dionysos's thyrsus-tipped lance is, by that very handing down, called on to master that lance, called on (one might say with Shelley) to become the conductor of that particular "burning atom of inextinguishable thought" called *Dionysos* as it comes to him and us "covered in the ashes of its birth" but still "pregnant with lightning." In short, the self-portrait's rod and staff of trembling responsiveness "vibrates" both to the thrum of this canonically ecstatic God and to the pulse of "the ever-beating heart" shaking "the weak hand that grasps it."

Such a collapsing into one another of the receiving and the mastering hand recalls the attention both the *Defence* and *Prometheus Unbound* pay to an endlessly reforming network of responsiveness and responsibility, in which cultural reception and cultural handiwork constitute the two polarities of a fully human way of being in the world. At the creative center of what the *Defence* pictures as a recurrently (re)formative event of poetic circulation and interchange, it positions a power of poetry capable of being struck by an intuition of Intellectual Beauty, and then further capable of "arresting" that intuition by "[veiling] it in language or in form" (*NS*, 532). What his future readers will still have available to them of Adonais are those arresting accounts of his that, line by line, constitute the monument of his writing. "The dead *live* there," but also just *there* the dead live. So, while all human flesh must trace the path of "dust to the dust," a writer of this stellar quality will become a star-like "splendor" of "lofty thought" in the firmament of time.

Like *smile, splendor* is a master-tone of Shelley's Italian period. Inherited from Dante, the term conceives of the refulgently achieved work of art as condensing or even (further) crystallizing the breath of our experience into radiant gists of representation, like the "'young dawn" of daylight (364) commissioned to "turn all thy dew to splendor." In *Adonais*, the first appearance of "Splendor" has one of Adonais's personified Splendours alighting on the dead poet's mouth and desperately applying a "caress upon his icy lips" (105) so as to kiss back into breathing life "that mouth, whence it [i.e. the Splendor] was wont to draw the breath/Which gave it strength to pierce the guarded wit,/And pass into the panting heart beneath/ With lightning and with music" (101–5). But this necrophiliac effort at mouth-to mouth resuscitation is instantly chilled into ineffectuality by the "icy lips" of its object, its futile bid for a literal resurrection of Adonais serving to intensify and focus the immediately prior dumb-show of despair, when all the "quick dreams" and other attendant spirits that gathered around Adonais neither kindled nor freely wandered, but instead drooped "round the cold heart" at which they could no longer either "gather strength or find a home again." This individually featured Splendor not only focuses the grief felt by all its fellows for the passing of the spirit that (literally) made them what they are. It also transforms that grief into the twinned affirmations of this writer's enduring voice and of his readers' posthumous draw toward the hearing and resounding of that valuable voice now left in their keeping.

Now that Keats has come to the end of his life, no further splendors of his writing can be expected to draw on the poet's enamored breath. But while the originating source of the poet's attained textual Splendors may be thus spent, that source or incentive remains preserved in what has become of it in a *Dichtung* resplendent with all that has been so densely gathered into its stay and keep. Like the (poetic) flowers troped into "incarnations of the stars when splendour/Is changed to fragrance" (174–5), these surviving Splendors of Keats' poetic labor must now be cultivated for their sweetly attractive savor and fragrance. The young English poet lodged with Death under the vault of the blue Italian sky has become a corpse, but what his English-speaking survivors will increasingly call "Keats" is a literally accomplished corpus that will be capable of coming to new life, but only in the "kindling brain" of its readers. That the inanimate body of Keats can never be restored to "the vital air" (26) is just the "law of mortal change," legible to Shelley since at least his writing of "Mont Blanc." But if the spirit in which the poetic corpus of this writer was framed is still to be found at animating play in the body of Keats's work, then perhaps one reason we cannot dream of *restoring* John Keats to the "vital air" is that he has *become* the vital air of the Desires and Adorations that breathed his poems into the variously expressive forms there right next to or before us.

In "The Poet," Emerson writes that "all language is vehicular and transitive, and is good, as ferries and horses are, for conveyance, not as farms and houses are for homestead" (*EL*, 463). What, from the moment of its conception, a Keatsian Splendor is charged with conveying is Keats's vital breath. Because this vital breath still lives on in Keats' poems, his spirit can, like Milton's, become a "clear Sprite [that]/Yet reigns on high" (35–6). Or, as is said directly of the "lofty thought" of *all* "the splendors of the firmament of time" (388): "the dead live there/And move like winds of light on dark and stormy air" (395–6). The regicide but reigning spirit of Milton is, in addition, named "the Sire of an immortal strain" (30). In one sense, this *strain* speaks of a musical air, in another of a breed or lineage. Put these two senses together, and you arrive at an illustrious genealogy of song, inscription into whose bloodlines *Adonais* would claim as the just deserts of a poet who devoted his work to a loveliness which he made more lovely. Keats has performed so well in this line, the poem claims, that precisely as he now "lies sepulchred in monumental thought," he must (to continue quoting *Hellas*'s way of putting it) be "ascribed to your bright senate," must be accepted as among the "progenitors of all that yet is great" (*Hellas*, 420–2).

That Keats "bought, with price of purest breath,/A grave among the eternal" (57–8) is *Adonais*'s early and deftly veiled intimation of his fated ascent to the "abode where the eternal are." This casual and economically turned reference to how for Keats the wages of pure breath were eternal life comes immediately after the stanza on Milton, where in one breath, as it were, this exemplary hero of both English poetry and the English commonwealth is named both an authoring parent and a son of light. The immediate implication for Milton is that this representatively great and enduring poet is now recognized as the sire of an immortal strain precisely because he allowed himself to become a son of light. The further implication for the entirety of the poem is that the correlates of an authoring paternity and the obediently listening filiation of a "nursling" of song (47) are here figuring the acts of writing and reading, as these in turn stand for the economies of cultural generativity and cultural inheritance, for the daily circulation of a culture's work that, lest it die or lapse terminally into a dead letter, must always be both receiving and rendering, with every laborer in the vineyard called on to become "the other to one's self, calling upon it with the words of others."

Adonais's pyramidal wedge of "flame transformed to marble" is the "beautiful idealism" of a quasi-scriptural writing or poetry congenitally on fire to arrest into recuperative form its own driving incentive. Although the incentive behind "Keats" or any other writer understood as a corpus of words is sealed into the inadequacy of a residual statement, the remains of this literal monument to a spiritual incentive can nonetheless be recurrently unsealed by such readers as can allow themselves to be read by these splendidly attractive structures of air. They can endlessly be unbound by such readers as, by the incantation of this verse, would let its volatile truth touch the enchanted chord, and so (as in the over-quoted but under-read figure of the fading coal) let the dearest deep-down things of one's desire and sore need flame out in correspondent acts of self-recognition and self-articulation.

Ever still burning, yet ever inconsumable

Fire plays a more prominent role in *Epipsychidion*, than in *Adonais*. It speaker climactically looks forward to how he and his love

> shall become the same, we shall be one
> Spirit within two frames, oh! wherefore two?
> One passion in twin-hearts, which grows and grew,
> 'Till like two meteors of expanding flame,
> Those spheres instinct with it become the same,
> Touch, mingle, are transfigured; ever still
> Burning, yet ever inconsumable:
> In one another's substances finding food,
> Like flames too pure and light and unimbued
> To nourish their bright lives with baser prey,
> Which point to Heaven and cannot pass away: (573–83)

The bonding flame on which these lines close is clearly sexual, but like the flame of "Love" that in Shelley's account of the *Commedia* led Dante "[serene] from the lowest depths of Hell/Through every Paradise and through all glory" (*The Triumph of Life*, 472–4), it is just as clearly aspiring toward becoming, like the pyramid of *Adonais*, a "wedge sublime" of fire that would indeed be about the business of subliming itself into the "heaven" of its ardent aspiration. Furthermore, these flames' capacity to be "ever still/Burning, yet ever inconsumable" more than hints at a significance and ontological staying power like what Moses found pulsing around the sacred ground of the burning bush.

Epipsychidion's breathless anticipation of these consuming flames, themselves inconsumable, marks the climax, soon to fall, of what a typical and remarkably pedestrian day spent in this favored place would be like now that indeed "The day is come and thou wilt fly with me" (388) to a walker's paradise that plays itself out according to the signature Shelley rhythm of the systole and diastole of an "ever-beating heart." A first, diastolic, movement of the lovers' daily ramble has them "wandering" out "under the roof of blue Ionian weather" and extending their "possessing and possessed" attention to the furthest reaches of this new world in which they so happily find themselves:

> We two will rise, and sit, and walk together,
> Under the roof of blue Ionian weather,
> And wander in the meadows, or ascend
> The mossy mountains, where the blue heavens bend

> With lightest winds, to touch their paramour;
> Or linger, where the pebble-paven shore,
> Under the quick, faint kisses of the sea
> Trembles and sparkles as with ecstasy,—
> Possessing and possessed by all that is
> Within that calm circumference of bliss. (541–50)

This "circumference of bliss" is fleshed out along both the vertical and the horizontal axis. As already noted, the horizontal is continually suffused and reconstituted in the ecstatically redundant kisses and ecstasies of shore and sea, while along the plumb-line of the vertical the blue heavens bend "with lightest winds, to touch their paramour" of earth. After this dilation to both the heavenly and the oceanic perimeters of their island-home of heart's desire, the course of the verse turns inward to an "old cavern hoar," which even at the island's high noon and "roof of blue Ionian weather" seems "yet to keep/ The moonlight of the expired night asleep" (553–4). Like the cave of Asia and Prometheus's restoration to each other in the third act of *Prometheus Unbound*, this cavern—so strikingly opposite to the cold "chaste, cold bed" (239) of Shelley's former incarnation of an anesthetized Endymion—is the burning heart and *thalamos* of the flowering island that *Epipsychidion* is in the process of imagining not only into the bloom of its "sound, and odour, and beam" (*Sensitive Plant*, 93) but also, and climactically, into its root. Being the origin of the poem's imagined world, this cavern is also the scene of its Cavellian *exit*, into "the intense, the deep, the imperishable/Not mine but me" (391–2) of the desire drawn toward this "delicious island," in whose own central "heart" there burns "like a buried lamp, a Soul/... An atom of th' Eternal, whose own smile/Unfolds itself" (477–80) into just this circumference of perfectionist bliss.

Having arrived at his anticipation of the cavern/*thalamos*, the poem's speaker gives what again turns out to be conspicuously inadequate expression to what he as a poet and a "world of love" would most pressingly speak of as both the end of his and his love's daily walk and their beginning or primal scene. There, he says

> we will talk until thought's melody
> Become too sweet for utterance, and it die
> In words to live again in looks, which dart
> With thrilling tone into the voiceless heart,
> Harmonizing silence without a sound.
> Our breath shall intermix, our bosoms bound,
> And our veins beat together; and our lips

> With other eloquence than words, eclipse
> The soul that burns between them, and the wells
> Which boil under our being's inmost cells,
> The fountains of our deepest life, shall be
> Confused in passion's golden purity,
> As mountain-springs under the morning Sun. (560–73)

With a climactic emphasis on the vertical axis arising from deep within this circumference of bliss, the speaker muses ecstatically on what he would have become his and his love's endless returns to the silently intense mysteries of delight and generation taking place in a *thalamos* whose most immediate progeny is their transport to an ever-renewed golden age of themselves as they become "confused in passion's golden purity/As mountain-springs under the morning Sun."

Epipsychidion's understanding of itself as a spiritual epithalamion out to give liberating expression to the incentive behind its own poetic construction of things dictates how at its end it must return to the inchoate womb of just these words in just this order. To be sure, the metaphoric vehicle here is an imagined or anticipated erotic union quickly progressing beyond a meet and happy conversation into its sexual expression. But if this poem is "essentially about the role of poetry as the most appropriate object of human desires" (*NS*, 391)—a claim about its motives that Cavell more or less makes for the whole of English romanticism—then the vastly more far-ranging tenor of this metaphor is the poet "singing of what he loves in dream" (*Prometheus Unbound*, IV.268) as he here approaches (and only in thought approaches) the incentive toward the constitution of writing we call *Epipsychidion*, an incentive to language that in Shelley's considered judgment no less than Cavell's, must logically be different in kind from the words in which that incentive finds its expression.

This is not the only place in his poetry where Shelley figures such navels or *thalamoi* of the fundamentally poetic language with which the ζοὸν ἔχον λόγον strives to make sense of where it finds itself. Nor is the cave the only figure with which he guesses at the "deep [and imageless] truth (*Prometheus Unbound*, II.iv.116) of "life, and the world, or whatever we call that which we are and feel" (*NS*, 505). He also is drawn toward calling it the "burning fountain," or "the *yes* the heart breathes," or the "liquid fire" of the blood that depends for its life-giving circulation on a "heart," which though here become "voiceless," is still (as in Détienne's account of Dionysos) the "muscle" that is the "internal maenad" of the human as it spontaneously keeps "leaping within" and announcing itself as a "power that draws from itself and by itself to liberate its energy, suddenly with [the] volcanic violence"[56] of "an eloquence other than words."

The run of verses anticipating this day-in-the-life of this paradise begins with the "meanwhile" concluding line 540 and rhyming with the "Elysian isle" of the preceding line. Just before this emphatically enjambed turning to the pedestrian joys of this flowering island, the poem projected itself not into the time remaining to the lovers, but further on into a vision of how the joys and delights of this poem will be posthumously received by its future readers. As he and his love will continue to live in these words (the speaker claims) they will become "the over-hanging day/The living *soul* of this Elysian island" (539–40, emphasis added). The lovers' earthly portion will suffer the inevitable when the "years heap/Their withered hours, like leaves, on [their] decay" (536–7), but these words will not so necessarily pass away. On the contrary, because they give expression to the "*yes* the heart breathes," they have a chance of being gathered up into the "Loveliness," in the maintenance of whose attractively vital signs the writer has here borne his part with such breathings of his desire as would make his turn on the *topos* of the flowering island so pulse with the animation of delight that it could, conceivably, become one of those "monuments of things . . . created indeed by one mind, but a mind so powerfully bright" in its perfectionist constitution of words "as to cast a shade of falsehood on the records that are called reality" (*Letters*, I.485).

Implicit in *Epipsychidion*'s hope that it will become both the "living soul" and the monumental tuition of this placeless heaven is the confidence that its vision of the two lovers securely imparadised in one another's arms is to be read and taken to heart as a memorable and animating "calling out" of human desire. This complements the poem's earlier insistence on how, when arrived at their heart's home in the tower, the lovers will settle into it as essentially readers and listeners not only of their own unmediated budget of desire and experience, but also of what, across the firmament of time, other members of the human form of life have made of their portion of human condition and experience. The speaker acknowledges these necessities of listening reception and erudite intertextuality with his enthusiastically itemized anticipation of all the specifically high-cultural appointments that will make his and love's tower over into an adequate venue for what they seek. The speaker assures Emily that to the "fitted-up chambers" of their tower

> I have sent books and music . . . and all
> Those instruments with which high spirits call
> The future from its cradle, and the past
> Out of its grave, and make the present last
> In thoughts and joys which sleep, but cannot die,
> Folded within their own eternity. (519–24)

An earth-sourced and sky-scaling construction of human hands and "high spirits," the tower is an emblem of civilization. And precisely as just such a civilized edification of the mind imagining it, this self-reflexive image for the city of words in which it occurs must represent itself not only as founded on volcanic fire but also as a listening post forever on the *qui vive* to hear both what's in the wind of one's own unexchangeable experience and what more largely is the wind in the sails of our culture's most telling and perduring monuments of unaging intellect.

The tower's finely fitted chambers are the scene and the speaker the impresario of what he looks forward to as an invigorating participation in what Wordsworth called the "one great society on earth:/The noble living and the noble dead" (1805 *Prelude*, 10.968–9). Essential to these "coming attractions" (as movie trailers used to be called) are such instruments of music and letters as will "call" from their graves the spirit of previously achieved forms, and thus, by the same stroke of τὸ ποιεῖν, "call/The future from its cradle." The perfectionist life the speaker here imagines for himself is, in other words, a life drawn toward the reception of what other similarly attuned "high spirits" have found counting for them, and so, in turn, a life drawn toward being the other to oneself, calling upon it with the words of others. Because this is a picture of cultural work sustaining itself by an endlessly recursive circulation of inspiring provocations and achieved tuitions, any one arrogating the right to "call out" and re-mark where we at present find ourselves must first be gifted in hearing the accumulated inheritance of his culture. And so the tower's attentive "hearing" of a select repertory of "books and music" draws out of the tower's celebrant and would-be renovator his thankfully provoked desire that the staying power of his own work in this kind be instanced in this presently unfolding poem as it contrives to make its flowering island of delight "last," not because it holds a winning ticket in the lottery of literary fame but because it bears provokingly expressive witness to "thoughts and joys which sleep but cannot die,/Folded within their own eternity."

Epipsychidion's concluding insistence on the naturalness of a "simple life" pursued in aversion to the "pale drudge Luxury" is designed to evoke the charmingly pristine place written up in even the most sophisticated versions of pastoral. But it is more than that. Juxtaposed with the tower and the highly cultivated pursuits of those planning to make it "[their] home in life" (536), this emphasis on the naturalness of the life there in prospect emphasizes that while this beautiful idealism of a gratified life of desire must be endlessly constructed and cultivated, it is not artificial in any impugning sense of the term. As already suggested by its fiery and chthonic origins "as it were Titanic," this perfectionist vision would be founded on what we desire, it would be turned around the fixed point of our real and sore need. Consequently, all but the poem's last word is reserved for the centrally secluded cavern where the lovers' flames burn companionately to heaven, seemingly exempt from the devouring jaws of time and claiming for themselves the sacredly persistent ground of the burning but unconsumed incentive of and to our human, talking form of life.

Like the transfigured Roman pyramid of *Adonais*, the constitution of writing called *Epipsychidion* would become what the one spirit's stress of *Adonais* makes of the "wedge sublime" of Cestius's pyramid. It would make its mark and enter its claim as "flame transformed to marble," the writer of this testament proposing that precisely this *literal* and thoroughly in-*character* survival of himself and his love bears perduring witness to an ardently attractive vision of himself and the animation of delight driving him. Only after thus settling on the final disposition and bequest of the flowering island to his future readers does the speaker modulate into the "meanwhile" of line 540 that psychopompically conducts those readers into the very heart of this island as, day by day, it raptly pulses its way back and forth between a circumference of delight and an ingathered cave forever bursting into "[flames] that point to Heaven and cannot pass away" (583) as if (drawing on Cavell drawing on Shakespeare's Cleopatra) the true marble constant of our human, talking form of life was an animating "life of life" that is all fire and air.

But the speaker's anticipation of the ego-annihilating communion of the cave is not the poem's last word. That privileged place is reserved for the poet's acknowledgment of his abrupt expulsion from this heaven of his heart's desire:

> Woe is me!
> The winged words on which my soul would pierce
> Into the height of love's rare Universe,
> Are chains of lead around its flight of fire.—
> I pant, I sink, I tremble, I expire! (587–91)

The disappointment with words packed into these concluding words about words is of a piece with the poem's self-reflexive preoccupations, but the lines' obvious disappointment with what it still calls its "winged words" is not the whole story about this writerly *cri de coeur*. In the *Defence* Shelley calls "Poetry and the principle of Self . . . the God and Mammon of the world." Keeping in mind that radical opposition, this poem about poetry now represents its poetically performing self as returning back over the threshold of a life imagined into intensely passionate identification with the beautiful one on whom he has staked the existence of "the world I say of thoughts that worshipped her."

The final word and drag of the self is particularly evident in the very last line, both in its spondaically weighted and four-fold repetition of "I." But while this last line *reports* the final triumph of leaden gravity over winged fire, it itself is not plodding. It is an agitated rush through four highly charged verbs, charged in themselves and charged in sparking attraction to their many cognates scattered throughout the rest of the poem. Word by sputtering word, the line frantically speaks of nothing but loss and want. At a mere ten syllables, "I pant, I sink, I tremble, I expire" pulses with a hectically animated account of losses: the loss of breath, of altitude, of resolution, of life. At the provocation of such poverties, expirations and falls as it cannot evade but must lament, the line enacts its own brand of passionately performative utterance. A ring-composition in miniature, the line is framed by one verb for labored and/or desirous breathing and another for the last life's breath of any animate being as well as for the expiring of a fire or the end of a lease. On a first reading, then, the poem's final "I expire" may be a first-person-singular-present enactment of the visionary speaker's dying back into ordinary life and, for this particular occasion, running out of any more breath made words. But given that the entirety of *Epipsychidion* has been represented as a testament coming from the hand of its already expired author, that final word might, on a second reading, be heard in yet another, but not contradictory, way. It might be heard as a locution analogous to the logical present of Descartes' "I think, therefore I am." It might be heard as the acknowledgment that "I am human, therefore I am mortal, therefore I expire." Heard this way, the last word of the poem becomes a performative taking on of human condition, where giving up the ghost is not just the empirically final but also the spiritually consummate living out of an earthly condition where "life no less than death ... [appears to be] a condition and process of dissevering" (*IQ*, 89) and where the "very image of [human] life expressed in its eternal truth" (*NS*, 515) is that it is internal to this human form of life ἔχον λόγον, that it must spend its life' in order to redeem it, and never so consummately so as in the generously expanding extravagances of an art where "the intense, the deep, the imperishable,/Not mine but me" is allowed to expire into such skillfully articulated witness as, *exempli gratia*, the "literal monument" of *Epipsychidion* or *Adonais*.

Envoy

In making the last line of *Epipsychidion*'s bear such an extravagant weight of experience, I would call into question what I sense is a common suspicion that its final lines are the work of a writer hastily extricating himself from a tangle of story, theme, and eloquence from which he can find no more graceful way of exiting. There is a considerable measure of truth in this, but the implication of hastily conceived and executed writing does not sit well either with the writerly self-consciousness that the ending is acting out or with the immediately subsequent sophistications of an envoy which (it is generally agreed) "restates the central theme of the entire composition" (*NS*, 407). The envoy is "highly wrought" in anyone's book. Here, it is in its entirety:

> Weak Verses, go, kneel at your Sovereign's feet,
> And say:—"We are the masters of thy slave;
> What wouldest thou with us, and ours and thine?"
> Then call your sisters from Oblivion's cave,
> All singing loud: "Love's very pain is sweet,
> But its reward is in the world divine
> Which, if not here, it builds beyond the grave."
> So shall ye live when I am there. Then haste
> Over the hearts of men, until ye meet
> Marina, Vanna, Primus, and the rest,
> And bid them love each other and be blest:
> And leave the troop which errs, and which reproves,
> And come and be my guest,—for I am Love's.

Addressed throughout to the verses of *Epipsychidion*, the envoy begins by commanding these words still vibrating in memory to go to the Court of Love and pledge their unconditional fealty. Though addressed as "weak," these verses—self-described as "flowers of thought"—are nonetheless instructed to announce themselves as the "masters" of the poet who, by this same reckoning, is himself a "slave" of Love. In obedience to this directive, this work of the poet's hand is to solicit an audience at the Court of Love and there ask its sovereign what she would make or have "of us" (verses) and "of ours" (our "maker"), and so most comprehensively and intensely of "thine," that is, of all and anything subjected to *Alma Venus Genetrix*.

Although the composer of these words thus declares himself the abject subject of a Love whose law, it will be remembered, is deemed "coincident with Necessity,"[57] he nonetheless issues a volley of commands to his "master" verses. With a confidently arrogated air of entitlement, he orders them to *go*, to *kneel*, to *say*, to *call*, to *haste*, to *bid*. In short, he represents his life with and in his language as Emerson's "stupendous antagonism" (*EL*, 953) of a subjection to the way things are (called) and a membership in the species ἔχον λόγον and so the inventor of the game. This complexity is not well captured by the one-sided axiom that the language writes the writer. Its necessary interplay of reception and taking steps word by word better answers to Emerson's maxim that "he who has more obedience masters me," a paradoxical aphorism unpacked by Cavell into the conviction of ordinary language philosophy that the fact of (having) a language is such that the more one obediently listens to its circulating values and forces the more one attains to their resounding mastery.

For the slave of these verses—who is also their summoner and commissioner—finally to sign off on them (to *subscribe* to them) as "Love's guest" affirms that the "not mine, but me" of the "boiling" well "under our being's inmost cells" (569–70) is that driving portion of him wholly given to Love and unstintingly attendant on it. Not surprisingly, then, this guest of Love is the writerly equivalent of the lovers in *Epipsychidion*. They are "possessing and possessed by all that is/Within that calm circumference of bliss"; he is so possessed by the daemon of his master-theme that he must seek to make it his own in a discourse of desire (enacting a desire of discourse) that would make it and its prerogative "be manifest and be obeyed" (*TN*, 45).

And the desire of which this writer would sing so authoritatively has a history, one invoked in the envoy's further charge to the verses of *Epipsychidion* that in their approach to Love's Court they call from "Oblivion's cave" their "sister" precursors in that line of poetry where "Love became a religion" and its votaries celebrators in song of "the dominion of love (*NS*, 525, 526). Recalling the intertextual play of the tower's "instruments," with which "high spirits" are wont to "call/. . . the past/Out of its grave, and make the present last/In thoughts and joys which sleep, but cannot die" (*Epipsychidion*, 520–3), this rallying of the poem's similarly attuned spirits is instructing it on how most accurately and persuasively to represent itself to the Court of Love. It is to identify itself as constituting yet one more authoritative announcement that, beyond the mystery of the "very pain of love [being] sweet," the reward of any pen dedicating itself to its service in "votive tears and symbol flowers" (*Hellas*, 1095) is a staying power in "the world divine," which "if not here, it [Love] builds beyond the grave."

And this love and its religion also has a future. For after its urging of all the preceding remarkings and tuitions of love starring the firmament of time, the envoy's concluding six lines proleptically affirm that when their writer is in his grave, his testamentary words will enjoy an afterlife of moving above and within their human receptors like the "form of love," so extensively imagined toward the end of the first act of *Prometheus Unbound*. For, in a studied recollection of this figure reaching back to Homer through Plato,[58] these words are told to hasten over the hearts of men until they meet listeners sufficiently of the "best and gentlest" (*Prometheus*, I.775) that they will not just hear them but take them to heart. "Marina, Primus, Vanna and the rest" are judged to be just such listeners. At their doorstep these words will arrive with the force of an invitation, bidding them to "come" and dwell with and on these words as the guests of a master builder, the rich promise of whose hospitality is guaranteed by his own habitual *entrée* into the house of Love.

All of which is to say that the envoy's final figure for his words of Godspeed to *Epipsychidion* is the Emersonian master-tone of the constitution, city or house of words. We are nowadays very knowledgeable about the prison-house of language, that telling metaphor for the daunting reality that, like the dyer's hand, we are day after day subdued to our native language as our primary medium of verbal communication. But what Shelley offers in aversion to any confining or penal image of the fact of language is a perfectionist city of words, which is neither the decay of our routinely "common, false, cold, hollow talk" nor a dwelling place capable of being forced upon its potential inmates or citizens. Rather, this enamored "world I say of thoughts which worship" Emily is there next to us, and only its attractive smile, not any collaring hand, can draw us into its fold. As has been very sensibly remarked by every poet of love I can recall, the god of their idolatry does not operate like the serially rapist Jupiter. The work of any poet/nightingale sitting in darkness and singing of what he loves in dream and only to cheer his solitude will find capable hearers and followers by nothing else but an "incantation of verse" ("West Wind," 65) that is capable of bringing back to life what, to Shelley's mind, are the "eternal truths charactered on the imaginations of men" (*NS*, 529) and so, at a still deeper register of human condition, the still enchantable chord of the dead or cold or sleeping image of beauty (*NS*, 532).

In the guise of an "editor" of *Epipsychidion* recovering for publication the manuscript's marginal jottings, Shelley closes his "advertisement" of the poem with the same sophisticated self-consciousness that distinguishes the envoy. Addressing his work with a translation of some lines from Dante's famous "Voi, ch'intendendo, il terzo ciel movete," he writes:

> My Song, I fear that thou wilt find but few
> Who fully shall conceive thy reasoning,
> Of such hard matter dost thou entertain;
> Whence, if by misadventure, chance should bring
> Thee to base company (as chance may do),
> Quite unaware of what thou dost contain,
> I prithee, comfort thy sweet self again,
> My last delight! tell them they are dull,
> And bid them own that thou art beautiful.

The echoing effect between this and the envoy is surely by design. Both of these very self-conscious runs of verse channel Dante, both address the poem they frame, and both are, in their different ways, heartening. In the first, the poem is counseled to comfort itself amid base company by constituting itself as a standing rebuke to the herd of the unawakened, which it cannot force to do as it bids but can precisely *bid* to acknowledge, one by one, their own unimpressionable dullness and so get on their own reluctant way to "own[ing] that thou [*Epipsychidion*] art beautiful." To the same effect, the closing envoy invites a readership prepared "to leave the troop which errs, and which reproves," and ready through their impressionable "hearts" to enter into this house of many mansions, and so become participants in that loveliness, which the present writer trusts he has by his own words made more felicitously inviting. This final and explicitly self-referring turn of *Epipsychidion* calls for an audience sufficiently receptive to be provoked into becoming rapt inmates of a flowering of mentality, whose air so sweetly recommends itself because their breather has himself been a guest and fosterling of Love, someone who, by the evidence of just these words, can justly say with Dante, "I' mi son un che, quando/Amor mi spira, noto, e a quel modo/ch'e' ditta dentro vo significando" (*Purgatorio*, 24.52–4). Because he has come to know and subscribe himself as "Love's " the writer of the envoy promises the stars to any reader ready to take the word-by word steps necessary to become his "guest" and so the guest of Love.

As an emblem for what the poem itself would be about, the "fitted-up" chambers of *Epipsychidion*'s tower stand "looking towards the golden eastern air,/And level with the living winds, which flow/Like waves above the living waves below" (516–18). A similar point about the tuition and structuring of a life spent in the reception of the life of life can be made for *Adonais*. What turned out to be this highly wrought capstone to the life's work of Shelley is composed of skillfully finished and blocked off *stanzas*. In Italian, *stanza* means "room" and its root of standing (shared by the English *constitution*) suggests set aside spaces where members of the human family can retreat or gather in such household activities or pursuits as repose, study, intimacy, refection, or conversation. The term can, however, also suggest a closed-down or closed-in space, and indeed the highly wrought Spenserian stanzas of *Adonais* typically achieve a satisfyingly expected sense of closure in their concluding alexandrines. But like the hypaethral Greek temples of Shelley's admiration, he designs the stanzas of *Adonais* to be "open to the bright and liquid sky" (*Prometheus Unbound*, III.iv.118). He takes pains to construct them into an emblem for the sacredly affirmative "acceptance of a certain revised form of life (philosophy may poorly call it animism) outside himself, outside any human power" (*PDAT*, 266). And never more so than when the master builder of these stanzas finally launches the vessel of his poetry toward the "Abode where the Eternal are." For in that climactic advent of the spirit, the speaker of *Adonais* calls on what is fast becoming the beckoning breath of his being to descend upon him and drive his "spirit's bark" up to what, as a metaleptic successor to Dante's "amor che move il sol et l'altre stelle," he has just now called that "Benediction" within the eclipsing but never quenching "Curse" of life as we routinely pursue it. For all its imposing stanza-by-stanza construction, then, *Adonais* would, in the end, aspire not to the condition of a completed edification but toward that edification's hypaethrally sustained reception of "the breath whose might I have invoked in song." Unit by unit, this house of words is built up so as endlessly to let come and happen there such breathings for incommunicable powers as would do for the mind in action what the invisible influence of an inconstant wind does for a fading coal: call it back into the resurgent flame and flower of mentality, which is always there next to us in that perfectionist "world within this Chaos, mine and me,/Of which she [Emily/Asia/Love] was the veiled Divinity,/The world I say of thoughts that worshipped her."

6

Reviewing the Vision of *The Triumph of Life*

> "What is the universal sense of want and ignorance but the fine innuendo by which the great soul makes its enormous claims?"[1]
>
> Emerson

> "Teach me now to listen,
> To strike it rich behind the linear black."[2]
>
> Heaney

Many years ago I concluded a book about Rousseau's English reputation with a chapter arguing that Shelley's last long but unfinished poem was a critique of the Enlightenment.[3] In that chapter, "The Breath of Darkness: A Reading of *The Triumph of Life*," I saw this dream-vision in terza rima as the work of the same man who in his "Defence of Poetry" represented the "French writers" (*NS*, 529) of the Enlightenment as the most recent chapter in a history of would-be bearers of light who produced precisely the opposite effect of the mind darkening itself to itself when their "wreathes of light/Signs of thought's empire over thought" led to a latter end where "for the morn of truth they feigned, deep night/Caught them ere evening" (210-15). Despite all the good works and intentions Shelley granted to the *siècle des lumières*, it was to him a false dawn because, as Simon Jarvis has written apropos of Wordsworth's supposed enmity to the Enlightenment, its ideal of "abstract rationality [failed], precisely, to be rational *enough*."[4] From the world-historical disappointment nested in this conviction, there springs the *Triumph*'s two mutually reinforcing paradoxes about glaring lights that blind and "the breath/Of darkness [that] reillumines even the least/Of heaven's living eyes" (390-2).

Stanley Cavell is not the only Western philosopher either to make epistemology his main concern or to intimate that the Enlightenment never really happened because the party of humanity was not partial enough to human condition. But the historical particulars of his discontent with philosophy's preferred standards of mindfulness fall out along the same implicitly romantic lines of thought that led to Shelley's verdict on a cast of mind so hotly in pursuit of an encyclopedically commanding knowledge of the world that it all but inevitably slighted the utterly specific and literally unending task of (self)acknowledgment, acerbically alluded to in the remark of his Rousseau that "their lore/Taught them not this—to know themselves" (211–12). For a host of reasons, Cavell locates his epistemological misgivings in either the Renaissance of Shakespeare or the post-Kantian nineteenth century, but those misgivings themselves suggest a similar dissatisfaction with the cultural climate of the Enlightenment, based on his frequently reiterated claim that our primary relation to the world is not in the knowing of it but in a more fundamental *receiving* of it.

In Wordsworth, Cavell found a kindred spirit as committed to "wise passiveness" as he was to the "philosophical power in passiveness," where "being at a loss" or "not knowing your way about" is the initially *suffered* incentive to thinking, not unlike the mysteriously provident darkness that makes its kerygmatic debut in Shelley as the "shadow" of Intellectual Beauty that "floats unseen among us" and is "to human thought. . . . nourishment/ Like darkness to a dying flame." (Another, more celebrated, expression of this characteristic romantic sensibility is Keats's "negative capability," defined by him as the "quality [that goes] to form a man of achievement especially in literature" when one is "capable of being in uncertainties, mysteries, doubts, without any irritable reaching after fact and reason.")

The value that these poets found under the burden of the mystery or in a mist or in a breath of darkness was, I strongly suspect, one of the obscurer promptings that led Cavell to acknowledge that his philosophy was calling for some version of what Alfred North Whitehead called the romantic "reaction" against the Enlightenment. But in this closing chapter and in the spirit of Cavell's teaching that thinking takes place "with every word, in every breath," I would like to get behind such imposing generalities as Romanticism and the Enlightenment and track how certain utterly specific words and individually ordinary words of *The Triumph*—"the breath of darkness" (390–1), "beside my path" (433), "native noon" (131), "the casual air" (532), "the Sun [springing] forth/Rejoicing in his splendor" (2–3)—have as a consequence of my reading of Cavell and Shelley in conversation with one another started "dilating in a new light,"[5] which could not but radiate back into my sense of the whole of *The Triumph* as indeed a critique of the Enlightenment, but one now revealed to have been provoked along the same forceful lines of attraction and repulsion as Cavell's persistent wrestlings with what "your philosophy" calls thinking, and thus something like a best case—or at least a test case—of how the work of Cavell and the texts of the English romantics call out and answer to each other in ways that sound out the world-historical depths of the questions and purposes animating their poetry and his philosophy.

I'll begin with the very ordinary "beside my path" in line 433 of the *Triumph*. So ordinary is this phrase that one might need to be reminded that the "beside" part of it occurs at the critical moment of *Epipsychidion* when with the withdrawal of the attractive vision of Emily, the protagonist finds himself addressed by an unspecified "voice" assuring him that the phantom just now fled from him is still "beside thee" (233). In the *Triumph*'s staging of this Shelleyan type-scene about finding one's passion and voice, "beside my path" concludes the protracted withdrawal of the "shape all light" out of Rousseau's ken but not out of his mind. For the track of that shape's withdrawal is very significantly likened to the early-morning fadeout of Venus/Lucifer as "veil by veil [its] silent splendour drops/. . . amid the chrysolite/Of sunrise" (413–15) so that (to both a veiling and an adumbrating effect) it "did keep its obscure tenour . . ./Beside my path, as silent as a ghost" (432–3).

More than a quarter-century ago when I was trying to find my way through this defining passage in Shelley's spiritual autobiography that he is here projecting onto Rousseau, I found some initial traction in the way this "light from heaven" (429) synesthetically modulates into the "obscure tenour" of its continuing heavenly course as the third sphere "whose light is melody to lovers" even as "the world can hear not the sweet notes that move" it (478–9). As impressive as the strong poetic hand behind "obscure tenour" is, I now find myself even more struck by the flamingly obvious notation of this shape's astronomical position as *"beside"* the path of Rousseau's earthly career, a noting of it that assigns to it the divinely absconded lode-star role in what Donald Reiman has succinctly described as the "symbolic universe"[6] of Shelley, where even as the daily returns of the atmospheric veils of daylight work to obscure the starlit heavens, they also, and with the same everyday recursiveness, make the "true sun" of desire—quite conventionally figured as the morning star of Venus—seem to beckon out beyond and along the upward withdrawing of its "intense lamp [narrowing]/In the white dawn clear/Until we hardly see—we feel that it is there" ("To a Sky-Lark," 23–5).

I will be the first to acknowledge that without Cavell's tutelage on the place in *Walden* where Thoreau emphasizes that "with thinking we may be *beside* ourselves in a sane sense" (*Walden*, 91), the "nextness" of the "shape all light" to the "hell . . . [of this] harsh world in which [Rousseau wakes] to weep" (333–4) would never have occurred to me either in itself or in its pertinence to Cavell's claim that the "most thoughtful" act of thinking is "to let true need, say desire, be manifest and be obeyed" (*TN*, 45). But having been introduced to "nextness" as a term of criticism, self-analysis and self-constitution in Thoreau, Emerson and Cavell, and having further heard the idea echoed in Shelley's prose reflections on an explicitly perfectionist "soul within our soul that describes a circle around its proper Paradise which pain and sorrow or evil dare not overleap" (*NS*, 504) and its "antitype" in "the soul out of my soul" (238) of *Epipsychidion*, I am confident that I am not, as it were, hearing things. The persisting nextness of the "shape all light" as an attractive specter of loveliness haunting the Western mind and staying its course just next to that mind's daily rounds, is audibly there. What Rousseau affirms to be lost to him but still audibly next to him is an obscurely hounding or haunting strain of attraction and provocation that he cannot put by or refrain from thinking about, because (to quote Wordsworth's *Intimations Ode*, one of the clear inspirations of *The Triumph*) he is on his way by this "vision splendid ... attended" even unto its apparent last of "[fading] into the light of common day," this a phrase from the *Immortality Ode*, which is commonly taken to mean that the light goes out, even though, as the author of *Must We Mean What We Say?* is quick to point out, "'fades into' does not *say* 'fades out,'" and so "may propose some other mode of becoming, a happier disillusionment" (*IQ*, 75, Cavell's emphasis).

The stationing of the shape all light beside the track of Rousseau's earthly life is not the *Triumph*'s only deployment of "nextness." An earlier instance occurs when the poem's narrator imagines what goes unheard by the multitudes "[pursuing] their serious folly as of old" (73). As the triumphal cortège hurtles its way along a "path where flowers never grew," we are told that just beyond its devastating track, there are "fountains ... [of] melodious dew" which this imperial mob, caught up in its own "savage [and] stunning music" (435), can no more hear than they can "feel" the breezes which "from the forest told/Of grassy paths , and ... violet banks where sweet dreams brood" (69–72). After my reading of *Epipsychidion*, I will not argue for these "telling" but unfelt and unheard breezes as a figure for what's there to be heard in the wind of the forest of our world, nor for these "grassy paths" as a standing offer of more naturally satisfying ways of spending your time in this world, nor for these "violet banks" brooding sweet dreams as flowerings of mentality. I will simply assert these significances and correspondences as but part of my over-all sense that with this elaborate nature imagery, the narrator of *The Triumph* diagnoses the affliction of those in thrall to Life as fundamentally a deafness to the promising possibilities just beside them both in their next self and in the "garden ravaged" (*Epipsychidion*, 187) of the world in which they find themselves so strenuously and so vainly laboring.

In the course of being pained and disheartened by his vision of a world seemingly gone "all amiss" (179), the speaker literally stumbles upon Rousseau, and then stays with him and copiously hears him out, because both he and his Rousseau are defined by their draw toward a lost figure of, call it, Intellectual Beauty that lies just beyond the broad and common way of those done in by Life, and is variously imagined as a *locus amoenus* of "melodious dew" just off the beaten track, a feminine object of desire in the fashion of Asia or Emily, or that same object of desire deified or "catasterized" into what Yeats called Shelley the star of infinite desire.

Rousseau's attraction toward the "shape all light" as toward his Immanuel (i.e. his God(dess) [still] with him) attracts the imagery of a Rousseau inextinguishably on fire, that dominates the portraits of Rousseau sketched by Byron, Hazlitt and other contemporaries of Shelley.[7] Byron, for example, judged that Rousseau's ardor was directed not toward any "living dame" but toward an "ideal Beauty, which became/In him existence, and o'erflowing teems/Along his burning page, distempered though it seems." This "apostle of affliction" was "Passion's essence—as a tree/On fire by lightning; with ethereal flame/Kindled he was, and blasted" (*Childe Harold*, III.77–8). The Rousseau of Shelley's *Triumph* also traces Rousseau's fiery nature back to a heavenly incentive and onward to the less than glorious way his earthly career played or flamed itself out:

> "If the spark with which Heaven lit my spirit
> Earth had with purer nutriment supplied
>
> Corruption would not now so much inherit
> Of what was once Rousseau—nor this disguise
> Stain that within which still disdains to wear it. —
>
> If I have been extinguished, yet there rise
> A thousand beacons from the spark I bore." (201–7)

The reader of *The Triumph* does not need to take Rousseau's word for it that, as he protests here, he had a constitution enflamed by higher things and leading toward what are still taken to be the manifest realities of both his burning page and his "wretched" life. The poem does not just say (or have Rousseau say) that he was passionately drawn toward a fervent proclaiming of the surpassing attractions of the "shape all light." It enacts this zealous motion of his spirit by presenting him as incapable of not sounding out the persistent calling out to him of this absconded vision. Rousseau's verbal performance, in short, witnesses if not to the full prophetic portion of a fire in the belly, then at least to that of a fading coal, still responsive to this now "invisible influence" and so forever ready to burst out into the "transitory brightness" of the charged language of praise that he all but uniquely reserves for this all but totally withdrawn "light from heaven."

According to the Rousseau of *The Triumph*, a "spoiler spoiled" (235) like Voltaire will have the intellectual work he habitually did done unto him. Shelley's Rousseau polemically represents himself as in a different fix. With no little vanity, he represents himself as a burnt-out case, an ardent soul done in "by [his] own heart alone" (241). But the consuming fire of Rousseau's heart is of the unextinguished variety so often invoked by Shelley. Having once been kindled (and blasted) with an ethereal flame, he finds himself unable to "uncreate" the turn in his life toward this object of desire. And so, like Actaeon, he is hounded by it. Any one experiencing this turn or tropism out beyond the bondage of life can, to be sure, openly abjure its dominion or muffle its call. But the call will not simply go away. Pushed underground, it will become "the mutiny within" (213). It will migrate into a sacred discontent with a (self)imposed "disguise" (204), which, while not totally repressing its own aversive stirrings, will fashion itself into a "mortal mould" (17) staining "that within which still disdains to wear it" (205).

 The poem's onrushing pageantry of imperial misery and disarray has led some of its best readers to see its representation of a world gone all amiss as indicative of its creator's belated access to a more darkly mature vision of human desire. There is some truth in this. In the end, perhaps the single most apt description of the human life and history pursued in *The Triumph* is "a living hell." But this hardly counts as news, coming as it does from a poet who, amid all the fervors of *Epipsychidion*, ever so casually wrote off "our life" as "this cold common hell." The "undeserving [because brutalizing] way [of our world]" which the Uranian Venus of *Adonais* was made to trod to such bloody issue figures how it is pointedly the best and finest qualities of our nature that are the most trashed. Since this is an insight that distinguishes Shelley's work from almost its beginnings, the spectacles of misspent desire streaming through *The Triumph* should be read not as palinode but as the brutally honest and sardonic parody of one acknowledging the endemic corruption of the "education of error" that has become our life, but still finding bitter consolation in the jealously guarded maxim that it is the corruption of this best of love that produces our worst of "sensuality and force" (*NS*, 526). The *Triumph* features a juggernaut of "Life" going about its Satanic business of "[confusing] all best things to ill" (*Prometheus Unbound*, I.628), but this entails neither that these best things of our aspiration no longer exercise any call on us to heed and follow their perfectionist lead. For all the poem's parodic gibbeting of our corrupted will, it does not deny, indeed it emphasizes, the attenuated staying with Rousseau of a fervent motion toward a "shape all light," persistently beside his path and repeatedly identified with both Shelley's star of infinite desire and Dante's female figure of beatifically saving grace. In this poem, both the powerful few and the hordes chained to Life's car are, like the dyer's hand, subdued to the element they worked in and sought to master. On that world they had set their hearts, and to that world they had turned their grasping hands. In the self-recounting of the life Shelley imagines for him, Rousseau is different, and different, it would seem, only because the "shape all light" beside his path is still calling on him as the tantalizing "nextness" of a world elsewhere, which, from the aggrieved perspective of his exile, now seems more his "native noon" (131) than where he presently finds himself not so much living as stuck or stalled, his thin discolored hair, like appallingly blighted grass, "vainly" seeking to hide the "holes" that "were or had been eyes" (187–8).

Native is cognate with *natality*, and although *The Triumph* does not use the word, least of all in Cavell's sense of "the idea of the birth of the human: that is the birth of a world," (73) that very idea is the semiotic matrix for the opening scene of the autobiography which Shelley imagines for Rousseau. This life is said to begin in

> the April prime
> When all the forest tops began to burn
>
> With kindling green, touched by the azure clime
> Of the young year (308–11)

Here, the green of spring kindles to the prompting touch of the young year and its azure clime. Here is not so much a *locus amoenus* as the recurrent *hora amoena* of the "April prime," a naming of spring composed of one element referring to first things in both time and excellence and another to that month of the year deriving its name from the Latin *aperio* and thus speaking of the responsive opening of Flora into its many flowers.

In the course of arguing in *Rousseau in England* for the *Rêveries d'un promeneur solitaire* as the Rousseau text most pertinent to *The Triumph*, I dwelt less on this primal kindling than on the "oblivious spell" (331) induced by the pervasive "sound" (318) and "music" (330) of the Lethean stream described at length in the approximately twenty lines coming after this ardent beginning. For anyone graced with even snatches of this neo-natal music (Shelley has Rousseau testify) there would be opened up a route toward the kind of earthly paradise, found at the summit of the *Purgatorio*, its iconic figure Mathilda gathering flowers and its necessary preliminary a total immersion in Lethe. Like *Epipsychidion*, the *Triumph* secularizes the two baptisms of water and fire, but it now seems clear to me that the former plays only its conventionally allotted role of the precursor.[8] The *Triumph* does represent the "oblivious spell" of its primal waters as both attractive and necessary, but only because it alone can wash away our "whole life [as] an education of error" and leave "what is too often the duty of the reformer in political and ethical questions to leave, a vacancy," a vacancy or opening, I want to say, for the exodus of desire in "unimprisoned flames" (*Adonais*, 161), or kindling green.

The progress of "natality" in this part of the poem runs from sap kindling in the April prime through a flood of light that comes streaming out of an "orient" cave and coalesces into the "shape all light" only to withdraw into her persistently thought and re-membered (after)life as what Cavell calls the "[lost] track of desire itself" (*SW*, 51). On their way to their climax in the coming of "the shape all light," these imagined beginnings of Rousseau ring the changes on the Cavellian master-tone of natality in almost every word: *April, prime, kindling, green, young,* the "bright omnipresence/Of *morning*" flowing "through the *orient* cavern."

Furthermore, the poem goes on to cast the ironically named "Life" to which Rousseau's "shape all light" so quickly yields the field as the morbidly overdetermined contrary of all this natal splendor. It represents Europe in 1822 as a death-in-life shambles where

> the old anatomies
> Sate hatching their base broods under the shade
>
> Of demon wings, and laughed from their dead eyes
> To reassume the delegated power
> Arrayed in which these worms did monarchize
>
> Who make this earth their charnel.
> (501–5)

This *tour de force* of the grotesque illustrates what according to Cavell is the self-appointed task of the romantic poet: not to argue its audience into a proposition about (whatever may be meant by) the death, loss, or withdrawal of life and the world, but to get that audience to see that this poetic vision "expresses the way you are living now" (*IQ*, 44), to get that audience to see, for example, that its vision has been hollowed out into "dead eyes" with the consequence that, without radical change, it cannot possibly become king over itself, its nature its own divine control (*Prometheus Unbound*, III.iv.196–7; IV.394–401), but instead will go on being the host to the plague of *worms* so well practiced at making this earth and flesh of ours their *charnel*. Pullulating embodiments of Jupiter's "He reigns," these worms do not even govern. They play at governing, they "monarchize."

This (almost) universal masque of death and anarchy finds its representative figure in a Rousseau who, to his special chagrin as both man and writer, remembers being favored by a "shape all light," whom he did not allow to be, as it were, his whole heart, mind, soul and interest. In Rousseau's own words, "I among the multitude/Was swept" (460–1) because he failed to be "delayed" by either the "phantom of that early form," or the attractions of "sweetest flowers," or the "falling stream's Lethean song" (460–4), and so by default he found "his *bosom*" [bared] "to the *clime*/Of that cold light whose airs too soon deform" and his entire self swept up into the triumph's "living storm" (466–8, emphases added). In Cavell's terms, he could not sit still, he could not "stop to think (say not for action but for passion), as if to let [his] needs recognize what they need" (*CH*, 20).

The result is that as he now stands Rousseau cannot be counted either as one who lived up to the perfectionist standard of "those two of Athens and Jerusalem" who "put aside the diadem/Of earthly thrones or gems, till the last one/Were there" (132–4), or as a member of that other more short-lived band of "the sacred few": the "young spirits" who "touched the world with living flame" and then promptly "Fled back like eagles to their *native* noon" (130–1, emphasis added). Fallen by the wayside and apparently devolved into a vegetable state, Rousseau has landed himself in the "wretched" fix and semblance of an "old root which grew/To strange distortion out of the hill side" (183–4). In sharp contrast to this fate, the brief account of the two cohorts of the sacred few strategically positions them at the natal and mortal termini of a human life. Together, they constitute what turned out to be a last valedictory manifestation of Shelley's consuming interest in what he steadfastly acknowledged to be our unknowable end and origin, but just as steadfastly persisted in imagining as united in the identity of desire or incentive that he repeatedly gave expression to in the dominant chord of his poetry that has been aptly named the "Venus-complex": his strikingly original and synesthetically rich response to the literary commonplace that it is the one sphere of Venus that in different seasons provocatively beams down on us from its two stations as now the morning, now the evening star.[9]

As we have seen, the identity of Lucifer and Hesperus in Venus is a major feature of *Epipsychidion* and also of *Adonais*'s twinned epigrams from Greek pastoral. The *Triumph* revisits this most significant of Shelleyan tropes when it focuses the everyday phenomenon of morning not, for example, on the sun rising above the eastern horizon, but on the vertically narrowing disappearance of the morning star out through our atmosphere and into "the presence of that fairest planet" beside our path, which though "unseen is felt by one who *hopes/That his day's path may end as he began it/In that star's smile* (416–19, emphasis added)."

Thus does even the ostensibly failed Rousseau give expression to his troubled affinity of hope (and fear) with two sets of admired figures, each of which the seer of this dream-vision identifies as the still remembered and treasured singers of their "native noon" of desire.

Rousseau loved many things Italian, but to my knowledge he never once in his voluminous writings mentions Dante. Nonetheless, Shelley very unhistorically has his Rousseau asserting that the gloriously auspicious beginnings of his life have turned into a living hell, imaginable as the semiotic equivalent of Dante's *selva oscura* or *Epipsychidion*'s "dark wood," and explicitly named a "mysterious dell" as astounding as "quella valle" (*Inferno*, 1.14) from which Dante had to begin his journey upward beyond the highest of earth's mountains and toward "l'amor che move il sole et l'altre stelle." This Dantean intertext becomes fully explicit when Rousseau introduces the pandemic hellishness which has come to be his world with an extended tribute to Dante, the opening where and when of which is that

> Before the chariot had begun to climb
> The opposing steep of that mysterious dell
> Behold a wonder worthy [of Dante]
> (469–71)

This mysterious dell is the proverbial "vale of tears" derided by Keats as "the common cognomen of this world among the misguided and superstitious"[10] but reimagined by Shelley ("Hymn to Intellectual Beauty," 17) as a comprehensively accurate way of naming any human inhabiting of the earth unresponsive to the visitations of intellectual beauty and therefore (in the openly damning and theological words of *The Triumph*) having "the action and the shape, without the grace/Of life" (523). The lay of the land that makes a dell a dell is its two "steeps" joined in opposition; but above this terrestrial field of our action, the *Triumph* projects itself out toward an astronomical field, in whose more capacious framing the "mysterious dell" of the poem's vision is overseen by the two "steeps" of first and last things that at day's end are imagined as one in the never-to-be-transfigured burning and beckoning of that Love which led Dante on through hell and toward the glories of the *Paradiso*. Not only, then, is *The Triumph* polarized along a horizontal axis, charged at one end with the visually occluded but obscurely sensed tenor of the initial "shape all light," and at the other with the hope of its smiling return, but it is also mounted upon an intersecting vertical axis, extending from the lowest depths of hell toward the loftiest star of unascended Heaven/Pinnacled dim in the intense inane" (*Prometheus Unbound*, III.iv.204). This is not accidental. At the advent of the poem's vision, its *Faust*-quoting seer explicitly and solemnly positions himself at the meeting of just these two axes. Behind him, he says, "rose the day" and "before him fled/The night," while there "above his head" was "Heaven," and "at his feet . . . the Deep." (26–8)

In addition to this anagogical framing of itself, *The Triumph* also deepens and extends its narrative of decline and fall beyond Rousseau's individual fate to the entirety of the "great crowd" filling "this valley of perpetual dream" (397) with its one recurring event of how "From every firmest limb and fairest face/The strength and freshness fell like dust, and left/The action and the shape without the grace/Of life" (520–3). On the model of the Tower of

Babel and in line with Paul DeMan's sense of *The Triumph* as a poem about our figurings and disfigurings of experience,[11] the poem's final variation on its master-theme of the fall is set forth in terms of the shadows or adumbrations of representation. Without exception, each member of the triumph projects a "shadow" that was

> Each, like himself, and like each other were
>   At first, but soon distorted seemed to be
>
> Obscure clouds molded by the casual air,
>   And of this stuff the car's creative ray
> Wrought all the busy phantoms that were there
>
>   As the sun shapes the clouds. (530–5)

What now strikes me as most powerfully original about this particular representational and linguistic variation of the Fall is that its agency is not any grand Promethean ambition of scaling the skies or stealing fire. It is, instead, the fleeting and tenuous phenomenon of the *"casual* air." Affixed to an explicitly molding "air," this *casual* is hardly itself a casual word choice. Its root meaning speaks of things haphazardly falling out as the product not of deliberation but of accident. The word points to a deficit of attention and interest that resonates with what the Spirit of the Hour in *Prometheus Unbound* deprecates as the idly "cold, hollow talk/Which makes the heart deny the *yes* it breathes," and chimes also with the way Cavell, speaking as an Ishmael of the spirit and thinking of all the *casualties* accruing from our first "casual step" (*TN*, 57) outside the terms or "lines" of the forms of life that grow (ordinary) language, curtly says, "call us casual" (*IQ*, 59). Call us the victims of the casual slaughters we ourselves daily and unthinkingly inflict on τὸ ποιεῖν as the principle of synthesis which "has for its objects those forms which are common to universal nature and existence itself" (*NS*, 510), and so in the event find ourselves adrift and hence an easy mark for being swept up into the triumph's "speed in the van and blindness in the rear" (101).

(More than 20 years after his turn to romanticism in *In Quest of the Ordinary*, Cavell will address this condition as the distinctively modern one of being "starless" and without any "sidereal orientation" (*LDIK*, 523, 529). These ominous words rise to the surface of Cavell's autobiographical *Little Did I Know: Excerpts from Memory* in response to Maurice Blanchot's *Writing of the Disaster*. To Cavell's apparent approval, Blanchot takes the etymological sense of the *disaster* (of the modern [human] subject) not as our being simply "ill-starred" but as "marking our being dissociated or disconnected or disengaged from the pertinence of the stars" so that for

Blanchot "disaster is revealed metaphysically to be, or to have become, the normal state of human existence, marked by the release from our ties to the stars, say from our considered steps beyond, a release that partakes of the oblivion of the transcendental draw of words, of their openness to a future, their demand for continuity with past and present" (*LDIK*, 522). Cavell further notes that for Blanchot "it follows as part of the disaster that consideration is no longer a usable mode of thought. Consideration (and reconsideration) speaks of a careful attention to the framework of stars, but Blanchot tells us that the bearing of stars no longer holds for us. There is now no sidereal orientation" (*LDIK*, 529). To this truly disastrous prospect of the modern subject living in exile from thoughtful consideration, Cavell counters with a "mode of thinking" which he calls "consideration, placing a constellation of ideas within whatever constellations you divine (reading intertextually, in its various forms, would produce examples), not with the idea of choosing one over the other but of expanding each inflected by the other," something (Cavell further remarks) that he has "often characterized as speaking without assertion" (*LDIK*, 530), as in his many calls for the neutrality of philosophical authorship and his appreciation of Thoreau's resolution to tell all and say nothing. To my mind, this mode of thinking in which one takes "considered steps beyond" cries out to be itself constellated or supplemented with whatever may turn out to be the partiality or incentive to any and all human considerations, frameworks or constitutions. And it is as just such an incentive to his flowers of thought that Shelley's "Venus-complex" claims its prominent and commanding place in his poetry. For that one star—itself constellated into morning star and evening star, *Alma Venus Genetrix* and load-star—takes up its place within this poetry as the incentivizing *mis en abyme* toward a constitution of writing, whose bent toward the divining and considering of its own provocations is exemplified in the oft noted abandon with which it constellates both metaphors (Emily seen as *benediction, star, glory, delight, refuge* and so on) and myths (the Greek Prometheus seen also as the Satan of Milton and the Jesus of the gospels) with, manifestly, the idea not of "choosing one over the other but of expanding each inflected by the other." Shelley was aware that this was the way to get on in his own craft of poetry. The imagination does its work, he wrote in *Epipsychidion*, by way of "a thousand prisms and mirrors ... [and their] reverberated lightening" (166–9).[12]

The disastrously casual effect of our starless and sleepwalking "education in error" is captured in the multitudes of the *Triumph* who, strangers to any considered reflection, endlessly sit "chattering like restless apes/On vulgar hands and voluble like fire" (494–5), but also and more pointedly in the haphazard and ephemeral riot of the reputedly grave deliberations which "like small gnats and flies as thick as mist/On evening marshes throng about the brow/Of lawyer, statesman, priest and theorist" (508–10). In the damning accents of "England in 1819," this says to post-Napoleonic Europe that this is your philosophy, this your religion, this your polis, this your law. In its aversion to this fetidly voluble swamp, *The Triumph* would reveal that the age's outwardly cold clime and "atmosphere of thought" (*Prometheus Unbound*, I.676–7) is paradoxically the breeding ground for a miasmal and overheated buzz, thronging about the brow and jamming the reception of any saving grace or sidereal orientation coming down from that particular "Light from Heaven" (429) which is the third sphere of Venus.

One of the more obvious ways *The Triumph* represents its author's quasi-Wittgensteinian misgivings about thought caught in the grip of itself and darkening itself to itself is how it has Aristotle "throned in new thoughts of men" that became "signs of thought's empire over thought," until the "spirit" of Bacon "leapt/Like lightning out of darkness" and supposedly put an end to the "jealous" watch of Alexander's tutor at "truth's eternal doors" by "[unbarring] the caves that held/The treasure of the secrets of [Protean Nature's] realm" (267–73). But after this brilliantly conventional account of a dogmatically enshrined Aristotle overthrown by an "empirical" and reality-craving Bacon, the Rousseau of the *Triumph* moves on from any and all claimants to the Aristotelian title of "il maestro di color che sanno" (*Inferno*, 4.131) to the "bards of old," and in line with the *Defence*'s briskly advanced claim that Rousseau was essentially a poet" and not a "mere reasoner," he associates himself not with the practitioners of τὸ λογιζεῖν but with the poets, engaged in the more fundamental of the "two classes of mental action, which are called reason and imagination" (*NS*, 510).

The field of action and writing in which the *Triumph* places Rousseau is not, then, what most of us most of the time call thinking. It is, instead, the field cultivated by the "bards of old," who "[sang] the passions" (275) in quest of what Cavell calls the exits of desire. *Prosateur* Rousseau goes so far as to judge himself more this kind of poet than any of the so-called "bards of old." For they, he asserts, "inly quelled/The passions which they sung." He, by contrast, "suffered what I wrote or viler pain!—/And so my words were seeds of misery—/Even as the deeds of others"—others, it is clear, like the Roman Emperors and Pontiffs who "rose like shadows between Man and god/Till that eclipse, still hanging under Heaven,/Was worshipped by the world o'er which they strode/For the true Sun it quenched" (279–91).

To Rousseau's positing of a moral equivalence between the misery deriving from these public men of action and his own individual work as a very articulate "apostle of affliction" (*Childe Harold*, III.77), the poem's narrator objects that his words were not "seeds of misery" in the same way as their deeds. Since this is a fraternal stroke of correction that Shelley's Rousseau very uncharacteristically suffers wisely, he quickly amends his thought to the judgment that the power of these others "was given/But to destroy," his own to "[create], even/If it be a world of agony"—a "world of agony" that is, I am suggesting, composed along the lines of a romantic book of losses in which the "modern subject" must come to know itself as, in Cavell's diagnosis, peculiarly susceptible to such modern world-historical afflictions as lostness, exile, devastation, a sense of disappointment, strangeness, perverseness, sickness, torment and a fear of suffocation (*PDAT*, 206).

After this preliminary sorting out of who this one generally acknowledged founding father of modernity was and what (writing) business he was about, Shelley has him curtly command, "now listen" (308). Listen (as Thoreau might say) not idly or casually but "on tiptoe" and "with your most alert and wakeful hours" (*Walden*, 71) to this poetically condensed autobiography that is the revelatory world of agony which I created for myself and infected my readers with. The unspoken assumption of this directive is that, as Shelley's *Defense of Poetry* puts it, "it is better to go to the house of mourning, than to the house of mirth" since "sorrow, terror, anguish, despair itself are often the chosen expressions of an approximation to the highest good" (*NS*, 529), this a Shelleyan gloss on *Ecclesiastes* that anticipates the confident rhetorical question of Emerson that is one of the epigraphs to this chapter: "What is the universal sense of want and ignorance but the fine innuendo by which the great soul makes its enormous claims?" (*EL*, 385).

The one, maddening, want here is of the "shape all light." But if like the Emily of *Epipsychidion* and the Asia of *Prometheus Unbound*, the *Triumph*'s "shape all light" is another of Shelley's figures for the perfectionist "better world we think, and know not to exist, with no acceptable reason not to exist," then that world is not one "that is *gone*, [and hence] not one to be mourned, but one to be borne, witnessed" (*PP*, 30). Just such steadfast bearing and witnessing is what the agonized Rousseau of the *Triumph* is about and fated to. By every one of the lingering words he lavishes on the withdrawing "shape all light," this Rousseau of Shelley's imagining shows that he is still attracted to what he still calls this "light from heaven." Furthermore, in the full acknowledgment that the withdrawal of this "star's smile" has left the world open to the "new vision" of the "cold bright car" and its "savage, stunning music" (435), he nonetheless trusts that its absconded shape and smile will remain beside his earthly path because the occluding veil of the earth's atmosphere also functions as the tenuous medium for such intimations of her abiding presence as have the light of that star's smile fade not just *into* the light of common day (as Cavell pointed out for the glory and the dream of Wordsworth's *Immortality Ode*) but into its smell and note and barometric pressure as well. For by the "seeing as" faculty of poetry, the "smile" of a star which is also a "shape all light" is further likened to

> the scent
> Of a jonquil when evening breezes fan it,
>
> Or the soft note in which his dear lament
> The Brescian shepherd breathes, or the caress
> That turned his weary slumber to content. (419–23)

Rousseau testifies, then, not only to a persistent memory of (call it) the thing itself of the shape's heavenly splendor but also to an equally persistent *experience* of her attractive draw and influence, which by its alternation of attraction and withdrawal "forever sought, forever lost" has led him into the kind of living hell *and* martyrdom imagined by Dante. That such an inferno of sacred discontent is where Rousseau finds himself is made clear from how, nearing the close of his spiritual autobiography, he introduces and, as it were, captions the final, most graphically hellish section of the *Triumph* as:

> a wonder worthy of the rhyme
>
> Of him who from the lowest depths of hell
> Through every Paradise and through all glory
> Love led serene, and who returned to tell
>
> In words of hate and awe the wondrous story
> How all things are transfigured, except Love;
> For deaf as is a sea which wrath makes hoary
>
> The world can hear not the sweet notes that move
> The sphere whose light is melody to lovers—
> A wonder worthy of his rhyme
> (471–80)

With its framing ring-composition of "a wonder worthy of the/his rhyme" (471–480) this conspicuously self-contained passage does more than simply name what is to follow that "hell" orthodoxly defined as a sense of utter and irreversible loss. It also preveniently contrives to place the "ghastly dance" (540) of the next sixty lines in the larger perspective of the *Commedia* as a whole. The result is that Shelley can at the same time say "damn you" to "this cold common hell, our life" (*Epipsychidion*, 214) and sound out the full-throated praise of the redeeming note of Love which he heard Dante faithfully following and singing through every kind of spiritual weather.

This lavishly redundant praise of Dante is pointedly directed toward him as a writer, a writer capable of returning from what he has been through so as "to tell/In words of hate and awe the wondrous story/How all things are transfigured, except Love." To this wonder, a starless world at sea in a wrathfully unreflective lather of interfering static may turn a deaf ear, but not so the deviser of this tribute, who in the same breath as he proudly draws attention to how his troping of the contemporary into the hellish "takes after" and is the equal of Dante, also implies that he can lay claim to such poetic mastery only because he has been himself so impressionable—so, in his word, "tempered"—to the sweetly provoking notes in which Dante tells how the psychpomp Love led him "from the lowest depths of hell/Through every Paradise and through all glory."

Contrary to the "sweet notes" and "obscure tenor" of Venus, the "clime" of Life's "cold car" brays out the triumphalist spirit of the age in a characteristically savage and stunning music. Of both musics, the human form of life is fated to be not only the creator and the creation, but also the battleground. What we give our interest and attention to is what we will become contributing constituents of, be it at one extreme the spirit breathed to their kind both from the world in its April prime and from the visions of the "sacred few," or at the other "the clime/Of that cold car whose airs too soon deform" into the headstrong disorientation of "speed in the van and blindness in the rear" by which the Car of Life sustains a culture of illusion and frenetically mindless conformity, the most recent counter to which has, in Shelley's accounting, been those mostly Renaissance writers (with Dante "the Lucifer of this starry flock" (*NS*, 528) and Rousseau its only modern) who "have celebrated the dominion of love, planting as it were trophies in the human mind of that sublimest victory over sensuality and force" (*NS*, 526). Of these two contending music in *The Triumph of Life*, William Hazlitt was quick to recognize "a new and terrific Dance of Death."[13] But the poem's other not quite still and not always small voice tells of a "light from heaven" which Shelley's Rousseau realizes too late he should have stayed in step with.

In summary, *The Triumph of Life* stages a *psychomachia* between the one, primally creative air from the heaven of *Alma Venus Genetrix* and the entropic blasts of "this cold common hell" (*Epipsychidion*, 214), which is the way we actually live now in this "valley of perpetual dream," reprising the Shelleyan variation on the Pauline body of our death, already found in *Adonais*'s exhortation of "Peace, peace! He is not dead . . . *We* decay/Like corpses in a charnel; fear and grief/Convulse us and consume us day by day,/ And cold hopes swarm like worms within our living clay" (343, 348–51, Shelley's emphasis).

About this life-and-death struggle, one needs to keep two things in mind. *First*, the side consistently championed by Shelley is not what to many it has often seemed: all and only wishful thinking. For this side explicitly requires the arduously sustained dedication and discipline so essential to the courtly-love poetry animating both Shelley and Dante before him. In the context of Shelley's entire body of work, moreover, this is a requirement which in him no less than in Dante amounts to an unremitting call for a steadfastly *thoughtful* dedication to, in his nineteenth-century case, the load-star of love, represented by him as the saving alternative to the routinely inattentive and uninterested fecklessness, which both Shelley's "casual air" and Cavell's "Call us casual" so emphatically name the very ordinary way the human form of life ἐχὸν λόγον has of all but inevitably getting on the path to "emptiness" with a first casual but decidedly "off" step, whose slight degree of turning can and will produce a world of difference down the road.

The second thing one needs to keep in mind about this *psychomachia* is that it is indeed a battle, not a disputation. The contention of the two (and the imagined prevailing of the one over the other in almost all of Shelley's work) does not entail any claim that the discourse of love and loveliness *refutes* what has been inexorably stamped on our minds and characters by the forms and pressures of the time. The *Triumph*'s framing of a world-historical crisis in our human form of life is worked out, rather, along the same lines as those pursued in the first act of *Prometheus Unbound*, where the facts of the furies' lacerating account of these "types of things which are" (*Prometheus*, I.645) are not denied by Prometheus. Rather, they are poignantly taken to heart by him and painstakingly entered into his account of his condition, with the consequence (apparently unforeseen by the archetypal foreseer) that precisely this process of coming to terms with the historical record of his beloved humankind exposes the furies' perversely driving interest in a narrative that would make the human soul, alone still unsubdued to Jupiter "like unextinguished fire" (*Prometheus Unbound*, III.i.5), falter in its attraction toward Asia. Again, the only available response either to the furies' torturing of Prometheus or to the juggernaut of Life presiding over "the action and the shape without the grace/Of life" (522-3) is not the *pons asinorum* of trying to refute what Shelley is manifestly making his own words represent as the accomplished facts of where we find ourselves. The "hope," rather, is to "prove the induction otherwise" by way of that "true theory ... Which seeks a "soul" not only of goodness (*Julian and Maddalo*, 204) but of a steadfastly star-oriented witness in things as notoriously ill as the poisoned cup of Socrates or Jesus's agonized and "thorn-wounded brow/ [streaming] with blood" (*Prometheus*, I.598-9).

The capacity of our every word to be not just one more link in "the chains of lead...[impeding the soul's] flight of fire" (*Epipsychidion*, 590) but itself a phenomenon of fire "instinct with spirit... and pregnant with a lightning [and looking for its] conductor" (*NS*, 528) plays a decisive role at the outset of the *Divine Comedy*, when, having tried some abortive first steps out of the darkly wooded valley, an all but terminally downcast Dante becomes the vigorously receptive conductor for the words of a Vergil who in his turn has been moved by the fervently compassionate appeal of Beatrice in "a relay of grace that extends from Heaven to Virgil, through three blessed ladies."[14] I note without documenting it that the medium for this call to renewal is very redundantly and self-consciously the provoking power of words. In the relative near term on the way through purgatory to paradise, Dante is being summoned down into the contracting and ultimately ice-bound depths of the inferno, but the most immediate (and comprehensively enabling) effect of Beatrice and Virgil's words on him is in the opposite expansive direction of his wholeheartedly responding to their call, and doing so under the sign of an epic simile whose tenor is the life's breath of "buono ardire" coursing back into his heart and whose vehicle is the opening flower:

> Quali fioretti del notturno gelo
>   chinati e chiusi, poi che 'l sol li'mbianca
> si drizzan tutti aperto in loro stelo,
>   tal mi fec'io di mia virtude stanca,
> e tanto buono ardire al cor mi corse,
>   ch'i' comincai come persona franca. (*Inferno*, II.127–32)

> (As little flowers that were all bowed and shut
> By the night chills rise on their stem and open
> As soon as they have felt the touch of sunlight,
> So I revived in my own wilting powers
> And my heart flushed, like somebody set free.)[15]

This is the same language of flowers that we have encountered as a major and insistently self-reflexive feature of Shelley's poetry from as early as his call to the writerly service of Intellectual Beauty in "that sweet time when winds are wooing/All vital things that wake to bring/News of buds and blossomings" to the late blooming and sumptuously self-reflexive flowers of *Epipsychidion*, and on finally to *The Triumph* where the life-provoking incentive of *Venus Genetrix* received, taken to heart, and kindling into answerable style is extended from flowers to the entire forest of our life in "the April prime/When all the forests tops [begin] to burn/With kindling green, touched by the azure clime/Of the young year."

After the scene for Rousseau's life-story has been set and identified as (call it) a forbiddingly dark and cold valley of spiritual bondage but one still capable of bursting out with "flowers of gentle breath; like incarnations of the stars" (*Adonais*, 173–4), the attention of the reader is directed to Rousseau as, so to say, an individual forester of this region, whose visitation by the shape all light draws out of him the same self-reflexive figure of an ardently responsive human self rising like a flower in self-transfiguring openness to the radiant visitant commanding him to "arise and quench thy thirst," so that

> as a shut lily, stricken by the wand
>   Of dewy morning's vital alchemy
>
> I rose; and bending at her sweet command,
>   Touched with faint lips the cup she raised.
>   (401–4)

The call to which Rousseau as shut lily here responds is literally the "cup" which the "shape all light" holds out to him, and which he "touches" with only faint lips and to the desolating effect of clearing the way for the "new vision and its cold bright car." *Cup* here is fairly obvious code for one's portion or fate, that given or received condition of the human which (not so obviously) Cavell locates in our terms as our condition(s) (what we say together) so that "language is our fate . . . [that] to which we are fated, and in which our freedom resides . . . as a struggle with the language we emit, of our character with itself" (*CH*, 39–40). What Rousseau finds himself so powerfully drawn to becomes (mostly) lost to him, largely because (as I contended in *Rousseau in England*) he touched the proffered cup with insufficiently ardent lips, this being the serious point behind Shelley's similar mockery of Wordsworth as "a kind of moral eunuch/ [who] touched the hem of Nature's shift,/Felt faint—and never dared uplift/The closest, all-concealing tunic" (314–17).)

But if Rousseau's inadequate response to the shape all light looks forward to the unfulfilled promise of his life, it also looks backward to the poem's opening proem or frame when on the occasion of just that "awakened earth" called for at the close of *Ode to the West Wind*, we have "*all* flowers in field or forest" (9, emphasis added) responding to "the kiss of day" not only with a fervent ecstasy but to a sweet and fragrant issue:

> Swift as a spirit hastening to his task
>   Of glory and of good, the Sun sprang forth
> Rejoicing in his splendour, and the mask

> Of darkness fell from the awakened Earth.
> The smokeless altars of the mountain snows
>   Flamed above crimson clouds, and at the birth
>
> O light, the Ocean's orison arose
>   To which the birds tempered their matin lay.
> All flowers in field or forest which unclose
>
>   Their trembling eyelids to the kiss of day,
> Swinging their censers in the element,
>   With orient incense lit by the new ray
>
> Burned slow and inconsumably, and sent
>   Their odorous sighs up to the smiling air
>   (5–14)

As it leads up to its manifestly self-reflexive flowers, this opening celebration of the april-prime and morning of the world becomes a ritually ordered splendor of responsiveness, the god of whose idolatry is itself an ur-wonder of responsiveness springing forth "swift as a spirit hastening to its task/Of glory and of good" (1–2). It is an opening that performs in a more serenely confident manner what *Epipsychidion* had already represented as "the green lizard and the golden snake" leaping toward the newly attractive heat of the vernal sun "like unimprisoned flames out of their trance awak[ing]" (161–2). It mythically enacts how behind its frenzied mask of "fearing, loving, hating, suffering, doing and dying" (200), this "astonishing thing" of "Life, and the world, or whatever we call that which we are and feel" (*NS*, 505) may be aptly figured as an altar turned toward the "*birth*/Of light" (emphasis added) with mountainously sacrificial flames that would not singe a sleeve and with an ocean breathing up orisons "to which the birds tempered their matin lay." Having thus set the scene of a sacredly burning and singing creation, the poem then turns its now openly self-reflexive eye on the flowers of the morning, which, as troped into trembling eyelids opening to the kiss of day cannot but ecstatically swing their "censers" into an element of "enamoured air" (39), steeped in the burning fountain of which they inconsumably send up to the smiling air their own contribution of "odorous sighs" and "orient incense." Like the "april prime" of the kindling forest tops, this opening marks off a hallowed moment of glorious natality, where flowers opening into their expression of "odorous sighs" and "orient incense" and wreathing the entrance to the *Triumph*'s visionary precincts take up their place as the "symbol flowers" (*Hellas*, 1095) of poesy that are in the poet's auspicious business of tuning in to and sounding out "the *yes* the heart breathes" so integral to finding our way back to both our (lost) human nature and our alienated world.

The morning flowers of the *Triumph* give poetic expression and tuition to an "intuition" of Cavell's about "language and world," which, while making room for the now too dominant intuition that language constructs (or "legislates") the world, would supplement it with this intuition turned in the "reverse direction, in which the world calls for words" (*AP*, 116) which in turn calls for such things of this world as the opening hand or flower as ready-to-hand figures for the initially listening or receiving faculty of τo ποιειν that must come before any mental grasping or handling of the world. This is, as said, the world-historical epistemological judgment that underlies both the rhetoric of the "Defence" pitting τo ποιειν against τo λογιζειν and the poetry of the *Triumph* about glaring lights that blind and sidereal orientations wafted our way only when "the breath/Of darkness reillumines even the least/Of heaven's living eyes" (390–2).

About the "breath of darkness." If one were to shift the emphasis of this phrase from the light imagery (that I confess myself to have been unduly fixated on in *Rousseau in England*) to the "breath" which is the specifically vital and resuscitating action of the darkness, the resulting "*breath*/Of darkness" might further suggest (there is an abundance of other contributing evidence) that underlying the poem's transvaluing battle of dark and light is, as said, a more fundamental "breath war," a psychomachia, between the "enamored air" of this framing proem and what becomes of its initial airing of things in "the clime/Of that cold light whose airs too soon deform."[16] At the mercy of a subsequently imposed and hardly enamored clime, almost everything and everyone in the *Triumph* suffers a monstrous transformation. That's what happens when one is left with "the action and the shape without the grace/Of life" (522–3). But in aversion to this vision of pervasive calamity and abomination, the poem crafts its opening lines into a performance of the sacred affirmative, according to which the life's breath of our (human, talking) form of life is, at the top of its bent, called to both the expending and disclosing of itself in an unbound discourse of desire, which would, in response to its "true Sun" (292) and with the inconsumable burning predicated of the divine, send the offerings of its "orient incense" and its "odorous sighs up to the smiling air."

This is a lovely picture, perhaps too lovely or flowery to be the whole truth. For even within the narrow compass of the proem, its composer and speaker experiences a falling off. The proem begins, *allegro*, with a swift spirit hastening to a good and glorious task that climaxes in the bravura strokes of all the flowers of thought and poesy burning up toward the heavens. But it then abruptly falls into a markedly slower and more *penseroso* tempo tracking how in "succession due" "Continent,/Isle, Ocean and all things that in them wear/The form and character of mortal mould" were mustered by the "Sun their father" and ordered to "bear/Their portion of the toil which he of old/ Took as his own and then imposed on them" (15–20). But these darker tones into which the music of what happens so quickly cadences is not the proem's final note. Several lines further into it, its speaker seems to anticipate the metaphoric possibilities of the breath of darkness gifting us with the stars, when on the pivot of "But I, whom thoughts which must remain untold/Had kept as wakeful as the stars/That gem the cone of night" he turns sharply away from what he has just presented as a world of constraining toil, and returns, in a "strange trance" which is expressly "not slumber," to the "freshness of that dawn," resumptively characterized as "sweet talk in music through the enamoured air" (39).

The now explicitly thoughtful composer of the proem thus reprises his opening theme with two related differences. One of these differences is critical to the poem's larger structure and import. The speaker makes the reprised morning music (which turns out to be not the first such sacred aubade in his experience) into the "enamoured" medium for the overwhelmingly hellish content of the vision that comprises the body of the poem as we have it. The thoughts of this seer of a world gone "all amiss" are so captivated by the strains of the enamored air of morning that they bring on a "strange trance," whose "[transparent] shade" conditions the entirety of the calamitously fallen world he subsequently sings the seeing of. Or, to assess his visionary and prophetic stance from the opposing, world- and history-bound perspective, the speaker's deep trance prevents neither the historical nor the natural "scene [from coming] through" as "clear as when a veil of light is drawn/O'er evening hills they glimmer" (30–33), because the whole of this spectacle of historical mischance is, from its inception, conditioned and made intensely and unavoidably clear by its grievous difference from the "enamoured air" in its evening or Hesperian aspect. (This is, I dare say, a quite deliberate lighting decision on Shelley's part. It works to the same framing effect as his placing of the Dantean "wonder" of Shelley's own infernal verses within the larger perspective of his *maestro ed autore* led from hell to Paradise by Love's soft note.)

The second, emphatically emphasized difference in the reprise of the "enamoured air" is its pronounced note of *dejà vu* or *dejà entendu*. "I knew" says the speaker "That I had felt the freshness of that dawn,/Bathed in the same cold dew my brow and hair" and "heard as there/The birds, the fountains and the Ocean hold/Sweet talk in music through the enamoured air" (33–9). With this emphasis, the poem's opening natality scene about the "birth/Of light" discloses itself as a moment of finding or reorienting one's self that has a history, the history of an open-ended but endlessly interrupted series of diurnal *re*findings that are there for the taking and the "going-on-with," but only, it would appear, after the daily rounds of drill and imposition have made one sufficiently receptive to them. The dawning aliveness common to all such refindings is not only shadowed by the knowledge that it is a routinely withdrawn gift of one's experience, forever leaving one with an intenser sense of how deplorable is "the action and the shape without the grace/Of life" (522-523). It is also graced with the news that this music whose "light is melody to lovers" is not next to one only in a spatial sense. It is also (potentially) next up in time as the sidereal orientation to which he may, as in a twinkling, find himself again "tempered" and so led on to something like the apparently founding but long deferred thought of Cavell that in one's utterly individual life "a blessing has to be seen to be offered, a promise of an authorization for me to become what I am" (*AP*, 38) as it is found there for the receiving in that gift for hearing things which Cavell calls "perfect pitch" and honors as the "title for experiences ranging from ones amounting to conversions down to small but lucid attestations that the world holds a blessing in store, that one is, in Emerson's and Nietzsche's image, taking steps, walking on, on one's own" (*AP*, 47).

In the proem of The Triumph of Life Adam's curse of mortality and toil comes after what is strategically positioned as the more primal event of a heliotropic world joyfully hastening to its task of glory and of good. And even after this resigned acknowledgment of the fated falling-off of the human, the visionary mind at play in the poem's framing narrative finds itself turning away from the encroaching gloom and returning, in entranced memory, to the treasured light, motion, note and odor of that earlier "enamored air" as both what this poem is to be written for and where it is to be written from. Even as the celebrant of the enamored air lays up his treasure in his own orient incense of praise song, he acknowledges that he has not been exempted either from his own human character or from the deplorable "types of things that are" (*Prometheus*, I.645). Very much to the contrary, he acknowledges that he bears the form and character of mortal mold with a Promethean increment of thoroughness and depth that is proportionate to how in precisely these flowers of the morning "opening their trembling eyelids to the kiss of day," he celebrates his own weakness for all that human flesh is heir to, not excluding his vulnerability to all he might hear coming his way from that star of love in the light of whose smile he, like his Rousseau, hopes to end his earthly path, and so also not excluding the possibility of Emerson's "induction otherwise" that this "universal sense of want and ignorance [is] but the fine innuendo by which the great soul makes its enormous claims" (*EL*, 385).

In "this cold common hell, our life," some even in the train of Life are said to have "subdued their age/By action *or by suffering*" (121–2, emphasis added). But what any actor or victim in this pageant of wretchedness is now most urgently called upon to suffer or bear is the gift of Promethean fire that, *in principio*, drove "man" into the distinctively human action of "speech [which] created thought,/Which is the measure of the universe" (*Prometheus*, II.iv.72–3). This is the magnanimous gift of intelligence and intelligibility which does not allow its recipients the miserable ease of turning a conveniently deaf ear to everything that is "is all here amiss," but it is also a gift which, at the dearest freshness deep down of "the *yes* the heart breathes," can vault itself into "the achieving of a promise of expression that can attract the good stranger to enter the precincts of its city of words" (*CH*, 7). For Shelley, this defining and never finally stifled aspiration of the form of life ἔχον λόγον recurrently finds its tuition in a gendered figure of desire that, precisely as "forever sought forever lost," calls on its humanly singled out hearers and bearers—those who cannot "uncreate/That world within this Chaos, mine and me,/Of which she was the veiled Divinity,/The world I say of thoughts that worshipped her" (*Epipsychidion*, 242–5)—to get each on their way toward what Thoreau would "call life" not in the manner of those "who are said to live in New England" but "direct on a tangent to this sphere, summer and winter, day and night, sun down, moon down, and at last earth down too" (*Walden*, 215), because, as Hugh Roberts puts it, the losses attendant on inevitable change open us to "the possibility of creative joy,"[17] open us to the possibilities of what Cavell calls our natality or "lively origination" or "heaven-born freedom" (*IQ*, 75).

Or, to give the last (shared) word to Shelley, Cavell and Emerson—all writers in the perfectionist business of inviting their readers to a position of "martyrdom ... in aspiration to an idea of the human" (*CH*, 56)—we, whose evidently mysterious doom it is to have been cast off into "our whole life as an education of error," are nonetheless, each and all, called to get on the necessarily aversive way of thinking through such "mysteries of human condition" (*EL*, 966) as are "after [my, our] constitution" (*EL*, 262) as a form of life, because for those "whose strife/Tills" our "garden ravaged" of a world "for the promise of a later birth," there is pregnant in the martyr's finely attuned "capacity for loss ... the chance of ecstasy" (*T*, 53), the chance of still further flowerings of orient incense, sent up to the smiling air of divinities of whom it can be confidently declared "Not gold, not blood, their altar dowers/ But votive tears and symbol flowers" (*Hellas*, 1094–5).

Notes

Preface and Acknowledgments

1 Stanley Cavell, *In Quest of the Ordinary: Lines of Skepticism and Romanticism* (Chicago: University of Chicago Press, 1988), ix, hereafter *IQ*. For a bibliography of works by Cavell through 1995, see Peter S. Fosl, "Stanley Cavell: A Bibliography 1955–1995" in Stanley Cavell and Stephen Mulhall, *The Cavell Reader*, Edited by Stephen Mulhall, Blackwell Readers (Cambridge, Mass.: Blackwell, 1996), 319–414; an earlier version of this bibliography also includes works about Cavell: *Bucknell Review* 32 (1989), 322–34, repr in Richard Fleming and Michael Payne, *The Senses of Stanley Cavell* (London. Toronto: Associated University Presses, 1989), 322–34. The most complete and up-to-date bibliography for students of literature is online at *OLP and Literary Studies Online*, <http: //www.olponline. wordpress.com/. . ./cavell-bibliography>.
2 Morris Eaves and Michael Fischer, *Romanticism and Contemporary Criticism* (Ithaca, NY: Cornell University Press, 1986), 230.
3 Stanley Cavell, *The Senses of Walden* (New York: Viking Press, 1972), 51, hereafter *SW*.
4 Ralph Waldo Emerson, ed., Joel Porte, *Essays and Lectures* (New York: Library of America, 1983), 479, hereafter *EL*.
5 Stanley Cavell, *Conditions Handsome and Unhandsome: The Constitution of Emersonian Perfectionism* (Chicago, IL: University of Chicago Press, 1990), 55, hereafter *CH*.
6 Unless otherwise noted, I will be quoting from the 1805 version of *The Prelude* as found in William Wordsworth, *The Prelude: 1799, 1805, 1850*, Jonathan Wordsworth, M. H. Abrams, and Stephen Gill (New York and London: Norton, 1979).
7 Eaves and Fischer, *Romanticism and Contemporary Criticism*, 230.
8 Stanley Cavell, *Little Did I Know: Excerpts from Memory* (Stanford, CA: Stanford University Press, 2010), 354, hereafter *LDIK*.
9 Stanley Cavell, *A Pitch of Philosophy: Autobiographical Exercises*, Jerusalem-Harvard Lectures (Cambridge, MA: Harvard University Press, 1994), 117, hereafter *AP*.
10 Eaves and Fischer, Romanticism and Contemporary Criticism, 230.
11 Ibid., 229.
12 Stanley Cavell, *This New Yet Unapproachable America: Lectures After Emerson After Wittgenstein*, Frederick Ives Carpenter Lectures (Albuquerque, NM: Living Batch Press, 1989), 45, herafter *TN*.
13 Stanley Cavell, *The World Viewed: Reflections on the Ontology of Film* (Cambridge, MA: Harvard University Press, 1979), 180, hereafter *WV*.

14 Ludwig Wittgenstein, *Philosophical Investigations*, Translated by G. E. M. Anscombe (New York: Macmillan, Blackwell, 1953), § 90, Wittgenstein's emphasis; hereafter *Investigations*. (Citations from the first part of the *Investigations* are by remark and indicated by §; citations from the second part are by page.).
15 Charles Altieri, "Wordsworth's 'Preface' as Literary Theory," *Criticism* 18(2) (1976 Spring): 128.
16 Stanley Cavell, *Themes Out of School: Effects and Causes* (San Francisco, CA: North Point Press, 1984), 51, hereafter *T*.

Chapter 1

1 Henry David Thoreau, *Walden; and Resistance to Civil Government*, 2nd edn., Edited by William John Rossi (New York: Norton, 1992), 1, 150; hereafter *Walden*.
2 Gerald Bruns, "Stanley Cavell's Shakespeare," *Critical Inquiry* 16(3) (1990 Spring): 612.
3 Stanley Cavell, *Must We Mean What We Say: A Book of Essays* (Cambridge [Eng.] and New York: Cambridge University Press, 1976), 19; hereafter *MW*. The phrase "linguistic phenomenology" is cited at *MW*, 99; it comes from Austin's "A Plea for Excuses," *Philosophical Papers*, 3rd edn, Edited by J. O. Urmson and G. J. Warnock (Oxford and New York: Oxford University Press, 1979), 182.
4 Stanley Cavell, *The Claim of Reason: Wittgenstein, Skepticism, Morality, and Tragedy* (Oxford and New York: Oxford University Press, 1979), xi; herafter *CR*.
5 Cavell is quoting from the Kemp Smith translation of Kant's *Critique of Pure Reason*, A 158, B 197. The German original reads, "die Bedingungen der *Möglichkeit der Erfahrung* überhaupt sind zugleich Bedingungen der *Möglichkeit der Gegenstände der Erfahrumg*" (Kant's emphases).
6 Stanley Cavell, *Disowning Knowledge in Seven Plays of Shakespeare* (Cambridge [Cambridgeshire] and New York: Cambridge University Press, 2003, updated edition); hereafter *DK*.
7 Cavell takes up the idea of the "father tongue" in *Senses of Walden*, 14ff, and in *In Quest of the Ordinary*, 133.
8 Stanley Cavell, *Contesting Tears: The Hollywood Melodrama of the Unknown Woman* (Chicago, IL: University of Chicago Press, 1996), 97; hereafter *CT*.
9 *Critical Inquiry* 13 (1987), 386–93. The piece is titled a fragment because its original placement was in a public lecture, which in 1996 would be published as the second chapter of *Contesting Tears*: "Psychoanalysis and Cinema: Moments of *Letter from an Unknown Woman*." In the latter, the fragment appears as pp. 90–7.

10 My use of "bill-filling" and "cap-fitting" draws on John Austin's elucidation of "name-giving" and "sense-giving" as two distinguishable directions in a speech act of identification: "How to Talk: Some Simple Ways," *Philosophical Papers*, 143.
11 Stanley Cavell, *Pursuits of Happiness: TheHollywood Comedy of Remarriage* (Cambridge, MA: Harvard University Press, 1981), 78; hereafter *PH*.
12 To underscore the pressure exerted on Cavell by this passage of fewer than fifty common and mostly monosyllabic words, I note the main sites and dates of its many returns over a decade: "Thinking of Emerson" (1978) and "An Emersonian Mood" (1980), both in *The Senses of Walden*; "The Politics of Interpretation" (1981), 50, and "The Thought of Movies" (1982), 19, both in *Themes* (1984); *In Quest of the Ordinary* (1983), 22; "Hope Against Hope" (1985), 134, in *Conditions Handsome and Unhandsome*; also in *Conditions* (1988), 55, 65, 79, 97–8.
13 The flamingly ordinary "sees . . . as" is in quotation marks and italics in order to indicate the phrasing's draw on what in a long section of *The Claim of Reason*, Cavell discusses as "seeing something as something" [which] is what Wittgenstein calls "interpretation" [and] is the principal topic of the chief section of what appears as Part II of the *Investigations* (354). The section is launched under the famous sign of the duck-rabbit, and involves what Wittgenstein calls the "dawning of an aspect."
14 See Edward Duffy, "From Proverbs of Ashes to Coals on the Tongue: The Scriptural Dynamics of Luke," *Genre: Forms of Discourse and Culture* XL (2007 Fall/Winter): 171–200.
15 Robert Alter and Frank Kermode, *The Literary Guide to the Bible* (Cambridge, MA: The Belknap Press of Harvard University Press, 1987), 31.
16 In J. P. Fokkelman's contribution on "Genesis" in *The Literary Guide to the Bible*, the scene of Jacob wrestling with the angel is brilliantly analyzed as an agonistic drama of acknowledgment in which a protagonist whose very name is Fraud is forced to "stand up for himself, take responsibility" (52).
17 John Keats, *The Letters of John Keats*, 2 Vols, Edited by Hyder Edward Rollins (Cambridge: Harvard University Press, 1958), I.243.
18 From *The Babylonian Captivity of the Church* in Martin Luther, *Three Treatises* (Philadelphia, PA: Fortress Press, 1970), 193.
19 Seamus Heaney, *Station Island* (New York: Farrar, Straus & Giroux, 1985), 19.

Chapter 2

1 Seamus Heaney, *Seeing Things* (New York: Farrar, Straus & Giroux, 1991), 25.
2 Stanley Cavell, *Philosophical Passages: Wittgenstein, Emerson, Austin, Derrida*, Bucknell Lectures in Literary Theory (Oxford: Blackwell, 1995), 103; hereafter *PP*.

3 See his *Science and the Modern World* (New York: The Free Press, 1967), 75–94.
4 Stanley Cavell, *Philosophy the Day after Tomorrow* (Cambridge, MA: Belknap Press of Harvard University Press, 2005), 266; hereafter *PDAT*.
5 Eaves and Fischer, *Romanticism and Contemporary Criticism*, 230.
6 From "Inniskeen Road: July Evening" in Patrick Kavanagh, *Collected Poems* (New York: Norton, 1973), 19.
7 Eaves and Fischer, *Romanticism and Contemporary Criticism*, 230.
8 William Wordsworth, *The Prose Works of William Wordsworth*, 3 Vols, Edited by W. J. B. Owen and Jane Worthington Smyser (Oxford: Clarendon Press, 1974), I.128–9.
9 Eaves and Fischer, *Romanticism and Contemporary Criticism*, 230.
10 Ibid.
11 I am indebted here to Timothy Gould's scrupulously patient tracking of the "story" of Cavell and the voice, indebted in particular to his underscoring of Cavell's acknowledgment of the "obscurity of the promptings" that may have led him into subjects where he had not yet found a firm footing: Timothy Gould, *Hearing Things: Voice and Method in the Writing of Stanley Cavell* (Chicago, IL: University of Chicago Press, 1998). A less obscure and immediately pertinent fact in the story of Cavell and the voice is that, as Cavell himself recounts in the Foreword to *The Claim of Reason*, this first part of the lengthily gestated *Claim of Reason* was its last written. It was, written, that is to say, at a stage in Cavell's philosophical progress where he was well on his way toward Emerson in particular and romanticism in general.
12 Stanley Cavell, "'Epilogue: The *Investigations*' Everyday Aesthetic of Itself,'" in *The Cavell Reader*, Edited by Stephen Mulhall (Cambridge, MA: Blackwell, 1996), 389.
13 Stanley Cavell, *Emerson's Transcendental Études* (Stanford, CA: Stanford University Press, 2003), 244; hereafter *E*.
14 "The wood-cock snaring episode [is] a 'dry run' for the boat-stealing episode." Joshua Wilner, *Feeding on Infinity: Readings in the Romantic Rhetoric of Internalization* (Baltimore, MD: Johns Hopkins University Press, 2000), 38.
15 For a further and bracingly antithetical development in this school of Wordsworthian criticism, see Paul H. Fry, *Wordsworth and the Poetry of What We Are* (New Haven, CT: Yale University Press, 2008). Fry finds in the authentic Wordsworth (the one not trying to be the kind of philosophical poet Coleridge wanted him to be) not much of either spousal verse or the transcendental imagination. Instead, he very pertinently harks back to Wordsworth's "fundamental intellectual framework, his adherence to the monist empirical tradition that passes from Locke through David Hartley" (xi), a positioning of himself and Wordsworth that leads him away from Hartman on the eruptive and

god-like Imagination of *Prelude* 6, and toward a Snowdon of whose representation of a "majestic intellect." Fry first asks "what is not natural here?" (127), and then briefly adduces even the Simplon Pass as one of many places in this authorship where you can find a Wordsworth for whom "the descendental pull of the natural sphere of things is so strong . . . that it renders transcendental belief staggeringly difficult . . . to achieve and sustain" (125).
16 William Wordsworth, *The Prelude*, 100.
17 David Bromwich, *Disowned by Memory: Wordsworth's Poetry of the 1790's* (Chicago, IL: Chicago University Press, 1998), 22.
18 Bromwich, *Disowned by Memory*, 22.
19 Ibid., 172.
20 Ibid., 109.
21 Seamus Heaney, *Seeing Things* (New York: Farrar, Straus & Giroux, 1991), 66.

Chapter 3

1 Henry David Thoreau, *Walden; and Resistance to Civil Government*, 2nd edn, Edited by William John Rossi (New York: Norton, 1992), 115.
2 William Wordsworth, *The Prose Works of William Wordsworth*, 3 Vols, W. J. B. Owen and Jane Worthington Smyser (Oxford: Clarendon Press, 1974), I.139.
3 Morris Eaves and Michael Fischer, *Romanticism and Contemporary Criticism* (Ithaca, NY: Cornell University Press, 1986), 229.
4 Jerome J. McGann, *The Romantic Ideology: A Critical Investigation* (Chicago, IL and London: University of Chicago Press, 1983), 1.
5 McGann, *Romantic Ideology*, 1.
6 Marjorie Levinson, *Wordsworth's Great Period Poems: Four Essays* (Cambridge, MA: Harvard University Press, 1986), 4.
7 Levinson, *Wordsworth's Great Period*, 12.
8 Ibid., 1.
9 Eaves and Fischer, *Romanticism and Contemporary Criticism*, 238.
10 Levinson, *Wordsworth's Great Period*, 5.
11 Ibid.
12 Ibid., 4.
13 Ibid., 10.
14 William Keach, *Arbitrary Power: Romanticism, Language, Politics*, Literature in History (Princeton, NJ and Oxford: Princeton University Press, 2004), 121. The German terms are quoted by Keach from Marx's *Dix-Huit Brumaire*. For a fuller discussion of Cavell's crucial distinction between the conditions of our natural (human) history and the historically

determined conditions of any given society, see Edward Duffy, *The Constitution of Shelley's Poetry: The Argument of Language in Prometheus Unbound* (London: Anthem Press, 2009), xxiii–xxvi.
15 McGann, *Romantic Ideology*, 26.
16 Alan Liu, *Wordsworth: The Sense of History* (Stanford, CA: Stanford University Press, 1989), 100.
17 William Wordsworth, *The Prelude: 1799, 1805, 1850*, Edited by Jonathan Wordsworth, M. H. Abrams, and Stephen Gill (New York and London: Norton, 1979), 9.
18 James K. Chandler, *Wordsworth's Second Nature: A Study of the Poetry and Politics* (Chicago, IL: The University of Chicago Press, 1984), 194.
19 Chandler, *Wordsworth's Second Nature*, 194.
20 Ibid., 188.
21 Charles Altieri, "Wordsworth's 'Preface' as Literary Theory," *Criticism* 18(2) (1976 Spring): 128; Paul H. Fry, *Wordsworth and the Poetry of What We Are* (New Haven, CT: Yale University Press, 2008). Wittgenstein's sense of our natural reactions as worked out in language and form of life points to a dimension of the natural, different from (though not incompatible with) the sense of the natural championed by eco-romanticists such as Jonathan Bate in his *Romantic Ecology: Wordsworth and the Environmental Tradition* (London: Routledge, 1991). I share Bate's exasperation with Alan Liu's exaggerated but still characteristic New-Historical claim that "there is no Nature" (Liu, *Wordsworth*, 38). Someone needed to say, "'Nature' is a term that needs to be contested, not rejected. It is profoundly unhelpful to say 'There is no nature'" (Bate, 56). But it seems to me that Bate is imagining a diminished, alienated, and too narrowly "green" nature, when, in assertions like the following, he draws an either/or line between romantic thinking and what that thinking must find itself called to think its way through: "The Romantic Ideology is not . . . a theory of imagination and symbol . . . but a theory of ecosystems and unalienated labor" (10). Romanticism is both of these things, and it is so in the nature of things, in the nature of human labor with and among things. The term "nature" has more recently been investigated and to an extent rehabilitated by Paul Fry's "stone-colored" (74) criticism, coming out of a "monist empirical tradition" (xiii) and proposing that Wordsworth's great poetic discovery and the point of his insistence on nature was the "ontic unity of the human and nonhuman in the sheer minerality of things" (59). Both the nature of Wordsworth's discovery and the degree of its insistence were, according to Fry, reactions against a regnant picture of "things" as they had been "neutralized and alienated by Kant." The upshot is not the Wordsworth of the egotistical sublime but the poet whose "attention to objects in his poetry and his theory of poetry is an almost monastic discipline aimed at *effacing* the ego" (201, Frye's emphasis). I find much of this congenial, but I feel somewhat like the young Shelley returning from his first (and

last) geology class at Cambridge with the exasperated exclamation that the professor talked of "stones, stones! nothing but stones!" (as quoted from Hogg in Newman Ivey White, *Shelley* [New York: A. A. Knopf, 1940], I.78). Fry makes much of the closing line of "A Slumber Did My Spirit Seal" but not enough, it seems to me, of the last item in its catalogue of the nonhuman things rolled round in earth's diurnal course, which is not of the mineral kind but of the sap-filled vegetable kind we call trees.

22 See David Ellis, *Wordsworth, Freud and the Spots of Time: Interpretation in "The Prelude"* (Cambridge, MA: Cambridge University Press, 1985), 17–34.

23 In her study of the 1804 five-book *Prelude*, Sybil S. Eakin shows how its intermediate placement of the Snowdon material *before* the concluding spots of time frames the latter and serves to draw out their maturing significance regarding "the power of the mind." Although the phrasing I have used shows up only in the 1850 version, its "sense conducting to ideal form" remains a formulation succinctly pertinent to the first spot's similarly vertical structure of pool, woman and beacon. One might even surmise that, once drawn into intimate compositional conversation with the Snowdon vision (which I will shortly be discussing), the verticality of the first spot of time played no small part in the fact of Wordsworth's discourse going on to this kind of summarizing statement about what as an image of the mind Snowdon was about. See Sybil S. Eakin, "The Spots of Time in Early Versions of The Prelude," *Studies in Romanticism* 12 (1973 Winter): 389–405.

24 Liu, *Wordsworth*, 390.

25 Thomas Weiskel, *The Romantic Sublime: Studies in the Structure and Psychology of Transcendence* (Baltimore, MD: Johns Hopkins University Press, 1976), 175–85; William Wordsworth, *The Prelude*, 578–9. Weiskel's reading of this scene is forceful, subtle and suggestive, but, in considering the girl in isolation from the pool and beacon, he sees her as an image of militant repression and regression. "The vision [i.e. of her] occurs in flight from the characters" (179) of writing at the sight of the gibbet, but not in the recuperative sense of a turning away from the dead letter. On the contrary, for Weiskel this flight represents a further turn of the screw of death-dealing repression. Defensively *seen* but not *read* by Wordsworth, she fights the visionary poet's battle "against the fact that things may come to signify" (180). As will become evident, this is a reading of this figure, very different, indeed opposite, from my own.

26 Jonathan Bishop, "Wordsworth and the 'Spots of Time,'" *ELH* 26 (1959 March): 56.

27 J. Douglas Kneale, *Monumental Writing: Aspects of Rhetoric in Wordsworth's Poetry* (Lincoln, NE: University of Nebraska Press, 1988). See also Robert Young, "'For Thou Wert There': History, Erasure and Superscription in '*The Prelude*,'" in *Demarcating the Disciplines: Philosophy*

Literature Art, Edited by Samuel Weber (Minneapolis, MN: University of Minnesota Press, 1986), 103–28; Mary Jacobus, *Romanticism, Writing and Sexual Difference* (Oxford: Clarendon, 1989), 16–27.
28. Kneale, *Monumental Writing: Aspects of Rhetoric in Wordsworth's Poetry*, 142, 142, 144, 147.
29. Levinson, *Wordsworth's Great Period*, 6–13.
30. Paul De Man, Burt et al., eds., *Romanticism and Contemporary Criticism: The Gauss Seminar* (Baltimore, MD: Johns Hopkins University Press, 1993), 82.
31. Liu, *Wordsworth*, 364; Frances Ferguson, *Wordsworth: Language as Counter-Spirit* (New Haven, CT: Yale University Press, 1977), 33.
32. William Wordsworth and W. J. B. Owen and Jane Worthington Smyser, *Wordsworth: Prose Works*, II.185.
33. William Wordsworth and W. J. B. Owen and Jane Worthington Smyser, *Wordsworth: Prose Works*, II.185.
34. Chandler, *Wordsworth's Second Nature*, 188.
35. Robert Alter, *The Art of Biblical Narrative* (New York: Basic Books, 1981), 52.
36. In retrospect, this seems an early step toward Cavell's later romantically induced claim about the fact and the necessity of a human self-authoring, which does not begin with "the dust of the ground and magic breath . . . [but rather with] an uncreated human being and [an incommunicable] power of thinking" (*IQ*, 111) whose medium is "our breath made words."
37. Liu, *Wordsworth*, 361.
38. Ibid., 400.
39. Ibid., 448.
40. Ibid., 361.
41. This increasingly insistent strain in Cavell's thinking has recently issued into Stanley Cavell, *Little Did I Know: Excerpts from Memory* (Stanford, CA: Stanford University Press, 2010).
42. Joshua Wilner, *Feeding on Infinity: Readings in the Romantic Rhetoric of Internalization* (Baltimore, MD: Johns Hopkins University Press, 2000), 10–11; Simon Jarvis, *Wordsworth's Philosophic Song* (Cambridge, MA: Cambridge University Press, 2007), 219–23.
43. Liu, *Wordsworth*, 449.
44. Ibid., 212.
45. Ibid., 222.
46. Ibid., 211, 211, 455.
47. John Keats, *The Letters of John Keats*, 2 Vols, Edited by Hyder Edward Rollins (Cambridge, MA: Harvard University Press, 1958), I.281.
48. In his psychoanalytic reading of Wordsworth, Joshua Wilner tellingly connects the spatial and dynamic arrangement of the infant-babe tableau with both Snowdon and the spots of time. In the former, resumptively named by Wordsworth "the first/Poetic spirit of our human life" (*Prelude*, 2.275–6), the "gaze passing between the mother's eye and the child evokes the line of force that [in Snowdon] connects the moon to the breach in

the mist, while this breach also, as a 'breathing place' that draws down to 'the voice of waters' rising through the mist, seems to have some disturbed relation to the mouth of 'the babe,/Nursed in his mother's arms.'" Wilner, *Feeding on Infinity: Readings in the Romantic Rhetoric of Internalization*, 11.
49 Jarvis, *Wordsworth's Philosophic Song*, 221.
50 Ibid., 221.
51 Ibid., 223. With "emphatically," Jarvis is recalling both Wordsworth's affirmation that "such a being" as the infant babe of his conjecture "emphatically . . . lives,/An inmate of this *active* universe" (Wordsworth's emphasis), and his own explicitly philosophical idea of an "emphatic concept," examples of which Jarvis finds in *life* and *art*, words which "are, ineliminably, normative or evaluative as well as descriptive" (Jarvis, 187), because they "are haunted by a desire, or a need, which makes of them more than can be exhausted in adequation to a state of affairs" (31). To call something "life" or "art," Jarvis argues, is not simply or not always simply a matter of placing it in a larger generic category. It is (often) to praise it and hence to imply that some things accurately enough grouped under these generic terms by the zoologist or the curator may not live up to the standard of life or art. Think of the outraged traditionalist saying of the latest would-be revolutionary breakthrough "That's not art," or of wisecracking Thoreau addressing his readers as "you who are said to live in New England."
52 Liu, *Wordsworth*, 447.
53 Ibid., 211.
54 Ibid.
55 Ibid., 369.
56 Ibid.
57 Ibid.
58 Ibid., 449.
59 Ibid., 38.
60 Jarvis, *Wordsworth's Philosophic Song*, 215.

Chapter 4

1 Donald H. Reiman and Neil Fraistat, *Shelley's Poetry and Prose*, 2nd edn (New York: Norton, 2002); hereafter *NS*. This is the edition from which, unless otherwise noted, I will be quoting Shelley's prose by page and his poetry by line number.
2 See especially Terence Allan Hoagwood, *Skepticism & Ideology: Shelley's Political Prose and Its Philosophical Context from Bacon to Marx* (Iowa City, IA: University of Iowa Press, 1988), 1–77.

3 I say mostly the West because Shelley also invokes such Eastern deities as Ahrimanes, Siva and Vishnu, undoubtedly due to the eighteenth- and nineteenth-century vogue of syncretic mythology, so copiously documented by Stuart Curran in his *Shelley's Annus Mirabilis: The Maturing of an Epic Vision* (San Marino, CA: Huntington Library, 1975). On the whole matter of Shelley's inheritance of his culture, one can find a bracingly authoritative counter to Santayana's much quoted characterization of him as a poet of voluntary disinheritance in C. S. Lewis's demonstration that he is a "more *classical* poet than" the Augustan Dryden. Santayana, *Essays in Literary Criticism* (New York: Scribner's, 1956), 188; Lewis, "Shelley, Dryden, and Mr. Eliot," *Selected Literary Essays* (London: Cambridge University Press, 1969), 188.

4 For the most complete exploration of the spirit-of-the-age trope in the romantic era, see James Chandler, *England in 1819: The Politics of Literary Culture and the Case of Romantic Historicism* (Chicago, IL: University of Chicago Press, 1998).

5 I derive this naming of the counters to Prometheus's furies from Earl Wasserman's apt application to the Prometheus story of the angels ministering to the Satanically tempted Jesus in *Mark* 1:12. See *Shelley: A Critical Reading* (Baltimore, MD: Johns Hopkins Press, 1971), 300.

6 This is one of the tasks of my reading of the play in *Prometheus Unbound, Constitution of Shelley's Poetry*, 57–239.

7 Reiman, *Shelley's "The Triumph of Life": A Critical Study* (Urbana, IL: University of Illinois Press, 1965), 13; Wasserman, *A Critical Reading*, 326ff; Hartman, *Criticism in the Wilderness: The Study of Literature Today* (New Haven, CT and London: Yale University Press, 1980), 102.

8 See Duffy, *Constitution of Shelley's Poetry*, 108–10, pages which are greatly indebted to John Hollander's *The Figure of Echo: A Mode of Allusion in Milton and After* (Berkeley, CA: University of California Press, 1981). His "regent of discourse" is on page 17, and the quotation from Bacon—from *De dignitate et augmentis scientarum* II.xiii—on page 10.

9 Judith Chernaik, *The Lyrics of Shelley* (Cleveland, OH: Press of Case Western Reserve, 1959), 32.

10 William Keach, *Shelley's Style* (New York and London: Methuen, 1984), 29.

11 See my reading of "Euganean Hills" in *Constitution of Shelley's Poetry*, 21–2.

12 Edward Duffy, "Where Shelley Wrote and What He Wrote For: The Example of 'The Ode to the West Wind,'" *Studies in Romanticism* 23(3) (1984 Fall): 351–72; and *Constitution of Shelley's Poetry*, 33–56.

13 See his brilliant reading of the beginning of *The Acts of the Apostles*, in *The Parasite*, translated by Lawrence R. Scher (Baltimore, MD: Johns Hopkins University Press, 1982), 40–7.

14 Donald H. Reiman, *Percy Bysshe Shelley*, Twayne's English Authors Series (Boston, MA: Twayne Publishers, 1990), 97.

15 See Keach, *Shelley's Style*, 154–83.
16 Harold Bloom, *The Visionary Company: A Reading of English Romantic Poetry* (Ithaca, NY: Cornell University Press, 1971), 7–15.

Chapter 5

1 All quotations from Dante are taken from Dante Alighieri, *The Divine Comedy*, Edited and Translated by Charles S. Singleton (Princeton, NJ: Princeton University Press, 1970). The Merwin translation of this is "And I to him, 'I am one who, when/Love breathes in me, take note, and as it is/dictated within, go setting it down," Dante Alighieri, *Purgatorio: A New Verse Translation*, Translated by W. S. Merwin (New York: Alfred A. Knopf, 2001), 235.
2 Thomas Pfau, "Tropes of Desire: Figuring the 'Insufficient Void' of Self-Consciousness in Shelley's *Epipsychidion*," *Keats-Shelley Journal* 40 (1991): 109.
3 Hollander, *Figure of Echo*.
4 See especially Earl Schulze, "The Dantean Quest of *Epipsychidion*," *Studies in Romanticism* 21(2) (1982 Summer): 191–216.
5 Dante Alighieri, *Purgatorio*, 145.
6 Frederick L. Jones, ed. *The Letters of Percy Bysshe Shelley*, 2 Vols (Oxford: Clarendon Press, 1964), 434; hereafter *Letters*.
7 Dante Alighieri, *Purgatorio*, 146.
8 See Duffy, *Constitution of Shelley's Poetry*, 79–88.
9 On the rhetorical figure of metalepsis, its relation to Echo as the regent of discourse, and the term's origin in μεταλαμβάνω, see Hollander, *Figure of Echo*, 133ff. The Greek word has a wide range of meaning from the partaking of something, to the pursuing or succeeding of someone. Hollander focuses on the term's etymological root in "taking after" and shows how that basic sense is at play in our way of "understanding a prior meaning" by taking after it in both the sense of trying to keep up with it and of emulating it.
10 Stuart M. Sperry, *Shelley's Major Verse: The Narrative and Dramatic Poetry* (Cambridge, MA: Harvard University Press, 1988), 169.
11 Carl Woodring, *Politics in English Romantic Poetry* (Cambridge, MA: Harvard University Press, 1970), 322.
12 Schulze, "Dantean Quest," 203.
13 As already indicated, Earl Schulze precedes me in assigning the Actaeon figure almost as large a place in *Epipsychidion* as in *Adonais*, but his reading of the figure as indicative of a pathological condition is very different from my own understanding of it as a beautiful idealism of heroically agonized witness, one where in this instance, the martyr almost gives up the good fight of witnessing to the world he thinks.
14 Kenneth Neill Cameron, "The Planet-Tempest Passage in *Epipsychidion*," *PMLA* 63 (1948): 950–72.

15 Denis de Rougemont, *Love in the Western World* (Princeton, NJ: Princeton University Press, 1983), 221.
16 Angela Leighton, "Love, Writing and Skepticism in *Epipsychidion*," in *The New Shelley: Later Twentieth-Century Views*, Edited by G. Kim Blank (New York: St. Martin's, 1991), 226.
17 Leighton, "Love, Writing and Skepticism in *Epipsychidion*," 226.
18 Ibid., 227.
19 Mary Wollstonecraft Shelley, *The Letters of Mary Wollstonecraft Shelley*, Edited by Betty T. Bennet (Baltimore, MD: Johns Hopkins University Press, 1980), I.223.
20 G. M. Matthews, "A Volcano's Voice in Shelley," *ELH* 24 (1957): 191–228.
21 Woodring, *Politics*, 257.
22 Seamus Heaney, *Finders Keepers: Selected Prose 1971–2001* (New York: Farrar, Straus & Giroux, 2002), 147, 154.
23 J. Hillis Miller, "The Critic as Host," in *Deconstruction and Criticism* (New York: Seabury Press, 1979), 217–53.
24 Matthews, "Volcano's Voice," 222.
25 Ibid., 206.
26 William Andrew Ulmer, *Shelleyan Eros: The Rhetoric of Romantic Love* (Princeton, NJ: Princeton University Press, 1990), 144.
27 Jerrold E. Hogle, *Shelley's Process: Radical Transference and the Development of His Major Works* (New York: Oxford University Press, 1988), 300–1.
28 Hugh Roberts, *Shelley and the Chaos of History: A New Politics of Poetry* (University Park, PA: Pennsylvania State University Press, 1997).
29 Roberts, *Shelley and Chaos of History*, 444.
30 Miller, "Critic as Host," 238.
31 Kenneth Burke, *The Philosophy of Literary Form: Studies in Symbolic Action* (Baton Rouge, LA: Louisiana State University Press, 1941), 45.
32 Pfau, "Tropes of Desire," 120–1.
33 Peter Sacks, *The English Elegy: Studies in the Genre from Spenser to Yeats* (Baltimore, MD and London: Johns Hopkins University Press, 1985), 138–65.
34 Pfau, "Tropes of Desire," 107 (Pfau's scare quotes).
35 Leighton, "Love, Writing and Skepticism in *Epipsychidion*," 226.
36 Ibid.
37 Adrienne Rich, *Diving into the Wreck: Poems 1971–1972* (New York: Norton, 1994), 23.
38 My own remarking of this pregnant phrase, twice used in *Prometheus Unbound*, I owe to Michael O'Neill, *The All-Sustaining Air: Romantic Legacies and Renewals in British, American and Irish Poetry Since 1900* (Oxford: Oxford University Press, 2007), 16. It's worth quoting here some of what O'Neill says about Shelley's use of the phrase: "The air we breathe is a hackneyed phrase, revivified by Shelley, for whom the 'world-surrounding ether' (1.661) serves as an image of the way in which humans are affected by, and affect, prevailing climates of thought and belief."

39 Richard Holmes, *Shelley: The Pursuit* (New York: E. P. Dutton, 1975), 657.
40 Jarvis, *Wordsworth's Philosophic Song*, 187.
41 On paradigm and syntagm as the axes of language, see Roland Barthes, *Elements of Semiology*, Translated by Annette Lavers and Colin Smith (New York: Hill and Wang, 1968); Ferdinand de Saussure, *Course in General Linguistics*, Translated by Wade Baskin (New York: Philosophical Library, 1959).
42 John Keats, *The Letters of John Keats*, 2 Vols, Edited by Hyder Edward Rollins (Cambridge, MA: Harvard University Press, 1958), II.167.
43 John W. Wright, *Shelley's Myth of Metaphor* (Athens, GA: University of Georgia Press, 1970), 29.
44 For Milton's use of "Anarch," see *Paradise Lost* II.988. For Shelley's, see Frederick Startridge Ellis, *A Lexical Concordance to the Poetical Works of Percy Bysshe Shelley* (New York: B. Franklin, 1968). His most pertinent uses of the word are at line 152 of "Lines Written among the Euganean Hills," and at lines 49, 318, and 934 of *Hellas*.
45 Edward Duffy, *Rousseau in England: The Context for Shelley's Critique of the Enlightenment* (Berkeley, CA: University of California Press, 1979), 142.
46 Sacks, *English Elegy*, 151.
47 Ibid., 164.
48 William Wordsworth and Alexander Balloch Grosart, *The Prose Works of William Wordsworth for the First Time Collected*, with Additions from Unpublished Manuscripts, Edited by Alexander Balloch Grosart, Illustrated by Alexander Balloch Grosart (London and New York: Moxon AMS Press, 1967), III.463.
49 Wasserman, *A Critical Reading*, 493.
50 Duffy, *Rousseau in England*, 142–3.
51 Marcel Détienne, *Dionysos at Large*, Translated by Arthur Goldhammer (Cambridge, MA: Harvard University Press, 1989), 35.
52 Détienne, *Dionysos at Large*, 59.
53 Ibid., 64.
54 Ibid., 46.
55 *Upaithric* is a coinage of Shelley's from the Greek ὑπαίθριος, meaning open to the air or, perhaps more pertinently, open to the αἰθήρ, the purer air of the heavens. The word can be found in an unabridged English dictionary as the more correctly transliterated as *hypaethral*. The passage from Shelley's letter from Naples merits quoting at length: "I now understand why the Greeks were such great Poets, & above all I can account, it seems to me, for the harmony the unity the perfection the uniform excellence of all their works of art. They lived in a perpetual commerce with external nature and nourished themselves upon the spirit of its forms. Their theatres were all open to the mountains & and the sky. Their columns that ideal type of a scared forest with its roof of interwoven tracery admitted the light & wind, the odour & the

freshness of the country penetrated the cities. Their temples were mostly upaithric; & the flying clouds, the stars or the deep sky were seen above" (*Letters*, II.74–5).
56 Détienne, *Dionysos at Large*, 59, 64.
57 Woodring, *Politics*, 257.
58 See Duffy, *Constitution of Shelley's Poetry*, 78ff.

Chapter 6

1 Ralph Waldo Emerson, *Essays and Lectures*, Edited by Joel Porte (New York: Library of America, 1983), 385.
2 Seamus Heaney, *Opened Ground: Selected Poems 1966–1996* (New York: Farrar, Straus & Giroux, 1998), 282.
3 *Rousseau in England*.
4 *Wordsworth's Philosophic Song*, 42, Jarvis' emphasis.
5 Heaney, *Seeing Things*, 75.
6 Reiman, *Shelley's "Triumph"*, 11–18.
7 See *Rousseau in England*, 73ff.
8 In this connection and in light of how the perfectionist writer is driven toward constitutions of words that would witness to "what he loves in dream" (*Prometheus*, IV.268), I will happily confess myself more receptive to Donald Reiman's contention that Rousseau's *La Nouvelle Héloïse* "provides the organizing metaphor for large sections of 'The Triumph of Life'" (*NS*, 482). The principle of this organization is Rousseau's avowal in his *Confessions* of the same perfectionist motive toward the writing of *La Nouvelle Héloïse* as that driving Shelley toward the creation of "beautiful idealisms of moral excellence." "Seeing nothing that existed worthy of my exalted feelings," writes Rousseau, "I fostered them in an ideal world which my creative imagination soon peopled with beings after my own heart," as quoted in *NS*, 482 from the translation of J. M. Cohen (Penguin Books, 1954). The French original, in Book 9 of the *Confessions*, is on p. 427 of the Pléiade edition.
9 "Venus-complex" is the useful coinage of Glenn O'Malley, *Shelley and Synesthesia*. (Evanston, IL: Northwestern University Press, 1964), 58–88.
10 *Keats Letters*, II.101.
11 Paul DeMan, "Shelley Disfigured," in *Deconstruction and Criticism*, Harold Bloom (New York: A Continuum Book, Seabury Press, 1979), 39–73.
12 I am grateful to Norton Batkin for so memorably choosing and constellating passages from these pages of *Little Did I Know* at the celebration of its publication preceding the conference, "Stanley Cavell and Literary Studies: Consequences of Skepticism," held at Harvard University, October 14–16, 2010.)

13 William Hazlitt, *The Complete Works of William Hazlitt, Twenty-One Volumes*, Edited by P. P. Howe (London: J.M. Dent, 1930), 16.273.
14 Dante Alighieri, *The Inferno of Dante*, Robert Pinsky (New York: Farrar, Straus & Giroux, 1994), 308.
15 Heaney, *Station Island*, 76.
16 This alternative phrasing of "the breath/Of darkness" might also cue a hearing of the *Triumph*'s opening lines as most interested in "the *birth/ Of light*" (6–7), most interested not in enlightened ideas or opinions or theses but in the conditions from which such intellectual goods emerge. This is a voicing and hearing of the two phrases that is very much encouraged by, in both cases, a tercet-spanning enjambment, emphasizing *breath* or *birth*, this a management of the verse line that is also evident in the "*burned*" predicated of the flowers' orient incense at the beginning of the fifth tercet.
17 Roberts, *Shelley and Chaos of History*, 397.

Bibliography

Alter, Robert. *The Art of Biblical Narrative*. New York: Basic Books, 1981.
Alter, Robert and Frank Kermode. *The Literary Guide to the Bible*. Cambridge, MA: The Belknap Press of Harvard University Press, 1987.
Altieri, Charles. "Wordsworth's 'Preface' as Literary Theory." *Criticism* 18(2) (1976 Spring): 122–46.
Austin, J. L. *Philosophical Papers*, 3rd edn. Edited by J. O. Urmson and G. J. Warnock. Oxford: Oxford University Press, 1976.
Barthes, Roland. *Elements of Semiology*. Translated by Annette Lavers and Colin Smith. New York: Hill and Wang, 1968.
Bate, Jonathan. *Romantic Ecology: Wordsworth and the Environmental Tradition*. London: Routledge, 1991.
Bates, Milton J. *Wallace Stevens: A Mythology of Self*. Berkeley, CA: University of California Press, 1985.
Bishop, Jonathan. "Wordsworth and the 'Spots of Time.'" *ELH* 26 (1959 March): 45–65.
Bloom, Harold. *The Visionary Company: A Reading of English Romantic Poetry*. Ithaca, NY: Cornell University Press, 1971.
Bromwich, David. *Disowned by Memory: Wordsworth's Poetry of the 1790's*. Chicago, IL: Chicago University Press, 1998.
Bruns, Gerald. "Stanley Cavell's Shakespeare." *Critical Inquiry* 16(3) (1990 Spring): 612–32.
Burke, Kenneth. *The Philosophy of Literary Form: Studies in Symbolic Action*. Baton Rouge, LA: Louisiana State University Press, 1941.
Cameron, Kenneth Neill. "The Planet-Tempest Passage in *Epipsychidion*." *PMLA* 63 (1948): 950–72.
Cavell, Stanley. *The Claim of Reason: Wittgenstein, Skepticism, Morality, and Tragedy*. Oxford and New York: Oxford University Press, 1979.
— *Conditions Handsome and Unhandsome: The Constitution of Emersonian Perfectionism*. Chicago, IL: University of Chicago Press, 1990.
— *Contesting Tears: The Hollywood Melodrama of the Unknown Woman*. Chicago, IL: University of Chicago Press, 1996.
— *Disowning Knowledge in Seven Plays of Shakespeare*. Cambridge [Cambridgeshire] and New York: Cambridge University Press, 2003, updated edition.
— *Emerson's Transcendental Études*. Stanford, CA: Stanford University Press, 2003.
— "'Epilogue: The *Investigations*' Everyday Aesthetic of Itself.'" In *The Cavell Reader*. Edited by Stephen Mulhall. Cambridge, MA: Blackwell, 1996.

— *In Quest of the Ordinary: Lines of Skepticism and Romanticism*. Chicago, IL: University of Chicago Press, 1988.
— *Little Did I Know: Excerpts from Memory*. Stanford, CA: Stanford University Press, 2010.
— *Must We Mean What We Say: A Book of Essays*. Cambridge [Eng.] and New York: Cambridge University Press, 1976.
— *Philosophical Passages: Wittgenstein, Emerson, Austin, Derrida*. Bucknell Lectures in Literary Theory. Oxford: Blackwell, 1995.
— *Philosophy the Day After Tomorrow*. Cambridge, MA: Belknap Press of Harvard University Press, 2005.
— *A Pitch of Philosophy: Autobiographical Exercises*. Jerusalem-Harvard Lectures. Cambridge, MA: Harvard University Press, 1994.
— *Pursuits of Happiness: The Hollywood Comedy of Remarriage*. Cambridge, MA: Harvard University Press, 1981.
— *The Senses of Walden*. New York: Viking Press, 1972.
— *Themes Out of School: Effects and Causes*. San Francisco, CA: North Point Press, 1984.
— *This New Yet Unapproachable America: Lectures After Emerson After Wittgenstein*. Frederick Ives Carpenter Lectures. Albuquerque, NM: Living Batch Press, 1989.
— *The World Viewed: Reflections on the Ontology of Film*. Cambridge, MA: Harvard University Press, 1979.
Cavell, Stanley and Stephen Mulhall. *The Cavell Reader*. Edited by Stephen Mulhall. Blackwell Readers. Cambridge, MA: Blackwell, 1996.
Chandler, James K. *Wordsworth's Second Nature: A Study of the Poetry and Politics*. Chicago, IL: The University of Chicago Press, 1984.
Chandler, James. *England in 1819: The Politics of Literary Culture and the Case of Romantic Historicism*. Chicago, IL and London: University of Chicago Press, 1998.
Chernaik, Judith. *The Lyrics of Shelley*. Cleveland, OH: Press of Case Western Reserve, 1959.
Curran, Stuart. *Shelley's Annus Mirabilis: The Maturing of an Epic Vision*. San Marino, CA: Huntington Library, 1975.
Dante Alighieri. *The Divine Comedy*. Edited and translated by Charles S. Singleton. Princeton, NJ: Princeton University Press, 1970.
— *The Inferno of Dante*. Translated by Robert Pinsky. New York: Farrar, Straus & Giroux, 1994.
— *Purgatorio: A New Verse Translation*. Translated by W. S. Merwin. New York: Alfred A. Knopf, 2001.
DeMan, Paul. "Shelley Disfigured." In *Deconstruction and Criticism*, 39–73. Edited by Harold Bloom. New York: A Continuum Book, Seabury Press, 1979.
De Man, Paul and Burt et al., eds. *Romanticism and Contemporary Criticism: The Gauss Seminar*. Baltimore, MD: Johns Hopkins University Press, 1993.

Derrida, Jacques. "Signature Event Context." In *Limited Inc*. Edited by Gerald Graff, Jeffrey Mehlman, Samuel Weber. Evanston, IL: Norhwestern University Press, 1988.
Détienne, Marcel. *Dionysos at Large*. Translated by Arthur Goldhammer. Cambridge, MA: Harvard University Press, 1989.
Duffy, Edward. *The Constitution of Shelley's Poetry: The Argument of Language in Prometheus Unbound*. London: Anthem Press, 2009.
— "From Proverbs of Ashes to Coals on the Tongue: The Scriptural Dynamics of Luke." *Genre: Forms of Discourse and Culture* XL (2007 Fall/Winter): 171–200.
— *Rousseau in England: The Context for Shelley's Critique of the Enlightenment*. Berkeley, CA: University of California Press, 1979.
— "Where Shelley Wrote and What He Wrote For: The Example of 'The Ode to the West Wind.'" *Studies in Romanticism* 23(3) (1984 Fall): 351–77.
Eakin, Sybil S. "The Spots of Time in Early Versions of The Prelude." *Studies in Romanticism* 12 (1973 Winter): 389–405.
Eaves, Morris and Michael Fischer. *Romanticism and Contemporary Criticism*. Ithaca, NY: Cornell University Press, 1986.
Ellis, David. *Wordsworth, Freud and the Spots of Time: Interpretation in "The Prelude"*. Cambridge, MA: Cambridge University Press, 1985.
Emerson, Ralph Waldo. *Essays and Lectures*. Edited by Joel Porte. New York: Library of America, 1983.
Ferguson, Frances. *Wordsworth: Language as Counter-Spirit*. New Haven, CT: Yale University Press, 1977.
Fleming, Richard and Michael Payne. *The Senses of Stanley Cavell*. London and Toronto: Associated University Presses, 1989.
Fry, Paul H. *Wordsworth and the Poetry of What We Are*. New Haven, CT: Yale University Press, 2008.
Gould, Timothy. *Hearing Things: Voice and Method in the Writing of Stanley Cavell*. Chicago, IL: University of Chicago Press, 1998.
Hartman, Geoffrey H. *Criticism in the Wilderness: The Study of Literature Today*. New Haven, CT and London: Yale University Press, 1980.
Hazlitt, William. *The Complete Works of William Hazlitt*, 21 Vols. Edited by P. P. Howe. London: J.M. Dent, 1930.
Heaney, Seamus. *Finders Keepers: Selected Prose 1971–2001*. New York: Farrar, Straus & Giroux, 2002.
— *Opened Ground: Selected Poems 1966–1996*. New York: Farrar, Straus & Giroux, 1998.
— *Seeing Things*. New York: Farrar, Straus & Giroux, 1991.
— *Station Island*. New York: Farrar, Straus & Giroux, 1985.
Hoagwood, Terence Allan. *Skepticism & Ideology: Shelley's Political Prose and Its Philosophical Context from Bacon to Marx*. Iowa City, IA: University of Iowa Press, 1988.
Hogle, Jerrold E. *Shelley's Process: Radical Transference and the Development of His Major Works*. New York: Oxford University Press, 1988.

Hollander, John. *The Figure of Echo: A Mode of Allusion in Milton and After*. Berkeley, CA: University of California Press, 1981.
Holmes, Richard. *Shelley: The Pursuit*. New York: E. P. Dutton, 1975.
Jacobus, Mary. *Romanticism, Writing and Sexual Difference*. Oxford: Clarendon, 1989.
Jarvis, Simon. *Wordsworth's Philosophic Song*. Cambridge, MA: Cambridge University Press, 2007.
Jones, Frederick L., ed. *The Letters of Percy Bysshe Shelley*, 2 Vols. Oxford: Clarendon Press, 1964.
Kavanagh, Patrick. *Collected Poems*. New York: Norton, 1973.
Keach, William. *Arbitrary Power: Romanticism, Language, Politics*. Literature in History. Princeton, NJ and Oxford: Princeton University Press, 2004.
— *Shelley's Style*. New York and London: Methuen, 1984.
Keats, John. *The Letters of John Keats*, 2 Vols. Edited by Hyder Edward Rollins. Cambridge, MA: Harvard University Press, 1958.
Kneale, J. Douglas. *Monumental Writing: Aspects of Rhetoric in Wordsworth's Poetry*. Lincoln, NE: University of Nebraska Press, 1988.
Leighton, Angela. "Love, Writing and Skepticism in *Epipsychidion*." In *The New Shelley: Later Twentieth-Cenury Views*, 220–41. Edited by G. Kim Blank. New York: St. Martin's, 1991.
Levinson, Marjorie. *Wordsworth's Great Period Poems: Four Essays*. Cambridge, MA: Harvard University Press, 1986.
Lewis, C. S. "Shelley, Dryden, and Mr. Eliot." In *Selected Literary Essays*. Edited by Walter Hooper. London: Cambridge University Press, 1969.
Liu, Alan. *Wordsworth: The Sense of History*. Stanford, CA: Stanford University Press, 1989.
Luther, Martin. *Three Treatises*. Philadelphia, PA: Fortress Press, 1970.
Matthews, G. M. "A Volcano's Voice in Shelley." *ELH* 24 (1957): 191–228.
McGann, Jerome J. *The Romantic Ideology: A Critical Investigation*. Chicago and London: University of Chicago Press, 1983.
Miller, J. Hillis. "The Critic as Host." In *Deconstruction and Criticism*, 217–53. Edited by Harold Boom et al. New York: Seabury Press, 1979.
O'Malley, Glenn. *Shelley and Synesthesia*. Evanston, IL: Northwestern University Press, 1964.
O'Neill, Michael. *The All-Sustaining Air: Romantic Legacies and Renewals in British, American and Irish Poetry Since 1900*. Oxford: Oxford University Press, 2007.
Pfau, Thomas. "Tropes of Desire: Figuring the 'Insufficient Void' of Self-Consciousness in Shelley's *Epipsychidion*." *Keats-Shelley Journal* 40 (1991): 99–126.
Reiman, Donald H. *Percy Bysshe Shelley*. Twayne's English Authors Series. Boston, MA: Twayne Publishers, 1990.
— *Shelley's "The Triumph of Life": A Critical Study*. Urbana, IL: University of Illinois Press, 1965.

Reiman, Donald H. and Neil Fraistat. *Shelley's Poetry and Prose*, 2nd edn. New York: Norton, 2002.
Rich, Adrienne. *Diving into the Wreck: Poems 1971–1972*. New York: Norton, 1994.
Roberts, Hugh. *Shelley and the Chaos of History: A New Politics of Poetry*. University Park, PA: Pennsylvania State University Press, 1997.
Rougemont, Dénis de. *Love in the Western World*. Princeton, NJ: Princeton University Press, 1983.
Sacks, Peter. *The English Elegy: Studies in the Genre from Spenser to Yeats*. Baltimore, MD and London: Johns Hopkins University Press, 1985.
Santayana, George. *Essays in Literary Criticism*. New York: Scribners, 1956.
Saussure, Ferdinand de. *Course in General Linguistics*. Translated by Wade Baskin. New York: Philosophical Library, 1959.
Schulze, Earl. "The Dantean Quest of *Epipsychidion*." *Studies in Romanticism* 21(2) (1982 Summer): 191–216.
Serres, Michel. *The Parasite*. Translated by Lawrence R. Scher. Baltimore, MD: Johns Hopkins University Press, 1982.
Shelley, Mary Wollstonecraft. *The Letters of Mary Wollstonecraft Shelley*. Edited by Betty T. Bennet. Baltimore, MD: Johns Hopkins University Press, 1980.
Sperry, Stuart M. *Shelley's Major Verse: The Narrative and Dramatic Poetry*. Cambridge, MA: Harvard University Press, 1988.
Thoreau, Henry David. *Walden; and Resistance to Civil Government*, 2nd edn. Edited by William John Rossi. New York: Norton, 1992.
Ulmer, William Andrew. *Shelleyan Eros: The Rhetoric of Romantic Love*. Princeton, NJ: Princeton University Press, 1990.
Wasserman, Earl R. *Shelley: A Critical Reading*. Baltimore, MD: Johns Hopkins Press, 1971.
Weiskel, Thomas. *The Romantic Sublime: Studies in the Structure and Psychology of Transcendence*. Baltimore, MD: Johns Hopkins University Press, 1976.
White, Newman Ivey. *Shelley*. New York: A. A. Knopf, 1940.
Wilner, Joshua. *Feeding on Infinity: Readings in the Romantic Rhetoric of Internalization*. Baltimore, MD: Johns Hopkins University Press, 2000.
Wittgenstein, Ludwig. *Philosophical Investigations*. Translated by G. E. M. Anscombe. New York: Macmillan, Blackwell, 1953.
Woodring, Carl. *Politics in English Romantic Poetry*. Cambridge, MA: Harvard University Press, 1970.
Wordsworth, William. *The Prelude: 1799, 1805, 1850*. Edited by Jonathan Wordsworth, M. H. Abrams, and Stephen Gill. New York and London: Norton, 1979.
— *The Prose Works of William Wordsworth*, 3 Vols. Edited by W. J. B. Owen and Jane Worthington Smyser. Oxford: Clarendon Press, 1974.
Wordsworth, William and Alexander Balloch Grosart. *The Prose Works of William Wordsworth for the First Time Collected*, with Additions from

Unpublished Manuscripts. Edited by Alexander Balloch Grosart. Illustrated by Alexander Balloch Grosart. London and New York: Moxon AMS Press, 1967.

Wright, John W. *Shelley's Myth of Metaphor*. Athens, GA: University of Georgia Press, 1970.

Young, Robert. "'For Thou Wert There': History, Erasure and Superscription in '*The Prelude*'." In *Demarcating the Disciplines: Philosophy Literature Art*. Edited by Samuel Weber. Minneapolis, MN: University of Minnesota Press, 1986.

Index

acknowledgement 7, 21–2, 52, 81, 88, 90, 97, 100, 103, 155
  see also reception
Actaeon 130, 143, 145–7, 175, 206
Aeschylus 118, 162, 170
Alter, Robert 18, 101–2
Altieri, Charles 16, 96, 230n. 21
animism 82–3, 199
  reconceived as interest 19, 44–7
  in romanticism 37–45
  in Wordsworth 64–78
Arendt, Hannah 75
Aristotle 213
Augustine 36, 83
Austin, J. L. xii, 1–5, 47, 49–50, 54–5, 57, 80, 105, 167, 226n. 3, 227n. 10

Bacon, Francis 120, 213
Batkin, Norton 238n. 12
Beckett, Samuel 13, 30–1
Bion 174
Bishop, Jonathan 98
Blake, William xi, 1, 11, 35, 123, 161
Blanchot, Maurice 211–12
Bloom, Harold 68–70, 130
Bresson, Robert 15
Bromwich, David 75
Bruns, Gerald 226n. 2
Burke, Edmund 94
Burke, Kenneth 166
Burns, Robert 48
Byron (George Gordon) Lord xi, 11, 85, 173, 175, 205, 213

Cameron, Kenneth Neil 148
Cavell, Stanley,
  "aesthetics and economics of speech" in 8–9, 23–4

animism in 47–8
autobiography in 54, 57, 105, 150
coinage of "secular mysteries" xiv–xvi
desire in the philosophy of xviii, 13, 85, 91
eschatology in 30–3
the "father tongue" of writing in 9–10, 14, 61
film in xiv–xv
"flowerings of mentality" in 122, 158
"interest" in 94–5, 100
the Kantian "settlement" of skepticism in 6–8, 38–40
knowing oneself as the capacity for placing oneself in the world 59–62
marriage in 43–4
"the modern subject" in 90, 116, 169, 211–12, 214
"other minds" skepticism in 48–52
"partiality" in the philosophy of xiii–xiv, 13, 177
perfectionist writing in 130
psychoanalysis in the thought of 11–12, 226n. 9
"reading" in xviii, 16–18
skepticism in xvii, 6–8, 15, 22, 37–8, 40–3, 48, 50, 166–7, 178, 239n. 12
turning to romanticism 10, 35–47
the two Kantian standpoints in 20–5
voice in 54–8
the "writer's faith" in xi, 13–15, 87
Works
  The Claim of Reason 4, 12, 17, 23, 35, 40, 43, 48–52, 56

Disowning Knowledge 53
"Emerson's Constitutional
  Amending: Reading
  Fate" 59, 78–82
*In Quest of the
  Ordinary* xviii, 10, 35, 46,
  54, 57, 59, 82
Little Did I Know 211–12
*Must We Mean What We
  Say* 3, 204
Philosophical Passages 47, 54
A Pitch of Philosophy 47, 54
"The Politics of
  Interpretation" 11, 227n. 12
Pursuits of Happiness 43
*This New Yet Unapproachable
  America* 102
The Senses of Walden xv–xvi,
  1, 10, 15, 52–3
*The World Viewed: Reflections
  on the Ontology of
  Film* xiv–xvi, 15
Chandler, James 94–6
Chaplin, Charlie 53
Chatterton, Thomas 172–3
Chekhov, Anton 32
Chernaik, Judith 120
the city or constitution of words 15,
  20, 91, 102–3, 117, 130, 172,
  177, 191–4, 198, 212, 224 see
  also perfectionism
  origin in Plato 61
Claremont, Claire 148
Coleridge, Samuel Taylor xiv, xvii,
  xxii, 10, 13, 15, 19, 22,
  35–42, 45, 72, 87, 124, 130,
  229n. 15
Collins, Williams 130
Curran, Stuart 234n. 3

Dante Alighieri 112–18, 125,
  137–9, 141–4, 148, 150, 155,
  158–9, 168–70, 176, 198–9,
  207, 209, 215–16, 222

DeMan, Paul 99–100, 163, 165, 211
Derrida, Jacques 3, 47, 54–5, 110
Descartes René xvii, 36–7, 195
De Sica, Vittorio 15
Détienne, Marcel 185, 191
Dionysos 175, 185–6, 191
Dreyer, Carl,
  his *Passion of St. Joan* 15

Ecclesiastes 214
Echo, the figure of 120, 136, 144–5,
  235n. 9
Ellis, David 231n. 22
Emerson, Ralph Waldo xiv,
  xvii–xviii, xx, 6–8, 10,
  15–27, 29–32, 36–7, 45–7,
  53, 57–63, 75, 77–82, 87,
  100, 102–6, 108–9, 111–12,
  114–19, 122, 126, 129, 134,
  176, 184, 193–4, 196, 264,
  275, 284, 288n. 12, 289n. 11
  reception in 7–8, 95, 100, 109,
    113–15
  words as the "horses of thought"
    in 19, 129
  Works
    "Divinity School Address" 17
    "Experience" 32, 77, 102
    "Fate" 19, 22, 53, 59–60
    "The Poet" 187
    "Self-Reliance" 28, 103
    "Transcendentalism" 35
Endymion 143, 145–8, 190

Faust 210
Fellini, Federico 15
Ferguson, Frances 99, 232n. 31
Fokkelman, J. P. 227n. 16
Fosl, Peter S. 225n. 1
Frankenstein of Mary Shelley 35
Freud, Sigmund 11, 25, 97
Frost, Robert 182
Fry, Paul 96, 228n. 15, 230n. 21
Frye, Northrop 165

Gaius Cestius, pyramid of   181–3
Gould, Timothy   228n. 11

Hartley, David   228n. 15
Hartman, Geoffrey   68, 120, 228n. 15
Hawthorne, Nathaniel   26
Hazlitt, William   205, 216, 227n. 1, 229n. 21, 236n. 22, 238n. 2, 239n. 15
Heaney, Seamus   81, 161
Heidegger   xvii–xviii, 7, 9–10, 15, 17, 31–2, 37, 53–4, 57–8, 69, 77–8
Hoagwood, Terrence Allan   233n. 2
Hogle, Jerrold   163
Hollander, John   120, 136, 235n. 9
  see also Echo, the figure of
Holmes, Richard   170
Homer   197
Hume, David   43
Hunt, Leigh   173–4

impressionability   xx, xxii, 63–4, 81, 83, 119 see also acknowledgement
incentive or interest   19, 86–8, 102, 122
Isaiah   18

Jacob   18
Jacobus, Mary   231n. 27
Jarvis, Simon   106, 110–11, 115–16, 201, 232n. 42, 233n. 51, 237n. 40
Jesus   16–18, 20, 29, 114, 176–7, 217

Kant, Immanuel   xvii, 6–7, 12, 15, 22–3, 38, 60, 69, 77, 87, 104, 122, 226n. 5, 231n. 21
Kavanagh, Patrick   161, 228n. 6
Keach, William   229n. 14
Keats, John   xi, 11, 20, 48, 164, 170–88, 202, 210
Kneale, J. Douglas   99

LeBrun, Charles   114–16
Leighton, Angela   149–50, 168
Levinson, Marjorie   86–7, 89–90, 105
Lewis, C. S.   234n. 3
listening   81, 111–12, 193, 221
  see also acknowledgement; obedience
Liu, Alan   93, 98, 104–7, 111–12
Locke, John   228n. 15
Lowell, Robert   16
Lucan   172–4
Lucretius   xiii–xiv, 118, 163
  his *Alma Venus Genetrix* in Shelley   xiii-xiv, 118, 196, 212, 216
Luther, Martin   20, 29

McGann, Jerome   86
Manhattan College   xii
Matthews, G. M.   151, 162–3
Merwin, W. S.   139, 141, 235n. 1
Miller, J. Hillis   161–5
Milton, John   44, 65, 71, 79, 118, 120, 170–3, 188
Moore, Thomas   173
Moschus   174

Narcissus   143–4
natality   44, 110, 155, 157, 207–9, 220, 222, 224
neutrality   60, 79, 86, 104–5, 212
  see also philosophical authorship
New-Historicism   90, 99, 114–16
"the next self"   61, 145, 175, 180–1, 203–4 see also perfectionism
Nietzsche, Friedrich   15, 32, 46–7, 79, 150, 223

obedience (as mastery)   64, 81, 111–12, 115, 197 see also acknowledgement; listening
OLP and Literary Studies Online   225n. 1

O'Neill, Michael   236n. 38
ordinary language philosophy   1–33,
   55, 112, 197
Ovid   144

Paul, St.   18
Penrith Beacon   93
perfectionism   xi, xxi, 61–2, 116,
   129–30 *see also* city or
   constitution of words
Persius   145
Petrarch   150
Pfau, Thomas   166–7
philosophical authorship   60,
   79, 86, 212 *see also*
   neutrality
Plato   55, 61, 130, 140, 197
Poe, Edgar Allan   26

reception
   in Cavell   50, 60, 78, 81, 122
   in Emerson   7–8, 95, 100, 109
      113–15
   in Shelley   119, 124, 153, 156–70,
      185–6, 200
   in Wordsworth   103–4
redemption   2, 10–16, 29–30, 54–7,
   88–9
Reiman, Donald   xxii, 119, 203,
   234n. 7, 239n. 8
Revelations   18
Rich, Adrienne   236n. 37
Roberts, Hugh   163, 224
romanticism   116
   animism of   xvii–xviii, 15, 64–78
   Cavell's philosophy calling
      for   xii, 10
   Cavell's turn to   35–47
   recovery of voice in   10, 35
Rougemont de, René   149
Rousseau, Jean-Jacques   xii, 20, 88,
   145, 169, 216
   as character in Shelley's *The
      Triumph of Life*   201–24

Sacks, Peter   166, 177
Santayana, George   234n. 3
Sausurre, Ferdinand de   3, 109
Schulze, Earl   145–7, 235n. 12
Searle, John   47, 55
secular mysteries   xviii, 135
Serres, Michel   127
Shakespeare, William   31, 58, 118,
   141, 170, 179
   Works
      Antony and Cleoptra   80
      Hamlet   53
      King Lear   30, 40
      *A Midsummer Night's
         Dream*   102
      Othello   43, 48
      The Winter's Tale   47–8
Shelley, Percy Bysshe   x–xiii
   attraction in   121, 124, 149,
      204, 215–16
   autobiography in   150
   desire in   118, 129, 182–5, 188,
      190–4, 197, 205–7
   the Enlightenment in the
      thought of   201–3
   flowers of thought and poetry
      in   120, 122–4, 136–7,
      156–7, 161–2, 168, 175, 184,
      196, 218–21
   high culture in   118
   impressionability in   122,
      127, 149, 153, 169–70, 181,
      199, 216
   "intellectual system" of   117,
      122–3, 167
   "interest" or incentive in   170, 177
   lightning in   xx, 125–9
   Lucifer/morning star in   27, 79,
      134, 154–5, 183, 203, 209,
      216
   "the mind in creation" as a fading
      coal   121–2
   natality in   157, 207–9, 220,
      222, 224

"nextness"in 203–7, 209–10, 223–4
the perfectionist writing of 117, 121, 124, 129–30, 135, 141, 145, 149, 154, 156–70, 172–3, 180, 190–4, 198–200
praising the hypaethral temples of Greece 199, 237n. 55
reception in 119, 124, 153, 156–70,185–6, 200
the "spirit of the age" in 119–20, 128–9
Venus in xiii–xiv, 141–2, 144–5, 148–50, 152–5, 173, 183, 196, 203, 206, 209, 213, 216
the "Venus complex" in 209–210, 212, 238n. 9
Vesper/evening star in 153–5, 176, 183, 209, 212
"the writer's faith" in 167
Works
    Adonais 12, 126–7, 131, 170–89, 199–200, 206
    The Cenci 153
    "The Cloud" 127
    A Defence of Poetry 121–4, 142, 152, 161, 165, 194, 201, 213–14
    "England in 1819" 127–8, 131, 213
    Epipsychidion 134–70, 175, 178, 183, 189–200, 203–4, 206–7, 209, 212, 224
    Hellas 162, 188, 197, 224
    "Hymn to Intellectual Beauty" 120, 141–2, 202, 210
    Julian and Maddalo 141, 217
    "Lines Written among the Euganean Hills" 124, 159
    "The Mask of Anarchy" 151
    "Mont Blanc" 120, 161
    "Ode to the West Wind" 125–8, 131, 147

    "On Love" 145
    Peter Bell the Third 130
    Prometheus Unbound 117–21, 127–8, 131, 134, 144, 149, 162, 167–9, 190–1, 199, 211, 217, 224
    "The Sensitive Plant" 120, 190
    "To a Sky-Lark" 203
    The Triumph of Life 134, 201–24, 239n. 16
    "With a Guitar. To Jane" 180
Sidney, Philip 172–3
Socrates 155, 217
Spenser, Edmund 163, 199
Sperry, Stuart 143
Stevens, Wallace 143

Tasso, Torquato 123
theodicy 79–80, 149
Thoreau, Henry David 6, 10–11, 14–15, 20, 25–30, 56–8, 60–6, 77–8, 88, 178–9, 233n. 51

Ulmer, William Andrew 236n. 26

Virgil 15, 218, 138
Voltaire 205

Walden see Thoreau
Walden Pond 27–8, 78
Wasserman, Earl 120, 184, 234n. 5, 237n. 49
Weiskel, Thomas 98, 231n. 25
Westbrook, Harriett 148
Whitehead, Alfred North 42, 148
Williams, William Carlos 58
Wilbur, Richard 47
Wilner, Joshua 106, 228n. 14, 232nn 42, 48
Wittgenstein, Ludwig,
    correction in 105
    de-sublimizing thought 38–40

forms of life in   5–8, 13, 21–4, 49, 69, 89, 95–6
the grammatical critera of   4–5
language acquisition in   36
the "scene of instruction" in   36
Works
   Philosophical Investigations   xii, 2, 10, 17, 36
   Tractatus Logico-Philosopicus   12
Woodring, Carl   144
Wordsworth, Jonathan   98
Wordsworth, William   x–xiii, 35, 79, 85, 90, 118, 124, 180, 193, 201–2
   animism in   64–78
   reconceiving animism as interest   44–7
   Works
      "Elegiac Stanzas"   110
      "Immortality Ode"   10, 44, 98, 109, 204
      The Prelude   xi, 16, 19, 70, 75, 65–8, 70–7, 92–116
      "Tintern Abbey"   86
World, concept of   69, 83
"the world I *think*"   80–1, 135, 140
   see also "the next self"; perfectionism
Wright, John   172

Yeats, William Butler   114, 153, 181, 205
Young, Robert   231n. 27

www.ingramcontent.com/pod-product-compliance
Lightning Source LLC
Chambersburg PA
CBHW071814300426
44116CB00009B/1309